D1563596

THE GERMAN COMMUNISTS AND THE RISE
OF NAZISM

Also by Conan Fischer
STORMTROOPERS: A Social, Economic and Ideological Analysis, 1929–35

The German Communists and the Rise of Nazism

Conan Fischer

Lecturer in History
University of Strathclyde

St. Martin's Press   New York

First Published in the United States of America in 1991

Printed in Hong Kong

ISBN 0–312–05352–5

Library of Congress Cataloging-in-Publication Data

Fischer, Conan.
The German Communists and the rise of Nazism/Conan Fischer.
    p.   cm.
Includes bibliographical references and index.
ISBN 0–312–05352–5
1. Kommunistische Partei Deutschlands—History—20th century.
2. Nationalsozialistische Deutsche Arbeiterpartei—History.
3. Labor movement—Germany—History—20th century.   4. Germany—Politics and government—1918–1933.   I. Title.
JN3970.K6F49   1991
322'2'0943—dc20

                                                        90—44602
                                                        CIP

For Kate and Jane

Contents

Acknowledgements

Any academic text is, to a greater or lesser extent, the outcome of a collective effort and as well as being grateful for the large body of published research and debate which has eased my path, I would like to thank those colleagues and friends who have assisted in various ways. Richard Hamilton, Elizabeth Harvey, Detlef Mühlberger, Karl Rohe and Rainer Zitelmann kindly provided me with copies of their own publications and research materials, or alerted me to the writings of others. Ian Kershaw, Tony Nicholls and Hartmut Pogge von Strandmann provided me with the opportunity to develop and sharpen my ideas at symposia or seminar series. Dick Geary, while not always in agreement with the thrust of my provisional conclusions, engaged in an extended and always courteous debate as well as an exchange of publications which stimulated me to follow up my enquiries more thoroughly. Eve Rosenhaft brought to my attention the potential of the Staatsarchiv Bremen which became a happy hunting ground over two summers. The staff of that archive and of the Bundesarchiv in Koblenz were extremely helpful and saw to it that I returned to Scotland with sufficient material to justify requests for more commodious office accommodation. The Wolfson Foundation, the German Academic Exchange Service and my former employers, Heriot-Watt University in Edinburgh provided financial assistance for my research visits to Germany for which I am very grateful. Paul Hare, my former boss at Heriot-Watt, deserves particular thanks for providing me with vital support and time to complete this work during a very difficult period.

The writing of the book itself has inevitably presented challenges and its subject matter and some of the conclusions I felt forced to reach have produced a sense of misgiving and unease from time to time. I am therefore very thankful for the advice and encouragement received from Bill Knox and Tony McElligott who read and commented on early sections of the draft and would particularly like to thank Peter Stachura for reading over the complete manuscript at very short notice and coming up with a number of valuable suggestions. For any deficiencies which have survived this range of assistance I, of course, accept responsibility.

CONAN FISCHER

Abbreviations

ADGB	Allgemeiner Deutscher Gewerkschaftsbund
AEG	Allgemeine Elektrizitäts-Gesellschaft
Antifa	Antifaschistische Aktion
BVG	Berliner Verkehrsgesellschaft
cf.	Compare with. Used here in a complementary sense, except when indicated otherwise
Comintern	Communist International
CPSU	Communist Party of the Soviet Union
DAF	Deutsche Arbeitsfront
DHV	Deutschnationaler Handlungsgehilfenverband
Dinta	Deutsches Institut für technische Arbeitsschulung
DMV	Deutscher Metallarbeiterverband
DNVP	Deutschnationale Volkspartei
ECCI	Executive Committee of the Communist International
FDJ	Freideutsche Jugend
GVG	Großdeutsche Volksgemeinschaft
IAH	Internationale Arbeiterhilfe
IKD	Internationale Kommunisten Deutschlands
Jungdo	Jungdeutscher Orden
KAPD	Kommunistische Arbeiterpartei Deutschlands
KJVD	Kommunistischer Jugendverband Deutschlands
KPD	Kommunistische Partei Deutschlands
MdL	Mitteilungen des Landeskriminalpolizeiamts
MSPD	Mehrheits-Sozialdemokratische Partei Deutschlands
Na	Nachrichtensammelstelle
NRI	Nachrichtensammelstelle im Reichsministerium des Innern
NSBO	Nationalsozialistische Betriebszellen-Organisation
NSDAP	Nationalsozialistische Deutsche Arbeiterpartei
PNPW	Politische Nachrichtensammelstelle für die Provinz Westfalen
P-PB	Polizei-Präsident in Bochum
P-PR	Polizei-Präsident in Recklinghausen
RB	Reichsbanner Schwarz Rot Gold
RdI	Reichsverband der deutschen Industrie
RGO	Revolutionäre Gewerkschaftsopposition
RI	Reichsminister des Innern

SA	Sturmabteilung
SS	Schutzstaffel
SPD	Sozialdemokratische Partei Deutschlands
Stas	Stahlhelm-Selbsthilfe
USPD	Unabhängige Sozialdemokratische Partei Deutschlands
USSR	Union of Soviet Socialist Republics
ZKA	Zentraler Kampfausschuß

Archival abbreviations are contained in the bibliography

Introduction

The Weimar Republic was beset by enemies to the right and to the left, even before its constitutional arrangements had been finalised. Much distinguished these radical extremes in terms of ancestry, ideology and social constituency, but they shared a common aim in the destruction of Weimar and both sought to mobilise a mass following to achieve this once their respective, early putschist adventures had failed. The radical left quickly crystallised into the Communist Party of Germany (KPD) which strove to fashion a coalition of working people around a hegemonial proletariat. The radical right concentrated more gradually around the National Socialist German Workers' Party (NSDAP) which sought support from all levels of society for its 'national' revolution which was deemed to transcend class divisions. Both groupings were therefore looking to most of the discontented sections of the population.

Neither movement enjoyed success across the board and each became aware that the other was attracting significant numbers of anti-republicans. It will be argued that both movements were, therefore, forced to wage a two-front war during the Weimar period; against the Republic itself, but also against each other, and that the latter struggle arose as much out of competition to attract as large a constituency as possible as from straightforward animosity. Both were forced to tailor their political strategies to deal with the challenge posed by the other and were in effect adjusting to the pressures and opportunities of the broader political and socio-economic environment of inter-war Germany. While not wishing to discuss the detailed evidence of later chapters at length here, it will emerge that as the smaller and more isolated politically of the two, the KPD came increasingly to fear the potential displayed by the radical right generally and, later, by the Nazis specifically for mobilising support which the Communists themselves required. The NSDAP and its affiliates came to be regarded as especially dangerous rivals for the anti-republican constituency and out of this concern developed an extended and complex relationship between the Communist and National Socialist movements.

An examination of this process provides a range of novel insights into the history of the Weimar Republic, particularly with regard to working-class political behaviour and ideology and this in turn casts doubt on some of the broader interpretations of twentieth-century German historiography which have become commonplaces, such as the tendency to provide Nazism with an explicitly reactionary, petty bourgeois pedigree. Yet relatively little has appeared on Communist-Nazi relations, for which the simplest and most convincing explanation arguably lies in the traditional view of their respective social constituencies; the radical left the home of the revolutionary working class and the radical right that of the reactionary lower middle class. There may have seemed little to consider beyond the violence which constantly punctuated relations between them and which has seemed to represent a crude form of class warfare. An impressive array of recent research, however, indicates that the Nazi movement succeeded to an unprecedented degree by any standard in gaining a mass following which transcended class, regional and confessional boundaries, even if this success was by no means uniform. The constituencies of the radical extremes, it now appears, overlapped and consequently the time has come to re-examine the relationship between them from first principles.

The Nazis' breakthrough at the end of the 1920s, which established them as a major actor on the German political stage, did not come out of a clear blue sky. The radical right had constituted a powerful and sometimes threatening force from the earliest days of the Republic. The KPD appreciated from an early stage that the ambitions of the right impinged on its own and consequently developed a range of strategies to meet the problem, and these were, by and large, employed later to deal with the Nazis during the early 1930s. The Communist movement's responses to National Socialism were therefore less reactive and better considered than has sometimes been assumed, and the KPD's relationship with the radical right generally during the 1920s is, accordingly, given detailed consideration here.

This study is substantially indebted to a number of specialist works which have examined particular dimensions of the relationship between the radical extremes. To that extent, earlier parts of the book in particular will have an intentionally familiar feel in some respects and, furthermore, given the absence of any comparable wider-ranging study, it has not been necessary to take issue with other works in their entirety. However, the primary sources utilised here in the cause of historical revision demand conclusions which may, at first sight, appear startling and even provocative. This is particularly so given the recent, often acrimonious debates between historians of Germany over the significance of Nazism and even over how best to study the

Nazi era. The conclusions of this particular work inevitably impinge on these debates, but, it will become clear, do not constitute a direct intervention therein.

The main emphasis is placed on the radical left's relationship with the right. This approach was suggested by the self-conscious response to the political challenges of the day which the Communists' inherent weakness precipitated. This consequently stimulated the Communist movement into producing an excellent range of highly articulate, sometimes introspective and often self-critical analyses which remain readily available, if under-exploited, in the German archives. One of the main objectives of this work, therefore, is to exploit these sources extensively to provide an insight into the KPD's view of events (distorted or otherwise) and thereby arrive at a fuller understanding of its role in the history of the Weimar Republic.

The hierarchical nature of the Communist movement allows examination of the development and transmission of policy from the Communist International in Moscow, to the Central Committee of the KPD in Berlin, to individual party districts and affiliated organisations and then down to the grass roots. Of course, this can amount to noting how and establishing why policy was adapted, subverted or simply ignored at subordinate levels on occasion. The transmission of information on the day-to-day unfolding of political life up the same hierarchical chain and the responses to this are similarly revealing.

The single-minded hostility of Hitler to rival political organisations and the almost unremitting aggressiveness of the Nazis' political campaign both at an organisational and at grass-roots level would not have allowed for such a differentiated picture of radical politics to be drawn from the far right as can be achieved from the KPD's perspective. That is not to say that evidence from the Nazi side, and elsewhere, is neglected here. The continuous monitoring of the KPD by officialdom and by political rivals, notably the NSDAP and SPD, allows for critical assessment of the KPD's own material by reference to these external sources and also allows the KPD's history to be placed in a broader context than the use of Communist material alone would have allowed.

This book, therefore, seeks to reveal and examine dimensions of the history of both radical extremes in Weimar which have either been incompletely understood, or sometimes ignored. It will become evident that the obstacles confronting the KPD were even more formidable than has hitherto been appreciated, given the problems posed for it by the right. The implications for our understanding of

National Socialism are also pronounced, for from an examination of the relationship between it and the Communist movement comes dramatic confirmation and also substantial elaboration of the hypothesis advanced recently that the NSDAP was indeed a mass movement. The history of the Weimar Republic and of its downfall were, perhaps, even more convoluted and controversial than hitherto believed.

1 The Early KPD: Responses to Weakness

Germany had witnessed decades of rapid economic and social modernisation by 1914, yet retained a hereditary monarchy whose powers exceeded those of the parliament. There was widespread pressure for constitutional reform which so alarmed the monarchist authorities that they eventually risked war in August 1914 as a means of deflecting this pressure. They hoped ultimately to restore the Imperial Government's credit through military success, but in the event defeat threw Germany into a state of turmoil during the autumn of 1918. The question arose of how to deal with 'an enraged and totally war-sick populace'[1] in the hour of defeat as crowds milled through the streets of urban Germany and Workers' and Soldiers' Councils began to take up the task of day-to-day administration.

In the face of this civil disorder, and Allied demands that Germany reconstitute itself on democratic parliamentarian lines, the Emperor William II abdicated on 9 November 1918 and fled to the Netherlands. Prince Max of Baden resigned his office of Imperial Chancellor, leaving the moderate, majority Social Democratic Party (MSPD) to assume office hesitantly and with considerable misgivings. A Republic was proclaimed almost as an afterthought and without consultation by the majority Socialist Philipp Scheidemann, to the consternation of some of his closer colleagues. Another Social Democratic leader, Friedrich Ebert, became Chancellor, uncertain of his prospects or even the legality of his position. The radical Socialists, by contrast, believed their hour had come. The veteran radical, Karl Liebknecht, proclaimed a proletarian republic from the gates of the Royal Palace in Berlin on the evening of 9 November. He declared to the cheering crowds that capitalist rule in Europe was at an end and appealed to workers everywhere to complete the world revolution which Lenin had begun in Russia the year before.[2] Liebknecht's optimism seemed well-founded. The revolutionary outburst of November 1918 was triggered by Germany's defeat, but it also marked the culmination of longer-term pressures. Even before the war sections of the working class were becoming more radical, and this radicalism coexisted uneasily with a Social Democratic, and a trade union organisation which functioned on increasingly bureaucratic and hierarchical lines.[3]

The privations of war exacerbated matters, not least because the MSPD and the trade unions seemed largely concerned with integrating and disciplining the labour force within the existing socio-economic order,[4] to the point where, in Moses' words: 'In the closing weeks of the Great War the determination of the union leaders to do all in their power to prevent industrial chaos overwhelming the nation as a result of a dictated peace caused them to throw in their lot with German industry.'[5] Furthermore the labour force itself had changed in character because of the war. Conscription had removed many workers from the civilian economy and their replacements – usually young and often female – were strongly influenced, and led, by experienced shop stewards who, in sectors such as metalworking, were themselves radically inclined. Most notable were the Revolutionary Shop Stewards (*Revolutionäre Obleute*) of the Berlin metalworking industry who stood on the far left of the Social Democratic movement. In addition, the labour force in the heavy, war-goods industries had also expanded explosively and in these large workshops a hard-pressed workforce, largely unschooled in the tenacious gradualism of German trade union practice, were natural adherents to the radical cause.[6]

This process of radicalisation had begun to express itself in institutional terms even before the outbreak of revolution. The Social Democratic Party (SPD) had supported the Imperial Government's war effort with misgivings at the outset, but by 1916 a sizeable minority of the Socialist deputies in the Reichstag were no longer prepared to vote for war credits. Differences between the majority and this minority peace faction culminated in a formal splitting of the SPD in January 1917. Henceforward the majority, the MSPD, continued to vote war credits (while supporting calls for a negotiated peace) while the Independents, the USPD, advocated an immediate peace without indemnities or annexations. Although this was not technically a split between left and right, the left did tend to concentrate in the USPD, while reformists and revisionists were to be found principally in the MSPD. Other developments also testified to the more radical political climate. Even before the war there were signs that some radical workers were adopting a syndicalist outlook, partly in response to the increasing bureaucratisation of the labour movement, with Bremen and Hamburg providing notable examples of this trend.[7] The spread of syndicalist thinking became more marked during the war itself,[8] but by 1916 disenchantment with the SPD's pattern of development had even extended into the higher echelons of the Social Democratic leadership. Karl Liebknecht – always an awkward radical – cooperated with Rosa

Luxemburg – a leading figure on the left of the SPD – to create in 1916 a small, radical pacifist pressure group known as the Spartacus League (*Spartakusbund*). Although initially weakly founded, the Spartacus League established itself as a faction of the USPD in 1917 and began to gain a certain following in radical circles and even to attract the attention of foreign revolutionaries such as Lenin.[9]

Imminent defeat for Germany seemed to strengthen the radicals' hand still further. On 23 October 1918 Liebknecht was released from prison (whence he had been sent in 1916 on a charge of attempted treason) to a rapturous response from crowds in Berlin.[10] Strikes and demonstrations, which had been increasing in frequency and intensity from 1916 onward, now spilled over into open insurrection. Workers, soldiers, and even peasants, took to the streets, attacking symbols of the old Imperial authority, occupying factories and forming local councils, or Soviets, which managed to assume an admittedly ill-defined role in day-to-day public administration. In some more radical cities, such as Düsseldorf and Bremen, the USPD had even forged links with the Russian Bolsheviks and endorsed the achievements of the 1917 October Revolution.[11]

The radical revolutionaries therefore had grounds for optimism, but this was tempered by unmistakable signs that the German Revolution might not follow the same course as that in Russia. The MSPD, with support from the army, began to consolidate its hold on power, while the USPD's leadership also made clear its support for parliamentarianism and accepted three of the six Cabinet posts in the provisional government. The composition and behaviour of the National Congress of the Workers' and Soldiers' Councils was particularly disappointing for the radicals. Dominated by the majority Socialists, it met on 16 December to debate, among other issues, Germany's constitutional future. In the event, government proposals to convene a National Assembly to frame a parliamentary republican constitution were accepted without discussion and the Congress merely debated awhile before settling on 19 January 1919 as the best date for elections to the Assembly.[12] The National Congress had thereby confirmed that, short of further revolutionary upheaval, Germany would not follow the former Russian Empire and become a union of Soviet republics.

Rosa Luxemburg had already lambasted the Ebert government in Spartacus's newspaper, *Die Rote Fahne (The Red Flag)*, and had little time for the USPD's leaders either. Now the National Congress of the Workers' and Soldiers' Councils was tarred with the same brush.[13] On 15 December a final attempt by Rosa Luxemburg to force the USPD to leave the Ebert government and reject the concept of a National Assembly was heavily defeated at a general meeting of the Berlin party organisation[14] and this increasingly public disagreement between Spartacus and the rest of the USPD on this set of fundamental issues made it 'pointless for the Spartacists to delay setting up a communist party'.[15] Suddenly time seemed short. Spartacus and its radical allies had to act before the Constituent Assembly could meet and effectively stabilise the improvised political order[16] and before, as seemed possible, the Revolutionary Shop Stewards and the left-wing Independent Socialists Müller and Ledebour moved to found a rival radical, but parliamentarian, party to the left of the USPD.[17]

As a result the founding conference of the Communist Party of Germany[18] (KPD) was hastily convened and held in Berlin between 30 December 1918 and 1 January 1919. The majority of the 127 delegates were from Spartacus, with 29 delegates from the Bremen radicals (by then reconstituted as the International Communists of Germany (IKD) making up the largest minority grouping. Formal designations apart, it quickly became apparent that the delegates fell into two distinct and inherently incompatible categories. The majority were radical utopians, more or less anarcho-syndicalist in character, who derived from a range of local associations which remained largely autonomous even after the founding congress.[19] As Borkenau commented:

> It was mostly the 'crazy fringe' which joined the Spartacists, and some of these newcomers were more than doubtful elements. On the whole they were sincere and self-sacrificing, but politically impossible.[20]

In addition to this utopian majority, which quickly fell under the influence of the IKD delegates, the conference included a small group of informed, revolutionary Marxists among whom were two leaders of the highest calibre in Rosa Luxemburg and Karl Liebknecht.[21]

A struggle quickly developed between these two groupings at the conference. Luxemburg believed unflinchingly in the principle of a democratic mass revolution and remained bitterly opposed to the élitist revolutionary strategy developed and applied by the Russian Bolsheviks.[22] She maintained that a mass revolution was feasible but, in contrast to most of the conference delegates, did not believe it would occur overnight – despite her sometimes inflammatory rhetoric in the columns of *Die Rote Fahne*. In a rousing speech to the conference

Luxemburg warned against putschism and proposed that participation in elections and the systematic education of the masses marked the surest way forward to revolution.[23] The conference delegates were warned that they 'stood at the beginning of the revolution' and even the more sanguine Liebknecht asked of the delegates: 'Was our parliamentary activity, even in the Reichstag, completely worthless?'[24] As a skilled and persistent critic of the wartime government in parliament Liebknecht should have known, but the conference delegates saw things differently: 'The delegates allowed Rosa to say what she liked in the theoretical field, but in political practice they went their own way'.[25] This was demonstrated most clearly when the conference came to vote on the issue of participation in elections to the National Assembly. For Luxemburg opposition in principle to the Assembly had been overridden by her practical appreciation of the situation in Germany, but the majority of delegates supported an IKD resolution rejecting participation by a majority of three to one.[26] It was not just that the delegates had rejected bourgeois parliamentarianism but, as Rosenberg argues: 'that the delegates, in contrast to their leaders, believed that the bourgeois republic would be toppled within a few weeks by revolutionary mass action.'[27] Many radicals outside the conference were unimpressed. The radical metalworkers of Berlin, represented by the Revolutionary Shop Stewards, broke off negotiations to join the new party – not least because of the KPD's attachment to a strategy of 'constant demonstrations and *Putschist* tactics'.[28] Thus, despite Spartacus's earlier claim to speak for 'the masses, the millions, of the socialist proletariat', its breakaway from the USPD had left it relatively isolated and its transformation into the KPD was to initiate a traumatic infancy rather than a triumphal march towards revolution.[29]

The confused and sometimes bloody events of early 1919 confirmed this gloomy prognosis. The dismissal of the USPD Police Chief of Berlin, Eichhorn, by the central authorities on 3 January[30] triggered massive popular protests on the fifth which emboldened some individual radical leaders to strike a blow at the Ebert government. Ironically, given their earlier stance on violence, these included the Revolutionary Shop Stewards and, fatefully (without authorisation from the KPD), Karl Liebknecht.[31] The rebels had counted on help from disaffected military units, but this was not forthcoming and of the 700 000 original demonstrators only a few hundred became involved in the subsequent fighting with government forces. Not only were the insurgents defeated, but had to observe that while factory workers might well be prepared to demonstrate, or strike, they were not prepared to participate in armed insurrection.[32] However much radical workers may have disapproved of specific government actions in January, they evidently disapproved as much of the utopian adventurism with which the young KPD was inextricably associated.[33] To compound the disaster, both Rosa Luxemburg and Karl Liebknecht were arrested and murdered by government forces, depriving the Communist movement of its two outstanding leaders.

The suppression of the January unrest, however, did nothing to stem the growing misgivings of many workers who regarded the actions of the Social Democratic government with mounting dismay. The problems went back to November 1918 when the MSPD's leaders had been sufficiently alarmed by the revolutionary turmoil to throw in their lot with the Imperial Army's Officer Corps, and were compounded when, in January 1919, the government embarked on a strategy of using right-wing volunteer forces (*Freikorps*) to defend, as it saw it, parliamentarianism and social and economic stability in the face of left-radical insurgency. Working-class unease over this strategy[34] was strengthened by the authorities' decision to treat the Workers' and Soldiers' Councils with benign neglect and brought to a head by the failure to initiate a programme of socialisation of heavy industry.[35] Unrest spilled over into fighting between workers and *Freikorps* units in many industrial cities during February and March and although much of this violence was spontaneous in nature, the KPD became involved and was thereby discredited when the insurgents were suppressed piecemeal by government forces.[36]

Liberal and socialist historians by and large agree that the SPD's fears were exaggerated and that the deals struck not just with the military, but with other elements of the old order such as the civil service and heavy industry, did much to facilitate subsequent attacks by the right on the very Republic the SPD purported to be defending.[37] At the time, however, Communist leaders saw matters in a decidedly conspiratorial light, accusing the MSPD's and USPD's leaders of naked treachery[38] and East German historians have to some extent evaluated the failure of the revolutionary left in 1918/19 in comparable, if more measured, terms.[39] The revisionist and reformist labour leaders were, they claim, able to rely on the 'misguided loyalty' of many workers to prevent revolution at the end of the war and then preserve the old order intact. The bourgeoisie, it is argued: 'could rely on the willingness of the right-wing Social Democratic Party and trade union leaders to leap into the breach and defend [their] interests'.[40] The USPD's leaders have been seen, by and large, as equally culpable. As one authors' collective has commented: 'The objective function of the right-wing USPD leaders during the November revolution consisted in using parliamentarianism and democratic illusions to restrain revolutionary-minded sections of the working class who were dedicated to the traditions of the German labour movement from taking up meaningful class struggle, and to bind them to capitalist state power.'[41]

Implicit in this argument is the assumption that a large proportion of the German working class was inherently revolutionary and that their revolutionary aspirations accorded, more or less, with those of the KPD. Non-Leninist historians, whatever their precise political viewpoint, have referred both to the KPD's internal weaknesses[42] and to the politics of the German working classes to provide explanations for the Communist Party's birth pains (not to forget the presence of a numerically strong, if politically disorientated, middle class[43]). For one thing the traditions of German labour were not necessarily radical. The Free Trade Unions were theoretically committed to socialism, but in representing the core of organised labour they strove for incremental improvements within the existing socio-economic framework and there is little evidence to suggest that most working men in pre-war Germany wished it otherwise. Furthermore, even this commitment to reformist-style socialism had generally appealed primarily to the employees of smaller firms 'where conditions remained similar to those of a workshop in a handicraft', and found less support in heavy industrial sectors such as metalworking or chemicals.[44] In the final years of peace there were unmistakable signs of radicalisation in some heavy industrial centres as exasperation mounted with the SPD's increasingly cautious and bureaucratic stance,[45] but the general picture was one of an underdeveloped socialist, let alone radical, consciousness in heavy industrial regions. Thus in 1913 the Metalworkers' Union had organised just 10 000 out of 150 000 employees in the big iron and steel works of the Ruhr District, while 20 000 workers there belonged to the employer-supported Company Unions.[46] Even the Ruhr coalminers, some of whom were to play a prominent part in the demands for socialisation and in the broader struggles of the early Weimar years, were before 1914 suspicious of union leaders who indulged in overt politicking – despite the strong personal political convictions of some of these same miners:

> What the miners wanted in a union, if they were to have one, was an organisation to defend and promote their shared economic interests as miners. When leaders tried to promote other interests, the miners just refused to follow.[47]

In fact, as Hickey notes, before the war: 'most miners remained outside any organisation at all while many of those who did join soon left again'[48] and this tenuous situation was bound to influence the character of the broader labour movement in the Ruhr: 'The emphasis on organisation and the cautious, non-radical policies and tactics which accompanied it can be seen – in the Ruhr at least – largely as a response to the realities of an unsettled, divided working class and the experience of industrial weakness.'[49] This evident dichotomy between the workers' movement and the socialist workers' movement in the Ruhr can also be explained to a significant degree by factors operating outside the workplace. Thus Rohe argues that in this industrial, and yet non-urban, setting, values based essentially on life and experience within its residential communities were crucial in the development of politics. The pre-modernist lifestyle and mentality of much of its industrially-employed population led the large Catholic element in the Ruhr at least to seek in support for the Catholic Centre Party a political expression of their hostility to secularised modernity. Even National Liberalism, the industrial bourgeoisie's expression of modernity could benefit from the parochialism of evangelical (and thus anti-Catholic) working-class life as much as from employers' pressure on workers to vote Liberal.[50]

However, despite important exceptions such as Bremen and Berlin, it was largely in heavy industrial regions (including the Ruhr) which lacked a deep-rooted tradition of trade unionism or Social Democratic politics that radicalism manifested itself most strongly towards the end of the war. As argued previously, this mounting radical sentiment was undoubtedly linked to changes in socio-economic conditions which had been precipitated by wartime circumstances.[51] The resulting combination of large numbers of new workers with increased material privation[52] created what Wolfgang Mommsen has described in the context of the miners' strike of December 1918 in the Eastern Ruhr as an 'elemental movement of great force'. The Ruhr miners hoped for changes in the running of the mines, such as humane working conditions and an element of worker control over day-to-day decision-making in the pits, but, he argues, they did not seek 'a fundamental restructuring of the social system as such'.[53] Far from being a legacy of Germany's mainstream Social Democratic tradition, this form of militancy was often very much at odds with the SPD and the Communists on matters of industrial policy, tending towards spontaneity, originating within specific workplaces and often assuming a utopian character.[54] Thus, Mommsen argues, all the major strike movements in the period November 1918 to March 1919 had little to do with any particular political ideology. Demands for nationalisation were not generally informed by any notion of theoretical socialism, representing instead a quest for immediate improvements in the social lot which had syndicalist rather than Marxist overtones. Disappointment, therefore, with the MSPD over its reluctance to press ahead with nationalisation did not make the workers concerned into committed Marxist-Leninists.[55]

Many historians have consequently distinguished between these radical, socio-economic aspirations and the politics of Social Democracy when studying the 1918/19 revolution. The majority of delegates elected to the Council of Soviets in December 1918 were supporters of the MSPD and most of the radical minority were supporters of the USPD, such as the Revolutionary Shop Stewards, who remained in favour of a parliamentary republic.[56] The views of these delegates on what precisely constituted socialism were vague and diverse and the committed revolutionaries of Spartacus were virtually excluded. Liebknecht and Luxemburg failed to win mandates.[57] Similarly the political demands of participants in the great munitions strike that had swept Germany in January 1918 were largely in line with those of the MSPD; an end to the war, fair negotiations with Russia and the establishment of political democracy in Germany.[58]

This longstanding view of a revolution whose political demands were inherently moderate has been challenged more recently from a number of sides. Thus Tampke has argued that: 'the claim that the "prevailing political goals were predominantly reformistic and radically democratic" is not really supported' and that the left-radical groups in the Ruhr which strove for fundamental political and social change 'were not in a minority but had considerable support from the start'.[59] Kocka agrees that the radicalism of this period possessed an identity in its own right, concluding that: 'Arthur Rosenberg's hypothesis that this "strangest of all Revolutions" ultimately rested on a misunderstanding – in the sense that what the great majority of the working class wanted had already been granted in the October parliamentarianism and in the coming armistice at the beginning of November – has rightly been modified from a number of different perspectives.'[60] However, such lines of argument do not lead one to conclude that prospects for Spartacus and the KPD were, after all, reasonably favourable. Kocka, for example, sees in the revolution of 1918 and 1919 not so much 'an attack by the working class on capital and industry', but more an attack 'against a bureaucracy that was no longer defended by anyone'. The state's predominant role in the prosecution of the war, combined with the extreme hardships the war brought about, left it isolated both from the masses and the entre-preneurial class who, in effect, formed a 'negative and anti-bureaucratic coalition' against it.[61] Tampke, in examining the revolutionary movement within the mines and factories of the Ruhr, does perceive a direct conflict between labour and capital, but notes that the radicalism of the time 'was anarcho-syndicalist in character'.[62]

This, however, almost brings the argument full circle. While one can support Winkler's observation that the troubles of March and April 1919 were indeed more than a protest movement, for there was mounting disillusionment with the MSPD,[63] the radicalism of the time nonetheless seemed to remain largely anchored in the workplace, or at best in the community and did not translate itself in the main onto the wider political stage.[64] Even in the radical city of Bremen, as Ryder observes, the MSPD gained about 70 000 votes in the elections for the National Assembly as against 30 000 for the USPD and 65 000 for the middle class parties. Similarly in municipal elections in March in the same city the MSPD's vote exceeded that of the KPD and USPD combined.[65] Individual KPD cells of an anarchist or syndicalist character were ill-equipped to enter national political life and thus Tampke himself observes that the Communist Party was little more than an 'insignificant splinter group' at this stage.[66]

Under these circumstances one can well appreciate Rosa Luxemburg's desire for caution at the KPD's founding conference, as well as her conviction that the pursuit of a Bolshevik strategy was both undesirable and inappropriate for German conditions. Her following in the young KPD was anything but Bolshevik, but it regarded the Russian revolutionary achievement with enthusiasm and was impatient for action in Germany. Rosenberg points to the significant numbers of radical utopians from the poorer, more embittered sections of the working class within Spartacus[67] who could not be relied upon to maintain discipline in the complex political environment of late 1918.

> Experience has confirmed all too often that this section of utopian-minded workers, predominantly recruited from among the unemployed, are easily demoralised and then lurch from one extreme to the other. . . . Because of their distrust, impatience and indiscipline they cannot promote any effective revolutionary policy, but only destroy. Marx, Engels and Lenin have opposed the utopian tendency with all possible vigour and warned against making concessions to it.[68]

This impatience was reflected in the radical utopians' assessment of the prospects for trade unionism after the war. The post-war strike movement, they believed, signalled the end of the old trade unions based on particular industries or crafts and heralded the formation of "one big union", built upon a revolutionary programme'. This, it is argued, 'spoilt their last chance to get a foothold within the mass movement'.[69] The same impatience and misplaced confidence in the imminence of revolution led, as noted, to their refusal to participate in parliamentary elections[70] at the KPD's founding conference and in agreeing to this decision Luxemburg and Liebknecht had effectively surrendered meaningful leadership of the KPD and 'condoned in advance any action that some gang of adventurers or another might precipitate'.[71]

The suspicion with which other revolutionary groups whose politics were more firmly anchored in the German political tradition – such as the Revolutionary Shop Stewards – regarded the KPD as perfectly understandable in this light. The KPD, it is argued, was too out of touch with the great majority of the working class for its broader revolutionary goals to have had any real chance of success; the objectives of the two groups did not coincide.[72] Thus while one can sympathise with the argument that the events of 1918/19 did represent a revolutionary upheaval rather than simply a collapse of the old Empire, it seems clear that the KPD was not the frustrated heir in the hour of the revolution's failure.[73] Perhaps the USPD lost an historic opportunity to effect radical changes in German society at the time, perhaps the revolution adopted too diverse a range of forms and objectives to have had real prospects of success, but throughout the period the KPD had played a subsidiary role and to a degree even a wrecking role in events.

By May 1919 it was becoming clear to the KPD's leadership that the wave of strikes that had swept Germany during the spring were not synonymous with political revolution and that disastrous episodes such as the Munich Soviet of April 1919 (with which the KPD was not directly involved) had only strengthened the hand of explicitly reactionary forces. The Workers' and Soldiers' Councils had all but lost any influence in public affairs and the KPD quickly lost any remaining interest in them as a potential vehicle for revolution[74] (if they had ever been that).

These setbacks initiated a bitter struggle within the KPD which eventually deprived it of much of its already limited following. The party's new leader, Paul Levi, concluded that his membership's relative indiscipline and isolation had contributed to the disaster of early 1919 and resolved to establish the authority of the *Zentrale* over the heterogeneous and disparate party.[75] He recognised that there was little prospect of immediate revolution and believed that the KPD had to purge itself of left-radicals so as to make possible the winning of mass support from radical sections of the working class who by then were largely within the USPD. With this in mind syndicalism was rejected as a 'disease' and KPD members were urged to stay in the mainstream, socialist-oriented trade unions, but to isolate the 'counter-revolutionary' bureaucracy.[76] At first Levi found himself relatively isolated within the party and also faced with a measure of support for his ultra-left opponents from the Soviet Union. Lenin and Zinoviev, Fowkes argues, welcomed insurgency in Europe at any price if it reduced the effectiveness of the Allied intervention in Russia and that of the anti-Bolshevik White Russian Forces.[77] By October, however, Levi was able to prevail at the so-called Heidelberg Conference where he demanded successfully a departure from syndicalist tactics, revolutionary adventurism, and insisted on the authority of the party's leadership over the movement. This victory was won at a cost. Over half the KPD's 107 000 members eventually left (including virtually the entire Berlin membership and many from the Rhineland, Saxony and northern Germany) and subsequently formed the left-radical Communist Workers' Party of Germany (KAPD) on 10 April 1920.[78]

Naturally there were recriminations all around. Karl Radek, who represented the Moscow-based Communist International (Comintern) at the Heidelberg Conference, condemned the departing left-wing delegates both for their syndicalist and their nationalist tendencies. He labelled them 'National Bolsheviks' and dismissed their ideas as of little significance for the revolutionary movement.[79] For their part the departing delegates, who included the leaders of the KPD in Hamburg, accused Levi of bolshevising the KPD and reportedly concluded that: 'The economic, social and political conditions in Germany provide no basis for specifically bolshevik methods and the transfer of Russian revolutionary methods onto German soil only strengthens the counter-revolution – something ever wider sections of the working class have understood.'[80]

At the end of its first year of existence, then, the KPD faced a very uncertain future. It had been reduced to the level of a minor sect with just a few pockets of organisational strength. However many radical workers there might have been in Germany, few had joined the Communist Party and of those few, many were in the process of leaving again. It appeared that the KPD had failed to strike roots within the German working class and that the positive attractions of Communism in Germany were distinctly limited. This is well worth remembering when one comes to consider the difficulties that the NSDAP was to have in the early 1930s in gaining a hold within the working class, for neither party found it particularly easy to gain a natural constituency therein at the outset and in that respect both differed from the well-established SPD during the Weimar era. For all the setbacks the latter suffered, or even inflicted on itself, it generally managed to maintain a large, stable mass membership and a sizeable core electorate, and was associated with the General German Trade Union Federation (ADGB) – a formidable organisation.

But for developments outside of Germany the KPD might never have become a significant political force. However, socialists in many parts of Europe respected or even admired the Bolsheviks' revolutionary achievements and because of this, membership of the new Communist International based in Moscow appeared attractive initially to many West European Social Democrats.[81] The KPD had adhered to Comintern more or less from the outset and this membership lent the small party a significance which its then size and level of support within Germany would never have justified. As the prospects for an internal revolution continued to fade, other German radical socialist and communist parties likewise looked to Comintern as a means of counterbalancing their domestic impotence. The KAPD, the USPD and later even the nationalist-minded League of Communists (*Bund der Kommunisten*) made approaches to Comintern in their own right and had they been admitted on an individual basis, the KPD might have enjoyed a marginal existence at best. The attitude adopted by Comintern was, therefore, to be crucial. In the event it decided, after some prevarication, that its most reliable and ideologically acceptable affiliate in Germany was the KPD and those sections of the KAPD and USPD that wished to adhere to Comintern were prevailed upon to do so by amalgamating with the first named.[82]

The winning over of the USPD with its 800 000 members, among them a significant proportion of industrial trade unionists, was the greatest potential prize for the KPD in these circumstances. It stood to gain thereby both a mass following and a substantial presence in the factories. In some respects the task was not a hopeless one. Rosenberg argues that the expulsion of the utopian activists at the Heidelberg Conference had potentially opened the way for a merging of the KPD and the USPD's left.[83] The matter seemed urgent, for the German right appeared ready by early 1920 to reverse even the limited revolutionary gains of late 1918. Dissident troops occupied Berlin in March without meeting military opposition and it took mass action by the non-communist trade unions to frustrate this so-called Kapp Putsch. The KPD's failure to gain control over either the strike movement or most of the ill-fated workers' risings that followed amply demonstrated its marginal position to the frustration of many of its own members.[84] However the USPD as a whole, and even parts of its left wing, were not communists and, as Hunt remarks, the sympathy of left Social Democrats in general for the Soviet Union and their wish to reunite the socialist working class movement did not amount to an endorsement of Leninism:

> Their traditions and mentality were essentially Social Democratic and not Communist; their mentors were Bebel and Liebknecht, the pre-war Kautsky, even Rosa Luxemburg, but not Lenin, Trotsky or Stalin; and their 'workers' fatherland' was Red Vienna, not Soviet Russia.[85]

Furthermore Comintern itself was changing significantly in character at this time from a relatively independent body into one increasingly dominated by the Russian government and reflective of Soviet foreign policy interests. Since membership of Comintern required acceptance of the Twenty-one Conditions which, Winkler argues, amounted to an insistence that all members of Comintern follow the directives of the Moscow Executive, USPD members were effectively being asked to contemplate subordination to the interests of a foreign power.[86]

In the event, when the USPD came to vote on affiliation to the Comintern and on an amalgamation with the KPD at its Party Congress at Halle in October 1920 it effectively split on the issue. On paper the left won the day, gaining 237 votes for affiliation with 156 opposed, and since this decision was taken in the face of opposition from most party functionaries and newspaper editors the victory can be regarded as a substantial one for the radical rank-and-file delegates.[87] The vote did not, however, deliver up the USPD to the KPD bag and baggage. Of the 800 000 USPD members fewer than half joined the KPD, estimates ranging between 300 000 and 400 000, leaving the KPD with a membership of between 350 000 and 450 000 at the end of the process.[88] This was sufficient, Klönne argues, for the KPD to represent the majority of the socialist industrial working class from late 1920 until the inflation of 1923,[89] but this claim is somewhat overstated. At least 300 000 independent socialists eventually rejoined the MSPD and among these were most of the active trade unionists, most of the skilled workers (including engineering workers) and most of those with a longstanding tradition of Social Democratic politics.[90] The KPD may have become a numerically more significant force and have recruited many younger, newly radicalised workers from the coal mining and chemical industries, but the remaining independents retained the party funds, 56 of the 69 party newspapers and the loyalty of 59 of the 81 Reichstag deputies[91] and these resources were re-merged into the SPD in 1922. As Borkenau concludes: 'The chief result of Halle and its aftermath was a considerable strengthening of the right-wing within the labour movement', while Rosenberg asserts, still more polemically, that once the right of the USPD had rejoined the MSPD they 'dominated without limits the free trade unions'.[92] On balance these sweeping conclusions do seem justified. The KPD's membership of around 400 000 contrasted with the reunited SPD's tally of well over one million.[93] In electoral terms the KPD did inherit some of the USPD's support, but its achievement was decidedly patchy and largely restricted to some former USPD strongholds in Catholic areas.[94] The trade union organisations were also dominated by the Social Democrats. At the 1922 ADGB Congress the KPD had just 90 of the 691 delegates,[95] and by the 1925 Congress just four KPD delegates remained.[96]

Although its merger with the USPD had only been a qualified success, the KPD could at least now claim to represent the dominant force on the radical left; the KAPD in early 1921 had only 45 000 members.[97] Differences persisted, however, between Levi and his close associates on the one hand, who advocated a long-term gradualist struggle to enhance the KPD's standing, and more left-wing leaders on the other who argued that the time had now come to seize the political initiative through a policy of open insurrection. At this point the KPD's adherence to Comintern was to prove fatal to Levi, for a complex dispute which had its origins in the International's treatment of the Italian Socialist Party led to the repudiation of Levi by Comintern delegates and the German left on the KPD's Central Committee and to the subsequent resignation of Levi and some of his closer colleagues. The new, activist Central Committee was all too receptive to Comintern appeals to initiate a fresh wave of open struggle in Germany, quite possibly to relieve pressure on the Russian government which was in difficulties at that time.[98]

The resulting 'March Action' was a disaster for the KPD.[99] Active support for the insurrection was limited to the Mansfeld copper mines and Leuna chemical works in central Germany and to a minority of workers in the Hamburg shipyards, and the authorities were well prepared. Elsewhere, unemployed Communists became embroiled in fighting against factory workers who wanted no part in the business and resisted attempts to bring them out on strike. Paul Levi, having opposed the March Action from the outset, detailed in his devastating critique of the rising fights in the Ruhr and Berlin: 'We learn that it was a terrible thing to watch how the unemployed, crying loudly at the pain of the thrashings they had received, were thrown out of the factories',[100] and Borkenau's polemical conclusion that 'the alleged offensive of the working class, undertaken in its name by the Communist Party, at once transformed itself into a fierce fight of the Communists, with the unemployed as their battering-ram, against the workers'[101] is echoed by Levi's plea that: 'Never again in the history of the Communist Party can we allow Communists to declare war on the workers'.[102] Many ordinary members of the party evidently sympathised with Levi's more cautious and more democratic line[103] and their disillusionment with the new leadership over the March fiasco is reflected in the fall in party membership from around 400 000 to 180 000.[104] Factory workers turned away in despair while to the left of the KPD the national revolutionary Communist League condemned the futile destruction of what military capacity the communist movement had possessed. Only in Thuringia where the Communist League's local leader, Lindemann, had stopped the rising did such a capacity remain.[105] Ironically, however, the instigators of the March Action retained their positions within the party while Paul Levi, who had attacked the 'lunacy' of precipitating such an undertaking with decidedly limited support, and also the role of the Executive Committee of the Communist International (ECCI) in the rising, was expelled from the Party on 15 April 1921. The leftists found his criticism of violent confrontation unacceptable while cooler heads could not forgive his criticisms of Comintern to which they remained loyal.[106]

It might appear that the KPD had demonstrated the limits of its potential yet again in disastrous fashion and that Rosa Luxemburg's fears for the party if it adhered to Comintern and adopted an insurrectionary strategy had been fully vindicated. Events within Germany indicated that most workers, let alone the lower-middle-class masses, had no time for the KPD's adventurism. Some had been prepared to strike and even fight when the Republic, or the social and economic gains it had brought them, were threatened by right-wing actions such as the Kapp Putsch. These incidents, however, can best be characterised as defensive struggles, far removed from the KPD's notion of a revolutionary offensive. Indeed, the majority of organised workers perceived the Republic as 'their' Republic and therefore worth defending at the very time the KPD wished to destroy it. In Russia too the situation altered to the disadvantage of the KPD's left-wing leadership. The government there had already abandoned its revolutionary economic strategy known as 'war communism' and, under the auspices of the New Economic Policy, tolerated private capital in order to restore the fortunes of the Russian economy. Now, as a consequence of this, Lenin's support for revolutionary adventurism abroad ended. Russia desired constructive trading relations with the West and, in any case, concluded that there was little immediate prospect of successful revolution in the capitalist countries. As part of this change the Soviet Union signed the Treaty of Rapallo with Germany as a basis for the restoration of regular economic relations and at this point the adventurers in the KPD were reined in.[107]

Neither Comintern nor the KPD abandoned revolution as the final goal, but the means to this end altered dramatically within the auspices of the United Front tactic. This tactic could involve forging common programmes with other socialist parties, or even entering coalition administrations, such as in Saxony and Thuringia in the autumn of 1923, and in this guise it was dubbed the United Front From Above. More often, however, the Communist movement appealed to the ordinary members of rival parties over the heads of their leaders in an attempt to win their support.[108] This United Front From Below was more frequently used during the Weimar era and it was in this form that the United Front was, later, to be significant in Communist/Nazi relations.

Thus in addressing the Third Congress of Comintern in mid 1921 Trotsky, with Lenin's support,[109] declared:

It is realised that the post-war revolutionary ferment is over. . . . The turn is taken to winning the masses, using the united front, that is, organising the masses on a programme of transitional demands.[110]

The KPD was, therefore, to concentrate on day-to-day affairs of the working class from within the factories. The factory cells formed for this purpose were to provide the future organisational base of the party and allow it to campaign on important bread-and-butter issues such as the defence of the eight-hour-day and against wage cuts.[111] These, of course, were the sort of issues German labour organisations had traditionally campaigned upon, prompting Rosenberg (who had himself been on the left of the party in the early 1920s) to conclude that a merger with the SPD was the logical consequence of such a tactic.[112] This, however, would have been to admit that the game was up and Trotsky's characterisation of the United Front programme as one of 'transitional demands' indicates that Comintern had no intention of abandoning its long-term objectives. The same held for the KPD itself. The development of the United Front strategy within Germany derived, ironically, from the writings of the disgraced Levi which convinced his successors of the advantages of this tactic:

> The workers who had not wanted to fight for revolution would surely fight about wages, hours, and taxes. And as they wanted to fight for these immediate objectives, against the wishes of their leaders, a rift would open between masses and leaders, and the former would gradually come over to the communists, who would lead them to revolution.[113]

On the surface this tactic proved extremely successful and enabled the KPD to regain and even exceed its previous peaks of popular support. By early 1922 party membership had recovered to the levels of early 1921[114] and this time Communist influence in the factories and other workplaces appeared to be growing. Certainly the Reich Commissar for the Surveillance of Public Order revealed his concern in a report of 7 April 1922:

> The Communists' strategy of creating a proletarian United Front and forming a workers' government to work with the Soviet Union against the Entente to remove the burdens of the peace treaty has found a resonance in broad circles. They have managed to achieve great success, by means of dedicated work of the most unscrupulous kind within the trade unions and other organisations, in detaching the masses from their leaders and actually turning them against their trade union leaders. . . . It would be wrong to assess the danger posed by the Communists in terms of their paid-up membership. In any future action they will receive strong support from hitherto non-Communist sections of the working class as well as from broad

sections of the civil service, state-employed workers and white-collar staff.[115]

The significant progress made on this level by the KPD left a deep impression on its leaders themselves but, contrary to the authorities' fears, attempts to translate this grass-roots success onto the national political stage during 1922 were disastrously unsuccessful and attracted harsh criticism from the ECCI.[116] In essence the KPD was faced with the same dilemma that had confronted it repeatedly since 1918. Once it behaved like a revolutionary Communist party (let alone a Bolshevik one) at national level, any support it could garner locally either melted away or proved ineffective in this wider context. This fundamental problem could not be faced, however, without the very meaning and purpose of the KPD being called into question and the party persisted in pursuing strategies such as the United Front tactic in the hope, eventually, of achieving the breakthrough that had thus far eluded it.

The logic of such a strategy involved great risks and contained the seeds of the disaster of early 1933. The KPD had rejected any longstanding formal alliance with other labour organisations (a logical enough decision from a Bolshevik viewpoint), but continued to believe that it represented the objective interests of the masses and could therefore win them over through the United Front tactic. Initially this strategy was directed exclusively against the SPD, but given that Bolsheviks regarded the Social Democratic leadership with loathing, there was no particular reason why a similar United Front strategy could not be employed against other hostile parties or organisations which enjoyed mass support. Thus first the Catholic unions and then, as will be seen,[117] the Nazi movement became objects of a United Front approach. The success or otherwise of this policy will be evaluated in due course, but, given that the KPD conducted the policy from a position of weakness rather than strength, the risk of contaminating the sizeable proportion of Communist supporters who were not committed Bolsheviks was always real. Zinoviev and Radek recognised the danger *vis à vis* Social Democracy from the outset,[118] but the possibility of building grass-roots bridges from Communism to yet another ideology, rather than from that ideology to Communism, even to one as distinctly opposed to Communist ideology as Nazism, could not be excluded.

Such problems lay in the future, but the KPD's weakness initiated other opportunistic strategies which also served as potential bridges between radical left and radical right. One such involved its attitude towards the lower middle classes. The Comintern perceived no long-term role for an autonomous lower middle class in the revolutionary scheme of things, as Lenin himself made clear at the First Comintern Congress in March 1919:

> When in capitalist society, the class struggle on which it rests becomes more acute, there is nothing between dictatorship of the bourgeoisie and dictatorship of the proletariat. The dream of another, third way is the reactionary lament of the petty bourgeoisie.[119]

Following on from this, Comintern and the KPD came to use the description 'petty bourgeois' to apply to all parties which pursued ideologies lying in some way apart from the notion of pure class struggle and in this way the description of a party as 'petty bourgeois' came to refer to its ideology rather than to its social composition.[120] However, the rejection of any distinctive 'non-proletarian' ideology did not necessarily prevent the Comintern from advocating the recruitment of the lower middle classes to the proletarian revolutionary cause. The USPD was condemned in 1920 for its 'useless attempts to win the lower middle classes before the revolution',[121] but in the Twenty-One Conditions presented to the Independents, among others, for entry to Comintern was the demand for agitation 'not only among the urban working-class masses, but among rural workers and small peasants'.[122] Here, perhaps, is demonstrated the Comintern's translation of the Russian revolutionary experience (in which the rural population played a vital role) to industrial Germany which did not lack a (predominantly right-wing) peasantry, but also possessed large numbers of white-collar staff and independent proprietors.

The KPD, therefore, had sought to gain influence within the broad masses of the lower middle classes in both the towns and the countryside. As its founding conference concluded: 'None of the parties engaged in the struggle can afford to neglect the mobilisation of the petty bourgeoisie for service in their armies',[123] and by 1920 Lenin himself agreed with this line of argument.[124] The Hamburg Communists – while still a part of the KPD in April 1919 – believed that the lower middle classes shared objective interests with the proletarian revolution because of their imminent ruin at the hands of the Versailles settlement,[125] which made their recruitment more than a cynical exercise. By late 1920 the KPD was putting much effort into winning over peasants and farm workers,[126] but there is no evidence of any notable success at this early stage. The problems that the KPD as an

avowedly proletarian party experienced in trying to attract lower
middle-class support, both rural and urban, have been widely
discussed, but nonetheless it had recognised the significance of the
lower-middle-class issue from an early stage. Once the NSDAP began
to dominate sections of this class, Communist concern was to increase
and the struggle between the KPD and NSDAP was to involve a battle
for lower-middle-class, as well as working-class, support.

All in all, the KPD was not in an enviable tactical position by late
1922. Its objective weaknesses were partly ameliorated by its
adherence to Comintern, by the adoption of tactical initiatives such as
the United Front From Below policy and not least by the opprobrium
the SPD had brought upon itself by its seeming readiness to crush any
open manifestations of left radicalism by whatever means available.
However, none of these factors served as a substitute for a positive
programme which might find broad acceptance within the working
classes, and throughout this early period of Weimar's history the
national question was to pose further, extraordinary difficulties for the
new party. Eventually, in 1923, the KPD's increasingly positive
perception of the national question was to combine with the United
Front policy to provide the initial set of linkages with the radical right
and even the infant Nazi movement.

2 The National Question 1918–1922

At first sight the national question might appear unlikely ground for cooperation between the KPD and the radical right. Karl Marx had regarded it as being of peripheral importance[1] and on balance European socialist parties could conclude from his, and Engels', writings that nationalist politics might divert attention from the revolutionary class struggle.[2] The founding fathers of the SPD had agreed; Karl Kautsky rejected nationalism as a phenomenon of the bourgeois capitalist era and saw no role for the national state or even distinctive national cultures in a future socialist world.[3] On the practical plane the use of nationalist sentiment by the German Imperial Government to reconcile the middle classes to an essentially non-democratic constitutional order reinforced Social Democratic hostility to nationalism.[4] It came to be an expression of social and political repression under the Imperial regime before 1914 and as Schüddekopf writes: 'For the working class the equation "national equals social reactionary" assumed increasing validity'.[5]

That said, German socialism contained elements of thought which perceived a positive role for the national state in the building of socialism, advocating the systematic intervention of the state to achieve a degree of national economic security commensurate with the well-being of the individual.[6] Ferdinand Lassalle echoed Fichte and Hegel in asserting that national independence and inner freedom belonged together[7] and his contention that the great nations were a locomotive of historical progress was also present in the writings of Marx and Engels.[8] The material, neo-mercantilist, dimension of this thinking found an echo in the social legislation of conservative Prussia during the early 1850s[9] and perhaps even that of the Imperial Government under Bismarck and Caprivi which afforded industrial workers practical reasons for at least channelling day-to-day grievances and longer-term political demands through the institutions of the national state.[10] In this vein the Social Democratic trade unions under Carl Legien espoused the principle of achieving concrete material improvements and, in the longer term, economic democratisation through the strength of the trade unions' organisation within the context of the Imperial German state.[11] In late 1913 his deputy,

Gustav Bauer, went further by recognising the relevance of the nation to its proletariat. In a war, he observed: 'Economic blocs would be fighting each other, and as long as the proletariat lived in closed economic blocs, they had a vested interest in seeing their own flourish.'[12] The SPD itself was divided in its response to the opportunities offered it by conservative 'state socialism' and economic growth, containing both principled orthodox Marxists and internationalists,[13] but also revisionists and reformists who regarded the existing state structures as a framework within which change could be achieved.[14] Prominent revisionists such as Eduard Bernstein advocated a forward German world policy so long as it stopped short of war,[15] while Josef Bloch, editor of the *Sozialistische Monatshefte*, proposed the integration of the working class, 'into a classless folk community (*Volksgemeinschaft*), in which a culturally defined nationality principle would form the main criterion of membership', through a policy of imperial grandeur.[16]

These were extreme views, but the growing identification of the SPD as a whole with the national state in a variety of contexts has been noted[17] and Moore argues that the SPD found it increasingly necessary to have the framework of an independent national state in which to resolve the longings of the downtrodden. This, he argues, 'amounted to a demand for acceptance in the existing social order', from which: 'it could only be a very short step to a positive willingness to defend this order when a foreign enemy loomed on the horizon'.[18] Put more dramatically: 'If the nation were defeated, [working-class gains] would be completely lost.'[19]

In these circumstances it is not surprising that the SPD's parliamentary fraction should have voted for war credits in August 1914 once they had concluded that the war was defensive and directed primarily at Tsarist Russia.[20] With the die cast, the majority of the Social Democrats found it hard to change tack, even after it became clear that the Imperial Government sought a 'victorious peace' to reinforce its authority and deny the masses the political and social gains they had been led to expect in return for supporting the war effort. The immediate predicament of the SPD's leaders and the legacy for them of pre-war ideological developments was characterised by one of their radical critics in telling terms: 'In the event of a defeat of the state to which they belonged, the proletarians would necessarily suffer greatly from unemployment and poverty, consequently it was their supreme interest and must be the supreme aim of their representatives to avoid this eventuality.'[21] The trade union leaders had come to similar conclusions, thus: 'The concept of thinking socialistically involved an awareness that it was not the private gain and advantage of the individual which guarantees victory but rather the sacrifices of the individual to the common weal of the nation.'[22] Comparable pronouncements were made in public. For instance, on replacing the more radical (and pacifist) Clara Zetkin as leader of the SPD women's movement in 1917, Marie Juchacz wrote in the movement's newspaper, *Die Gleichheit,* that: '*Gleichheit* would now put national interests above international; a strong Germany was a pre-requisite for a strong working-class movement.'[23] During the early stage of the war many workers evidently felt similarly. Even before the war patriotic, militarist and zenophobic tendencies had surfaced in some longstanding Social Democratic strongholds such as the Saxon industrial city of Chemnitz.[24] With the outbreak of hostilities nationalist fervour was sufficiently widespread within the working class to demonstrate the fundamental and instinctive importance of nationalist feeling to people who, just weeks earlier, had been committed in theory to the principle of international proletarian solidarity.[25] As the left-wing Social Democrat Henriette Roland-Holst commented in 1915: 'The present war has not only demonstrated that internationalist thought is infinitely less firmly anchored in the proletariat than we believed ten or twelve years ago, but, above all, that such sentiment (and all others) is impotent against feelings, moods, tendencies and passions which burst out from the subconscious with irrepressible force.'[26] In areas without a Social Democratic tradition patriotism and quiescent labour relations were the norm during the early stages of hostilities. Writing of the Ruhr Moore concludes that: 'To the end of 1915 the workers gave the war full and disciplined support, despite reductions in pay and many discharges, to the point where even the owners in the area praised it as a model.'[27]

As seen previously this quiescent, patriotic mood did not last.[28] The cost in lives, and mounting suffering on the home front, left workers increasingly ill-disposed towards a war effort which had as one of its objectives their political emasculation, and as popular discontent mounted the pacifist, internationalist left of the SPD began to reassert itself. The left of the SPD in parliament had, initially, voted for war credits out of respect for party discipline rather than from conviction[29] and had subsequently found that the emergency of the war provided the SPD's right with invaluable ammunition with which to curb and silence their radical colleagues.[30] So it came to the formal splitting of the SPD in 1917 and given that prominent future Communists such as

Luxemburg, Liebknecht, Zetkin, Levi and others were among those leaving the majority (and patriotic) SPD, the prospects for nationalism providing a bridge between radical left and right in the future must have seemed slim. Furthermore this pacifism and mounting working-class militancy were perceived by right-wing nationalists as akin to treason and their own existence was justified by their struggle against what they termed Bolshevism.[31]

However, in the mercurial political atmosphere of late 1918 the radical left, more notably in Hamburg and Bremen, developed a new form of revolutionary nationalism vaguely reminiscent of Robespierre's and in part inspired by events in Russia. Even before the armistice the prominent radical Bremen journal *Arbeiterpolitik*[32] was arguing that the German proletariat would need to fight a revolutionary war against the Western Entente to achieve revolution in Germany and safeguard the Russian revolution.[33] Similar sentiments were expressed by the radical leaders Heinrich Laufenberg and Fritz Wolffheim when they launched the revolution in Hamburg on 6 November with a mass meeting on the Heiligengeistfeld. With a Greater German Soviet Socialist Republic as their objective they demanded: 'The immediate organising of national defence by revolutionary means and in alliance with Russia to protect the revolution against the imperialist Entente.'[34] The programme was startlingly new, the logic somewhat less so. Just as the reformists had defended the integrity of the Imperial German state (against Tsarist Russia) so as to preserve a context within which they could achieve their gradualist objectives, so the radicals now required the survival of a revolutionary national state (free from Western capitalist influence) if they were to achieve their objectives. Socialism of any sort, it seemed, could not be realised in a territorial or institutional vacuum.[35]

This new form of radical socialism labelled itself 'national communism' and in its wish to stave off the capitalist West did not rule out cooperation with right-wing radicals at least on a temporary basis. Even cooperation between the revolutionary proletariat and the *Freikorps* was conceivable to fight Entente capitalism within the framework of a 'revolutionary *Burgfriede*' – a temporary truce between the proletariat and the nationalist bourgeoisie to permit a revolutionary war of liberation; with the proviso that the bourgeoisie subsequently recognised the exercising of state power by the proletariat.[36] Far-fetched though this strategy might now appear, its attraction in the desperate circumstances of post-armistice Germany were understandable. The war had radicalised many of its youthful participants, irrespective of their class or politics and these youthful radicals were ready for a reckoning with the old order. All soldiers, it was observed, had experienced the kind of suffering and deprivation that had justified working-class radicalism in peacetime, but Germany's defeat prevented them from achieving any sort of revolution, socialist or otherwise. In other words, the defeat may have enhanced right-wing hatred of the left, but it also created conditions in which cooperation between the radical extremes was not unthinkable, in spite of the obstacles to this. Therefore when groups such as the Hamburg National Communists advocated a defensive national revolutionary war to make possible changes which an Entente victory appeared to prevent,[37] their appeal was not exclusively to left-wing radicals.

The authorities noted that nationalist feeling of a similar kind was present within wider sections of the working class, whether revolutionary or reformist. At a Cabinet meeting on the 23 January 1919 at which Rhineland separatism was discussed, it was observed that the strongest resistance to any such moves came from the working class.[38] On 21 March Erzberger reported on the mood of the working class in Alsace and Lorraine where demands for autonomy from France were mounting. A wage of 3.50fr. for a ten-hour day had soured the workers' experience of liberation from 'Prussianism' and similar sentiments underlay much working-class nationalism.[39] Identification with Germany, or against the Entente, was intimately linked with the perception of likely material, social and political gains which would derive from a free, revived German state, or with the expectation of possible losses under the French, or Polish, state.[40]

Under these circumstances it is not surprising that revolutionary nationalist sentiment was present within the fledgling KPD and the presence of former IKD members within the party – to whom Laufenberg and Wolffheim had a particular appeal – reinforced nationalist sentiment still further.[41] At the very least the new Communist Party could ill afford to antagonise these numerous national communist members, for radical revolutionaries faced difficulties enough at the time without indulging in further fragmentation of the left. Schüddekopf goes further, arguing that had the KPD espoused a national communist programme 'at the outset, even before the signing of the Treaty of Versailles, [it] could have come to dominate revolutionary developments in Germany.'[42] In fact the KPD's leaders took quite the opposite course, becoming embroiled in a fierce struggle against the party's national communist and syndicalist elements which culminated in the loss of half their membership both nationally and in key centres such as Berlin.[43]

This opposition to the nationalist cause was part ideological and part pragmatic. Rosa Luxemburg had, in Borkenau's words: 'made it almost the core of her programme, both in Poland and in Germany, to disregard nationalism'.[44] After her death Paul Levi regarded the syndicalist tactics and revolutionary adventurism of the left radicals as the major problem and condemned them in these terms at the Heidelberg Conference in October 1919.[45] The nationalism of these same radicals remained an issue, however, attracting the disapproval of Comintern's delegate at Heidelberg, Karl Radek.[46] For the latter, economic links between a pre-revolutionary Germany and Russia were potentially the most useful and any political or military alliance between the two countries would have to await the destruction of the existing social order in the Reich.[47] In other words Radek doubted that the national communists, or national bolsheviks as he dubbed them, had a revolution to defend and it was not open to the Soviet Union to forge links with bourgeois states. If there was to be any cooperation at all between nationalists and the revolutionary left, Radek demanded that nationalists subscribed to the KPD's social revolutionary aims rather than the KPD according primacy to national liberation.[48] In May 1919 Lenin argued similarly when attacking German national bolshevism in his pamphlet, *'Left-Wing' Communism*: 'It would be petty-bourgeois to give liberation from Versailles precedence over promotion of the international Soviet revolution.'[49] Not surprisingly Comintern agreed, requiring in Point Six of its *Aims and Tactics* 'the complete union of the countries where the socialist revolution has triumphed'.[50] Thus, during the early months of Weimar, nationalism had established a presence on the radical left, but only to help split it and keep left and right well apart.

Changes began to occur after the presentation of the Entente's peace terms to Germany. Many radical intellectuals were driven to seek solutions on the right – where nationalism was always assured a warm welcome – but the prospect of harsh peace terms also had an impact on Comintern and the KPD. Even in March 1919 the first Comintern Congress observed that the Allies were strangling the revolution in the occupied parts of Germany and it condemned the Allied policy of indemnities and confiscations. It continued:

In addition the prisoners of war are to be made the slaves of the

victors. Proposals for compulsory labour service for German
workers are being discussed. The Allied Powers intend to impoverish
them and make them the hungry slaves of Entente capital.[51]

In its subsequent *Manifesto on the Versailles Peace Terms* the
Comintern argued similarly that:

> The entire weight of the Versailles peace falls in the first place on the
> German working class. If it were to endure for any length of time, it
> would mean that the German working class would have to groan
> under a double yoke – that of their bourgeoisie and that of the
> foreign slave-holders.[52]

Similar nationalist noises began to emanate from within the KPD. 'The
Versailles peace', wrote Erler, 'makes impossible simultaneously both
a capitalist and a socialist economy in Germany',[53] and later the KPD
was to reject Versailles and begin to advocate an anti-Western alliance
between Germany and the Soviet Union.[54]

At this stage, however, these implicitly nationalist utterances were
little more than straws in the wind. Lenin condemned those elements
in the KPD who opposed signing the peace treaty, arguing that: 'Even
a German socialist workers' government would have had to sign the
Treaty of Versailles in the first instance.'[55] The KPD's leadership
acceded to this view, commenting in its *Theses on the Peace* that: 'The
liquidation of war and the Peace of Versailles coincide with the
liquidation of the counter-revolution they therefore require an active
policy of revolution.'[56] The Comintern argued similarly that only
proletarian revolution throughout the Entente lands and in Germany
and Austria could overthrow the exploitative Versailles system and
continued: 'So long as the present German government is at the helm
the conflict between Berlin and Paris remains only a legal dispute
between the bourgeoisie of two coalitions.'[57]

The suppression of nationalist sentiment within the KPD took little
account of public reactions to Versailles and the other consequences of
Germany's defeat. The pacifism and war-weariness of 1918 was
superseded by a defensive nationalism as the harshness of the peace
terms became apparent and during 1920 this was reinforced by the
Allies' disarmament demands and mounting uncertainty over Upper
Silesia. Many workers and working-class organisations shared these
views so that by August Prussian officials considered national

bolshevik sentiments within broad sections of the population to represent an increasingly acute threat to internal security.[58] Later in the same month preliminary reports began arriving in Berlin of clashes between workers and French occupation troops in Upper Silesia,[59] and as trouble mounted in many Silesian cities left-wing radicals stormed the Polish and French consulates in Breslau on 26 August.[60] Pro-Polish elements struck back. Attacks and robberies upon, and even the murder of, pro-German workers were reported in November from the cities of Beuthen and Myslowitz and from the districts of Rybnik and Hindenburg.[61] The official labour movement in Upper Silesia expressed doubts in February 1921 about a Polish takeover, fearing that it could undermine the strength of organised labour: 'An important factor would be the undoubted flood of unemployed people from Poland itself which would have a confining and disruptive effect on the German trade unions because of their lack of schooling in trade union affairs and their lack of political consciousness.'[62] In other words, Germany's territorial integrity was linked with the integrity of the labour movement and in this sense the national question came to be of profound importance to German socialists. In mid March, just days before the plebiscite which brought victory for Germany but, nonetheless, partition of Upper Silesia, Entente troops occupied further parts of the territory. The working class in the newly occupied area reportedly responded by planning a protest strike, only abandoning this plan when it became clear that it would harm rather than help the German cause.[63]

The Upper Silesian workers were not isolated in their struggle. In Bavaria where the working class was, in any case, decidedly nationalist in reaction to the Allies' demands upon Germany,[64] the Communist Party itself eventually urged its Saxon colleagues not to obstruct trains carrying *Freikorps* units from Bavaria during mid 1921 to fight against Polish insurgents in Upper Silesia.[65] Whether this request was granted or not, workers in Saxony and Thuringia showed solidarity with their Upper Silesian comrades from an early stage. In September 1920 a Polish munitions train which was passing through Erfurt, presumably on its way from France, was attacked by workers and its cargo destroyed. The police arrested the ringleader, but even then had to beat off an attempt to free him which was organised by the local workers' council.[66] By February 1921 the authorities noted the growing concern in radical working-class circles throughout Germany over the Silesian question, observing that: 'The overwhelming majority of the German working class is supporting the retention of

Upper Silesia within the Reich with the utmost determination.'[67] The actions of some workers suggest that this official assessment of their mood was essentially accurate. For instance in Saxony workers in a number of factories offered to put in an hour's overtime without pay so that the money could be donated to the Fighting Fund for Upper Silesia. In Greater Dresden the Factory Councils decided to contribute an hour's wages to Upper Silesia, with the collection to be organised by the official trade union organisation, the ADGB. Similar meetings were widespread in the rest of Germany, demonstrating the importance attached by the working classes to the national question when it appeared to affect their own interests.[68] In fact the workers in the industrial heartland of western Germany soon had a national issue of their own. A combination of 'preposterous' Allied demands and German maladroitness on the reparations question soured relations between the two sides during 1921.[69] The Entente also became suspicious of covert German rearmament and occupied three Ruhr cities, Düsseldorf, Duisburg and Ruhrort, in March in response to these difficulties. Organised labour in the cities affected was in no doubt where its loyalties lay, and an official account of negotiations between the occupation authorities and the leader of the Metalworkers' Union in Duisburg provides a striking illustration of this:

> The leader of the German Metalworkers' Union answered the first question on the state of food provision to the working population with the reply that food supplies sufficed for the time being and that the working class would refuse to accept food from the Entente. Furthermore, the French District Officer was told that working class wages were not sufficient, but that the German worker was not so naive as to believe that Entente capitalism would raise German workers' wages. When the District Officer asked how the occupation was being received, he was told that it was felt by the working class to be dishonourable.[70]

Developments of this kind threw the KPD into disarray. Paul Levi's left-wing opponents on the Central Committee had their sights set on confrontation with the authorities by early 1921[71] and therefore tried to divert attention from the national question which, after all, seemed to demand some collaboration between classes. Versailles was judged to be a problem for the bourgeoisies of Germany and the West[72] and Ruth Fischer went further at a meeting of party functionaries in Berlin in early February 1921. After launching a bitter attack on the nationalist currents within the KPD she continued:

> In western Europe there is no such thing as a national working class. Russia drew the sword to defend revolutionary achievements, not to fight Entente imperialism. German revolutionaries too will not defend Germany – that is, the nation – instead they will defend their revolutionary gains.[73]

The KPD's *Hamburger Volkszeitung*, which strongly opposed national communist sentiment in a city where it was widespread, agreed with Fischer. The war and reparations, it maintained, had not benefited the British or French working classes, despite the robbing of the German proletariat,[74] while it considered the national question in Upper Silesia to be insignificant. Workers in Upper Silesia who were pro-German or pro-Polish would eventually realise their mistake.[75]

This was all very well, but national communists could still ask how Germany was to achieve a revolution in a world dominated by the capitalist Entente. The Soviet Union seemed to sense this, for its representative in Berlin, Vigdor Kopp, maintained relations between Comintern and the nationalist League of Communists during early 1921[76] and even the KPD hedged its bets as it negotiated with the League on plans for practical cooperation in early March.[77] The fiasco of the March Action effectively wrecked these moves, however, and precipitated the desertion of tens of thousands of KPD members to the nationalist KAPD or League of Communists. Even within the shrinking KPD many found the official anti-nationalist line espoused by Fischer and others hard to swallow. By February 1921 popular fury against the Allies' reparations demands had reached such a fever pitch in Munich that the KPD's local leaders, Thomas and Graf, identified openly with national communism. 'We Communists', declared Graf, 'support a revolutionary war against the Entente.'[78] Days later the SPD newspaper *Vorwärts* reported that Graf and Thomas had begun to collaborate with nationalist youth groups and had held joint propaganda meetings with the Pan German League,[79] while communist and nationalist activists began to appear together on the streets.[80]

The reaction of the KPD's national leadership was confused, with Comintern adding to the muddle. In clear contravention of his organisation's formal policy, the President of Comintern, Zinoviev, ordered Paul Levi to forge contacts with right-wing extremist circles, particularly with students. He was to win their cooperation by arguing that only if the far right cooperated with the radical left would they gain Russian help in the inevitable war that was looming between the Entente and Germany. If Zinoviev had been frank he might have added that the Russian government was anxious to divert attention from its own difficulties by any means available. In any case, Levi travelled to Munich where he did indeed begin to recruit right-wing extremists[81] as well as identifying publicly with Thomas's and Graf's stand.[82] Other local communist organisations were responding to events in a similar way. In the Silesian city of Gleiwitz the local leader, Rau, broke with party policy and, along with his members, declared for the German cause.[83]

Levi's colleagues in Berlin were not impressed. They rebuked him[84] and observed with deceptive blandness that the actions of the Munich KPD: 'were not in accordance with the fundamentals of the Communist Party'.[85] Disciplinary moves followed, with the Munich leaders being demoted and transferred from their posts,[86] but rumours circulated within the party that they had actually been expelled. The response to these rumours showed the strength of nationalist feeling within the KPD at large, with the authorities observing that: 'Many communists do not agree with the move and dissatisfaction with the *Zentrale* and with Levi is increasing.'[87] In fact, Levi's position as leader of the KPD had become untenable. His following of Comintern instructions on the national question had lost him support among senior party officials who no doubt felt that they themselves were remaining faithful to Comintern procedures. The denunciation of national communism and the punishment of the Munich leaders by the *Zentrale* had, as seen, aroused much opposition in the ranks and this too had rubbed off on Levi. Finally, as previously noted, Comintern's representatives in Berlin demanded in late February against Levi's inclinations that the KPD engage on a much more activist policy.[88] Levi consequently resigned along with other right-wing leaders, citing the difficulties he had experienced in carrying out Comintern policy in Germany as the reason for his move.[89]

Ironically, the authorities in Moscow decided at this point to clear up the muddle surrounding the national question in Germany and, despite reservations on the part of Zinoviev,[90] to exploit nationalist sentiment more openly for the Communist movement's own ends. The Hungarian economist, Eugen Varga, who had become Comintern's chief economics expert, assessed Germany's position in highly nationalistic terms. The reparations, foreign debts and the level of foreign control over the economy had made Germany the first example of a new style of colony. Its highly developed industry would be integrated into the Western economic system lock, stock and barrel, which seemed to justify tactical cooperation with bourgeois nationalists in revolutionary situations.[91] The Soviet representative in Berlin, Vigdor Kopp, was to instruct the KPD's leaders to abandon their previous opposition to nationalism and instead propagate national bolshevik ideas themselves.[92] Comintern statements on the situation in Germany during the remainder of 1921 and during 1922 reflected the new importance attached to the national question while continuing, understandably, to relate it to the question of class struggle. The German bourgeoisie was portrayed as a cowed and defeated class. Terrified of its own proletariat, defeated in war by the bourgeoisie of the Entente countries, its final desperate throw involved sucking the last drops of blood from its own proletariat to pay tribute to its new Entente masters: 'The bourgeoisie, aware that they cannot rely on the defeated working masses, will yield to the demands of victorious world capital in order to unload all the burdens imposed by the Entente on to the backs of the German proletariat.'[93] The Comintern appealed on several occasions to the French working class to realise that reparations were being extracted in the last resort from their German class brothers: 'they condemn the German proletarian to the life of a coolie',[94] and to oppose their own government's reparations policy,[95] but it expressed its belief in the inevitable ultimate demise of the Versailles reparations system in terms that a certain populist right-wing leader would have found perfectly acceptable: 'If [the German bourgeoisie] accept the conditions put forward by the Entente userers [*sic*], Germany's economic situation will get so much worse that the workers, driven to desperation, will be forced to rise against the robber Entente and its underlings.'[96] By the time of its Fourth World Congress during November and December 1922, it is argued, Comintern's position on the national question was 'fully in accordance with that of Hamburg national communism', with the important proviso that nationalism remained a tactic in the struggle of the international proletariat against world capitalism.[97]

Comintern, then, had recognised the potency of the national question in German politics and was prepared to exploit it, even to the extent of making the occasional exploratory overture to the German right. For the KPD itself the transition was less easy, which is understandable given the ferociousness with which the party's leaders had fought against nationalists and nationalism within their own ranks.

They began to issue appeals to the German working class to fight foreign, as well as German, exploiters[98] and to resist the Versailles Treaty – albeit in the cause of world revolution.[99] The party's behaviour was far from consistent, however. By mid 1921 it had with some difficulty finally purged its local organisation in Upper Silesia of all places of outspoken nationalists. Despite this the local party had advanced by advocating class struggle rather than nationalist struggle, but it remained a minority group in the province and had isolated itself from the rest of the working class which was German nationalist in sentiment.[100] The latter was hardly surprising. The Poles were no less disappointed than the Germans over the partition of Upper Silesia and by June a guerilla war, triggered by Polish insurgents, was raging in the German part of the province. Throughout Germany workers took a nationalist view of the question and found the KPD's official line unacceptable. As the authorities reported:

> The Upper Silesian question has a national rather than a commu-
> nist significance for very broad sections of the working class. Even
> in the Ruhr coalfield there exists, even among the younger radical
> miners, exceptional hatred against the Poles.[101]

From the summer of 1921 until late 1922 the KPD's leaders ducked and wove on the problem. On 10 May 1921 the *Zentrale* circulated a commentary on the reparations question and the possibility of the further occupation of German territory which discussed the national question very much on its own terms rather than subordinating it to the issue of the class struggle:

> The occupation of the Ruhr coalfield would not only represent an
> economic guarantee, a source of income and a means of putting
> pressure on the industry and trade of the rest of Germany. It would
> simultaneously be a political instrument with which to dismember
> and weaken Germany and a military position which would give
> France the greatest possible security against Germany – whether
> revolutionary or counter-revolutionary.
>   The disarmament issue gives France the means to attack southern
> Germany and, if necessary, occupy further territories there. We
> must also reckon on the possibility of France giving Poland
> permission to impose 'sanctions'; that is to occupy part of the Upper
> Silesian industrial basin.[102]

In July it accused the other parties of 'plundering the German working class and bringing it to its knees' through their acceptance of the reparations terms.[103] Small wonder, then, that the right wing of the USPD regarded the KPD's nationalism as 'damned similar to the war-mongering of the Pan German League'.[104] In September, by contrast, the KPD saw international revolution as the way forward,[105] but then, in another turnaround, the communist press joined newspapers of virtually all persuasions in welcoming the Treaty of Rapallo, signed between Germany and Russia in May 1922, as a putative alliance against the Entente.[106] By October 1922, however, the KPD reverted to calling for a common class struggle by the French and German proletariat against Versailles.[107] Finally, in November, the KPD backed Reich Chancellor Cuno's policy of national resistance against France as the Ruhr crisis loomed.[108]

The KPD, then, operated during the early 1920s in an environment where nationalist sentiment of a distinctly working-class kind was widespread and, initially, had had a firm hold within the KPD itself. In order to be true to their own convictions regarding international class struggle and to comply with conditions laid down by Comintern, the Communist Party's senior leaders initially declared war on nationalism and through expulsions and through the resignation of many thousands of members eventually reduced its potency within the party. They did so at considerable cost in terms of membership and support and once the Soviet authorities needed a powerful Communist presence in Germany in late 1920 and early 1921, the national issue was seen as a crucial means of winning back mass support. The KPD's leaders were slower to respond, but eventually they were prepared to recognise the significance of the national question for the revolution-ary cause. In a tortuous and sometimes self-destructive fashion the KPD had reached a point where a measure of cooperation with the radical right on the national question was inherently possible.

That said, what were the prospects of such cooperation when matters were viewed from the perspective of the far right? Despite the profound differences between the two extremes, both shared a hatred of parliamentarianism which sometimes seemed to obscure these differences and provided a bond of sorts which did not exist between the majority of the organised working class – committed as it was to parliamentarianism – and the far right.[109] Even within the *Freikorps* there were many admirers of Communist extremism: 'Because it attacked what they most hated: liberalism, parliamentary democracy and the "smug complacency" of the *bürgerlich* mentality.'[110] However, to share enemies was not to share aims and the KPD's demand for 'social liberation and a working class monopoly of political power'[111] was something the radical right could not contemplate. Thus the authorities of the day noted that mutual enmity nourished both movements. Plots and plans on the far right evoked a reaction on the far left and *vice versa*,[112] with a periodic risk of this activity spilling over into open conflict.[113] The Reichs Commissar for the Surveillance of Public Order noted in his report of 1 December 1922 that left and right did not merely react to each other's provocations. In addition: 'In their agitation both extremist parties justify the necessity of arming themselves above all else on the grounds that the government no longer has the power energetically to counter the opposite party.'[114] Of course this line of argument was disingenuous to say the least, for neither extreme wished to see a strengthened Weimar Republic and had in a roundabout way again implicitly acknowledged shared negative aims.

Thus it was that fighting rather than any cooperation first brought left and right together in concrete terms. The *Freikorps* were used repeatedly to crush demonstrations, strikes and risings staged by radical workers during the early years of Weimar and since the KPD was involved in this left-wing insurgency to a greater or lesser extent it too became involved in armed conflict with the far right. However, the physical proximity which fighting necessarily involves can sometimes produce unexpected examples of fraternisation, or the development of a fighting man's ideology, which can appear to transcend the original differences between the combatants. The fraternisation between British and German troops on Christmas Day 1914 is a well-known example of this phenomenon, but there were many other less spectacular instances during the First World War. The same occurred in post-war Germany. The ordinary *Freikorps* soldiers were not necessarily entirely socially distinct from their communist opponents; the *Freikorps* Oberland, for instance, contained 'many workers and woodcutters' within its ranks,[115] while as Mai has shown, the *Freikorps* Haas was overwhelmingly working class in 1919.[116] Thus the description of the *Freikorps* in general as 'consisting of the unemployed, or predominantly of youth in search of fighting and adventure'[117] need not have excluded the working class by any means. No doubt the workers involved were usually anything but socialist at the outset, being recruited from among the *völkisch*-minded population,[118] but with the passage of time some of these workers could become less unsympathetic to the Communist cause where the national question provided linkages between them. The same held true for one or two *Freikorps* leaders, such as Beppo Römer of Oberland, who were themselves later to end up in the KPD. Indeed Oberland, which helped to crush the Soviet Republic in Munich in April 1919 and fought against the Ruhr workers in March and April 1920, refused to break a strike in the Silesian city of Ratibor in mid 1921 (after a victorious engagement against the Poles), by which time Römer was already in contact with the KPD.[119] The participation of some former members of the Ehrhardt Brigade on the Russian side in the Russo-Polish war of 1920[120] was striking practical evidence of the way in which nationalism (here in the form of anti-Polish sentiment) could short-circuit the ideological gulf between the radical extremes and, given the increasing resonance of nationalism in Communist circles, it is understandable that some Communist organisations regarded the *Freikorps* contribution to the defence of Upper Silesia in a positive light.[121]

In more abstract terms, intellectuals on the German right perceived close links between Conservative and Bolshevik ideology which the Communists either refused, or were unable, to see at the outset. Alfons Paquet, a member of the Prussian Academy of Arts who was later to stand out against the Nazis, commented that Bolshevism was merely: 'the social expression of utter national despair in the wake of a lost war'.[122] The radical right was increasingly impressed by the Red Army's recruitment of former Tsarist officers – one in five had joined the Red Army – and for that reason too began to regard Bolshevism as a patriotic Russian phenomenon.[123] The right, then, were conscious that the boundaries between themselves and other ideologies were not impermeable and in exceptional instances adapted their political behaviour accordingly. *Freikorps* units were certainly instrumental in crushing the Ruhr workers' rising in the spring of 1920, but Schüddekopf remarks that the KPD had been able to recruit a significant number of *Freikorps* officers (who had participated in the right-wing Kapp putsch just weeks earlier) to lead the Ruhr workers in their struggle – which had been triggered primarily by the same Kapp putsch.[124] This was not an isolated incident, for the authorities observed that the favourable outcome of the reparations and disarmament negotiations at Spa was producing a 'national bolshevik' backlash among many former right-wingers:

It has been reported from all parts of the Reich that the outcome of the Spa negotiations has resulted in a considerable increase in 'national bolshevism' in originally right-wing circles. The intention of cooperating with Russia to throw off the Entente yoke is spreading with increading rapidity.[125]

The presentation of the final reparations demands to Germany in January 1921 would, the authorities feared, have a similar effect on many right-wingers:

> The despairing mood of many patriotic Germans will make it easy for them to conclude that it would be better to experience an overall collapse of the existing world order at the hands of Bolshevism than to be slaves of foreign nations.[126]

Therefore just as many Communists had come to see nationalism as an indispensable revolutionary tool in the Germany of the early 1920s, some nationalists had come to see certain attractions in Communism. Of course the scale and character of this convergence has to be kept within proportion. The few formal approaches for cooperation that the KPD made to right-wing organisations failed. The Communist Party failed to absorb any part of the ideologically eclectic *Freideutsche Jugend* (FDJ), which formed an important part of the essentially middle-class German youth movement. Even the KPD's approaches to avowedly left-radical elements of the FDJ at Hofgeismar in the autumn of 1920 and later to the FDJ more generally at Meißen in the autumn of 1923 failed because the FDJ rejected the Communists' uncompromising advocacy of the primacy of the class struggle.[127] Schüddekopf observes that contacts between the two sides during 1921 were aimed, basically, at attracting recruits from each other rather than at initiating cooperation on an open, equal basis and this observation has a wider temporal validity.[128]

With regard to the emerging National Socialist movement, it lacked the coherence and significance outside Bavaria, and more particularly Munich, for its attitude to be specially important at this stage. The nationalism within the Munich working class provided Hitler with possibilities for recruiting workers to his infant party,[129] but the local KPD's enthusiasm for the nationalist cause brought him competition from an unexpected quarter. Thus he felt obliged to adopt a relatively positive public attitude to the Communist Party during 1920, which did not necessarily entirely run counter to his inner convictions.[130] At one meeting he declared a preference for seeing half a million rifles in Communist hands rather than their being surrendered to the Entente, and just as Thomas, the Communist leader, might demand a popular rising and a struggle against the Entente, so Hitler was prepared to call for a national general strike.[131] Two days before the May 1920 general election Streicher, then a member of the German Socialist Party, appealed to the 'brothers' of the Social Democratic and Communist parties to support his own – a move that failed,[132] but which indicated nonetheless the perception on Streicher's part of some sort of community of interests between the ordinary supporters of the radical right and left. During late 1920 the Nazis began to use former left-wing political activists as speakers at their meetings,[133] and all in all, as Zitelmann has argued, the ambivalent position occupied by the NSDAP between left and right forced Hitler to defend himself simultaneously from accusations: 'that in truth he was a Communist or Bolshevist, or by contrast that he was a reactionary, monarchist, capitalist underling'.[134] However, the Nazis' apparent flexibility was of little immediate significance given their limited membership and limited geographical base. The parties of the left reportedly feared the NSDAP's potential by late 1922,[135] but the attitudes of more influential and powerful groupings within the amorphous coalition that made up the radical nationalist right were more important.

This element of ideological overlap and of, as yet, limited contact between the radical extremes must be seen as a response by these organisations to the objective situation in which Germany found itself after the war; a response reinforced by the reactions of some of their actual or potential supporters to the same situation. Both national and social revolution constituted plausible elements of any radical resolution of Germany's difficulties and this had drawn the far left and right closer together in spite of formidable initial obstacles. In 1920 Lenin compared the German situation with that in Russia in 1905: 'We see in Germany a similar unnatural coalition between Black Hundred members and Bolsheviks; a distinct "reactionary-revolutionary" type has emerged'[136] At Rapallo in April 1922 Radek was to speak of the need to 'unite Communists and right-wing Bolsheviks [sic] for a final struggle against West European capitalism'.[137] By late 1922, then, although national communists or national bolsheviks had failed to create or come to dominate a mass party, the radical left had become sufficiently influenced by national issues and the radical right had become sufficiently willing to grant guarded and qualified recognition of this to prepare the ideological ground for more significant cooperation during the crisis year of 1923. The KPD's United Front tactic was to provide the practical means for this cooperation to develop.

3 The 1923 Crisis

The reparations demands presented by the Allies to Germany in May 1921 proved unworkable for a variety of reasons[1] and a partial German default on payments provided the ostensible grounds for the occupation of the Ruhr District by French and Belgian troops on 11 January 1923 to extract reparations in kind. As the French Prime Minister announced to the National Assembly on the same day: 'We are fetching coal, that's all.'[2] There were, however, deeper-seated reasons for the occupation. During the peace negotiations at Versailles France had entertained the hope of weakening Germany economically on a long-term basis while strengthening herself. The demands for reparations had formed part of this strategy, but France's territorial ambitions were equally important. Before the war the economies of Lorraine (Lothringen), Luxemburg, the Saar Basin and the Ruhr had been economically interdependent, with the Ruhr drawing heavily on supplies of iron ore (minette) from Lorraine in particular.[3] French reannexation of Lorraine and the severance of Luxemburg and the Saar Basin from the German customs' union therefore constituted potentially a heavy blow against Germany, but from France's view the results were disappointing. Ruhr industrialists substituted Swedish and Spanish iron ore for the minette and by 1922 Germany possessed the same capacity for steel production as she had had in 1913. In northeast France, by contrast, the collapse of German demand for raw materials led to depressed conditions and seen in broader terms German industrial output was recovering rapidly by 1921, while French output was falling.[4]

The Treaty of Rapallo between Germany and Russia alarmed the French government still further since Germany appeared to be escaping the political isolation it had endured since Versailles and, perhaps, acquiring a potentially powerful military ally.[5] In these circumstances France activated its longstanding objective of occupying the Ruhr District in order to engage Germany in a general trial of strength, with the further specific aim of establishing a separate Rhineland Republic in the longer term.[6] The German government responded vigorously with a policy of passive resistance within the occupied zone which, although popular, effectively deprived the country of its industrial heartland. Government revenues consequently fell just as expenditure rose to provide welfare and other compensatory payments for those involved in the passive resistance, providing a final twist to the inflationary spiral that had begun after the war.[7] As printing presses churned out ever larger quantities of banknotes the value of bonds and cash deposits was destroyed entirely, leading to unprecedented levels of bitterness and despair among the middle classes. Eventually output too was adversely affected with most workers finding themselves either unemployed or on short time and the remainder finding that rampant inflation was undermining the value of their wage packets. Yet again, national and socio-economic problems had combined to bring the Republic to the point of crisis.[8]

Even before the Ruhr crisis the working class in the Rhineland had been hostile to the French occupation authorities[9] and 11 January brought about, in Kochan's words, 'a resurrection of the mood of August 1914' in Germany as a whole.[10] Defensive nationalism became widespread within the working class which resorted to spontaneous passive resistance even before the authorities and working-class organisations had fianlised their plans.[11] Social Democratic and trade union leaders were swift to react, however, and to a degree even anticipated the crisis. Shortly before French forces entered the Ruhr, ADGB leaders opened negotiations with the *Reichsverband der deutschen Industrie* (RdI) to determine, in cooperation with this employers' association, how limited strike action might best contribute to a programme of passive resistance.[12] On 7 February leading Social Democrats, including the Prussian Interior Minister, Carl Severing, agreed to cooperate with the Chief of the Army Command, Hans von Seeckt, in the formation of special paramilitary forces.[13] The SPD's main newspaper, *Vorwärts,* underwrote this working-class patriotism and former USPD members such as Rudolf Hilferding, Karl Kautsky and Eduard Bernstein took space in the paper to support resistance and condemn the French government's action.[14]

Despite this renewed wave of working-class patriotism, and despite its own painful experiences during previous years, the KPD played a minimal role in the initial phases of the Ruhr struggle. Fear of complete isolation prompted Communist participation in the half-hour protest strike called by the authorities in the Ruhr on 15 January,[15] but beyond this the Ruhr crisis was perceived within the context of the international class struggle. The KPD's leaders opposed the objectives pursued, as they saw it, by the French bourgeoisie in the Ruhr, but remained equally opposed to the German bourgeoisie.[16] Any patriotic pact to resist the French incursion was, therefore, out of the question. As Clara Zetkin declared at the KPD's Eighth Party

Congress in Leipzig on 21 January: 'Germany's working class will never form itself into a nation in league with the bourgeoisie, only through bitter life-and-death struggle against it.'[17] Similarly Paul Frölich had declared at the end of the Reichstag debate on passive resistance: 'We feel ourselves to be the brothers of our French comrades at this moment. No national united front. Instead the united front of the proletariat.'[18] The local party in the Ruhr itself followed this line with the result, the authorities observed, that it became conspicuously isolated from the majority of the working class in the area.[19] The KPD as a whole maintained an anti-nationalist stance during the early spring and although the Ruhr question continued to dominate German politics, the Communists and, intriguingly, the NSDAP, concentrated on domestic issues with limited support as their reward.[20] When the KPD did discuss the Ruhr issue it did so within the context of the international class struggle.[21]

The KPD's leading theorist, August Thalheimer, who stood on the right of the party, was the first to suggest, tentatively, that the national question was of significance to the Communist movement. Writing in *Die Internationale*, he ascribed a qualified revolutionary role to the German bourgeoisie in matters of foreign policy,[22] although national liberation remained primarily the task of the proletariat. It would: 'bring about the unity of the nation through the *Anschluß* of German Austria and thereby complete Bismarck's work'; a task in which the petty bourgeoisie and 'semi-proletariat' might participate in a subordinate capacity.[23] The left, grouped around Ruth Fischer and Arkady Maslow, resisted fiercely the notion of nationalist struggle at the cost of class struggle,[24] but by May the KPD's Central Committee appeared to have united on a policy of anti-French resistance with surprising conviction. As will be seen,[25] Comintern had much to do with this change of heart, but the KPD could hardly have failed to observe the opportunities that the Ruhr crisis offered it at domestic level. It only remained for the German Communists to abandon the rather tenuous construct of proletarian internationalism and dust down the national bolshevik tendencies which had been developed in earlier years. Bitterness in the Ruhr had reached new heights with the shooting dead of thirteen workers at the Krupp Essen works during French moves to requisition food lorries on 31 March leaving, in the authorities' estimation, little room for notions of class struggle between Germans for the time being.[26] A month later the KPD fell into line with other working-class organisations by denouncing repeatedly any talk of a negotiated settlement between Germany and

France, but did so in terms which, the authorities observed, appeared to build bridges towards the radical right:

> [The Communists] argue that the French and Belgians must proceed with the immediate evacuation of the Ruhr District and of all occupied German territories. With these demands the Communists are in complete agreement with those made by the right-wing radicals, and equally so in the opinion that the matter must be decided through action of some sort; they propose a general strike in this context.[27]

The KPD's tactical position had improved at a stroke. Even in March the SPD in the Reichstag had found the bourgeois parties unwilling to levy additional taxes on corporate profits and on the wealthy to underwrite the costs of passive resistance.[28] In May the Cuno government found itself in a parlous situation economically, yet unable to resolve the Ruhr crisis since France insisted that passive resistance end before talks begin, while working-class organisations reasserted their determination to continue passive resistance even if negotiations over the Ruhr began. The KPD recognised that the situation was critical and that a failure by the government to win the Ruhr struggle in decisive fashion might trigger major unrest.[29] In mid May the Central Committee predicted imminent bourgeois capitulation, commenting with not a few crocodile tears: 'The German bourgeoisie will capitulate at any moment in spite of the very costly resistance put up by the proletariat against the French imperialist incursion.'[30] In early June a delegation from the Central Committee, which included the previously anti-nationalist left-winger Ruth Fischer, visited the KPD's district leadership in Rhineland-South Westphalia to assess the situation. Stöcker, a member of this delegation, forecast that however the Ruhr crisis ended the area would probably be separated from the rest of the country. In such a situation, he told the local party, the proletariat would act as the saviour of the nation:

> It will be an historic task of the German proletariat – and this cannot be stressed strongly enough – to conduct the most bitter struggle against every foreign imperialism. It goes without saying that the KPD must take the lead in this struggle.[31]

The Reichs Commissar for the Surveillance of Public Order became alarmed both by the fact that the German government had painted itself into a corner and by the potential use the KPD could make of this. Passive resistance had undoubtedly caused great hardship in the Ruhr and was ruining the country's economy, but the population of the occupied area showed no weakening in its resolve to resist the French authorities. As the Commissar concluded: 'The mood in all sections of the Ruhr population, particularly in civil service and working-class circles which have been worst affected, demonstrates beyond doubt that people there will not understand it if the German government gives way on the issue.' This smoothed the way for Communist agitation:

> It must be stressed that the Communists in particular, who have indeed always understood how to recognise the mood of the population and exploit it for themselves, are ascribing to the present German government the intention of capitulating to French imperialism and capitalism. This accusation has unleashed an unpleasant style of agitation among the working class.[32]

In other words the KPD had latched on to the intense nationalist feeling present within the working class, and its self-appointed task was to lead the working population to social and national liberation.[33]

This renewed interest in the national question was also fuelled by Communist reactions to mounting fascist success in Germany which ultimately complicated the KPD's attitude to the radical right in a variety of ways. Despite the intensity of the Communists' struggle against the SPD they were not, as is sometimes suggested, blinded thereby to the threat posed by right-wing radicalism in general and National Socialism in particular.[34] *Die Rote Fahne* warned on 30 January 1923 that Hitler's growing success in Bavaria had alarming parallels with Mussolini's rise to power in Italy:

> Hitler is aping Mussolini; he has declared, 'To Berlin!'. The alliance between big capital and the fascists threatens the German proletariat with unprecedented slavery. The economic war on the Ruhr has engendered the danger of a victory of German fascism, just as it will strengthen the most decidedly counter-revolutionary elements in France.[35]

The May Day Manifesto of the Comintern was no less aware of the dangers posed by fascism, arguing that it represented the final phase in the struggle between capital and labour: 'Every single worker must be summoned to fight against fascism; against the united front of the exploiters – the united front of the proletariat.'[36]

This ideological opposition was reinforced by the prospect of exploiting a confrontation with fascism to benefit relations with the SPD's rank and file to the detriment of the latter's leaders. Attacks by the far right on ordinary Socialist working men prompted Communist attempts to mobilise joint KPD-SPD grass-roots resistance to this violence which in turn provided an opportunity to create the desired United Front from Below with Socialist workers.[37] This attempt to undermine the authority of the SPD's leaders, however, failed in the main. Even the ordinary Social Democrats had ample grounds for suspecting the KPD's motives on the basis of past behaviour and their leaders were even more wary. The Proletarian Hundreds were formed by the Communists in early 1923 purportedly to resist fascist violence, but, as Diehl observes: 'Social Democratic leaders, realising that the true purpose of the Communists was to gain control over large masses of socialist and unorganised workers, dragged their feet, avoiding cooperative ventures or forming separate SPD organisations.'[38] In addition, despite all the declarations of opposition to fascism, the KPD also made overtures to the right which did nothing to reassure the SPD.[39]

These overtures were symptomatic of the carrot and stick approach that the KPD adopted in its dealings with the far right. In this vein the Central Committee held a special conference of parliamentary members and senior officials in Stuttgart on 27 December 1922 to discuss the increasing threat posed by the Nazi movement. This was followed by further meetings all of which were assessed by the authorities as rather dreary failures, but at Stuttgart the Berlin leadership presented the *Guidelines for Combating National Socialism and Fascism* which laid down the future basis of Communist–Nazi relations. In essence a dual strategy of confrontation and collaboration was mooted. The radical right was, where possible, to be prevented from holding meetings, but National Socialism and fascism were also to be countered more positively: 'by the political influencing of circles attached [thereto] and by forming organisational links with the same'.[40] By approaching Nazis directly in this fashion the KPD's leaders had confirmed, implicitly at least, earlier suggestions[41] that the United Front from Below might be applied to the right as well as to the SPD's members. The presence of two Nazi representatives at the Stuttgart meeting who were allowed time to counter arguments of two of the KPD's speakers[42] pointed to one form of organisational link that was to become common in later years.

The KPD felt threatened on its home ground because the *völkisch* parties in general had for the working classes an attraction, extending even beyond the national issue, which was regarded as disconcerting and even menacing. In late 1922 it noted the influx of *völkisch*-minded young workers into the factories as some managers sought to dilute the influence of the political left within the economy. These workers' separate electoral lists for seats on the factory councils were perceived by the KPD as one threat to the left, another being their perceived role as agents of management.[43] However, the radical right was believed to pose a broader danger than the narrowly conspiratorial, for it seemed to be genuinely popular among some workers. Even the relatively small NSDAP was recognised as a competitor for 'sections of the population which the Communists expected to win for themselves' and the KPD was forced to accept that within a democratic environment some account had to be taken of this problem.[44] At the Leipzig Party Congress attention was paid in January 1923 to the increasing popularity of the NSDAP within Bavaria where it was estimated to have 50 000 members. 'It was dangerous', the Congress concluded, 'because of its sympathetic attitude towards the workers, on account of which it had already established a presence within the working class.'[45] With regard to the National Socialist programme, as contained within the *Twenty-Five Points*, the *Communist Party Correspondence* evaluated Points 2, 4, 5 and 24 as showing the true face of Nazism: 'imperialism, nationalism, and as a consequence anti-Semitism'. However it recognised that Points 10 to 14 and 'the remaining similar demands form the social bait to win over the petty bourgeoisie and the workers',[46] and elsewhere the KPD interpreted these parts of the *Twenty-Five Points* as 'posing the demands of the KPD'.[47] Thus the NSDAP was never taken by the KPD for an authentic socialist party, but it was recognised that the Nazis might win popular support from some of the social groups to which the left-wing parties appealed or sought to appeal and the Comintern went rather further when later assessing the NSDAP's socialistic demands as 'a healthy drive towards a final break with the Old Regime'.[48] The KPD's concern persisted during the spring of 1923 when Nazi success among the unemployed was noted and feared.[49] Indeed the left-wing leader Maslow concluded in April that the fascists had become serious competitors in the struggle for disappointed Social Democrats and politically unorganised workers.[50]

The problems posed by fascism for the European Communist movement were debated in March at the International Conference organised by the KPD in Frankfurt-am-Main.[51] The attraction of fascism to sections of the working class was recognised implicitly in the Conference's call for: 'systematic exposition of the class-hostile character of the fascist movement among the working class'. Youth in particular was considered vulnerable to fascism, with the Conference therefore calling for: 'particular attention to be paid to anti-fascist propaganda among working class youth, from whose ranks the fascists gain most of their supporters'.[52] This message was carried by Clara Zetkin to the enlarged ECCI meeting in June 1923. She stressed that fascism had a wide popular appeal with a social basis 'which extended beyond the petty bourgeois classes and into the proletariat'.[53] She did not question the orthodox Comintern interpretation of fascism as being a consequence of decaying capitalism and as constituting 'the bourgeoisie's ally and "instrument of class struggle" ', but added that because of the character of its mass support, fascism also contained elements 'which could become extremely uncomfortable, yes, even dangerous, for bourgeois society'.[54] Thus fascism was regarded at this stage, and in contrast to Dimitrov's later, famous interpretation,[55] as a mass phenomenon which could, possibly, slide into conflict with the ruling classes. The ECCI as a whole accepted Zetkin's view in their closing resolution 'On Fascism' which demanded that: 'the vague and unconsciously revolutionary elements contained within fascism [must] be directed into the proletarian class struggle against the bourgeoisie's class rule and powers of expropriation'.[56] This interpretation implied that fascism offered the KPD opportunities if it could harness the revolutionary forces contained within it (thus reinforcing the justification for extending the United Front tactic rightwards), but that it simultaneously threatened Communism through its ability to recruit and organise mass support which, the ECCI believed, properly belonged within the Communist movement. In any event, a constructive response to fascism was required.

Fascism's growing appeal to the petty bourgeoisie attracted the KPD's attention as much as its appeal to the workers and here the party found another stick with which to beat the SPD. As Brandler declared to the Leipzig Congress:

> The victory of fascism is the greatest defeat that the German proletariat has suffered so far. The Nationalists' following is recruited in part from social groups who were ready to participate in an active Socialist policy and who, in their disappointment at the betrayal and incompetence of Social Democracy, have now transferred to the opposite camp.[57]

In its resolution on 'The Political Situation and the Immediate Tasks of the Proletariat' the Leipzig Congress developed this theme by arguing that it was above all the lower middle classes who had been alienated from the revolutionary cause by the SPD's betrayal of the same: 'The bankruptcy of Social Democratic policy and the appalling suffering of the urban *Mittelstand* which has followed from this forms the main impetus for the burgeoning of a fascist movement in Germany.'[58]

The KPD's *Zentrale* had, as noted earlier, embarked on an ideological campaign in late 1922 to involve petty bourgeois Nazis in Communist-led struggles, or failing that, to neutralise them and had instructed subordinate party organisations accordingly.[59] The Leipzig Congress confirmed this strategy, stressing that there was no middle way for the petty bourgeoisie between the proletariat and capital. The petty bourgeoisie had to be shown that its salvation lay in a common struggle with the proletariat against big capital. Significantly, the Congress believed that only in this way could the Communist Party hope to defeat fascism: 'The proletariat will break up and beat down the rising fascist flood, which is a consequence of its own passivity if, during this struggle, it ruthlessly supports the interests of the collapsing petty bourgeoisie as against those of the big bourgeoisie.'[60] In May the propensity for white-collar staff to support fascism was noted and counter-measures within the trade unions proposed,[61] and the ECCI and the Central Committee of the KPD issued a joint warning in the same month regarding fascist successes within the lower middle class as a whole:

> The party must not repeat the Social Democrats' mistake of paying most attention to the winning of the working class. It must pay far more attention to winning over small peasant circles and those parts of the *Mittelstand* which were proletarianised after the war. At present they have lurched into the right-wing radical and nationalist camp.[62]

Their support was regarded somewhat cynically as a means of establishing a purely proletarian dictatorship,[63] but the potential importance of the lower middle classes for the political future had been recognised by the KPD and efforts were made to win them over, thereby 'weakening the class enemy and strengthening the forces of revolution'.[64] Thus Brandler for one justified the KPD's interest in nationalism partly because it represented a means of gaining support from middle-class circles.[65]

Communist hopes in this regard might seem to have been far-fetched, both because of the forthright manner in which the KPD emphasised its role as the party of the proletariat and because of the apparent readiness of petty bourgeois Germans, particularly Protestants, to support parties of the extreme right during the later part of the Weimar era. However, white-collar staff were not necessarily right wing in their political sympathies during the early twentieth century[66] and during the early 1920s this was no less the case for the lower middle classes in general. The hyperinflation, Flechtheim argues, caused the petty bourgeoisie to swither between fascism and Communism[67] and official reports on the political mood of the rural population lend some credence to this view. In March 1923 the Reichs Commissar for the Surveillance of Public Order noted that support for the KPD was increasing in the factories, but continued:

> In particular it must also be noted that in many rural districts with little industry Communist agitation among the agricultural population has, recently, enjoyed markedly more success. It has been established in case after case that collections made precisely in these circles have brought in large sums of money.[68]

The same official reported in similar vein in September 1923, noting Communist success in organising the small peasants. In southern Germany matters had progressed sufficiently for the KPD to contemplate convening a South German Workers' and Peasants' Congress which could subsequently be expanded into a Workers', Peasants' and *Mittelstands* Congress.[69] This is not to argue that the KPD was establishing a permanent presence within parts of the lower middle classes. Just over a year later, in December 1924, official reports spoke of Communist failure among the rural population[70] and by 1926 officials may still have regarded Communist rural agitation as a grave potential threat, but could not identify any significant successes.[71] Nonetheless, the KPD had become aware of the significance of the lower middle classes in German politics and at no time did it treat right-wing advances therein with equanimity. Furthermore, although the results of the KPD's middle-class agitation were very modest, there was, apparently, sufficient potential to ensure its continuation so as to combat the radical right on its home ground.

By mid 1923 the KPD could regard its overall progress with mixed feelings. The Ruhr crisis and the inflation had combined to inflict great suffering on the German population with: 'the ballooning price and frequent shortage of essential foodstuffs . . . causing widespread malnutrition and the reappearance of diseases that had been common during the worst days of the Allied blockade'.[72] The KPD benefited from this heightened misery and also from the employers' ability to whittle away at the gains made by the labour movement during and after the 1918 Revolution. By early 1923 party membership exceeded 200 000 and by the end of the year was approaching 300 000.[73] To this growth in membership can be added a number of notable electoral successes[74] although their significance has remained debatable. At one extreme they have been taken to demonstrate a collapse in SPD support to the benefit of the KPD,[75] at the other to indicate a switch by politically unorganised victims of the economic and political crisis over to the Communist Party,[76] but Winkler's conclusion that the KPD had progressed well without necessarily ousting the SPD as the majority working-class party appears to be a convincing overall assessment of the position.[77] However, against this rise in popular support must be set the continued Social Democratic dominance of labour organisations. Furthermore, the growth of fascism was regarded by the KPD as threatening and alongside this there remained the refusal of the national question to be subsumed somehow within the ideological framework of proletarian internationalism.

Fascism and nationalism posed separate problems in their own right, but the latter also contributed towards a unified Communist response to the two issues. Once the KPD came around to the view that Germany was a colonised and oppressed land and that the Communist movement had to stand at the head of the struggle for national liberation,[78] it was talking a language not entirely strange to the fascists. Diehl's comment that: 'while the Communists dreamed of revolution, the rightists dreamed of war',[79] is too crude a distinction both in descriptive terms and because it was precisely on foreign policy issues, which centred around nationalism and anti-French resistance, that a form of ideological rapprochement between radical left and right became possible.[80]

These issues became immeasurably more important because of the stance adopted by the Soviet government and, ultimately, Comintern during 1923. Germany had always represented the best hope for revolution in Soviet Russia's eyes, but after the signing of Rapallo pre-revolutionary Germany became Russia's ally in a hostile, capitalist world.[81] France's ambitions in the Ruhr threatened that ally and the Soviet government particularly feared Polish involvement on the French side, for if the Franco-Polish enterprise succeeded then even in conventional strategic terms Russia's position would have been greatly weakened. As *Isvestia* commented on 21 January: 'Soviet Russia, in her own vital interests, cannot allow the final subjugation and destruction of Germany by an alliance of France and her vassals, of which Poland is the first; . . . a Polish attack on Germany at the present moment is a direct blow at Soviet Russia.'[82] Of Central Committee members Bukharin was the most prominent in arguing that social revolution lay some years off in Europe and that, in the meantime, Russia had to seek temporary accommodations with: 'oppressed bourgeois states – with weak and threatened states – against the stronger and threatening'.[83]

This line of argument militated against Comintern's role as an agent of world revolution, which led its Secretary General, Zinoviev, initially to oppose the involvement of the KPD in any kind of patriotic united front.[84] However, Comintern was coming to function increasingly as an instrument of Soviet foreign policy interests by 1923 and Zinoviev eventually accepted that the KPD was relatively weak and that effective resistance by the German bourgeoisie to the demands of the Western capitalist powers was, in the immediate term, probably more useful to the Soviet Union than any contribution the German proletariat might eventually make (yet seemed unwilling to make!) to world revolution.[85]

Comintern's pronouncements during early 1923 reflected this change of mood. At the outset it had in January interpreted the Ruhr occupation as a facet of the class struggle and German workers were urged to form an alliance with the French proletariat and with Soviet Russia to destroy the system that had engendered the occupation:

> Workers of Germany! What awaits you? A sea of suffering, a double oppression, starvation and decay. The bourgeoisie are not even able to assure you your daily bread. They are doing business with their French colleagues at your expense, at the expense of the working class. . . . Unite . . . in a single powerful proletarian front for the fight to win a workers' government.[86]

The same theme was repeated in March in a letter from the ECCI to the Franco-German Workers' Congress at Frankfurt the purpose of which was to organise the fight against war and fascism. Here the German working class was urged to defeat French imperialism by defeating its own bourgeoisie and allying itself with Russia and with the French proletariat.[87] However even in January Comintern had made use of a nationalist vocabulary and of forms of analysis which it had developed in earlier years to qualify this rather simplistic line of analysis. Germany, it observed, had become a colonial country which would only regain national independence under the leadership of the KPD.[88] Admittedly this was to be achieved through class struggle, but on 16 January in an open letter to the Second and Vienna Internationals Comintern accepted that the national question and nationalism might acquire an ominous dynamic of their own:

> Reports are already coming in of preparation for mobilisation in Poland. France will set its vassals on the move against Germany. But even if that were not contemplated, there might at any moment be clashes between French troops and the closely packed population of the Ruhr which would drive nationalist feeling in Germany up to boiling point. If the military elements in France exploit Poincaré's difficulties in the Ruhr to push him further in his Rhineland policy, the policy of dismembering Germany, forces in Germany may easily be set in motion which will drive on to war in order to make use of nationalist fever to win power by a counter-revolution.[89]

Radek remained Comintern's acknowledged specialist on German affairs and although he had supported the expulsion of the National Bolsheviks from the KPD at Heidelberg in 1919 he had considered nationalism as a significant factor in German politics from the earliest days of the Republic.[90] Now he threw his weight behind Thalheimer and the other advocates within the KPD of a United Front approach to the Ruhr crisis. There seems little doubt that its potential usefulness for the Soviet Union lay uppermost in his mind,[91] but nonetheless, his exploitation of the German national question in this way involved recognition of its potency as a political force and Radek had doubtless observed that mounting conflict between workers and the occupation authorities in the Ruhr was stretching the KPD's internationalist stance beyond reasonable limits.[92] He indicated as much when addressing the KPD's District Party Conference in Essen in late March. In the face of opposition from the left, he demanded Communist participation in the national resistance against the Ruhr occupation: 'Unconditional refusal to obey occupation officials and the cessation of work in all militarily occupied factories'.[93] *Die Rote Fahne* published Radek's speech, but it found relatively few friends within the KPD at this stage.

The left of the KPD's Central Committee continued to regard a United Front Policy, even towards the SPD, as a diversion from the overriding aim of winning the class struggle within Germany, but at a meeting in late April in Moscow the ECCI insisted that the German left accept the United Front policy which Brandler and Thalheimer were attempting to pursue in the face of considerable opposition from Fischer and Maslow in particular. In return for their compliance the left was rewarded with extra seats on the KPD's Central Committee.[94] The authorities in Moscow, in particular Radek, feared that the German bourgeoisie was moving towards resolving the Ruhr crisis through agreement with the Western Allies and this strengthened Comintern's resolve to seek allies from wherever it could within the German social and political spectrum to sustain national resistance. In this vein it was hoped to divert some of the activists from the increasingly assertive fascist movement into the KPD which meant that from the Soviet viewpoint too there were grounds for some convergence between the radicals of left and right.[95]

The ground had, therefore, been well prepared for discussion of the issues involved at the Third Enlarged Plenum of the ECCI in June. During the early stages of the conference Zinoviev betrayed his inherent preference for principled class struggle when praising the KPD's internationalist stance at the outset of the Ruhr crisis, only regretting that the party had not pursued this line with even more vigour. Radek, by contrast, argued that 'in Germany emphasis on "the nation" was a revolutionary act, as it was in the colonies' and accused the bourgeoisie of plotting to sell out their country.[96] Shortly after this he wrote of the KPD's need to make 'such compromises as were necessary with the proletarianised petty bourgeoisie'[97] in order to build up support. His famous open overture to the right, the 'Schlageter Speech', which followed logically from these arguments,[98] came on 20 June during the Third ECCI Plenum on Fascism.[99] Schlageter had been an active participant in the struggles of the *Freikorps*, first fighting against the Russian Red Army in the Baltic states, then participating in the Kapp Putsch and in the crushing of the Ruhr Workers' Rising that followed it. He fought against the Poles in Upper Silesia before becoming involved with the NSDAP and in the underground struggle against the French in the Ruhr. In March he destroyed a railway bridge, was arrested, and eventually executed on 26 May.[100] He immediately became a national hero and a symbol of German resistance even for the KPD[101] and it was to this spirit that Radek appealed. Replying to Zetkin's speech on fascism which, among other things, called for working-class defence against fascist-terror, he declared:

I could not follow Clara Zetkin's speech all the way through because all the time I had before my eyes the corpse of the German Fascist, our class enemy, condemned and shot by . . . French imperialism . . . The fate of this German nationalist martyr should not be passed over by us in silence, or with a contemptuous phrase . . . Schlageter, the courageous soldier of the counter-revolution deserves honest and manly esteem from us, soldiers of the revolution. . . . Against whom do the German nationalists want to fight? Against Entente capital or the Russian people? With whom do they wish to ally themselves? With the Russian workers and peasants, together to shake off the yoke of Entente capital, or with Entente capital to enslave the German and Russian peoples?[102]

Radek continued that Schlageter's comrades had to side with the workers in a struggle against Entente and German capital; only this could save Germany from foreign invasion and dismemberment at the hands of the victor powers.[103]

The Plenum responded positively to Radek's speech on the whole, although the Czech delegate Neurath expressed misgivings over the KPD's apparent policy of 'competing with the German nationalists' on the latter's terms[104] and the French Communists expressed similar doubts retrospectively: 'Was [the KPD] out to win the support of the nationalist German petty bourgeoisie and lose the support of the French working class for the German revolution?'[105] The majority on the Plenum, however, showed little sympathy for Neurath's position and with reference to the French situation Radek argued that a defeat for France there would help undermine the Versailles system, adding that for him a revolutionary war against France was a just war.[106] In more general terms the widespread popularity of nationalism in Germany was admitted and it was accepted that the KPD would have to adjust its political stance further to gain mass support: 'To win the masses to their side they must take their national ideology as the starting point; the nationalism created by the occupation of the Ruhr was a revolutionary factor which the KPD must exploit.'[107] Radek had further stressed the revolutionary potential of this strategy in his own speech: 'The workers of the brain must unite with the workers of the hand in a steely phalanx; the great majority of the nationalist-thinking masses belong not in the capitalist camp, but in the camp of labour.'[108] Even Zinoviev now approved of this line of argument if it helped the USSR's geopolitical situation[109] and later, in August, the Comintern extended the mark of revolutionary respectability to the German fascists themselves: 'Fascism is not a bourgeois movement. It is primarily a movement of broad popular masses whose basic economic interests are hostile to the exploiting and impoverishing policy of the bourgeoisie.' There were no 'irreconcilable class contradictions' between fascism and the revolutionary working class, but Social Democratic treachery had driven these facists into the enemy camp from which the Communists would seek to reclaim them.[110]

The shockwaves from the Schlageter Speech quickly reached Germany. Radek himself took space in *Die Rote Fahne* to present his line of argument to a wider audience than had been present in Moscow. On 27 June he claimed, somewhat disingenuously, that the KPD had always given primacy to the anti-French struggle during the Ruhr crisis rather than to the cause of domestic revolution: 'If we had said at the time of the French invasion of the Ruhr that we wanted *first* to fight Cuno and *then* to throw out the French, we would then, whether we wanted to or not, have become the allies of Poincaré.'[111] On 5 July he wrote on the need to confront the problem of fascism which was not 'a clique of officers', but a mass movement. The KPD, he argued, had to establish how far the nationalist masses who were suffering socially were prepared to make common cause with Communism.[112] The German party leaders themselves had, as shown, begun to realise the importance of nationalism and to recognise the nature of the challenge posed by fascism some time earlier,[113] so their subsequent support for Radek's speech was not surprising.[114] Speaking for the KPD in Moscow, Böttcher rejected any role for his party as a 'branch of an intransigent internationalism'; the KPD had to understand how to act as 'leader of the nation'.[115] Days later Brandler argued similarly at a conference of the Berlin Brandenburg District Committee which basically endorsed Radek's line. The KPD must try, he argued: 'to divert "the small stream of honest national enthusiasm" into its own movement'.[116]

The authorities, understandably, paid considerable attention to these developments. The similarity with and continuity from earlier forms of national bolshevism was recognised, but in addition the Reichs Commissar for the Surveillance of Public Order argued that the KPD had developed its nationalist line during 1923 in response to popular pressure, some of which had originated within the party's own ranks:

Even the Communists have realised, albeit with some help from Moscow, that their tactic of fighting on two fronts [against the French and German governments] which ultimately amounted to supporting the French incursion, was not even understood by a large proportion of their own supporters. . . . The fact that such ideas are being propagated confirms how the Communists have assessed the mood among large sections of the German people.[117]

Perhaps most significant was the near unanimity within the KPD's national leadership on the issue. In earlier years disagreement and division had characterised Communist Party attitudes both to nationalism and to the radical right. During 1923, it is true, left-wing party leaders such as Fischer and Maslow had, initially, resisted the notion of any rapprochement with the radical right, but by June this opposition had evaporated, which indicates the degree to which expediency could determine tactics even in a party as hidebound by ideological considerations as was the KPD.[118] It also indicated, by the same token, that radical left and right, along with their actual and potential constituencies, shared a sufficiently large number of interests to make possible Radek's Schlageter line.

After the Schlageter speech cooperation appeared to blossom between the KPD and the radical right alongside mounting physical confrontation. This apparent incongruity derived from the Communist Party's need to maintain relations with rank-and-file Social Democrats who, in numerical terms, represented the largest pool of potential recruitment. As seen, the paramilitary Proletarian Hundreds were regarded by the KPD as the most plausible medium for recruiting Social Democrats[119] and therefore in June it presented them as a means of 'protecting the Republic against fascist conspiratorial organisations'.[120] In practice, however, the Hundreds became a medium for violent confrontation between the Communists and right-wing *Verbände* which, the authorities noted, was by July beginning to feed on itself:

> On the Left-radical side there is increasing intolerance of right-wing organisations, which gives the latter grounds for increasing their own self-defence capacity. Consequently a series of clashes between right-wing organisations and Communists have been observed which have sometimes developed into full-scale battles.[121]

Confrontations of this sort continued throughout the month, and were one factor behind the holding of a Communist-organised Anti-Fascist Day on 29 July in which the Proletarian Hundreds played a leading role.[122] The Anti-Fascist Day was intended to demonstrate the numerical superiority of the radical left over the radical right, attack the Cuno government for its wavering resolve in the Ruhr crisis, and seek an improvement in relations with the SPD.[123] In the event, the Social Democratic authorities in Prussia had banned the Hundreds in May and interpreted the planned Anti-Fascist Day as evidence of an increasingly insurrectionary mood within the KPD. It therefore banned open-air meetings and thereby undermined the impact of the occasion.[124]

Furthermore, there remained the more positive side of relations with the right. Even at the time of the Anti-Fascist Day the need to play the nationalist card was recognised: 'Making the people's cause into the national cause makes the national cause into the people's cause.'[125] This could have done little to reassure Social Democrats[126] and Winkler argues that the 'Schlageter line' had also threatened to irritate the KPD's proletarian supporters who were to be mollified through the party's policy of anti-fascist defence.[127] No doubt some ordinary Communists were irritated by the 'Schlageter line' but, as shown, nationalist sentiment among working-class, and even Communist, Germans had contributed as much to its inception as had pressure from Radek and the Soviet Union.[128] Although a proletarian, revolutionary party, the KPD had become trapped between these interests and others which could not easily be reconciled within the bolshevik ideological framework. Nationalism had become a wide-spread, radicalising force which seemed to threaten the political status quo to a greater extent than any insurrection which the German labour movement might have staged. Indeed, much of the labour movement favoured the constitutional status quo, albeit with misgivings, while the more socially heterogeneous fascist and right-radical movement opposed the status quo. Cooperation with the far right, therefore, seemed to enhance the prospects for change while cooperation with the Social Democrats at executive level contained the risk of stabilising an order the Communists ultimately wished to destroy.[129] The Social Democrats, on the other hand, enjoyed mass support which the KPD had to win over. No single policy could cope with these conflicting demands; the KPD consequently tailored a variety of policies to tackle the different challenges it faced, however contradictory these appeared and however opportunistic and risky they may have been.

During the summer of 1923 the KPD made repeated overtures to right-wing organisations and to their actual or potential constituencies. On 25 July, just four days before the Anti-Fascist Day, the party appealed to the radical right more or less on the latter's terms:

The Entente and the Jews are characterised by the *Völkische* as the only exploiters of the German people. Without doubt the Entente capitalists exploit the German working masses and without doubt Jewish capitalists fatten themselves through exploiting the German people.[130]

The appeal went on to remind the right that German capitalists of the Christian faith were equally culpable, but an unmistakable attempt had been made to gain approval from the radical right. As on other occasions the KPD believed that this effort was born of necessity, for the Central Committee concluded in early August that the German petty bourgeoisie had turned to fascism through disappointment with the Social Democrats' handling of affairs after the war:[131] 'They conceive of their suffering not as a consequence of the capitalists' class rule, but of the parliamentarian-democratic methods of the Social Democrats and of national oppression by the victorious Entente.'[132] The KPD had to wage an ideological campaign for the souls of this middle class and draw them into the Communist camp.

On several occasions when Communist leaders appealed directly to fascists at public meetings, their verbal utterances were particularly compromising. In July Ruth Fischer addressed Nazi students at a meeting in Berlin where she declared:

Whoever declares against Jewish capital, gentlemen, is already a class warrior, even if he doesn't know it. You are against Jewish capital and want to crush the stock market jobbers. Quite right! Crush the Jewish capitalists, hang them from the lamp posts. But, gentlemen, what is your attitude to the big capitalists, to Stinnes and Klöckner? . . . Only in alliance with Russia, gentlemen from the *völkisch* side, can the German people drive French capitalism from the Ruhr.[133]

Ruth Fischer had been a firm and determined advocate of proletarian internationalism until mid 1923, opposing Levi's national bolshevik line during 1920 and 1921 and Brandler's attempts in early 1923 to exploit the wave of nationalist outrage that accompanied the French occupation of the Ruhr. Thus her speech was not only remarkable for its anti-Semitism, but because her qualification thereof was couched in national bolshevik terms which Laufenberg and Wolffheim would have found perfectly acceptable. The speech appeared in written form in the Social Democratic newspaper *Vorwärts*, which makes mis-reporting a possibility, but Fischer did not trouble to refute it at the time, only doing so twenty-five years later[134] by which time, of course, it was embarrassing for different reasons. Furthermore her line of argument was in accordance with the contemporary Communist line and with that of a speech made by Hermann Remmele on 2 August. Remmele, a longstanding member of the *Zentrale*, found himself in difficulties at a joint nationalist/Communist meeting in Stuttgart as he tried to dismiss anti-Semitism as a diversionary tactic by the ruling classes. Changing his tune he declared:

> You only have to go to the slaughterhouse during the Stuttgart cattle market to see how the cattle dealers, most of whom are Jewish, buy cattle at any price while the Stuttgart butchers have to come away empty-handed because they simply don't have so much money for buying cattle.[135]

Eight days later Remmele addressed another meeting attended by Social Democrats, Nazis and Communists at which he declared a preference for working with the Nazis rather than the Social Democrats whom he branded with the familiar nationalist smear 'November Traitors'. The Social Democrats left the meeting in protest after which Remmele commented to the Nazis and Communists remaining: 'In this meeting after the Social Democrats have withdrawn there are not so many differences of opinion.'[136] Remmele disputed the accuracy of this report, which also appeared in *Vorwärts*,[137] and it must be remembered that he and Ruth Fischer had been addressing heated meetings where much could have been said in haste and regretted later. Nonetheless, it would be mistaken to dismiss these utterances as purely accidental or anomalous. The concerted attempt to build bridges to the radical right, which went as far as some practical cooperation between the KPD and the National Socialists,[138] made such incidents more than likely.

Radek continued to encourage such a stance in his writings, repeating in late July that the revolution could not be achieved by the workers alone and that the petty bourgeoisie would have to be won over to Communism.[139] The constant growth of the fascist movement complicated that, however, and necessitated compromises on the part of the Communists to broaden their base of support:

We must be prepared to form alliances with those sections [of the petty bourgeoisie] who, although unwilling to accept our ideology and retaining their own ideological framework, in practice want to fight for the same thing as us during this historical epoch.[140]

Thus, since a victory for Poincaré in the Ruhr would, for Radek, amount to a counter-revolutionary victory, the nationalist right had acquired an objective national revolutionary quality which required Communist support.[141] In early August Radek continued to argue that the KPD remained too weak for the final, decisive struggle and therefore had to recruit support from among the Social Democratic working class and the petty bourgeoisie. The latter were ascribed revolutionary qualities which the Social Democratic movement lacked;[142] an argument which bore an intriguing resemblance to Remmele's anti-Socialist outburst of 10 August.[143]

The Communist movement, therefore, had concluded that nationalism was a force to be ignored at its peril and that a revolutionary movement based on the working class alone might not succeed. Given the reformism of many Social Democrats which contrasted with the mounting disillusionment of the petty bourgeoisie with the Republic, the KPD's increasing interest in the radical right is understandable,[144] but its opening to the right was flawed in a number of ways. It applied Marxist–Leninist class analysis to phenomena which might have been better considered on different terms and, having nonetheless found a niche for anti-Semitic fascism in the revolutionary camp, the KPD became prepared to make compromises with fascism à la Radek, Fischer or Remmele. As Daycock concludes:

> The Communists tried hard to convince their Nazi audience that the racial question was irrelevant to their real (class) concerns. What went unnoticed, but was apparent in speeches such as Fischer's and Remmele's, was that too much was conceded (perhaps everything). Brandler was right on this point. As Fischer and Remmele borrowed some of the worst images from the anti-Semitic vocabulary, one has to wonder just who was influencing whom.[145]

In 1923 these indiscretions were not to prove too damaging to the KPD given their essentially opportunistic and tactical nature,[146] but the question remained of how far such a line could be pursued without becoming integral to the party's ethos.[147]

Despite the Communists' ambivalence, there were voices on the radical right who responded positively to the Schlageter line. The right was operating in changed circumstances by mid 1923. After playing a major role in the political affairs of the Reich in its founding years, the *Freikorps* and other *Verbände* found that their presence as an organised force had become unwelcome everywhere except Bavaria. The *Verbände* tried to maintain an independent existence through direct negotiations with Chancellor Cuno during early 1923, but the army, while valuing individual recruits from the right, would not tolerate any institutional competition from that quarter. The government, understandably, sided with the army and from March 1923 a clear split emerged, except in Bavaria, between the *Reichswehr* and the government on the one hand and the *Völkische* and the *Freikorps* on the other.[148] The radical right, therefore, found itself relatively isolated from any sources of power and influence and had to observe how sections of the pre-Republican establishment, if still anti-Republican in spirit, were reaching various forms of makeshift accommodation with the existing system. In such circumstances the prospects of cooperation with the KPD were less remote than previously.

Speaking in terms not dissimilar to those employed by Radek, albeit with a different underlying meaning, Moeller van den Bruck declared: 'We are on the way to becoming a proletarianised nation',[149] and some of his young followers evidently blamed sections of the German establishment for this as much as they did foreigners and Jews: 'Yes, if the capitalists' readiness for sacrifice in the Ruhr struggle collapses, then we want to join the KPD.'[150] It should be remembered that German business did resist any increase in corporate taxation to help cover the financial costs of the passive resistance.[151] Right radical groups were sometimes prepared to give former Communists positions of responsibility, such as on the founding committee of the *Deutsche Freiheitsbund*, which included a factory worker from Essen who had previously belonged to the KPD,[152] but more significant was their willingness on some occasions to regard Communism as one variant of a generic whole of which they too formed a part. The Bolsheviks' achievements in Russia were often regarded with admiration, as illustrated by Maurenbrecher's call in the *Deutsche Zeitung* of 2 May 1923 for a strong man to take over in Germany:

In such dangerous circumstances there is only one salvation; from the surging enthusiasm of our people a man must once again rise up who possesses the strength to seize the rudder of the ship of state and steer it in the direction he desires. Caesar, Napoleon and the supreme leadership that is presently constituting itself in Russia are examples of this development.[153]

Radek's Schlageter Speech can be set against this background and it was received with interest in some right-wing intellectual circles. Moeller van den Bruck debated with Radek over the Communist movement's new-found interest in nationalism. Reventlow exchanged views cautiously with Frölich in *Die Rote Fahne* over the relationship between nationalism and revolution in the context of Radek's proposals. Certainly the right was interested in what he had to say, but the suspicion remained that the KPD was trying to detach the *Völkische* from their leaders and subordinate Germany to the authority of the Comintern.[154] Furthermore there is little evidence that the KPD succeeded in winning over the nationalist masses and some right-wing groups were decidedly hostile to Radek's approaches. His Jewish background was attacked in the right-radical press[155] and the NSDAP's leadership issued a warning against contacts with national bolshevik circles couched in decidedly anti-Semitic terms.[156]

The Communist movement itself, therefore, did not consider the Schlageter line an unreserved success. On 13 July Radek confessed in Moscow that his efforts had not convinced the nationalist masses and that the KPD had to attempt to win over these masses – a message he repeated again in September.[157] Borkenau, who participated personally in the Schlageter campaign, also subsequently judged it a failure:

> The author . . . was struck by the self-assured feeling of the young university students of various nationalist organisations, who did not doubt that they were infinitely stronger than the communists; which was only the truth. And the weaker side never exerts attraction over the stronger one.[158]

The authorities too were dismissive of the Schlageter line and did not expect much to come of it. A report of 6 August regarded cooperation between the two sides as an indication of their mutual weakness and of shared negative aims which would prevent any common long-term constructive programme.[159] On 25 August the Reichs Commissar for the Surveillance of Public Order elaborated somewhat when observing that fraternisation between the far left and right only appeared to occur in situations where their strength was more or less evenly balanced. Thus in northern and central Germany simple considerations of power politics kept the *völkisch* coalition on reasonable terms with the KPD, while in southern Germany where the KPD was much weaker, the National Socialists had rejected any cooperation 'in a remarkably blunt fashion'.[160]

On the other hand the debate with the nationalists had enabled contacts to develop relatively widely and Communist leaders were, later in 1923, to evaluate their opening to the right as successful by virtue of the divisions it had created among the *Völkische* themselves.[161] Communists had been able to speak at nationalist meetings and each side had contributed to the other's journals.[162] It has been argued that this element of success did as much to prompt Nazi opposition to contacts with the left as did any fundamental aversion to the KPD:[163] 'Even Hitler', Daycock notes, 'recognised Communists as particularly valuable recruits for the NSDAP.'[164] Therefore when Brandler reported to Profintern in September 1923 on the success the Communists had had in penetrating fascist meetings, he may have displayed exaggerated optimism, but his claims were not groundless.[165]

Furthermore, the rather disappointing outcome of the Schlageter campaign was quickly eclipsed by a disastrously botched attempt to seize power through a tactical alliance with left Social Democrats in Saxony and Thuringia. In August a wave of strikes against the economic policies of the Cuno government, which was supported although not organised by the KPD,[166] appeared to signify a potential for insurrection within the German working class. However, both the Russian government and Comintern had assessed the prospects for revolution in Germany as dim and therefore encouraged the Schlageter line, and cooperation with the SPD to establish a broadly-based workers' government.[167] Any serious preparation for revolution by the KPD was, therefore, lacking at a time when conditions seemed potentially favourable.[168] Moreover, the period of profound unrest passed relatively quickly. The strikes themselves destroyed the Cuno government, and its successor moved to end the passive resistance against France (with an eventual settlement of the crisis on 27 September) and initiated steps to stabilise the mark, with a new currency introduced on 15 November. This new government, under Stresemann, also addressed itself to the problem of labour unrest. Four Social Democrats were admitted into the Cabinet as wage rises were granted to offset at least in part the inflationary wave, and as steps were taken against the strike leaders.[169] This combination of measures sufficed to defuse the situation and Brandler concluded that the objective conditions for revolution were again lacking. The ECCI, however, concluded too late in the day that the potential for revolution in Germany existed once more and plans were made for the Communists to enter the left-wing SPD governments in Saxony and Thuringia so as to obtain police weapons for a rising.[170] On 12 and 13 October 1923 Communist leaders gained ministerial posts in these two governments, but failed to take over significant numbers of weapons with which to arm the Proletarian Hundreds. The army, meanwhile, took countermeasures which culminated in the military occupation of the two states on 21 October. Lacking both weapons and support from the SPD (which had been interested in forming broad-based workers' governments, but not insurrection) the KPD decided to back down. On 21 October the *Zentrale* called off the rising; a decision confirmed on the next day by the Comintern delegates Radek and Pyatakov. A futile rising in Hamburg and a largely unsuccessful call for a strike on 29 October were all that remained.[171]

Brandler was blamed for the disaster, his earlier opposition to the rising conveniently forgotten, but so was the SPD. At an ECCI meeting in January 1924 Zinoviev denounced the 'United Front From Above' tactic which had been attempted in Saxony and Thuringia and declared that in the future the 'United Front From Below' was to be the only permissible strategy.[172] The Comintern confirmed this line in its *Instructions for Communist Fractions in Workers' Organisations and Bodies outside the Party* where it declared:

> The leading strata of German social-democracy are at the present moment nothing but a fraction of German fascism wearing a socialist mask. . . . The slogan of the united front tactic in Germany is now: Unity from below![173]

The United Front From Below was never intended to be any sort of democratic alliance or coalition with the SPD, but instead a means of mobilising support from members of it, or other parties, whose policies the Communist movement opposed.[174] As Zinoviev had admitted in June 1923, the United Front From Below was a strategic manoeuvre designed to compensate for the Communist movement's relative lack of popular support: 'What is this strategic manoeuvre? It consists in our appealing constantly to people who, we know in advance, will not go along with us.'[175] The Comintern had, therefore, admitted the weakness of its position and abandoned any attempt to work constructively with the reformist wing of the labour movement.

Ideological developments within the KPD mirrored this trend, for the German Communists were increasingly unwilling, and perhaps unable, to diverge from the general line of strategy laid down by the Comintern. Too many independently-minded leaders had been lost and, given the party's failure to achieve revolution in Germany, its ability to remain relevant as a revolutionary party in a non-revolutionary environment could best be achieved through its association with the Soviet Union and with Comintern.[176] Among the KPD's leaders Thälmann had argued, even at the beginning of 1923, that the United Front From Below was the only permissible way forward and that the United Front From Above, which implied cooperation with other parties to achieve a working-class government within a bourgeois-democratic political system, would surely end in failure.[177] Now this view became general. Fascism was defined as all forms of government other than Communism, and the SPD consequently became an enemy. 'In the KPD's view,' the authorities observed, 'the struggle for the dictatorship of the proletariat cannot, as previously, be waged in alliance with the SPD, but only against it.'[178] Indeed, the 1923 October rising had failed because of the SPD's alleged treachery[179] and at the Ninth Party Congress in Frankfurt-am-Main in April 1924: 'The tactical strategies linked to the use of democratic institutions were abandoned, the complete liquidation of the SPD was recognised as the central task.'[180]

As in earlier years, Communist condemnation of the SPD and the use of the United Front From Below against it had implications for relations with the far right. The same tactic could, logically, be used against any other political grouping whose membership the KPD wished to subvert and, ultimately, recruit. Certainly the opening to the right had never met with such decisive failure as had cooperation with the SPD (perhaps because hopes had never been set so high), even if *völkisch* leaders had placed limits on the development of the Schlageter course. Thus the KPD did not entirely abandon its approaches in this direction during the closing months of 1923 and its efforts concerned both right-wing leaders and the authorities. Hitler warned the Bavarian government in October 1923 of dire consequences if it failed to act quickly against Berlin: 'There is no more time. The economic misery drives our men so that either we must act, or our people will go over to the Communists.'[181] This threat might have been exaggerated to pressurise the Bavarian authorities into action in the weeks before his ill-starred rising which, incidentally, the KPD regarded with profound distrust.[182] Nonetheless, the expression of similar fears by the commander of the Munich SA to Hitler at this time[183] suggests that a problem did exist.

The KPD also continued its efforts to gain middle-class support. The central authorities in Berlin noted the success of Communist agitation among white-collar workers and civil servants in the occupied Rhineland in November, notably in Cologne and Stollberg, the economic misery of whom made them targets for both the far left and right:

> All these groups, who believe they can attribute their current miserable economic situation to the parliamentary-democratic form of government, are obviously accessible to the KPD's ideology. On the other hand others of the same social background have jumped into the arms of the Right radicals and even the fascists in the hope of obtaining help and salvation from this quarter.[184]

The KPD therefore continued to compete with the far right for the loyalty of the *Mittelstand* while, at the same time, making further overtures to elements on the far right. In December attempts were noted by the authorities to attract retired nationalist officers to the Communist side 'through written and verbal means in a form that "will not repulse these circles" '. In this way, it was hoped, the fascist movement would be deprived of their services in any coming civil war and some officers might, along with their organisations, come to side with the Communists.[185] The potential of this strategy was demonstrated by an official report on growing divisions within the *Freikorps* group *Bund Oberland* in December:

> Within the *Bund Oberland* in Silesia two factions are fighting it out. One faction recognises Dr Weber, who was arrested in Munich because of his participation in the Hitler Putsch, as leader and sympathises with the National Socialist movement. The other faction remains loyal to the old *Oberland* leaders Horadam and Beppo Römer.[186]

This was essentially a split between left and right with Römer eventually joining the KPD, which again indicated that overtures to the right were not entirely hopeless. Similarly, at least some working-class Nazis went over to the KPD after Hitler's abortive putsch.[187]

Early in 1924, however, the Schlageter line appeared to fall victim to the struggles between left and right both within the KPD and within the Soviet Union where Stalin was beginning to consolidate his hold on power. The KPD's left, who gained control of the party after Brandler's downfall, not only dissociated themselves from the botched October rising, but from the relatively ambiguous outcome of the opening to the right. Rediscovering their distaste for national bolshevism and, no doubt, suffering a severe bout of collective amnesia, the left-wingers castigated the former as a right-wing deviation[188] for which the hapless Brandler was held responsible. In Moscow Radek was out of favour with the left, leading the Russian Politburo to dismiss the Schlageter Line in January 1924 as an 'opportunistic overestimation of the differences in opinion within the Fascist ranks'.[189] The KPD's Ninth Congress continued the attack which was further pursued by the Fifth Comintern Congress in June and July. A German delegate declared:

> It is clear that Fascism and Communism oppose one another like fire and water and an alliance between them is an impossible thing. Today we see in the tendencies which were expressed in the Schlageter article and in the whole campaign, a deviation from the methods which we should have used in the fight against counterrevolution and that special form of counterrevolution, Fascism.[190]

However, while condemning the Schlageter Line in name, both this and other individual speakers, and also the resolutions of the Congress, endorsed the continuation of the strategy in substance.[191] The United Front opening to the radical right and to the middle classes was to continue. Public debates with the fascists were to be encouraged and the same were to be compelled to honour the revolutionary aspects of their programme[192] – a strategy which demonstrated unequivocally that the Comintern persisted in regarding parts of the fascist programme as revolutionary.[193]

In essence, then, little had changed and developments during the mid 1920s were to confirm that the United Front From Below tactic would continue to be applied to the right as well as to the SPD. At the Berlin-Brandenburg District Party Conference of March 1924 the Political Secretary questioned the very concept of the United Front tactic when he observed: 'The way in which the masses were won by means of Schlagetism and the United Front also shows that the resulting growth in the party has been a very temporary phenomenon which rapidly plays itself out.'[194] In other words, to mobilise fresh support around particular issues rather than through an appeal based on a coherent political programme was bound to be a high-risk strategy. However, his was a voice in the wilderness. The KPD's leaders and the Comintern persevered with the United Front From Below tactic, whatever the risks.[195] To be fair, there might have been little choice if the KPD were to gain significant reserves of fresh support, but the party had moved a stage nearer to the disastrous experiences of the early 1930s.

4 The Stabilisation Era, 1924–1928: General Developments

When Stalin enunciated his policy of 'Socialism in One Country' in late 1924, he accepted that any immediate hopes for world revolution had disappeared with the KPD's failure to trigger an uprising in Germany during the autumn of 1923.[1] Russia stood isolated in a capitalist world which was entering a period of relative stabilisation and the Soviet government therefore sought to pursue a more-or-less conventional foreign policy to protect its interests in this hostile environment. Germany was the linchpin of this strategy. As long as she remained detached from the Western alliance and maintained a policy of benevolent neutrality towards the USSR, the latter felt relatively secure from Western aggression,[2] but under Gustav Stresemann's direction German foreign policy was becoming increasingly equivocal.[3] A series of international agreements left her at best, less dependent on the Soviet Union than hitherto and, at worst, a potential tool of aggressive Western capitalism.[4]

Stresemann reassured the Soviet Union, with some difficulty, that Germany's stance towards her had not altered substantially and the signing of the Treaty of Berlin in April 1926 appeared to reiterate the principles of Rapallo.[5] Nonetheless it did not escape the notice of the authorities in Moscow that the German right – in heavy industry, the military and politics – remained unequivocally opposed to accommodation with the Western Allies.[6] The Social Democrats, by contrast, were decidedly pro-Western to the point where, in December 1926, they publicised in the Reichstag and in the British press details of secret Russo-German military cooperation.[7] In this potentially threatening atmosphere, the KPD's main task during the mid 1920s was, at Fowkes observes, to hinder any rapprochement between Germany and the West, which to a significant degree put it on the same side as the right and the NSDAP on foreign policy issues.[8]

The Soviet Union therefore watched anxiously for any signs of a thaw between the KPD and SPD during this period, to the point where any show of independence by the German Communists became suspect. Thus, when the KPD's leaders, Fischer and Maslow, exhibited signs of independent-mindedness during 1924 and 1925[9] the ECCI accused the party in August 1925 of being influenced by Social Democratic, 'West European', traditions which were prompting it to attack Russia and its Communist Party and which also led 'straight towards social democracy or to an alliance with it'.[10] In March 1926 Stalin expressed hostility to the strong national tendencies in Western Communist parties for similar reasons[11] and in early 1927 Zinoviev continued the attack, accusing oppositional elements in the KPD of being anti-Soviet and 'anti-Muscovite'.[12] By this stage, however, these 'pro-Western' elements within the KPD only enjoyed minority support and were roundly condemned by the majority at the party's Eleventh Congress in Essen in early 1927. As Jansen, one of the KPD's delegates to Comintern, declared: 'Our entire policy must be built on the basis of our doing everything, to the end, for the Soviet Union.'[13]

When nationalist interests contributed to the 'weakening and overthrow of imperialism', rather than to the weakening of the KPD, Stalin and the Soviet government found them much more congenial.[14] To this end the KPD denounced the Treaty of Versailles (again), the League of Nations, and demanded a revolutionary campaign for national and social liberation as vehemently during 1924 and 1925 as it had during 1923.[15] The Comintern argued similarly, condemning the Dawes Report (which in 1924 had rescheduled and liberalised Germany's reparations obligations) for transforming Germany 'into an international colony, a field of exploitation for the robbers of all countries' in July 1924[16] and declaring two years later that:

> The only real way out for the German proletariat is the way of its emancipation from the double yoke of native and foreign capital. The only way out of the blind alley of economic decline, falling living standards, permanent political crises, enslavement and a semi-colonial status for Germany is the way of a Soviet Germany.[17]

The radical right, of course, could not subscribe to these ultimate objectives and some right-wingers, including Friedrich Heinz of the Stahlhelm's Political Section and Mahraum of the Jungdo, therefore vetoed any cooperation with the Communist movement and the Soviet Union,[18] but others were attracted to the KPD's programme, as were some Communists to the right's, within the limits defined by their shared negative aims.[19] Moreover there was a growing realisation in German right-wing circles that Stalin was directing the revolution onto an increasingly Russo-centric, nationalistic path at the expense of

Comintern's internationalist stance.[20] Under these circumstances Russia became a more attractive ally for the far right than had been the case even in 1923 and the Soviet Union in turn saw in the German radical right a means of putting pressure on the German government and the West in general.[21]

In the realm of domestic policy matters were more ambivalent. As in 1923 there were personal contacts between *völkisch* and Communist leaders, involving among others the *Freikorps* leaders Römer and Ehrhardt,[22] and both sides expressed some sympathy for the other in speeches and articles. Remmele reportedly urged voters to support the nationalists rather than the SPD during a local election campaign in Lübeck during 1927[23] and in the previous year the prominent *völkisch* politician, Graf Reventlow, wrote approvingly of the KPD's domestic policies in the *Deutsches Tageblatt:* 'Voltaire's attack on the Church represents our view of capitalism: "Grind down this vile apparition!"'; we turn the Frenchman's words against capitalism, against the democracy of capital ruling Germany.'[24] He continued that the *Völkische* welcomed the Communist struggle against this 'democracy of capital' and he was not alone in his partial approval of the KPD. Plaas of the *Wikingbund* wrote positively in 1927 of the Red Front in the national revolutionary newspaper, *Der Vormarsch*, while Ehrhardt appealed in the columns of *Die Rote Fahne* for Red Front cooperation in the overthrow of Weimar in return for an eastward orientation in *völkisch* foreign policy: 'We see the road to salvation lying in cooperation with Russia.'[25]

This community of interests was reflected in the increasing cooperation between far left and right in parliament during late 1924[26] with a marked tendency for the KPD and the *Völkische*, including the NSDAP, to vote together in parliamentary divisions between 1924 and 1928. In 145 out of 197 divisions (73 per cent) they voted together, while in 135 out of 197 divisions (68 per cent) the KPD and SPD were on opposite sides.[27] Resulting Social Democratic displeasure surfaced in derisive and hostile press reporting of cooperation between the radical extremes during the period and the prompt Communist denials these reports often elicited betrayed an underlying unease among Communists over just where fraternisation with the right might lead.[28] A KPD delegate to the Sixth Comintern Congress in 1928, Grube, felt obliged to condemn rank-and-file doubts within his own party on this matter and in particular supported the continued use of the United Front From Below tactic towards the right: 'The German Communists had several examples of where they had succeeded, through skilled subversion work, in detaching large sections of the Stahlhelm's membership from the organisation, at least where they were proletarian in composition.'[29] This, however, serves as a reminder of the essentially uneasy basis on which relations between the two sides rested. For Communist advocates of an opening to the right, the destruction of these organisations' mass support through fraternisation with their members was prominent among their objectives. For the radical right, it might be fair to conclude, explicit hostility to the working classes was largely absent by the mid 1920s, but, as Diehl observes, their 'national' socialism or 'front' socialism 'was in fact little more than an idealised appeal for the total mobilisation of German society for the war of revenge which they had hoped someday to lead'.[30]

In any event the KPD wished, if possible, ultimately to mobilise all discontented groups in German society and therefore found the degree of support for the *Völkische* in early 1924, and the breadth of that support, alarming. The KPD maintained that the *Völkische* represented little more than 'the main protective force for endangered German capitalism' in objective terms, but understood that ordinary folk supported them for very different subjective reasons:

> In order to appreciate their role correctly, one must take into account not of what they are, but what the people take them for. The *Völkische* appear to be anti-capitalist, with procedures resembling those of a revolutionary party; they make a show of placing themselves at the head of a national opposition against the fulfilment policy. While their electoral success is a success for the far right, they therefore provide an indication of the despair and an, admittedly unclear, rebellious mood among the masses.[31]

The Central Committee therefore regarded right-wing radicalism as the greatest single threat to the Communist movement because of its capacity for exploiting disillusionment among supporters of both the moderate bourgeois parties and the SPD. Similar fears were expressed at the Frankfurt Party Congress in April 1924 where the *Völkische* were described as 'a mass movement which threatens to infect the proletariat with its poison',[32] and at a meeting of Berlin District functionaries in the same month Maslow was especially gloomy about the challenge mounted by the *Völkische* who 'posed an extraordinary danger for the working class'. This resulted from increasing success by the far right in recruiting working-class members, for as Maslow reportedly continued:

It is downright scandalous that great masses of proletarians, among them the unemployed who have become increasingly separated from the KPD, have already gone over to the *Völkische*, with yet more following. To save the unemployed at least, the Party *Zentrale* had appointed a special Unemployment Officer, whose task was systematically to work these circles for the benefit of the party.[33]

These fears were, evidently, sincerely held, but they were shown to be exaggerated when the electorate voted twice during 1924. In the May Reichstag elections the *Völkische* stood for the first time and won 32 seats, as against the KPD's 62; a result greeted with relief in Communist circles. The campaign against the far right was deemed a success and the main danger was now perceived to lie in the conservative German National People's Party (DNVP) which had attracted many working-class voters 'who despaired of the prospects for class struggle and who hope that a DNVP government will restore the peaceful conditions of 1914'.[34] Indeed, the KPD was confident that internal frictions within the *völkisch* movement were hastening its collapse.[35] The December Reichstag election results confirmed the KPD's optimism to some degree, for although it lost some support and only retained 45 seats, the *völkisch* alliance held a mere 14 which reduced it in parliamentary terms to no more than a sect. Seeing matters in a decidedly conspiratorial light, the KPD concluded that the radical right no longer assisted agrarian and industrial capitalism in gaining popular support for their own interests. The stabilisation of the economy and the settlement of the Ruhr dispute with France pointed to the use of more conventional parliamentarian methods, thus assuring the future of the DNVP.[36]

If the KPD's earlier fears regarding the radical right had been exaggerated, the same could be said of their new-found confidence. The radical right, as much as the KPD, was forced to adjust painfully to the more stable conditions of the mid 1920s, but it did not disappear and continued to demand of the Communist movement some degree of attention. In August 1925 the Red Front noted that rival paramilitary organisations (including the republican Reichsbanner which it regarded in pretty much the same light as the right-wing *Verbände*) were successfully recruiting and proselytising among 'enormous masses of the working population; industrial proletarians, half-proletarians, small farmers and farm workers'.[37] The temporary rise in unemployment seemed to benefit the fascist leagues during 1926,[38] and sporting courses organised within the factories for young workers and for the unemployed were regarded as a problem in 1927,[39] as well as the appeal of monarchist and nationalist propaganda to many workers.[40]

The Communist movement responded by trying to recruit as many working-class members as possible from the *völkisch* organisations. The paramilitary Red Front was considered the most apposite medium for this task once it turned its attention from brawling with members of the republican Reichsbanner to combating the 'greater enemy' of the nationalist leagues,[41] but in its annual report for 1925 the Red Front's national leadership was unimpressed with results. For instance in Mecklenburg the Stahlhelm, and not the Red Front, had profited from the collapse of radical, right-wing leagues, including the NSDAP, and in Württemberg the Communist organisation had failed to proselytise among the proletarian members of an already weak *völkish* movement.[42] In July 1926 the Red Front responded to this disappointing start by developing guidelines for work among the members of rival organisations, which in essence were a refinement of the United Front From Below tactic, involving a stress on the need for Red Front members to develop personal contacts and even friendships with members of other groups while playing down their own political loyalties. Opposition Section leaders would subsequently organise the sympathetic members of rival bodies into oppositional blocks within their own organisations. It was not intended to induce widespread transfers into the Communist movement itself, for these converts were regarded as more useful in their original political homes as a disruptive and subversive force, and as a source of information.[43] Under the circumstances it is hard to assess the degree of success the KPD had, although this tactic does explain, at least to some degree, the lack of overt Communist recruitment from the right between 1924 and 1928 which has been noted elsewhere.[44] Such recruitment was only mooted after the 1928 Reichstag elections as the KPD's self-confidence began to grow.[45]

The Comintern did not expend much energy on the NSDAP during the stabilisation era. The SPD, and even other right-wing groups, were regarded as greater problems than the small and divided National Socialist movement but, that said, the Nazis were not ignored. Mussolini's seizure of power in Italy lent all fascist movements an importance for one thing; the somewhat perverse association of fascism with Social Democracy focused attention on it for another.

In early 1924 Bukharin argued at the Thirteenth Russian Communist Party Congress that fascism and labourism were 'both manifestations of the bourgeois united front', with fascists predominating in defeated countries and where the class struggle was most intense.[46] At the Fifth Comintern Congress Bordiga advanced a similar view of fascism which, he argued, resembled Social Democracy as a bourgeois movement seeking mass support and which shared sufficient interests with the Social Democrats to ally with them against the revolutionary movement.[47] That said, Social Democracy was regarded as a movement in decay, while fascism, through its exploitation of nationalist rhetoric and of the crisis on the democratic left, was still threatening to attract working-class support which the Communists themselves needed. As an ECCI letter to the Ninth KPD Congress warned in April 1924:

> We should not underestimate the first successes of the fascists among the workers. They are extremely dangerous symptoms, to which the party must direct the most serious attention. If we fail to consider the national question as bolsheviks should, we shall not win over the little man from the fascists, and to fail in that means to surrender hegemony in the revolutionary movement.[48]

Similar allusions to the national dimension resurfaced from time to time, and even the Ruhr KPD argued in mid 1925 that its attempts to re-establish its organisational base were threatened by popular support for nationalism.[49] However, the Social Democrats' lacklustre record was seen as a more significant factor. The Fifth Comintern Congress observed in its *Resolution on Fascism* that the latter's roots lay partly 'in the embittered proletarian elements whose revolutionary hopes were disappointed';[50] a conclusion that made fascism a strange and particularly dangerous hybrid. Directed in the interests of the bourgeoisie it might have been, but the revolutionary appearance given to it by its style of political and military organisation allowed it to attract frustrated working-class revolutionaries as well as the disgruntled petty bourgeoisie.[51] Thus a KPD delegate to the Fifth Comintern Congress noted fascist success in the May 1924 Reichstag election in 'a number of strongly industrial areas where the communist vote was also large'. The way to remedy this problem was to fight the reformists: 'In this fight against the social democrats we shall win back from fascism, for the proletarian class struggle, all those elements and groups which are the foundation of the fascist mass movement.'[52] In other words, by destroying Social Democracy the KPD would eradicate the source of the workers' disillusionment with the left and thereby reclaim them for the Marxist–Leninist revolution. However unconvincing the argument may appear, and however much it may conflict with some recent typification of working-class Nazis as 'the Tory working class',[53] it must be remembered that this interpretation persisted into the early 1930s and continued to be acted upon. Working-class fascists were commonly regarded in Communist circles as disillusioned revolutionaries who had gone astray and could, therefore, be reclaimed.[54]

Turning specifically to the KPD's relations with the NSDAP, the fragmentation of the party after the failed Munich putsch was a visible enough sign of disarray and, in any case, Nazism like the wider *völkisch* movement was at first presumed to have declined in importance as the bourgeoisie turned back to supporting conventional political parties.[55] However, the Nazi movement did not collapse, and by 1926 was re-establishing a relatively coherent organisational structure following Hitler's release from prison (he served a brief term in Landsberg fortress for organising the 1923 'Munich Putsch') in the previous year. In social terms the NSDAP apparently impinged to a degree on the KPD's constituency, enjoying some success in recruiting workers during the mid 1920s. At a conference between the Reichs Commissar for the Surveillance of Public Order and the Intelligence Bureaux of the individual states in January 1925 the NSDAP was characterised as 'a workers' and *Mittelstands* party by composition which was founded by workers and small-time people' and which was hostile not just to Jewish capital, but to large-scale capital in general.[56] Kater confirms that over 40 per cent of the entrants to the Nazi Party were workers during 1926 and 1927, but it appears that a relatively high proportion of these workers came from the immediate vicinity of industrial cities, unlike the mass of Communist support which was located in the cities themselves.[57] Even so, in March 1927 an official report identified the NSDAP's key strongholds as Nuremberg, Elberfeld, Chemnitz, Plauen, Berlin and the Thuringian industrial area[58] and a report from the Red Front's leadership in the same month noted a decline in Nazi strength in rural northern Germany.[59] In October the Reichs Commissar observed that the NSDAP was making a systematic attempt to recruit Communist workers with a certain degree of success:

It has led to brawls and punch-ups in some cases, but also certainly results in some recruitment. It has been established recently with increasing frequency that Communist workers are transferring to the National Socialists and are actually being given positions as officials.[60]

Schüddekopf argues that this transformation 'from a petty bourgeois to a proletarian party' attracted national bolsheviks such as Reventlow, Stöhr and Kube from the wider *völkisch* movement[61] and the first signs were emerging that the NSDAP would become the centre of gravity of the radical right.

That said, the KPD quite understandably considered the Nazis to be more a potential than an actual threat. Communist officials observed the intensified Nazi recruitment among the industrial proletariat, notably the unemployed, but concluded that nationally this required little more than a watchful eye.[62] As much as anything the relatively small size of the NSDAP during this period, measured as it was in tens of thousands, must have reassured the KPD. Concern was therefore largely confined to localised upsurges of Nazi activity[63] and to any potential danger National Socialism might pose if, for instance, its mobilisation of 'backward proletarian elements' enabled industrialists to use the Nazis as a tool against the revolutionary working class,[64] or if it came to dominate rural Germany and thereby leave the urban proletariat dangerously isolated.[65]

As in earlier years, the Communist movement combated Nazism (like the radical right in general) with a combination of force and persuasion.[66] The sporadic clashes between the KPD and the Nazis and the disruption of Nazi meetings proved quite popular with the Communist Party's following, as did virtually any paramilitary activity,[67] and sometimes enabled the KPD to mobilise Social Democratic workers against a common enemy.[68] However, while it might have been enjoyable, violence seemed an inappropriate tool for winning over proletarian and petty bourgeois fascists. In its early days, the Red Front's leader, Willi Leow, actually forbade attacks on the right because 'nothing effective could be accomplished',[69] and in November 1927 the Communist group in the Red Front observed that the KPD would only win over those workers who had joined the fascists out of genuine conviction (rather than for economic reasons) by persuading them of the clearly anti bourgeois-democratic line of the KPD.[70]

This policy of personal involvement with members of the Nazi movement did lead occasionally to desertions to the KPD[71] and, as was always the risk, from the KPD to sections of the Nazi movement.[72]

However, transfers of membership never assumed significant proportions and could be counter-productive in various ways. Communist fraternisation with the Nazis could enrage the SPD and lead to embarrassing accusations in the Social Democratic press, such as in April 1927 when the *Bremer Volkszeitung* accused the Red Front and SA in Berlin of signing a non-aggression pact which agreed that the SA should attack the Reichsbanner while the Red Front went for the right-wing *Verbände*.[73] Similarly, Nazi recruitment from the KPD could easily irritate its lower-middle-class following.[74]

Some Nazis found a certain attraction in bolshevik-style Communism, as in 1923, and were even prepared to regard Communism and Nazism as analogous rather than antagonistic in certain important respects. Reventlow noted that the KPD and NSDAP had been prominent in opposing the Dawes Plan and that both sought a thorough social, political and economic transformation of society.[75] Following Hitler's internment in Landsberg the NSDAP split into three groups, one of which was the anti-parliamentarian *Großdeutsche Volksgemeinschaft* (GVG) led by Wiesenbacher. It strove to recruit among the working classes and consequently appealed to Communists to abandon their 'Jewish members' and fight alongside the GVG. This led Communists at one meeting to suggest a sensible compromise: 'Good, we'll work together; you hang the Jews and we'll hang the other capitalists!'.[76] Communist appeals to Nazi groups could also elicit encouraging responses, such as the declaration by an SA commander that he would never lead his units against the KPD and would prefer to work with it,[77] or another Nazi official's observation that in his opinion the only group, apart from the *Völkische*, to have a half-acceptable policy was the Communists.[78]

The theoretical basis for this potentially congenial relationship lay partly in a shared aversion to parliamentarianism and to the West, but also in mounting Nazi approval for the direction in which Stalin was taking the Russian revolution.[79] His policy of Socialism in One Country was regarded as essentially similar to the plans Nazi radicals had for Germany, and perhaps even a model for Nazis to follow. Thus at a meeting in Duisburg in October 1925 a Nazi speaker applauded the Soviet government's record which had 'liberated the Russian people from the Tsarist mire and put them on the right path'. He continued that Nazis would march alongside their Communist brothers on the orders of the Soviet government against Social Democratic profiteers and the Western alliance and comparable sentiments were expressed at meetings elsewhere in Germany.[80]

The National Socialist press advanced similar views, particularly in Gregor Strasser's *Nationalsozialistische Briefe*, but also in the Strasser brothers' and in Goebbels' contributions to the official party organ in Munich, the *Völkischer Beobachter*. Otto Strasser regarded Stalin as a Russian nationalist who proclaimed a cosmetic adherence to international Communism, which meant that: 'The official KPD in Germany, has therefore, become a nonsense and should, in Stalinist spirit, rename itself the NSDAP!'[81] Goebbels predicted that the world would see a 'national miracle' in Russia's resurgence[82] and went on to depict Russia as a model for Germany: 'because it is a natural ally for us against the devilish temptation and corruption of the West'.[83] Strasser's publishing house propagated the image of a radical, almost Marxist, Nazi movement with some success in northern Germany during 1926,[84] but Hitler could not accept these tendencies which flatly contradicted his intention, one day, to wage a war against Russia. The north German wing of the Nazi movement had an organisational focus in the *Arbeitsgemeinschaft Nord-West*, but it lacked coherence and effectiveness, just as the views of the radical Nazis represented a collection of opinions rather than a coherent ideology.[85] Hitler, therefore, found the subordination of these dissident voices a relatively easy task. At a meeting in Bamberg in February 1926 the north German leaders were prevailed upon to abandon their independent and iconoclastic line on relations with the Soviet Union. By October Gregor Strasser had announced the dissolution of the *Arbeitsgemeinschaft* and Hitler was in undisputed control of the party.[86]

These developments reduced the influence of the northern radicals, but did not entirely eliminate it, or their relatively positive attitude to the KPD.[87] In October 1928 at the NSDAP's Leaders' and General Congress in Munich, Hitler was yet again obliged to forbid fraternisation with the Communist movement. Josef Goebbels in particular had exceeded limits by portraying the advent of the Third Reich as the product of a future reconciliation between the Red Front and the SA in his newspaper, *Der Angriff*, during August 1928.[88] Hitler, rather more accurately as it happened, prophesied that either Communism or Nazism would annihilate the other,[89] but for the moment the KPD had observed that even the leadership echelons of the Nazi movement were not wholly barren ground. Some Nazis, leaders among them, appeared potentially susceptible to the United Front strategy.[90]

5 The Stabilisation Era 1924–1928: The KPD and Right-Radicals in the Factories

As the dust settled on the German body politic in the aftermath of the 1923 crisis, the KPD was forced to adjust to a variety of changed circumstances. The revolutionary environment of the early 1920s, which had repeatedly saved it from the worst consequences of its own deficiencies, was replaced by an uneasy truce – between republicans and monarchists within Germany and between Germany and the victor powers. Social Democratic theorists began to consider the possibility of working for the eventual democratisation of the capitalist economic system rather than for its overthrow in the foreseeable future.[1] The economy itself certainly looked healthier during the mid 1920s. Although unemployment remained high (in large measure because of widespread rationalisation within the manufacturing and heavy industrial sectors), the regulation of the reparations question and the provision of American loans and credits allowed the economy to recover by 1928 to something like its 1913 levels of prosperity. Increased spending on schools, housing and social welfare further improved the living standards of ordinary folk. The Communists (and the radical nationalists) remained unreconciled to this apparent stabilisation, predicting that it represented little more than a breathing space between crises. Nonetheless, the KPD was forced to explore the possibility of pursuing its revolutionary goals in gradualist fashion and through conventional channels such as the trade union movement, contradictory though this may have seemed.

The party was not only constrained by the relative tranquillity that had descended on Germany, but by a further tightening of Russian control over its activities. The new leadership which had replaced Brandler, notably Fischer and Maslow, successfully defied Russian wishes on a number of occasions during 1924 and 1925,[2] but were unable to sustain this show of independence for long. Its fragility was demonstrated when they were summoned to Moscow in August 1925 and condemned for their intellectualism which allegedly distanced them from the masses, and for their hostility to Communist involvement in the free trade unions (ADGB). Fischer was forced to stand down and was replaced by the compliant and anything but intellectual Ernst Thälmann. From then onward the KPD did not deign to challenge Moscow's judgement on matters of grand strategy and therewith lacked the flexibility and adaptability which were to serve the NSDAP so well in later years.

This is not to argue that the KPD's subsequent development and policies were merely a reflection of Soviet interests, however large an influence these exerted. Many radical socialist workers found that the SPD had little to offer them and were prepared at least to give the KPD passive, electoral support as an expression of their alienation from Weimar republicanism.[3] Thus the party polled reasonably well in Reichstag elections during the mid 1920s, albeit with a decline in support from 12.6 per cent in May 1924 to 9.0 per cent in December 1924. In May 1928 its share of the poll rose slightly to 10.6 per cent. This performance, however, emphasised the KPD's position as a minority party, and in other respects it emerged from the 1923 crisis and its aftershocks as a profoundly weakened force. From a little below 300 000 in 1923, the party's membership fell to around 125 000 or less in 1924, at which level it remained until 1930.[4] The KPD did succeed in establishing a paramilitary wing in 1924, the *Rote Frontkämpferbund* (Red Front), to counter the attractions of the Stahlhelm and the Reichsbanner for German youth, but its membership (which overlapped that of the party) reached 130 000 at best and, like the party's, was highly unstable.[5]

Most worrying, however, was the relative failure of the KPD's trade union policy and the party's consequent organisational weakness in the factories, for it was here that the main revolutionary effort was to be located[6] and where the right was soon to be perceived as a serious threat. This weakness in the industrial economy was disguised to some degree by the high level of support enjoyed by the Communist *Union der Hand und Kopfarbeiter* in the Ruhr District, in particular in factory council elections, but this passive voting support was never transformed into a paid-up mass union membership and, in any case, declined sharply after 1924.[7] Similarly the KPD contained a particularly high proportion of industrial workers,[8] but, given the restricted size of the party, they constituted a very small proportion of the industrial working class overall.

A further possibility was afforded the KPD by a policy of entryism into the free unions, and this was not neglected. However, a variety of factors militated against a successful outcome to this policy. Firstly, many workers had little time for the Communist movement, or indeed for political radicalism, and this placed limits on the KPD's potential. Even in the relatively radical Ruhr mining district, the Communist and Syndicalist unions together won only 43 per cent of the factory council seats in 1924 – their best performance during the 1920s.[9] Secondly, the economic crisis which struck in 1923 gave the employers an opportunity to purge their factories of radical activists. As Borkenau comments: 'Most of them found themselves unemployed instead of in power, as they had expected.'[10] The union leaders themselves, understandably, were extremely unwilling to assist the KPD in its enterprise. In essence the ADGB was anxious to preserve its independence from any political party under the watchword of 'neutrality'. This policy, which could militate against the SPD (let alone the Communists!) was intended to allow unions to formulate policy 'solely in the light of union needs', and to maintain a mass membership and a coherent union structure at a time when union members' political loyalties were divided between a number of parties. In this way the unions' bargaining strength was preserved and members were allowed to subscribe to whatever political or religious belief they chose. The KPD and, the union leaders argued, the Communist International, had very different plans for the unions, which justified the regular expulsion of KPD activists who betrayed the oath required of union officials not to pursue party politics.[11]

In such circumstances the KPD had problems enough, but it compounded them through excessive prevarication over the union question. During 1923 the Communist right had cultivated support within the official unions with some success. Perhaps a third of trade union members were Communist-influenced, with particularly strong support in the key Metalworkers' Union.[12] With Brandler's fall, however, confusion developed. In late 1923 the majority of left unionists voted to remain in the ADGB and to fight the expulsion of their activists, but a large minority voluntarily left the official unions to form or join independent organisations.[13] Notable among these was the previously mentioned *Union der Hand und Kopfarbeiter* with 55 000 members, most of whom were Ruhr miners.[14]

At this point Communist labour was split three ways: those remaining in the ADGB, those expelled from it or sacked by their employers, and those in the new, breakaway, unions. The ECCI was not impressed and in two letters to the KPD's Ninth Party Congress in March 1924 condemned the formation of independent unions which threatened to isolate the Communists from the masses. The Congress bowed to this pressure and resolved that KPD members could no longer voluntarily leave the official unions,[15] but this did not solve the problem of the existing independent unions. In July the Fifth Comintern Congress criticised their continuation, thus forcing the Fischer leadership in Germany to order the members of the independent unions back into the ADGB, while expelling many of their leaders and activists who resisted this from the KPD.[16]

The rout of Communist trade unionism was complete. Membership of the discredited Communist unions fell to 36 000 by late 1925 and the Communist and Syndicalist unions together had 64 000 members as against 188 000 members in the right-wing Company, or 'yellow' unions.[17] Even within their Ruhr stronghold the Communist and Syndicalist unions won only 30 per cent of the factory council mandates in 1925 as against 43 per cent in 1924.[18] Within the ADGB too, Communist influence was greatly reduced, despite Thälmann's efforts to reintegrate KPD members within them. Overall, around 400 000 or 10 per cent of the ADGB's membership were Communist supporters at this time[19] and while the Communist opposition still controlled a good third of the Miners' Union branches in late 1925,[20] the KPD group in the Metalworkers' Union fell from 400 in October 1923 to 42 in spring 1925, and from 100 to 6 in the Transport Union.[21] The KPD group in the ADGB overall fell from 2700 to 200, with its representation at congresses never again above five delegates.[22] The ECCI reflected on the scale of the disaster in a letter to the KPD in August 1925, noting the party's reduced organisational strength in industry and confessing that: 'Our ideological influence on the 80 per cent and more members of the free German unions not organised in political parties has dropped steeply',[23] and concluded: 'Only those communist workers can have substantial influence in the German unions today who have influence in the factory; but it is precisely in the factories that Communist influence has recently grown weaker, and we should not conceal this fact.'[24] The Comintern's primary concern was the disadvantage at which this left the KPD in its struggle against the SPD,[25] but the Communist Party was also going to confront right-wing attempts to gain a foothold in the factories through the establishment of company (Yellow) unions from a position of organisational weakness rather than strength.

Several factors contributed to the re-emergence of these right-wing, company unions during the mid 1920s.[26] Big business, particularly the heavy industrial sector, displayed an increasingly hostile attitude to the trade unions and the labour movement in general at this time. Before the 1918 Revolution the German employer had regarded himself as 'master in his own house', with big business showing scant regard for the trade unions' claims to represent the interests of labour.[27] Employer-organised company unions played a considerable role in some individual firms, allowing each employer substantial powers to dictate terms on working conditions and wage rates, not least because many workers in the Ruhr District's metallugical sector in particular identified with this company-based ethos.[28] However, the revolutionary situation of late 1918 forced the employers to reassess their position. Fearing the prospect of outright social revolution and the nationalisation of much of the economy, they concluded a series of agreements with the official unions which were seen as a timely preemptive compromise, not least to stave off nationalisation or other forms of direct state intervention.[29] The unions were recognised as equal and sole partners in wage bargaining which was to be conducted on a collective basis; industry by industry rather than firm by firm. With that and with the persecution of former company union members by their left-wing colleagues, last-minute wartime attempts by heavy industry to re-vamp company unions as nominally autonomous bodies collapsed.[30] There is no doubt that the powers of corporate labour had been considerably enhanced, but big business at least seemed ready to accept this as a satisfactory resolution to the problems created for them in this sphere by Germany's defeat.[31] Certainly the unions became a relatively conservative factor in German political life during the Weimar period and were willing to accept (and even welcome) sweeping rationalisation measures during the mid 1920s and to cooperate in a series of lay-offs and wage cuts during the ensuing depression.

Within a few years, however, heavy industry came to regard the earlier agreements with labour, such as the move to an eight-hour day (largely abolished in 1923), less favourably – not least by the mid-1920s because of the demise of the KPD as a revolutionary threat.[32] The unions were still recognised as negotiating partners for the time being, but firms tended to seek greater autonomy in wage bargaining and within heavy industry the Ruhr coal syndicate in particular began to question and even undermine the fundamental tenets of the post-1918 settlement.[33] In this atmosphere heavy industry regarded trade unionism increasingly sourly. January 1921 saw the establishment of the *Deutsche Volkshochschule* at which selected workers and salaried staff participated in short courses which were designed to create a new cadre within the workforce which was opposed to trade unionism.[34] Soon enough the employers went further. Some began to support the re-establishment of company unions openly, or to subsidise them as early as 1922 and found support for such actions in the conservative press.[35] In 1926 Borsig advocated the waging of a 'defensive struggle' against the trade unions, while Thyssen claimed that at heart the workers were not interested in class politics; their souls were 'German'.[36] Similar attitudes prevailed elsewhere, with the Hansa-Bund of north-west Germany arguing for the withdrawal of recognition for the trade unions, and as Preller observes, this increasingly common tone among employers 'finally led them away from their initial readiness to recognise the Weimar Republic and its class-based social policy'.[37]

Manufacturers and light industry in general took somewhat less extreme a line. Silverberg, for instance, expressed a preference for dealing with labour through the trade unions, rather than through company unions, and felt that major macro-economic problems, especially the reparations question, had to be solved in conjunction with the trade unions.[38] In pursuit of this partnership Silverberg was prepared to accept the Weimar constitution, but only if it allowed the employers to strengthen their position. And this indeed was the rub. There was no question of meeting the SPD and the unions on questions such as economic democratisation – a sound entrepreneurial class was regarded as indispensable – and were unions to accept cooperation on Silverberg's terms they would effectively have had to abandon the class struggle.[39]

Silverberg received rather passive support from the chemicals, electronic and exporting industries, but they were not a unified group and, in any case, tended to pursue a double strategy of cooperating with the unions after a fashion while working to undermine them through secret support for the yellow unions.[40] It could be argued that Silverberg was pursuing similar objectives to the heavy industrialists' by more subtle means, but even this was too much for the latter. The western heavy industrialists were instrumental in opposing him and were able to block attempts to recognise an active role for the unions in the economy.[41]

There was also a widespread conviction within big-business circles, which had originated before 1914,[42] that, specific disputes with the labour movement apart, economic growth and advancement provided a better guarantee of a sound social policy than did the allegedly ideologically-inspired and costly social policy legislation of the

Weimar Republic.[43] It was in this unwelcoming atmosphere, coupled with mounting labour unrest in the Ruhr metallurgical and coalmining industries,[44] that the SPD and ADGB introduced plans in 1928 for the democratisation of the economy; the Naphtali Programme. Worker participation in the management of the economy was regarded by Naphtali as a vital incremental advance along the road to social ownership. As one might expect, many industrialists were enraged, seeing this programme as the prelude not only to economic disaster, but also to political catastrophe as Germany's traditional leadership was replaced by a 'trade union élite' administering a centralised, monopolistic economy.[45]

With prevention better than cure, heavy industry had launched its own campaign for the hearts and minds of the workers in May 1925 through the creation of the German Institute for Technical Labour Training (Dinta). Working alongside the formally autonomous company unions and the nationalist leagues, Dinta was intended to overcome the alienation of most workers and salaried staff from their work at a time when a major rationalisation drive was in any case demanding major changes in work practices and accompanying attitudes. Among the specific aims of Dinta, the training of apprentices and young workers in company schools and sporting organisations, and the systematic education of workers in 'economic' thought and to accept the notion of the 'company community' (through the dissemination of work newspapers), were uppermost.[46] Although Dinta was largely targeting specifically on the young and the unorganised workers, this aim could potentially, as a contemporary observer noted: 'deprive the working-class movement of its pool of recruits and drain it dry, slowly but surely, like water from a field'.[47]

As the employers' attitude to the Weimar settlement and to the direction of policy in Weimar hardened, a rather different process occurred on the radical right. The paramilitary leagues had, as noted found the going increasingly difficult even in 1923. Now, in the more stable atmosphere of 1924 and after they found their prospects much diminished. The right-wing political parties and their trade union associates were increasingly ready to work within the framework of the republican constitution after a fashion,[48] which led to increasing differences between themselves and the paramilitary leagues which still believed that they formed the cadre for a future revolutionary army. The government too became ever less prepared to tolerate paramilitary activity, especially by 1926 when it was recognised as prejudicial to an early withdrawal of the Inter-Allied Military

Commission from Germany. The army, which in the early 1920s had utilised the paramilitary leagues as a frontier defence force on Germany's eastern borders, also lost any remaining interest as the threat of foreign invasion receded after the settling of many outstanding difficulties between the Allies and Germany at Locarno in 1925.[49] The leagues responded by toning down their military-revolutionary stance and attempting to adopt a more 'political' and gradualist tone, but this was not particularly successful.[50]

Indeed, the only league to retain its former significance during this period was the veterans' association, the Stahlhelm. It had eschewed the openly putschist tactics of the more radical *völkisch* leagues during the early 1920s, but even so its paramilitary character was never in question and its anti-republicanism and opposition to reparations payments and to Locarno left it with credit on the far right. The disappointed members of many smaller *Verbände* now joined the Stahlhelm[51] and its ranks were further swollen by a recruitment drive among German youth. This began in late 1923 as relations with another league, the Wehrwolf, to which the Stahlhelm had initially left much youth recruitment, broke down. This campaign was undoubtedly a success. Around half the Stahlhelm's membership was of the post-war generation by 1928/29 which not only provided it with vital new blood, but simultaneously satisfied a desire in conservative circles that as many young Germans as possible in the largely disarmed Republic should receive a military training, despite the provisions of the peace settlement.[52]

These young Germans were recruited to an organisation which saw itself as the peacetime embodiment of the 'front-line socialism' which had purportedly united Germans of every social and political background in the trenches of the Great War.[53] The Stahlhelm recognised that if such a spirit were to prevail in peacetime Germany, then the recruitment of workers and particularly working-class youth, which was very much exposed to Marxist influence, was especially important and a variety of means were employed to achieve this.[54] In December 1924 the Stahlhelm established an Office for Social Policy, through which financial help and food were offered to the out-of-work; it ran its own housing programme and, most telling of all, it provided an employment allocation service for its working-class members.[55] Employers were offered 'ideologically-sound' workers just at a time when they were coming to regard the official unions with mounting disfavour. In these circumstances the Stahlhelm's job allocation scheme was evidently a success.[56] The saying grew up: 'If you're not in the Stahlhelm you won't get any sort of work', and by 1929 even some local authorities, such as Potsdam, made Stahlhelm membership a precondition of appointment.[57]

From 1925 onwards the Stahlhelm developed links with like-minded employers' associations and with the yellow unions which were re-emerging as a minority presence in some factories at this time, and which could even allow discussion of matters as specific as the breaking of strikes in a particular industry.[58] In mid 1925 the Stahlhelm attempted unsuccessfully to establish its own union, the Union of National German Workers,[59] but then, in 1928, did form its own union organisation, the *Stahlhelm-Selbsthilfe* (Stas). The Stas was essentially corporatist in outlook and sought to integrate the worker in his occupational estate by operating as a 'synthesis of the company union and the trade union'. In this way the shared responsibility of employer and worker for the performance of any industry would eradicate the Marxist notion of class struggle. Indeed, the Stas consciously took on the official unions, who came to despise it as a strike-breaking organisation,[60] but it was able gradually to gain ground in the small and medium-sized firms of central Germany and Berlin by the early 1930s in the face of opposition from all other unions, including the Nazi NSBO.[61]

The KPD, therefore, witnessed a more aggressive attitude on the part of many employers to labour relations, and also was faced with the re-emergence of the yellow unions which were strengthened by the Stahlhelm's involvement. To compound this, the KPD's own position in the factories was, as noted, parlous.[62] This unpleasant situation was to make the KPD an especially painstaking observer of the radical right within the factories during the mid 1920s and, as will be seen, a mood of profound pessimism came to grip the Communist movement in this regard long before the NSDAP became a force in factory politics.

The yellow unions had virtually disappeared by 1918, retaining only 46 000 members, but numbers had recovered to 246 000 by 1921 – close to pre-war levels – and the yellow unions' membership fell proportionally less than that of their rivals in the wake of the 1923 upheavals in Germany. The ADGB dominated the German trade union movement, of course, with over 4 million working-class members in 1925, and the Catholic unions retained almost 600 000, but then came the yellow unions with 188 000 members, followed by the liberal unions with 158 000 workers and, finally, the Communist and Syndicalist unions which, as noted earlier, numbered just 64 000.[63]

The latter grouping could count on substantial passive support in factory council elections in the centres of heavy industry, but even in the Ruhr mining district a handful of yellow union delegates reappeared on the factory councils in 1924. Their eleven mandates might have appeared a pinprick when set against the 1310 Communist and Syndicalist mandates (or the 10 against 893 in 1925),[64] but the KPD regarded these tentative *völkisch* successes as a portent of a greater danger which arose out of Social Democracy's alleged betrayal of the working classes. The latter had produced a mood of apathy and even despair within sections of the working class and those who were 'insufficiently class conscious' had sometimes supported the super-ficially radical *völkisch* candidates rather than voting for the oppositional or openly Communist candidates. The KPD acknow-ledged that the *völkisch* successes were isolated, but was convinced that they demonstrated 'the terrible danger into which the entire working-class movement could run because of the passiveness of the reformist trade union bureaucracy'[65] and urged that a 'life and death struggle' be waged against the *Völkische*.[66]

During 1925 the KPD's objective position weakened, while the far right grew stronger. In July the Red Front noted the increasing tendency of employers to recruit from within the right-wing *Verbände*, thereby undermining the political cohesiveness of their workforces. In the countryside matters were worse, for some estate owners even made membership of a nationalist league a condition of employment.[67] Even in the radical Ruhr District, however, the local Communist party was concerned by the tendency of the far right to switch the main basis of their activities from the street to the factory. With help from employers, nationalist workers and staff were present 'in almost all factories', and, the KPD warned, 'if our factory councillors and officials are not sufficiently alert, then one fine day we'll have the suprise of our lives'.[68]

Specific mention of the Stahlhelm in this connection also became more common during 1925, whether it involved the body's growing influence among the rural working class where the material benefits of Stahlhelm membership were considerable,[69] or the Stahlhelm's presence in the factories. In the latter case the Communists were to approach the right-wingers man to man to discuss matters of common interest so as 'to convince the misled workers in the Wehrwolf, the Stahlhelm and so on of the disgracefulness of their behaviour and to make them into class-conscious proletarians, marching in the Red Front'.[70] At this point, therefore, the United Front From Below tactic had been extended to the right in the strategically critical context of the factory and the precedent set for similar approaches to factory-employed Nazis during the early 1930s. By the end of 1925 the national leadership of the Red Front regarded matters particularly seriously and the struggle against the nationalists on the land and in the factories became an issue of first importance.[71] The Red Front believed that 'a large percentage of industrial and rural proletarians' were organised in the Stahlhelm and similar bodies, with young proletarians comprising 'a large proportion of the members of these organisations'. The best prospects for remedying this situation were seen to lie in the workplace where these workers were free from their organisations and, given that many workers were more or less blackmailed by employers into joining nationalist leagues, this task was not seen as hopeless: 'Many workers having to choose between unemployment, or entry into the fascist organisations and work, choose the latter out of necessity.'[72]

During 1926 the Red Front in particular began to pay systematic attention to the social composition of the nationalist *Verbände* and their youth sections. The arithmetic of the situation was not to the Red Front's liking, for it concluded that not only was it outnumbered decisively by the republican Reichsbanner, but also by the nationalist leagues. The Stahlhelm alone was reckoned to have 400 000–500 000 members to whom could be added the 200 000 or so members of the smaller *Verbände*,[73] while the Red Front had just over 100 000 members. The social composition of the *Verbände* made matters worse. It is commonly assumed today that these leagues were overwhelmingly middle class, but although the KPD also described them as 'bourgeois', this tag referred to their political function, not their social composition. With regard to the latter, the Stahlhelm nationally was estimated by the Communist Party to be 80 per cent proletarian (as against an official Stahlhelm estimate of 88 per cent)[74] and although this figure seems very high, an East German estimate has set the figure at 50 per cent[75] and it appears that the proportion of specifically industrial workers in the Stahlhelm in 1926 could have approached 30 per cent.[76] To this would be added craft and agricultural workers and since the presence of the latter in the Stahlhelm in large numbers is nowhere disputed, it seems probable that a majority of rank-and-file Stahlhelmer were indeed workers.

Looking specifically at the far right's appeal to youth, the Red Front reached even more depressing conclusions. The membership of left-wing youth organisations (political, cultural and sporting) was estimated at 700 000–800 000 as against the 3–3.5 million young workers in the bourgeois organisations.[77] Elsewhere the Red Front described a 'high proportion' of these 3.5 million as proletarian[78] and looking at the Young Stahlhelm its claim of 80 per cent proletarian was noted without comment.[79] Similarly the leagues' womens' groups had recruited a very high proportion of workers 'under the cloak of representing specifically women's interests of female workers'.[80] Whatever the exact figures, the Red Front was in no doubt that it faced an uphill task in organising the mass of working-class youth, concluding: 'It is a fact that the majority of working-class youth is influenced by the bourgeoisie, even though we can establish that young workers belong to the most oppressed section of the proletariat as a whole.'[81]

The Red Front claimed to detect a numerical decline in the Stahlhelm's strength in early 1926,[82] which was probably little more than wishful thinking, but its belief that the Stahlhelm and other *Verbände* suffered from considerable internal dissent was more soundly based.[83] As one might expect, the Communist movement attributed this dissent to increasing contradictions between the class interests of the Stahlhelm's leaders and their largely working-class following: 'The Stahlhelm's cannot show its numerous proletarian members any escape from their economic predicament.'[84] This said, the Red Front's leaders had to admit that any such difficulties stemmed largely from this 'objective economic and political situation rather than any systematic, determined oppositional work by our organisations'.[85]

In general terms the Red Front conceded that the militaristic character of many right-wing organisations and their exploitation of 'war-romanticism' appealed strongly to many young workers, thereby weakening the left still further domestically and, it was asserted, arguably rather less objectively, producing prospective recruits for a war of intervention against the Soviet Union.[86] The best counter to this appeared to lie in matching the right's militarism within the Red Front and its youth wing, both to block off further recruitment by the right of young workers and to win over individual working-class members of the leagues.[87] In addition to militarism, it was recognised that nationalism continued to appeal strongly to many workers 'and ties a section of them to the right-wing organisations'.[88]

These problems apart, it seemed appropriate to use the United Front From Below tactic, as mooted in 1925, to agitate among the rank-and-file members of the *Verbände* to subvert them and then detach them from their leaders and ultimately their organisations.[89] The factory was perceived as a key area in this struggle for a variety of reasons. Firstly the KPD believed that the growth of the yellow unions, or 'white factory cells' as it called them, had reached serious proportions. Again the Stahlhelm was a key actor, for whatever internal problems this organisation might have suffered, it constituted, in the KPD's estimation: 'a dangerous opponent in the realm of economic struggle as one of the principal advocates of the white factory cells'.[90] These cells were becoming stronger and more numerous, particularly in the mining and smelting industries where foremen and older workers were active in organising them.[91] Ideally the Communists would have liked to organise all trade unionists and then set up red factory cells within the trade unions themselves,[92] but this was hardly realistic and the use of the United Front From Below tactic to approach right-wingers was regarded as the next best solution. This strategy was not used solely within the factories; there were instances when Red Youth Front formations came upon Young Stahlhelm groups during camping trips or whatever and tried to fraternise with them on the basis of common class interests, but it was in the factory that Communists and Stahlhelmer came into daily, regular contact and shared similar material concerns. 'Discussion with the individual man at the work bench' therefore marked the surest way forward,[93] although it would be supplemented by the opportunities that unemployment offices, public parks and public transport provided for approaching right-wingers and patiently discussing a range of issues with them.[94] As the Red Front in Württemberg demanded publicly of its members:

> The working class elements of the fascist organisations . . . demand a particular attitude of every comrade. Try to convince them by matter-of-fact discussion, don't lump them together with their leaders. We must fight for the soul of every proletarian who still stands apart from us or who is actually hostile. A good measure of patience is necessary here. Remember, even we once belonged somewhere different from today politically.[95]

During 1926, therefore, the German Communist movement had come to accept that the growing strength of the right in the factories, 'much better organised, much better armed, and operating in a much more unified fashion [than hitherto]'[96] had made physical confrontation an insufficient defence. The struggle would henceforward be conducted in large measure through proselytisation and personal contacts.

The Communists' resulting countermeasures failed to contain, let alone eradicate, right-wing influence within the industrial working class during 1927 and concern consequently mounted. The employers themselves had been far from idle. Ninety-five firms in the iron and coal-mining industry had Dinta schools, as against twenty-three in 1926 and dozens of firms had begun to distribute Dinta works newspapers[97] against which the KPD had little answer. The factory council election results began to reinforce the impression of Communist impotence just as the right-radical threat was growing. Thus, in the mining industry, the yellow unions received 41 mandates (0.63 per cent thereof) in 1925, but 90 mandates (1.4 per cent thereof) in 1927. The Communist union received 845 mandates (12.99 per cent) in 1925, but had collapsed and received none in 1927. The Syndicalists failed to benefit from this disaster with their tally of mandates declining from 75 in 1925 to 49 in 1927: well below the figure for the yellow unions.[98] In the metal industry the yellow unions received 1097 mandates in 1925 (4.1 per cent thereof) and 1350 mandates in 1927 (5 per cent) while the combined Communist and Syndicalist tally fell from 126 (0.5 per cent) in 1925 to 94 (0.4 per cent) in 1927.[99]

Leaving aside factory elections, the bourgeois women's organisations were recruiting proletarian members through the offer of jobs, by arranging discounts on the purchase of groceries and household articles, and by dispensing charity. The Red Women's and Girls' League feared that once recruited in this way, working-class women could be indoctrinated with bourgeois values and come to perceive themselves as mothers and home-makers in the first instance. The League was to prevent women from joining bourgeois organisations and win over for the class struggle those proletarians who had already joined them.[100]

This implicit criticism of the KPD's women's work was eclipsed by that of the movement's youth campaign. The latter had been designated as a priority, indeed as the priority, at the Red Front's Third National Congress in March 1926, but with little to show for this. As the Fourth National Congress lamented in March 1927: 'It is indeed a farce that we speak of the struggle against fascism and imperialist war while we simultaneously leave the young proletarians to the bourgeois paramilitary leagues without a serious struggle and deliver them up to nationalist indoctrination of the very worst sort.'[101] The Young Red Front concluded, not unreasonably, that it had a lot to learn from its more successful right-wing rivals: 'With regard to our campaigning methods, we should learn in particular from rival organisations and reflect over why the greater part of the young proletariat stands on the side of the class enemy', which, given the pecularities of the KPD's terminology, might have included the Social Democrats. Among its conclusions, the Young Red Front observed that the romanticism of young people and their wish for comradeship were of great importance. The rambles, scouting and camping activities of the right-wing leagues were very attractive for young workers, and therefore had to be copied by the Young Red Front.[102] The first attempts at this in northern Germany did enjoy some success and were soon extended to the southern states.[103]

However, recreational activities were also used specifically by the right to achieve rapid and effective penetration of factory workforces. In the Ruhr, for instance, the Red Front and the Young Red Front had become well established, but the same was true of the Stahlhelm, not least because of its sporting activities: 'There are a very large number of factories there in which up to 70 per cent of the workers are organised in "Factory Sporting Clubs" set up by the Stahlhelm', as a delegate to a KPD conference in Stuttgart reported. Of course most of these workers did not join the Stahlhelm itself (although its sporting activities and job allocation service did bring it 'a large number of members in the Ruhr District'), but its potential ability to influence many workers over and above its paid-up membership in Germany's industrial heartland clearly worried the Red Front.[104]

The Communist movement also remained convinced that the major *Verbände* derived much of their numerical strength from specifically working-class recruitment. The Stahlhelm was taken to be 65 per cent industrial and rural proletarian in 1927, with 25 per cent of its membership from the lower middle classes and 10 per cent (the leaders) from the bourgeoisie. Of the smaller leagues the Wehrwolf, with perhaps 100 000 members, was considered even more proletarian; 75–80 per cent workers, 15–20 per cent lower-middle-class, and a scattering of bourgeois members.[105] This resulted partly from a Wehrwolf policy, applied particularly in central Germany, to recruit workers only, and partly from the extremely radical stance adopted by some Wehrwolf leaders which attracted workers anyway. Thus in the left-wing stronghold of Hamburg the Wehrwolf alone of the leagues had recruited a sizeable membership of 900, precisely beause of this radicalism. The Jungdo was more lower-middle-class, but still apparently drew 30–40 per cent of its members from the working class.[106]

This disturbing pattern was accentuated by the organisation of many of these workers within the company unions. The Stahlhelm had won 'substantial influence in important large factories in the Ruhr District', as the Red Front reported in February 1927, and had also gained support in the middle Rhine lignite fields and in the industrial towns of the Erzgebirge/Vogtland and Silesia.[107] By midsummer the Red Front possessed somewhat more detailed information on the Stahlhelm and other *Verbände* which identified Halle-Merseburg, Baden-Pfalz, the Ruhr District and some towns near Berlin as centres of strength for their company unions, although it confessed that its information 'did not in the slightest way provide a picture of the extent of factory fascism in Germany'.[108] Nonetheless, it was able to identify some individual factories where the Stahlhelm had established unions, such as the huge Leuna chemical works with a payroll of 48 000 workers and a 400-strong Stahlhelm union, and the sugar refinery in Halle with 480 of its 600 workers so organised. These two factories were among forty in Halle-Merseburg with Stahlhelm unions which had an overall membership of perhaps 4000. In the Ruhr District the Gelsenkirchener Mining Company was identified as a Stahlhelm stronghold with 500 members,[109] and overall here the Red Front was able to identify twenty-five nationalist company unions in nineteen separate towns. Mines such as the Zeche Gustav (with 90 out of 1800 employees so organised), the Zeche Brassert (300 out of 2800) and the Zeche Dahlbusch (300 out of 5500) were joined by the iron works of Schildte and Knaudel (263 out of 1600) and the zinc smelter in Hamborn (100).[110] Subsequent East German research shows this list merely to scratch the surface. Key enterprises in Berlin, such as Siemens and AEG; in Chemnitz, such as Wanderer Werken and Vomag; in the Ruhr, such as Krupp and Thyssen; and other factories throughout Germany, including the Opel Werke in Rüsselsheim, had Stahlhelm groups.[111] Thus can be understood Kaasch's report to the Comintern in May 1927 that: 'The big factories are dominated above all by the SPD, followed by the Centre Party or the Fascists, especially the Stahlhelm.'[112]

However, the factory council elections revealed the limitations and potential weakness of these company unions. In the Leuna Works, it is true, the Stahlhelm union gained 1500 votes in the 1927 elections, which comfortably exceeded its 400-strong membership, but in many factories the vote for the 'yellow' candidate was well below the strength of the company union, especially in the Ruhr District. Of the 500 Stahlhelmer employed at the Gelsenkirchener Mining Company, only 54 voted for their candidate in a shop steward's election and in factory council elections the proportions were 137 out of 300 at the

Dahlbusch mine and 25 out of 100 at the Hamborn zinc smelter.[113] Many workers evidently had divided political loyalties, not least because of the ways in which the Stahlhelm had gained a foothold in the factories.

Leaving aside the convinced Stahlhelmer, some workers evidently joined to acquire various material benefits which membership of a company union could bring. In secret ballots, it seems, they hedged their bets by choosing non-yellow (presumably socialist) candidates to represent their interests as workers within privately owned and managed companies and therefore got the best of both worlds. The Communists' self-perceived task in these circumstances, however dubious the tactic might now seem, was to appeal to their sense of class solidarity 'so that they return to the ranks of the class-conscious workers and rejoin their organisations'.[114] In the countryside in particular employers could force workers into the Stahlhelm through 'economic terror', giving employees the stark choice of thereby remaining in their job (and quite possibly retaining rented or tied accommodation) or of refusing to join the Stahlhelm and thereby losing everything.[115] No doubt the victims of such tactics were the most likely to assume a split political identity, belonging to a right-wing organisation while voting left, but open defiance of their employers' wishes would hardly have been a practical option, rendering the Communists' task very difficult.

As well as influencing, or coercing, existing workforces, employers and company unions had the option of reconstituting workforces to their liking. Even in stable economic times older workers retire and are replaced by the young, but during the mid 1920s there was a particularly high turnover of labour. New employees were taken on in the wake of the 1923/24 economic crisis, but unemployment rose sharply in 1926 before falling equally sharply in 1927. Coupled with the intense rationalisation drive within German industry, employers were thereby given ample opportunity for changing the composition of their workforces quite dramatically. As intimated earlier, the Stahlhelm offered employers the chance of appointing politically reliable workers through its job allocation scheme and it appears that many took advantage of this.[116] In some cases, the KPD observed, hand-picked Stahlhelmer were transported across Germany to work in particular factories from which employers wished to remove radical workers, as in the case of the Knorr Bremse Works in Berlin in September 1927, and in more general terms the build-up of company unions was regarded as 'an important instrument for corrupting part of the working class, for undermining the Free Trade Unions, and for driving revolutionary influence out of the factories'.[117].

From time to time the KPD spoke of driving the 'fascists' from the factories in cooperation with the official unions, but, given its own weakness, its poor relations with the ADGB, and the glaring reality of the powers employers enjoyed in appointing and dismissing their employees, this was little more than rhetoric. As in 1926 the only realistic course open to the KPD was to take advantage of the many opportunities for personal contact between Communist and nationalist workers to try to convince them to change sides:[118] 'It is necessary to make these people aware of their duties as members of the proletariat; if they are handled properly, many of them will come back to where they belong.'[119] The immediate objective remained to persuade converts, while staying in their original organisations, to proselytise among their comrades and to provide the Communist movement with intelligence information. Public entry to the Red Front (which was theoretically open to members of all parties)[120] was regarded as a last resort when membership of the Stahlhelm, or whatever, became impossible.[121]

As was so often the case the Communist movement's ambitious and unrealistic plans were not transformed into deeds. In July the Red Front's leadership complained that with the exception of the Berlin and Halle-Merseburg districts, organised work among rival bodies, the Reichsbanner included, had been largely absent.[122] The Red Front was urged to repair the damage, but reports for 1928 show a remarkably similar pattern. There was mention periodically of crises in the Stahlhelm, not least because of its strikebreaking activities in a year of increasing industrial unrest which caused many workers to leave it, but, as the Red Front's leaders complained: 'Where has this favourable situation been exploited for us by the comrades of our District Organisations?'[123] At its Fifth National Congress the Red Front's leaders complained yet again about the lack of effective intelligence work on the right's activities in the factories, no doubt in part because of the KPD's own organisational weakness there:[124] 'Reports on the strength and activities of the fascists in the factories are very deficient, with the result that detailed figures on the activities of company unions and other fascist factory organisations cannot be given.'[125] Working-class youth reportedly remained at risk and yet the Communist movement had still failed to take on the nationalist sporting organisations or to counter the militaristic stance of the nationalist leagues: 'We must not ignore the fact that the bourgeoisie's nationalist war propaganda is often successful among the uninformed proletarian youth, all the more so because today's youth has no longer directly experienced a war.'[126] The situation was not hopeless. The Red Front claimed to have restricted the growth of factory fascism in the Ruhr, although this must be taken on trust and even the Red Front admitted that the area remained a stronghold of the same despite a combination of sabotage, physical confrontation and use of the United Front tactic which could sometimes disrupt the Stahlhelm and other groups, and even win over members from them.[127] At the end of the day, then, one is left with the impression that the KPD had been confronted by an unwelcome new dimension to its struggle against the far right of whose importance it was in little doubt, but against which its countermeasures were of limited value.

Although the company unions had failed to achieve their primary objective of undermining the ADGB and had therefore failed to fulfil the hopes vested in them by some industrialists and by the paramilitary leagues, their return cannot be dismissed as insignificant.[128] Well before the 1929 slump key sections of heavy industry had shown themselves prepared to use company unions as a weapon in their struggle to undermine the gains achieved by organised labour in 1918. This went as far as their using the Stahlhelm's job allocation service to recruit purportedly 'patriotic' workers to replace potential left-wing troublemakers within their factories, and it is clear that this strategy was initiated long before the mass unemployment of the early 1930s made its execution very much easier.

Ironically the 'stabilisation' of the Weimar Republic during the mid 1920s had helped to make this feasible, for with the clampdown on open paramilitary activity by the state, right-wing radicals had turned their attention to the workshops and factories of Germany.

Equally significant were the implications of this process for the political and social future of the German working class. As has been shown, the KPD was especially concerned. It had pinned its revolutionary hopes during this period on organising and mobilising the factory-employed proletariat which, given its organisational weakness in the factories, would have been a daunting task under any circumstances. However, at least the ADGB could be regarded as a relatively passive target which also had few friends among the employers and the wider establishment. The KPD argued, not without reason, that many ordinary trade unionists were more radical than their leaders and might, therefore, under suitable circumstances, be won for the revolutionary cause.

The yellow unions and their paramilitary allies posed completely different problems for the revolutionary movement. Not only were they working hand-in-glove with the employers and with the Dinta, but they were regarded as a new and highly threatening dynamic. Although they had failed to neutralise the reformist unions, they and more particularly their sporting and leisure auxiliaries had received a disturbing degree of support from individual workers, including many in Germany's industrial heartlands. Before 1930 this was manifested largely through membership of auxiliary organisations, but then began to translate into votes in factory council elections, notably in mining and chemicals.[129] This demonstrated the opportunism (or fearful impotence) of many employees and, as was shown, revealed the ability of individual workers sometimes to wear two or more political hats. This lays open to question the degree to which individual workers can necessarily, or usefully, be labelled as 'Socialist', 'Tory' or whatever and suggests that apparent shifts in formal political allegiance on the part of individuals were not necessarily so very dramatic an act. The 'change' might have involved stressing one part of their political persona at the expense of another.[130]

As the KPD understood, this called into question the prospects for the revolutionary movement within the factories. It would enter the depression years weak and isolated while the radical right had, even during the relatively stable mid 1920s, begun to undermine the apparent coherence of the labour force which the unions had, painfully, attempted to forge out of the 1918 agreements with the employers. These radical right-wingers did not necessarily serve as the direct forerunners of Nazism. There is little evidence to suggest that the Nazi trade union, the NSBO, drew its main working-class strength from these yellow unions during the early 1930s despite some transfer of members between the two sides.[131] The membership of the yellow unions remained more or less stable at this time and their working-class vote in factory council elections tended to rise.[132] However, it seems clear that the Nazi movement did not face quite the monolith in its bid for factory-based working-class support that has sometimes been suggested, for the edifice had already been fractured during Weimar's 'Golden Years'.[133]

The dramatic appearance of the NSDAP as a major political force was soon to overwhelm the pattern of development peculiar to the political economy of the mid 1920s, but the Communist movement believed that the tactics and lessons learned at that time and applied to the Stahlhelm and the yellow unions could also be applied to the

National Socialists as they began to organise in the factories. Indeed, all the points of contact between the KPD and the radical right which had developed during the 1920s were subsequently to define the character of the relationship between the Communist and Nazi movements during the early 1930s. It remained to be seen whether the KPD's organisational strength and internal discipline would be equal to the challenges therein.

6 Communist–Nazi Relations 1928–1932: The Ideological Dimension

Comintern abandoned any notion of further cooperation with reformist socialism in early 1928. The period of capitalist stabilisation was said to be over and an imminent economic crisis heralded a new revolutionary era.[1] In these circumstance cooperation with reformist socialist organisations was regarded as entirely inappropriate and the imminent struggle of 'class against class' required a policy 'totally antagonistic to the Social Democrats'.[2] In this spirit the official trade unions were condemned as a major support of the capitalist system and a barrier to revolution[3] which would be breached through the utilisation of the United Front From Below, to be directed against trade union leaders, and by the establishment of Communist factory cell organisations to confront the official unions on the shop floor.[4] For Comintern fascism was now perceived as a weapon in the bourgeoisie's economic struggle against the working class.[5] The increasingly equivocal line taken by many Social Democrats towards the abolition of capitalism and the increasing tendency for trade unions to develop methods of operating within the capitalist system compromised them irrevocably and made them part of this emerging fascist order in Comintern's eyes. As the ECCI official Piatnitsky commented: 'There was not a single strike, not a single lockout, not a single conflict between labour and capital in which the trade unions did not take the side of capital.'[6] The relatively open debate that had characterised Comintern meetings during the early 1920s was now a thing of the past and the characterisation of Social Democracy as 'Social Fascist' rapidly became a new orthodoxy within the member parties of the Third International. Thus, before the opening of the Tenth ECCI Plenum in July 1929 *Pravda* described Social Democracy as 'a component part of the fascist system' against which the Communists had to organise in the factories, while at the Plenum itself Kuusinen argued that Social Democracy merely obscured its fascist character 'behind a smoke-screen'.[7]

Looking specifically at Germany, Comintern again noted Social Democratic participation within the existing socio-economic order with distaste: 'The Social Democratic Party . . . has strangled the workers' strikes with the noose of compulsory arbitration; has helped the capitalists to declare lockouts and liquidate the gains of the working class', and, more emotively: 'Social Democracy prohibits May Day demonstrations. It shoots down unarmed workers during May Day demonstrations.'[8] Given this apparent 'reign of terror' unleashed by the Social Democrats on the working class, it is understandable that Comintern would regard the rise of Nazism as a complementary and, indeed, secondary problem and regard the NSDAP with no more or less aversion than it did the SPD. As *Pravda* was to write in March 1932: 'The SPD's "hysterical outcry" against the fascist danger concealed its alliance with fascism, and would deceive only the inexperienced into thinking there was a difference between the two.'[9] Indeed, it could at least be said for the Nazis that they promised to introduce an element of instability and uncertainty into the operation of the capitalist system, which could not, from the Communists' viewpoint, be said for the SPD.[10]

Many national and local KPD leaders regarded Comintern's new course with profound misgivings, feeling that far more united Social Democrats and Communists than divided them. A sharp struggle ensued between the majority, pro-Comintern, faction led by Thälmann and the 'conciliators', but the Stalinists prevailed and removed these 'conciliators' wherever possible.[11] Soon enough the only real debate occurred between a pro-Comintern KPD and outsider groups or the supporters of Leon Trotsky who urged a common front between Socialists and Communists against fascism, which was identified as a qualitatively new phenomenon.[12] The victorious faction had good reason to back the new strategy, however. As Ulbricht observed at a Central Committee meeting in October 1928, if the party did not quash its own right it would draw nearer to the Social Democrats and effectively liquidate itself.[13] With this the Comintern agreed and although there was brave talk of a new revolutionary offensive, the fear of cooperating with the Social Democrats was surely as much an admission of weakness as an expression of purist revolutionary zeal.

During 1928 the KPD adjusted its official view of the SPD accordingly. The founding of the Red Front in 1924 was now celebrated for mobilising 'great masses against republican indoctrination of the working class' with little said about its potential use against the radical right. Indeed in early 1929 it was argued that the bourgeoisie hardly needed the right at all any longer, 'relying in the present period primarily on the reformist organisations and in paramilitary terms particularly on the Reichsbanner',[14] and the formation of the *Norddeutscher Arbeiterschutzbund* in Hamburg was seen as much as a defence against 'attacks by the Reichsbanner fascists on workers' as it was a defence against the Nazis.[15] The events surrounding May Day 1929 gave this hatred a more concrete basis. Confrontation was in the air well before 1 May, with ECCI's May Day Manifesto declaring that: 'The social-democrats, by lulling the vigilance of the working class with the help of pacifist prattle, ideologically disarm it in the face of the bourgeoisie and deliberately drive the workers to complete and unconditional surrender.'[16] Separate Communist-led May Day demonstrations in Berlin resulted in fighting with the SPD-controlled police, with a number of deaths and injuries occurring. Communist leaflets subsequently denounced Social Democratic leaders in the bitterest of terms as 'the Social Fascist lackeys of finance capital' and the SPD as a whole as the 'Social Democratic Murderers' Party'.[17] Reflecting on events several months later, the KPD's Central Committee appeared convinced that its quarrel with the Social Democrats comprised the essence of the anti-fascist struggle, as the KPD 'stood up as the only organised mass force against social-fascism and the Reichsbanner, and stirred up broad masses of the workers against the bourgeois republic'.[18] Thus, while Thälmann noted Nazi electoral successes in Saxony with some concern, he concluded at the KPD's Twelfth Party Congress that 'Social Fascism' was the decisive form' of fascist development in Germany.[19] Nazism, therefore, occupied a subordinate position in Thälmann's demonology, which placed entrepreneurs and bourgeois state power as the key dangers alongside Social Democracy.[20] Again, the linking of fascism with Germany's existing economic and political order was, in theoretical terms at least, to allow the KPD to perceive the Nazi movement in rather less negative terms from time to time once it became a force to be reckoned with.

Russian foreign policy interests provided a further dimension to Communist–Socialist enmity, for the Soviet Union noted the SPD's continuing relatively pro-Western stance with concern. A Germany estranged from the West would, as before, provide the Soviet Union with a potential friend in the capitalist world and thus 'the Soviet Union sought common cause with German nationalism as distinct from Nazism',[21] while condemning the SPD for attempting to work, however reluctantly, within the constraints of the Treaty of Versailles. Thus the Tenth ECCI Plenum on the International Situation regarded the Young Plan negotiations on the rescheduling of German reparations payments with distaste because of their potential impact on Soviet–German relations. Germany, Comintern felt, remained the weakest link in the anti-Soviet front, and the Young Plan was regarded as an attempt to tie it in more closely: 'the stronger Germany was, the further it withdrew from Rapallo'.[22] The KPD's leadership echoed these concerns, understanding that the SPD's *Westorientierung* was, with the party in government, losing the USSR important advantages in Germany and this led Thälmann at the KPD's Twelfth Party Congress to stress the danger the SPD posed for the Soviet Union.[23] Just as the adoption of the 'class against class' policy had met with resistance within the KPD, so this adherence to Soviet foreign policy interests caused disquiet within the party, with some figures demanding a more 'national' stance that took account of German conditions.[24] However the orthodox Comintern line was to prevail and during 1930 the Young Plan and the Versailles system of which it was a part were attacked remorselessly along with the Weimar parties which tolerated the situation.[25]

Just as the KPD and Comintern perceived fascism essentially as an economic phenomenon, so the Young Plan and Versailles were presented as instruments in the class struggle which furthered capitalist interests. Thus the *Süddeutsche Arbeiterzeitung* declared in September 1930 that 'the robbing Young Plan will be paid for with the sweat of the working people, so that German and foreign capitalists can make huge profits'.[26] The national enslavement of Germany would only be ended when social liberation was achieved and that, *Die Rote Fahne* repeatedly declared, would come through the creation of a Soviet Germany.[27] Similarly, as the KPD declared in 1931, it was 'the only German party to wage a struggle for the national liberation of the German people from Versailles slavery and Young slavery . . . and the only one, leading the proletarian masses, which can complete the task of national and social liberation'.[28] The attacks on the SPD in this particular context assumed an especial virulence, with the same accused of 'justifying and endlessly prolonging the existing desperate situation'.[29] At times the language used against the Social Democrats could plumb the depths of hatred, as, for instance, when the Comintern declared in 1931 that: 'The German Social Democratic Party, the accomplice of the German militarists in the robber peace of Brest-Litovsk, in the occupation and plundering of the Ukraine . . . is the most active of all German parties organising the anti-Soviet front.'[30] By 1932 attacks of this sort on the SPD in the context of foreign policy were routine, as with the Central Committee's reaction to the conclusion of the Lausanne Conference which suspended German reparations payments in July 1932. At first sight the KPD's violent reaction to Lausanne might seem perverse, for the Conference had, after all, decided in Germany's favour, but the Central Committee's anger focused on the SPD's perceived role in an agreement which promised to improve German–Western relations. Lausanne was regarded as an agreement between factions of international capitalism with which virtually every corporate group in Weimar Germany had connived:

> The united front of the captains of industry, bankers and stock market speculators, of Junker, big agrarians, generals and followers of the swastika, the Reichsbanner leaders, trade union bureaucrats and police presidents – this supporters' front of the bourgeois dictatorship and the capitalist system – are now trying to absolve themselves in the eyes of Germany's working folk through mere words 'against' the plundering Young-system.[31]

Social Democracy's role in this policy of fulfilment was regarded as particularly despicable: 'Social Democracy is the slavish protagonist of a policy of subordination to the dictates of French imperialism, of the voluntary surrendering up of German working people, *Volksgenossen*, in the east of Germany to the jackboot of Polish Pilsudski-fascism.' The Central Committee remarked that although the NSDAP might sound every bit as nationalist as the KPD, its equivocal attitude to capitalism rendered its nationalism invalid. The Nazis would do the work of 'international finance capital' in the same way 'as the rest of the bourgeoisie and Social Democracy'.[32] Thus, once again, the Nazis were condemned for their alleged similarity to Social Democracy; a grave charge indeed.[33]

  In ideological terms, therefore, the KPD was playing a dangerous game. In its foreign policy pronouncements the party repeatedly used language, intentionally or otherwise, that was reminiscent of the Nazis' vocabulary. In 1929, it is true, the KPD fought shy of actually participating in the right's Young Plan referendum (which sought to reject the Young proposals), but in subsequent Reichstag debates it did line up with the Nazis and the traditional right on foreign policy matters.[34] Then, in 1930, during the campaign for the Reichstag elections in September, a senior KPD leader, Heinz Neumann, drafted at Stalin's behest a Programme of National and Social Liberation[35] which borrowed much from the 1923 Schlageter campaign and, indeed, Radek himself was likely involved in its formulation.[36]

At domestic level some local KPD organisations continued to defy the new orthodoxy, with the *Leipziger Volkszeitung* describing it as a concession to the Nazis.[37] Comintern complained on several occasions of this defiance, accusing some local officials of 'even going so far as to sabotage party decisions' concerning the confrontation with Social Democracy.[38] Similarly in July 1932, following a Comintern complaint that the KPD was going soft on Social Democracy because of its exaggerated fear of the Nazis,[39] a Berlin official of the KPD deplored: 'the neglect of our principled struggle against the SPD in certain cases, accompanied by a one-sided struggle against the Nazis (who are regarded as the sole embodiment of fascism)'.[40] However, this type of defiance was kept within limits and the KPD's capacity for enforcing an orthodox line was rated by the Comintern as second only to that of the CPSU;[41] again, most criticism came from left-wing radicals outside the party.[42] With orthodoxy therefore in the ascendant, the danger of a blurring of differences with the NSDAP at domestic level existed as much as in the realm of foreign policy. The SPD noted that it, and not The Nazis, was sometimes subjected to furious attack which did not necessarily even spare the children of Social Democrats: 'The Communist school children's organisation *Rote Lanzen* was, at one point, instructed to throw its little 'Social Fascist' rivals out of the playgrounds.'[43] On other occasions Communist officials could express an open preference for the Nazis as when the leader of the KPD's Chemnitz-Erzgebirge District, Sindemann, who was also a member of the Saxon Landtag, declared:

> Oh yes, we admit that we're in league with the National Socialists, that we together with the National Socialists, want to destroy the existing social system . . . Bolshevism and Fascism share a common goal; the destruction of capitalism and of the Social Democratic Party. To achieve this aim we are justified in using every means.[44]

Such utterances were not to the SPD's liking; even less so that of a local KPD official in Schivelbein, Pomerania, who somewhat tactlessly informed Reichsbanner members at a meeting during the 1932 Presidential election campaign that Communists 'would rather vote for Hitler than for Hindenburg'.[45]

Of course the Central Committee regarded these pro-Nazi deviations with as much displeasure as they did unauthorised fraternisation with the 'Social Fascists', but the SPD argued that pro-Nazi outbursts followed logically enough from the KPD's ideological stance. In a discussion between SPD delegates and Thälmann shortly before the July 1932 election the Socialists expressed particular doubts about the KPD's nationalist line:

> Have the Communists made concessions to National Socialism in their struggle against Versailles and the Young Plan? Can we as internationalists draw up a programme of social and national liberation like that drawn up by the Communists?[46]

Thälmann denied any basic connection: 'National Socialism is rubbish with gravy on it',[47] but, revealingly, he was best able to dissociate his own party's stance from that of the Nazis on the basis of chronology. The Comintern had launched the struggle against Versailles in 1919 when 'there was still no National Socialist Party in Germany, thus an accusation that we somehow come together with the Nazis merely represents an insult to our party that does not accord with the facts'.[48] In a more considered response to such accusations the KPD alluded to its emphasis on the role of class struggle in the process of national liberation – something far removed from the Nazis' notion of racial struggle – but the party nonetheless confessed that it was walking an ideological tightrope. On the one hand Rosa Luxemburg was condemned for underestimating, even neglecting, the national question, while on the other Brandler was accused of having treated the national issue as self-evident rather than in conjunction with social liberation. This had led to the KPD going 'a step along the way together' with the nationalists against Versailles which – and again the precariousness of Communist ideology is evident – was as ludicrous as going 'a step along the way together with the Social Democrats against fascism!' at that time.[49] Since the Social Democrats were authentic fascists and represented the main thrust by fascism in Germany, it was logical enough to seek reasons for Nazism's success within the politics of Social Democracy. On the one hand the two movements were regarded as essentially similar with Socialism 'only distinguishable from the Hitler Guards through words, not deeds',[50] and with the Nazis 'like the Social Democrats using a social and sometimes an anti-capitalist demagogy to hold back the masses from struggle and from the formation of a united front'.[51] On occasion the Nazis were regarded as a deviation from fascism itself, albeit dependent on it: 'The methods of the SPD represent pure fascism. The Nazis too cannot govern without the help of the SPD.'[52]

However, even the KPD found it hard to sustain this simple equation with any real consistency, not least because the NSDAP's radical and anti-Weimar rhetoric lambasted the SPD in particular.[53] From time to time, therefore, Social Democracy was regarded as Nazism's pathfinder rather than as its Siamese twin. This particular interpretation focused on the shortcomings of, and alleged betrayals by, Social Democracy which had driven many disillusioned workers to a Nazism which served as a staging post between reformism and revolution. Thus the Central Committee argued that the 1929 Mecklenburg elections 'showed that the National Socialists used the SPD's social fascist policies in particular to attack it "from the left" '.[54] In 1932 the Pomeranian KPD noted that:

> Particularly in rural areas and in the small towns, workers form the most active elements of the NSDAP. . . . We must never forget that Hitler fascism is only possible because the SPD has smoothed its path; thus we must direct our main attack against the SPD so as to be better able to drive Hitler fascism from the field.[55]

Likewise in the factories there was alleged to be a causal relationship between Social Democracy's betrayal of the working classes and the rise of Nazism, both because reformist trade unionism had led to 'Stahlhelmer and Nazis . . . sprouting like poisonous mushrooms in the factories'[56] and, in more sinister vein, because Nazi factory cells 'were to be established at the behest of the Social Fascist leaders'.[57]

An element of *Schadenfreude* had crept into the KPD's observations, which resembled those made *vis à vis* the *Völkische* in 1924,[58] but the Central Committee also feared that a successful Nazi offensive against the SPD could rub off on themselves. They did, after all, share a common ideological ancestry with the Social Democrats and even in 1929 the Nazis 'were trying to tar the KPD and SPD with the same brush; so wherever the KPD commits opportunist errors the National Socialists are very successful'.[59] The danger was again apparent during the Nazi/Nationalist campaign of early 1931 to achieve the dissolution of the SPD-dominated Prussian Landtag in the hope of winning the subsequent elections. The Central Committee complained that the right 'had gained mass support with the deceitful slogan "Down with Marxism", by which they meant the SPD and the Prussian government'.[60] In other words the Nazis were equating Marxism with the bureaucratic misery of the early 1930s and the KPD consequently had to discredit the SPD's Marxist credentials to escape a share of the opprobrium: 'The only Marxist party, the KPD, has no intention of taking any share of responsibility for the Social Democrats' bankrupt policy of coalition, for the SPD's betrayal of Marxism.'[61]

The KPD regarded Nazism's ideological offensive against Social Democracy 'from the left' with particular concern because it appeared to be relatively successful. The *Sturmabteilung* (SA) and *Schutzstaffel* (SS) contained 'a high percentage of industrial workers and especially unemployed proletarians'[62] and although unemployment itself had driven many workers to the SA the 'decisive factor is the SPD's betrayal of socialism and the lying, pseudo-socialist demagogy of the Hitler Party'.[63] The same was said for workers in the Nazi Party itself: 'Sections of the Social Democratic working class have switched to the Nazi camp through their disillusionment with the treacherous role played by Social Democracy'.[64] while in some factories workers had joined the Nazis 'because of dissatisfaction with the SPD'.[65] In electoral terms too, 'the SPD's policy of toleration has distinguished itself through a heightened flow of electoral support to the National Socialists'.[66] Thus the KPD was particularly worried because, it believed, some of its most promising potential recruits, disillusioned Social Democrats, were turning to the Nazis. Equally worrying, however, was the continued designation of the bureaucratised and allegedly ineffectual SPD as Marxist by the Nazis since the KPD, as before, risked being discredited thereby. As *Die Rote Fahne* wrote in April 1932:

> Who are the new Nazi recruits? In part they are elements who were ready to participate in the Revolution of 9 November 1918 and then saw themselves sold down the river by the SPD leaders. A whole generation of adolescents were told: 'This is how the Marxists are ruining us!' and many of these young people confused the 'Marxism' of the SPD leaders with uncorrupted Marxism. Through their method of government the SPD leaders succeeded in discrediting Marxism among broad sections of the population.[67]

This view of working-class Nazis conflicts irreconcilably with the recent characterisation of the same as 'Tories' who had 'some lingering affection for the monarchy, for the German nation, and for the lost Reich' and had 'a considerable respect for authority'.[68] No doubt the

KPD were tempted to equate Nazi success with Socialist failure out of self-interest, but the empirical evidence the Communists produced to support their contentions and, for that matter, the very 'un-Tory' behaviour of the working-class stormtroopers,[69] contrasts with claims for the Tory argument which rest on sociological studies of working-class behaviour in other countries, or in Germany after the Second World War, rather than on empirical evidence from Weimar Germany itself.[70]

The implications of the KPD's line of reasoning are profound indeed. Many political scientists and historians have, understandably enough, perceived political struggle during the early 1930s as a conflict between a divided, quarrelling left on the one hand and an increasingly united right on the other. However the KPD saw the world rather differently. 'Left' and 'right' were only significant within the KPD's and Comintern's ideological framework when used to contrast the revolutionary KPD with a range of 'fascist' opponents who included the SPD as much as the German Army's High Command. Furthermore, although the NSDAP was regarded as an important fascist opponent, it was not necessarily considered to be more conservative or 'right-wing' than the SPD and the trade unions; indeed in some respects the reverse evidently applied.

Passing, at this stage very briefly, to the world of workaday politics, one finds widespread evidence of sporadic cooperation between Communists and Social Democrats at local level. In part this reflected defiance by local KPD organisations or groups of their party's ideology, but more often this cooperation was intended to undermine the Socialist movement by way of the United Front From Below. This fraternisataion, therefore, formed no part of any love match, but instead represented an underhand method of waging war against 'Social Fascism'.[71] Sporadic cooperation with Nazis was rather more common than hitherto recognised and will be discussed in detail in due course. Within the framework of Third Period Communist ideology it can be understood in similar terms to Communist–Socialist cooperation. It was not anomalous, or necessarily perfidious, but formed a part of the KPD's campaign to mobilise mass working-class support from within a vast and heterogeneous 'fascist' camp for the revolutionary movement.

Ultra leftism was not the only force at work, however, for a style of Communist nationalism which derived from the experiences of 1923 and before also influenced the shaping of KPD–Nazi relations during the early 1930s. The KPD had been forced to acknowledge the strength of nationalist feeling within the German working class during the early 1920s and the same problems confronted the Communist movement a decade later. Local KPD organisations experienced the impact of working-class nationalism during the NSDAP's and DNVP's anti-Young Plan campaign to which, they felt, their own party had no effective answer:

> *All* comrades in *all* district groups, as much in Pomerania or the Erzgebirge as in Hessen, have complained that the party has let them down over the Young Plan and the German Nationalist and Nazi referendum campaign. Only some of our squandered support could be reclaimed at election meetings and the strengthening of the Nazis can be attributed to this.[72]

Even the Comintern was quick to recognise that this nationalist feeling could not be ignored and the KPD's 'Programme of National and Social Emancipation of the German People', although partly aimed at dissident left-wing Nazis,[73] was intended to resolve this wider problem. As Piatnitsky explained at the Twelfth ECCI Plenum: 'Since the Nazis opposed the Young Plan, and the KPD opposed the Nazis, the idea might spread among the workers that the KPD supported the Plan; therefore the KPD "with the assistance of the ECCI proclaimed its programme of national and social emancipation"'.[74] Similar motives underlay the launching of the 'Scheringer Strategy' in March 1931. Convinced of the 'working class's nationalist sentiment', the former Reichswehr lieutenant and Nazi, Richard Scheringer, sought to use the national question as a basis for mass action by the KPD against the Nazis and in particular the SA.[75]

As in 1923 the national question was also seen as a promising vehicle through which to attract radicalised middle-class support for the KPD and thereby divert from the NSDAP a crucial part of its constituency. To this end Scheringer and other leading Communists developed the concept of the 'People Revolution' as an element in the new national revolutionary programme. This created disquiet among some traditionally-minded KPD members who had no time for anything that diluted the party's commitment to class struggle and perhaps because of this the 'People's Revolution', or *Volksrevolution*, was declared to be synonymous with the 'Proletarian Revolution'.[76] In fact the 'People's Revolution' was designed to 'immunise' the middle classes against National Socialism and win them over to the KPD.[77] It was 'the rebellion of all socially oppressed sections of the German people against the capitalist system'[78] and from July 1931 the KPD produced a journal, *Aufbruch*, aimed specifically at the nationalist middle classes which was later edited by the former *Freikorps* leader Beppo Römer.[79] Individual members of the radical nationalist *Verbände* did find their way to the Communist Party as a result of this campaign,[80] but party membership figures testify to the absence of any wider success and by 1932 it was, in any case, being dampened down.[81] The appeal to working-class nationalist sentiment, however, was pursued with greater consistency and vigour since it sought both to defend the KPD and its potential constituency from further Nazi encroachments and to reclaim Nazism's significant working-class constituency for revolutionary Communism. Alluding to the defensive side of the strategy, Thälmann commented in June 1932 that: 'because of the great upsurge in chauvinism it will be impossible to drive back Hitler fascism unless we expose it on the national question and proclaim our revolutionary road in the liberation struggle against Versailles to the masses'.[82] By October 1932, with the Nazi movement in growing difficulties and with Nazi desertions to the KPD mounting,[83] the offensive dimension became more apparent, as an article in the Ruhr KPD's newspaper, *Pionier des Bolschewismus*, illustrates:

Very many Nazi voters expected national liberation through their party, which it can never deliver. We must stress the national question more strongly than before in our agitation and propaganda and show that the KPD is the only party waging the struggle for Germany's national liberation from the tribute burdens of the Young Plan. The radicalisation particularly of proletarian elements in the Nazi Party is manifesting itself clearly through the switching of individuals and even whole groups of SA members to the *Kampfbund gegen den Faschismus* or to the KPD.[84]

This form of ideological struggle became closely linked with the use of the United Front From Below tactic which became a decisive element in Communist–Nazi relations during 1932. More than at any other time, the KPD appeared successfully to be fracturing the barriers between itself and working-class Nazis[85] with results, however, that were to be disastrous in the unforeseen circumstances of early 1933.

In addition to the ideological demands of the Social Fascism theory and of nationalism, the very success Nazis enjoyed towards the end of Weimar demanded an ideological response of a more ad hoc kind. At times the National Socialist advance seemed to hold no terrors, as in

September 1930 when *Inprekorr* argued that the very success of Nazism in gaining working-class support 'carries within itself the seeds of the coming disintegration of the fascist party'.[86] Similarly in October 1931 Remmele declared in the Reichstag that the Communist Party did not fear a fascist military takeover since this would merely bring the contradictions of capitalism into the open and hasten the collapse of the system.[87] However, during mid 1932, as the Central Committee moved hesitantly to mend its fences with the SPD (a tactic condemned by Comintern and soon abandoned),[88] it perceived Nazism in terms with which even Leon Trotsky might have sympathised: 'We must also refute the error, which has found expression among some impatient workers, that the seizure of power by Hitler – that champion of open fascist dictatorship – could hasten the revolution, improve the prospects for our victory and reduce the suffering of the proletariat.'[89] Perhaps, the KPD mused, there were important differences between Social Democracy and Nazism after all. *Der Revolutionär* argued in May 1932 that the class bases of Socialism and Nazism differed and thus 'it is clear that in recognition of this difference we must put an end to the very frequent and very damaging lumping together [of the two movements] in our tactical and agitational work'.[90] *Die Rote Fahne* went further still in June, perceiving the gains made by the SPD during the 1918 Revolution and its aftermath in a particularly positive light.[91] However, even during this brief period the SPD was still usually regarded as fascist, even if the threat it posed might, after all, have been less deadly than Hitler's[92] and, as noted, this more reflective attitude to Social Democracy was quickly abandoned.

Furthermore, reflecting on the likely consequences of a Nazi takeover could not reverse the Nazis' increasing mobilisation of working-class support. By mid 1930 the KPD recognised that National Socialism was becoming a mass movement with a concomitant working-class electoral following and even the first signs of a presence in some factories. Most Nazis may have been middle class but, the Berlin KPD concluded: 'We must by no means ignore the fact that a section of the working class is taken in by the Nazis' radical vocabulary.'[93] This perception of working-class Nazis as the victims of demagogic deceit left open the possibility of ideological countermeasures through mass meetings, individual contacts and even direct mailing of known Nazi supporters.[94] The September 1930 elections confirmed the KPD in its view of Nazism's constituency as a 'crazy heap of malcontents'[95] and this simply reinforced the belief that an ideological struggle was the most appropriate response to the problem. The Reich Interior Ministry commented on this mood in November 1930, noting that the emphasis of the KPD's anti-fascist campaign '*today* no longer lies in the physical struggle against the fascists, but in political mass agitation to detach the working-class elements from the fascist and social fascist organisations'.[96]

During 1931 the KPD continued to argue, in private at least, that the socially diverse Nazi movement could only effectively be tackled through an ideological offensive. In March a KPD Instruction Letter argued:

> As long as the national fascist movement was not a mass movement and had not won proletarian elements in large numbers, it was correct [to beat down the fascists wherever you meet them], and a broad ideological and political struggle was unnecessary. However, things are different now. The Nazis have set out particularly to win over the working-class masses and do have very many workers indeed as members (especially in the SA) and considerable proletarian support (for instance in Saxony). Today a struggle with fists alone would be just as pointless and wrong as it would be, for instance, against the SPD and the other bourgeois parties.[97]

The Nazis for their part were not backward in using offensive physical terror against their Communist rivals and some local KPD groups responded in kind, but the leadership of the KPD was convinced that it had to complement a defensive physical struggle with:

> the improvement and greatest possible intensification of the ideological mass struggle against this rapidly growing popular movement. Any weakening in the face of Nazi terror, those murderers of workers, would be fatal, but the neglect of ideological mass work among Nazi supporters is already costing us dearly. To tolerate further neglect of this mass work would result in our political work losing considerable impetus, particularly in the factory council elections and the Prussian state elections.[98]

This line of argument, unequivocal in its perception of the KPD and NSDAP as competitors for support, prevailed during the decisive political struggles of 1932 and early 1933. Nazism was still perceived as a weapon with which the bourgeoisie waged open terror against the proletariat[99] and the role of the largely working-class SA in this

campaign could hardly be ignored.[100] However, a distinction
continued to be made between the role of organised Nazism and the
interests and aspirations of individual Nazis, particularly those from
the working class. As *Pravda* wrote in August 1932:

> National Socialist demagogy against Versailles and the Weimar
> Republic has also ensnared some retrograde elements of the
> working class, particularly unemployed workers. One of the most
> important tasks before the German Communists is the re-acquisi-
> tion of these sections of the working class who have been betrayed
> by the bourgeoisie.[101]

Die Internationale, reporting on the Twelfth ECCI and KPD Plenum,
wrote in September that the 1.5 million additional working-class votes
gained by the Nazis in the July 1932 Reichstag elections simultaneously
presented the KPD with challenges and opportunities:

> A large proportion of working people in the NSDAP want to fight
> honestly against capitalism and for socialism. We must win these
> working people for Communism. The whole party membership
> must recognise that because of the NSDAP's mass support the
> victory of the proletarian revolution in Germany is impossible
> without breaking into the ranks of the NSDAP.[102]

With the Nazi movement facing obvious difficulties at the end of 1932
the KPD's Central Committee stressed all the harder the importance
of pursuing an ideological campaign against National Socialism.[103]
   The KPD's leaders were able to identify specific incidents which lent
credibility to their strategy, such as an occasion in the Silesian resort
town of Schreiberhau where the police tried to enlist SA support to
break up a Communist demonstration in July 1932: 'A section of the
SA proletarians joined the demonstration in full uniform and said to
their leaders who sought to restrain them, "Our place is here, where
they're fighting for work and bread!" '[104] However, the constant
allusions to the need for an ideological (rather than a purely physical)
anti-Nazi campaign betrayed a frustration over rank-and-file reluctance to play this game in some areas. In August the Ruhr KPD's
newspaper, *Der Pionier des Bolschewismus*, reasserted that it was
impossible to combat a mass movement with 13 million supporters
with physical force alone and continued that the time was ripe for
subverting the SA and winning over hundreds of thousands of Nazis.

However, the paper observed: 'In this regard we shall find serious inhibitions within the party with a mood of: "Do you seriously mean that we should talk with scum like that?" ' It went on to urge its readers to cast doubts aside and pay attention to factory politics in particular.[105] In the event, the rank-and-file response to such demands was equivocal during the early 1930s, varying from time to time and place to place. This, along with the Nazi response to such overtures, is discussed in subsequent chapters, but it is clear that grassroots contacts between radical left and right during the early 1930s were far from freakish or insignificant. Comintern's ultra-left strategy, Communist responses to the challenges of German nationalism, and the ideological questions thrown up by the very success of National Socialism among social groups that the KPD considered as their own provided an extensive and relatively systematic ideological framework within which confrontation and collaboration between the Communist and Nazi movements could occur. As far as the Central Committee was concerned, rank-and-file contacts between Communists and Nazis were normal in ideological terms, the refusal to fraternise was deviant.

7 The Sociology of Communist–Nazi Relations

The National Socialists claimed to have transcended the divides of class, region and confession which had restricted the appeal of their main rivals, and to have gained support throughout society for their vision of a popular ethnic community (*Volksgemeinschaft*). When looking beyond the great divide of 1933 at the Nazis' record in government, however, serious reservations have been expressed by historians over the regime's integrative capacities, even if they have not necessarily been dismissed out of hand,[1] but a comparable consensus on the social basis of Nazism during the Weimar era is lacking.

On the one hand it has been argued that Nazism represented a broad coalition of lower-middle-class interests and that other social groups, notably the working class, were largely unattracted by Hitler's programme.[2] The electoral sociology of the early 1930s has been utilised to buttress this argument, for the NSDAP evidently gained many votes at the expense of the conservative and liberal parties, whose support declined in 1930 and collapsed in 1932, while the KPD's vote rose as the SPD's fell.[3] Attempts to examine systematically the relationship between Nazism and the working class, or Nazism and the left, have therefore been criticised for tackling issues which, psephological data suggested, did not exist. As one reviewer wrote of Kele's *Nazis and Workers*:[4] 'He goes one better than those who wish to have their cake and eat it – he tries to eat a cake he has not even got.'[5]

Recently, however, a number of detailed computer-based studies have created a more heterodox range of views on the psephology of National Socialism.[6] It now appears that Nazism appealed electorally to numerically significant sections of the working class[7] and this has invited a reappraisal of Nazi electoral strategy. 'Nothing', Childers observes, 'could be farther from the reality of National Socialist electoral strategy than Bracher's assertion that "in the final phase of the republic, National Socialist propaganda was directed almost exclusively towards the middle classes".'[8] Childers reaffirms the importance of the middle-class electorate for Nazism, but accepts,

118

with reservations, the Nazis' claims to have transcended the class divide in the electoral realm at least: 'The NSDAP by 1932 had become a unique phenomenon in German electoral politics, a catchall party of protest . . .'.[9] Hamilton's study of urban voting patterns employs a different methodology from Childers', but comes to similar conclusions. He stresses that the urban, protestant upper middle class voted for the Nazis in disproportionate numbers during the early 1930s, but also remarks that in absolute terms around half the urban Nazi vote came from working-class districts, despite lower relative levels of support in such areas.[10] Falter too has emphasised the sociological heterogeneity of the National Socialist electorate in a range of studies, concluding that 'the propensity of all voters to turn out in favour of the Nazi Party increased',[11] and has calculated that around 40 per cent of the Nazi electorate was working class from 1930 onwards.[12]

Although the psephological roadblock to a study of Nazi–Communist relations might thereby seem eliminated, objections have persisted, albeit on a more subtle terrain. It is sometimes argued that different types of worker voted Nazi and Communist which would have reduced the prospects of the radical extremes competing for similar pools of support.[13] It does appear that the Nazis' electoral performance in many urban, working-class communities was weaker than in specifically protestant, rural localities which were usually strongly middle class, but even so the NSDAP increased its vote in industrial, working-class settings from around one or two per cent in 1928 to near 30 per cent by July 1932 and in some cases to almost 40 per cent.[14] A sizeable number of former SPD and KPD voters switched to the NSDAP at each election during the early 1930s[15] and many Nazi and Communist supporters lived in close physical proximity in the cities of Germany, with all the implications that this entailed for political campaigning by the radical parties.[16] It has been argued that Nazi support in working-class districts derived in some measure from the lower-middle-class minority therein,[17] but a range of ecologically-based psephological studies suggest that no working-class groups were completely immune from the Nazi contagion. The NSDAP performed well within the protestant working class as a whole between 1928 and 1932[18] with a particularly strong showing within the handicrafts and small-scale manufacturing working class, according to Childers.[19] This key group, which employed up to 33 per cent of German workers[20] became, he concludes, 'one of the most powerful predictors of the National Socialist vote'[21] and yet it was precisely here, as his results indicate, that the SPD also showed well consistently and where the

KPD's performance improved in late 1932 as the Nazis' sagged.[22] In industry too the NSDAP performed respectably among protestant workers[23] and even among the metalworkers and miners where Childers indicates a below-par Nazi performance, there were signs of a dramatic improvement by late 1932.[24] The Nazi performance among Catholic workers was, like the party's performance among Catholics as a whole, altogether less impressive (while the KPD did do well among Catholic miners and metalworkers),[25] but all in all it seems clear that although no two major parties in Weimar Germany had identical patterns of electoral support, there were significant areas of overlap between the Communist and Nazi constituencies.[26]

Perhaps some of the confusion on this score has derived from a temptation to confuse the relative picture gained from regression coefficients with actual levels of support gained by a party in a particular setting. In awareness of this danger Falter demonstrates that while unemployed blue-collar workers were less likely to vote Nazi than the electorate as a whole (and therefore produce a negative regression coefficient) the Nazis nonetheless obtained support from 13 per cent of those employed blue-collar workers who were registered to vote, as against the 29 per cent who voted Communist in July 1932.[27] If it is accepted that the propensity to vote at all among the unemployed was relatively low,[28] then it is conceivable that a good fifth or more of those who did vote supported the Nazis.[29] Even here, therefore, the overlap between Nazi and Communist constituencies was evident and on turning to workers in work one finds that their predisposition to vote Nazi was little different from that of the general population.[30] As Manstein remarks; 'The high level of support for the NSDAP from the workers, as party members and electoral supporters, is one of the most important results of recent, methodologically-sound research.'[31]

Manstein notes that the absence of opinion poll returns precludes any conclusions on the behaviour of individual voters,[32] but no one has thought to remark on the unavailability of any detailed and reliable evidence (such as is supplied by modern opinion polling) on voters' second preferences. The KPD believed as early as 1923 that some Social Democratic voters were displaying a second preference for the radical right which sometimes translated itself into an actual vote, or first preference.[33] Historians have sometimes argued that certain Nazi voters had the KPD as their second preference and vice versa, which left these voters hanging like a latter-day sword of Damocles over their current first preference party.[34] Certainly the KPD believed that some types of Nazis could be susceptible to their message[35] and this, as much as recorded voting trends, was to influence Communist strategy during the early 1930s.

However, the recorded trends were daunting enough, and with the proportion of industrial and manufacturing workers who voted Nazi increasing eightfold between 1928 and July 1932[36] it would have been brave (or foolish) of any working-class party to ignore them, and the KPD's performance was pedestrian by comparison. Except in some Catholic cities, its urban vote stagnated, or even fell, between September 1930 and July 1932 as the Nazi vote there doubled.[37] The KPD therefore had every justification for paying close attention to the Nazis' electoral performance and the evidence it accumulated reinforced yet further its fears of Nazism's potential as a mass movement.

The first signs of an improvement in the Nazis' electoral fortunes came in in 1929 with some notable successes at local and state level.[38] Communist party officials noticed an increasing tendency for Nazis, workers among them, to attend Communist election meetings and to enter into debate with the KPD's speakers.[39] In the autumn of 1929 the Nazis chalked up gains in the Communal elections which, the KPD's Central Committee complained, had sometimes occurred through the mobilisation of potential Communist supporters.[40] *Die Rote Fahne* enlarged on these fears in October, noting that the biggest Nazi gains in the Baden state elections had occurred in the urban centres of Mannheim and Karlsruhe: 'That means', the paper wrote, 'that the social demagogy of the Hitler party has succeeded in influencing even some elements of the working-class electorate.'[41] In the left-wing stronghold of Saxony the KPD echoed these sentiments when it attributed a strong Nazi showing in the 1930 state elections to deficiencies in the Communists' own campaign.[42] Implicit in this self-criticism was the recognition that the KPD and NSDAP were, to some extent, competing for similar pools of support. The authorities were uncertain at this stage whether the KPD's fears were justified. The police in Baden observed that the Nazis only made sizeable gains from left-wing parties in the towns of Weinheim and Schwetzingen in the 1929 state elections. Elsewhere the Nazi vote came largely from former right-wing electors, but this would not preclude some of these converts being workers who, in an ideal world, the KPD would have wished to incorporate in its 'class front'. Certainly the Hessian Minister of the Interior believed that the NSDAP was attracting working-class support, some bought off with material inducements, but some constituting 'a voluntary and enthusiastic membership from proletarian circles', and the authorities in Berlin concluded similarly that: 'It would be a mistake to assume that the whole working-class movement has adopted a thoroughly negative attitude to the National Socialist movement.'[43]

The Reichstag election of September 1930 provided the revived NSDAP with an important national test of its electoral potential at a time of deepening economic gloom. Its spectacular breakthrough into important sections of the middle-class electorate was recognised by the KPD which felt it had been badly upstaged. The Communists admitted that they had not succeeded in attracting votes from those proletarianised sections of the middle class 'who were abandoning the bourgeois parties . . . to the Party, and in preventing their transfer to the Nazis'.[44] Matters did not stop there, for the KPD argued that the SPD's electoral decline had benefited the Nazis as much as, or even more than, themselves[45] and while not all SPD voters were workers, the Central Committee noted strong support for the Nazis in areas 'with a severely deprived working class (home, small-scale and medium-scale industry) which still maintain very strong, old Social Democratic traditions'.[46] The SPD also lost heavily to the NSDAP in East Prussia and the city of Breslau which further reinforced the KPD's conviction that the National Socialists were dangerous rivals for the votes of disillusioned Social Democrats.[47]

A study of results in individual electoral districts by the KPD revealed, predictably enough, that the greatest and most consistent Nazi electoral gains had occurred in protestant rural areas and that in many industrial districts where the Communists polled well the NSDAP had fared relatively poorly. However, this was not universally so, with the Central Committee identifying Magdeburg, Dresden, Chemnitz and Hamburg as industrial cities and Thuringia and North Westphalia as industrial regions where the KPD was relatively strong, but had still been outpolled by the Nazis.[48] The Central Committee's information derived from individual, detailed reports from each Communist Party District and many of these commented on the social basis of the Nazi vote. Four such districts detected no significant working-class support for the NSDAP, these being Württemberg, South Bavaria and the important industrial regions of the Ruhr and the Lower Rhine. In the three districts of Mecklenburg, Magdeburg-Anhalt and the Palatinate the Nazis were believed to have made limited inroads into the working-class vote and elsewhere the picture was bleaker. Upper Silesia and Pomerania had seen rural workers swing substantially to the Nazis, often under the influence of estate managers, and other districts reported a more general Nazi advance which affected the workers of town and country alike and often occurred at the expense of the SPD's vote. East Prussia, Hessen-Frankfurt, Lower Saxony, North Bavaria, Saxony, Thuringia and Halle-Merseburg were cited in this context, with the KPD in the last-named district noting a significant Nazi vote among the miners of the Geiseltal and Mansfeld and among the railwaymen in Falkenberg, Elsterwerde and Delitzsch.[49] Eight further districts – Baden, Berlin-Brandenburg, Franconia, Hessen-Waldeck, Middle Rhine, North-West, Silesia and the Wasserkante – made no comment on the social basis of the Nazi vote.

The NSDAP of September 1930 was clearly a world apart from the NSDAP of May 1928. The KPD's Central Committee predicted a particularly fierce struggle between itself and the Nazis for control of the proletarianised middle classes,[50] but the dimensions of the NSDAP's electoral triumph extended further than that. The Nazis had also won working-class votes and while their performance here fell well short of an unreserved triumph, there had been significant advances in important areas, sometimes at the cost of the SPD and in the extreme case of East Prussia even at the KPD's expense.[51] In private Thälmann eschewed the triumphalist tone of the party press, noting that the KPD had too few members as against voters and compared badly with the NSDAP in this respect. Communist functionaries were overstretched and the party had a lot of work to do among factory workers and even the unemployed.[52]

State election results subsequently reinforced the KPD's fears. In the case of Oldenburg a rise in the Communists' vote of 35.6 per cent was eclipsed by the Nazis' gains in spring 1931 and the details of this relative failure were particularly disturbing. Without enumerating the exact extent of the SPD's losses, the KPD complained that it had only picked up 5000 of these lost votes and pointed to its own failures in the state's industrial centres: 'The result was particularly unfavourable in the town of Delmenhorst where, in spite of the industrial population, we made next to no progress and equally in the second industrial town, Rüstringen, where our vote only rose by 20 per cent.'[53] The Presidential elections of March and April 1932 heightened the mood of uncertainty as a respectable first round vote of over 5 million for the KPD's candidate, Thälmann, fell to 3.7 million in the second round. The Central Committee had characterised the original 5 million voters as 'unconditional supporters of the proletarian revolution', only to find in April that the loyalty of many to the revolution was distinctly conditional. The Landtag elections of 24 April brought some recovery in the KPD's vote, but Communist commentators noted that the urban vote had been particularly soft in the Presidential elections and the subsequent recovery there only partial.[54] The Nazis, meanwhile, continued to record spectacular gains and Communist analysts were convinced that many of these new Nazi voters were potential, but squandered, Communist supporters. In Württemberg, the KPD believed, many unemployed workers in particular had voted for Hitler or the NSDAP[55] and a post-mortem of the spring elections by the Pomeranian KPD's leaders also acknowledged the Nazis' ability to gain working-class support, even in urban settings. As a delegate from Stralsund observed: 'It must be openly acknowledged that the NSDAP has succeeded in advancing further into the ranks of the working class; many proletarians are already roaming about with the swastika attached to their tattered overalls.'[56] The crisis was felt by the KPD in most parts of Germany with the police observing 'a near catastrophic uncertainty' within the KPD's leadership which had 'been particularly exacerbated by recent electoral setbacks'.[57]

The KPD launched its campaign for the July 1932 Reichstag elections in these menacing circumstances, but in the event was encouraged by the outcome and declared that : 'The party has emerged from the elections as the only winner, while in 1930 the first great National Socialist upsurge coincided with the KPD's electoral victory.'[58] At first sight this appears at best a curious assessment of the results, for the KPD's vote had edged up from 4.592 million to 5.283 million between 1930 and July 1932 while the Nazi vote had surged from 6.383 million to 13.769 million,[59] but this apparent euphoria was probably born of relief on two counts. The KPD's vote had recovered sufficiently from the disastrous Presidential election campaign and the disappointing Landtag elections to reach a new high and although the Communist Party was not interested in achieving a parliamentary majority to obtain power, it did regard electoral success as of plebiscitary and propagandistic value. In addition the overall level of support for the National Socialists appeared to have stagnated around that achieved during the Presidential and Landtag elections which suggested that the Nazi tide had peaked.

The pattern of Communist gains, however, ensured that competition with the NSDAP for similar pools of electoral support would, if anything, intensify. The KPD had experienced a striking upsurge in its rural vote which had been decisive in lifting its national tally in July 1932 above that of September 1930. It was not as if the Communists had suddenly grown stronger in the countryside than in the towns, but the party's rising rural vote did compare very favourably with its decidedly mixed fortunes in the cities. The KPD's district-by-district surveys testify almost universally to this trend which had first begun to show in 1930.[60] The Pomeranian KPD identified its strongest gains: 'in the rural areas and particularly in the decidedly agricultural county of Köslin while, for example, our vote rose by only 10 per cent in the city of Stettin and by 25 per cent in the industrial Randow District – as against 83.2 per cent in the County of Köslin'. The report concluded that this strong showing had been due to support both from rural workers and from 'petty bourgeois circles and the small fisher folk'.[61] Similarly the KPD's largest proportionate gains in Mecklenburg were on the land and even in absolute terms the rural vote had contributed substantially to the party's advance. Thus in Mecklenburg-Schwerin the KPD received an additional 8970 votes of which 4224 were from the countryside and small farmers as well as land workers had contributed to this trend.[62] It could be argued that Pomerania and Mecklenburg were largely rural in any case, but even in Upper Silesia with its significant heavy industrial electorate the rural vote had been decisive in lifting the KPD's tally from 111 167 in 1930 to 118 235 in July 1932. As the local KPD reported:

> The biggest gains by the party since the 1930 Reichstag elections both in absolute and relative terms occurred in the countryside. The rural contribution to the Communist vote has risen from 43.4 per cent in the 1930 Reichstag election to 45.5 per cent in the July 1932 election.[63]

In central Germany the picture was essentially similar. The Halle-Merseburg District had witnessed strong KPD gains in rural areas and setbacks in industrial districts during the Presidential and Landtag elections and having occurred, this shift was not reversed in the subsequent Reichstag election during which the party polled unevenly in both rural and urban areas.[64] Likewise in Thuringia the local KPD reported that: 'A general assessment of the election result . . . throws up the remarkable fact that the rise in our vote was 10 per cent in the urban districts as against 16.5 per cent on average in the rural districts.'[65] The KPD in Magdeburg-Anhalt observed similarly that: 'The party's electoral successes occurred in the open countryside and particularly in areas where "rural worker" or "unemployed" campaigns took place.'[66]

The Lower Rhine area formed one of the KPD's electoral bastions, not least because of its heavy industrial character. It included, for Communist administrative purposes, the west bank of the Rhine from Kleve (Cleves) on the Dutch border southwards to Rheydt and Grevenbroich, and then a bulge on the east bank running from south of (and thereby excluding) Duisburg eastwards to include Hagen and much of the County of Arnsberg, then southwards and westwards to embrace the County of Siegen, the cities of the Wupper Valley and the Rhine Valley as far south as Opladen. In the heart of this district stood the great metallurgical and commercial centre of Düsseldorf. However, the industrial cities produced relatively few additional Communist votes in July 1932 when compared with 1930. 'The strongest rise', wrote the local KPD, 'is identifiable in the open countryside – equally in places with a mixed population (industrial and farming populace) and in purely farming areas', and it continued by noting particular success in Catholic rural areas to the west of the Rhine and in the Upper Ruhr valley.[67] The details of the survey confirmed the overall trend. The average increase in the KPD's vote in the great cities was restricted to 1110, with the best returns in the textile towns of Gladbach-Rheydt and Krefeld and the worst in the metallurgical centres of Solingen, Remscheid and Hagen. Indeed in Hagen the KPD's overall vote fell slightly. The medium-sized towns witnessed an average increase of 505 in the Communist vote, while in purely rural parishes the average rise was 301. This final figure was achieved, as often as not, from a tiny base. Thus in Freienohl the Communist vote rose by 472 from 36 to 510 and in Breckerfeld by 650 from 319 to 969. By way of contrast the KPD's vote rose in Wuppertal by 230 from 57 805 to 58 035, in Solingen by 462 from 35 053 to 35 515, and in Hagen it fell by 85 from 21 903 to 21 818.[68] Thus, while the distribution of the Communist vote in the Lower Rhine confirms the party's appeal to sections of the urban industrial proletariat, it also confirms the impression given by many other district surveys that additional Communist voters were, rather surprisingly, often from a very different socio-economic environment. The same arguments applied to a degree in the Ruhr District where, the KPD concluded, the biggest electoral gains were either in SPD strongholds or 'in areas with a less heavy industrial and more agricultural character', rather than in the Communists' traditional strongholds.[69] The Middle Rhine, Hessen-Frankfurt, Baden-Pfalz and North Bavarian parties reported gains in industrial as well as rural areas,[70] but police reports detailing results in Bavaria and in Württemberg emphasise the rural dimension of the KPD's electoral advance in striking fashion.[71]

Scattered reports from other parts of Germany give a similar impression; of a high, but stagnant, Communist vote in many urban, working-class locations and of advances in rural (and also some urban middle-class) settings. Thus in village after village in the Saxon electoral districts of Chemnitz-Zwickau and Dresden-Bautzen the KPD piled up fresh votes while in the towns, such as Plauen, Chemnitz or Freiberg, the Communist vote either stagnated or even fell.[72] In Plauen, for example, the KPD's vote was 887 lower than in 1930[73] and in Chemnitz the Communists' below-par performance and a transfer of SPD votes to the Nazis made 'a serious critique of the party's organisation necessary'.[74] Likewise in Hamburg the KPD's share of the vote fell, particularly in working-class areas,[75] and in Berlin a tentative rise in the Communists' vote had occurred in a remarkable fashion: 'In Berlin the situation is such that in comparison to 1930 we have lost ground in the working-class districts and made considerable gains in those areas where the working-class element is not pre-dominant.'[76]

It must be stressed that this line of argument does not challenge the manifest reality of Communist electoral strength in many urban and industrial locations. It does, however, indicate that the Communist vote was, to a certain degree, sociologically diverse and that in July 1932 new KPD supporters often came from those social milieux associated with the NSDAP's electoral breakthrough or, for that matter, the Centre Party's core electoral support. In psephological terms, therefore, one is considering simultaneously significant Nazi inroads into the urban, working-class vote and some Communist penetration of the rural electorate.

The Communists interpreted events in a comparable manner and therefore concluded that since class or broader social identity had not been an exclusive predictor of Nazi electoral performance, their own political strategy must have affected the NSDAP's fortunes in a variety of settings. As the Ruhr KPD wrote:

> The Nazis suffered losses [as against the Landtag results] in cities where the Communist Party has enjoyed dominance over Social Fascism in the past. In all those industrial areas where the SPD was significantly stronger than our party the National Socialists have, with isolated exceptions, won.[77]

It could be argued that the KPD was underplaying the ethnic and religious factors at work in Rhine and Ruhr which undoubtedly influenced voting behaviour,[78] but the KPD's belief, founded partly on ideological conviction and partly on experience, that disappointed Social Democrats could turn to the Nazis in areas where the KPD lacked credibility is equally clear.[79] To that extent the radical parties were in direct competition and by extension of this logic could lose votes to each other. The Communists therefore sought specific reasons for exceptional National Socialist gains in urban industrial settings such as Zwickau, Merseburg, Chemnitz and Frankfurt-am-Main in the July elections,[80] and noted with concern instances such as Apolda where, it was believed, Communist supporters had switched to the Nazis.[81] On the other hand it appeared that some Nazi voters in Pomerania and the purely rural parts of the Middle Rhine district and North Bavaria had transferred to the KPD,[82] leading *Pravda* to conclude that the rural masses were, at last, turning from the NSDAP to the Communist Party which 'had strengthened significantly its influence in the villages'.[83]

The November Reichstag elections brought the Communists further gains and dealt the Nazis a sharp reversal in their fortunes, but the pattern of the KPD's advance was, again, surprising and even disconcerting. The rural electorate played a decisive part in raising the Communists' vote,[84] whether in the Lower Rhine district,[85] East Friesland,[86] the Bremen area,[87] or Mecklenburg-Strelitz where the urban vote rose by 5.4 per cent, but the rural vote by 20 per cent as against July, which was also a greater increase in absolute terms.[88] The KPD's performance in the Ruhr District was also disappointing, increasing by 7.1 per cent in the area as a whole (as compared with an increase of 13 per cent in the KPD's vote nationally) and by only 2.4 per cent in the Ruhr's industrial core. In some individual cities – Wanne-Eickel, Wattenscheid, Essen, Herne and Witten – the KPD's vote actually fell, leaving cities outside the Ruhr proper such as Bielefeld, Osnabrück, Münster and Herford to save the day.[89] The authorities noted a similar pattern of voting in Württemberg where the Communists chalked up strong gains in the countryside.[90]

At least the KPD found itself in the novel position of determining the pattern of Nazi losses and their significance for the KPD's own performance. Conclusions were mixed. The Lower Rhine party believed that most of the 89 500 voters who had deserted the NSDAP in the area had simply abstained,[91] but nonetheless, of the Nazis' erstwhile working-class supporters, a significant number had switched to the KPD in the urban settings of Hagen, Mönchen-Gladbach, Wuppertal, Neuss and Düsseldorf and in the rural areas around Olpe,

Brilon and in the County of Arnsberg.[92] In Bremen railway officials had been among those switching from the NSDAP to the KPD[93] and the local Social Democratic press noted that some Nazi voters from the hinterland of Bremen had also switched to the Communists.[94]

Although the preceding discussion does not seek to establish that patterns of electoral support for the NSDAP and KPD were identical, it does identify some important similarities which put into question the tendency of some writers to interpret the struggle between the two main radical parties as one between 'cowboys and Indians'; in electoral terms these areas of similarity and even overlap between them were growing in some cases as time went on. The NSDAP's electoral offensive on the working-class citadel (if there really was an all-embracing citadel in the first place) was not entirely repressed. The KPD's capacity for counter-attack was not entirely absent; its vote in the countryside was rising sufficiently rapidly by mid 1932 to attract official attention, and by November the KPD felt it was beginning to harry the Nazis in their own strongholds. The KPD may have been 'a class party through and through',[95] but even as such it had begun to broaden its electoral appeal and, in spite of itself, began to show signs of obtaining that which had come so spectacularly to the NSDAP: a mass following.

This may have pleased the KPD's leaders, but a Marxist–Leninist party such as theirs could hardly be satisfied with the garnering of a protest vote within a bourgeois electoral system.[96] There was a certain irony in the KPD's electoral advances as compared with the great difficulties experienced by the party in recruiting a stable, reliable membership and achieving a significant presence in (let alone dominance of) the great factories of capitalist Germany,[97] which makes comparison of the Communists' and Nazis' support in these critical contexts particularly important. Fortunately, less need be inferred when discussing membership patterns, for which records exist, than when considering the results of secret ballots, which allows in turn for a somewhat briefer discussion.

In 1927 and 1928, the last years for which detailed figures are available, some 80 per cent of KPD members were workers, this figure including: 40 per cent skilled industrial and 28 per cent unskilled industrial workers, ten per cent craftsmen and two per cent farm-workers. Of the remaining 20 per cent of members over half were housewives (most, presumably, working class) and the rest clerical staff, officials and members of other middle class groups. Almost all party members (95 per cent) had only received a basic, *Volksschule*, education and the great majority were aged betwen 25 and 50 with rather fewer youngsters and elderly members.[98] The more fragmented figures from the early 1930s suggest that in terms of occupation little had changed. Thus of recruits to the party in Saxony in early 1932 – 14 130 in all – 40 per cent were skilled workers, 35 per cent unskilled, and six per cent housewives, the rest deriving from a variety of middle-class and miscellaneous occupations[99] and of the delegates to a KJVD (Young Communists) conference in Nuremberg a year earlier 85 per cent had been workers.[100] After Hitler's takeover the persecuted rump of the KPD was, possibly, even more strongly working class.[101] What had changed by the early 1930s, however, was the proportion of members who were unemployed, for although many Communist party members were out of work even in 1927, by the early 1930s the jobless had come to dominate the party's social profile.[102]

The NSDAP's membership was only around 35 per cent working class during the early 1930s as against 65 per cent middle class[103] and this very different social profile might suggest that there could have been relatively little competition for membership between the Communists and National Socialists. Indeed, many historians have used these relative, percentage figures to adjudge the Nazis' attempt to gain a working-class membership a failure, but the use of absolute, rather than relative, figures alters the picture dramatically. The respective sizes of the two parties are important here. The KPD's membership rose from 120 000 in September 1930 to about 300 000 during 1932[104] of which around 80 per cent were workers (broadly defined);[105] that is about 100 000 in 1930 and 240 000 in 1932. Seen in this light the NSDAP's performance was more encouraging, for while most party members were middle class, the party became much larger than the KPD. It still had only 129 563 members, among them 33 944 workers, in September 1930, but by mid January 1933 (and thus before Hitler's takeover boosted membership) the at least 849 009 strong NSDAP included a minimum of 267 423 workers,[106] excluding housewives and old age pensioners from working-class backgrounds. The Nazis had, therefore, outpaced the KPD in terms of working-class recruitment during the early 1930s to the tune of 80 000 or more and, while these figures must be treated cautiously, it is conceivable that the NSDAP contained more workers than did the KPD by early 1933. Of the Nazis' new working-class recruits perhaps 60 000 were city dwellers,[107] and it is likely that of the KPD's net tally of 150 000 working-class new members a higher number were urban, but here the NSDAP's auxiliary organisations provided compensation. The KPD freely admitted that the SA, which grew much larger than its banned Communist counterpart, the Red Front, served as the major vehicle for Nazi urban working-class recruitment,[108] with many of its members not belonging simultaneously to the Nazi party and therefore appearing in the SA's membership profile as a complementary working-class element.[109] The relatively small Hitler Youth was, in all likelihood, very strongly working class[110] and the Nazis' expanding factory cell organisation, the NSBO, attracted during 1932 a large working class following as well as many salaried staff.[111] Thus the KPD and the Nazi movement recruited comparable numbers of workers (which means effectively that the Nazis had caught up with the Communists from an initially modest base) even if the Nazis' success in mobilising still greater numbers of the disaffected, protestant lower middle class has often allowed this significant achievement to be underplayed, ignored or even forgotten.[112] The KPD remained largely proletarian and gained limited support, while the NSDAP, although relatively less attractive to workers than to sections of the middle class, developed into a rapidly expanding mass movement which the Communist Party's leaders and veteran members came to fear.

Other KPD members, however, proved capable of switching to the Nazi movement and their behaviour was simply a particularly extreme manifestation of the devastating levels of membership turnover that plagued the Communist Party and made a mockery of attempts to forge it into a disciplined body of committed Marxist–Leninist revolutionaries. Almost half of all new recruits left the party again almost immediately[113] and the inevitable disruption this caused fed upon itself and triggered still more resignations. Veterans, understandably, were reluctant to trust new recruits with important tasks, leading to boredom or frustration among the latter,[114] and this steady stream of new recruits and of simultaneous desertions made the collection of dues (and hence proper identification and control of members) a nightmare.[115] By 1932 the crisis had engulfed the lower echelons of the Communist movement's leadership, with more than three-quarters of party functionaries able to boast no more than eighteen months' membership of the party in some areas.[116] Subsidiary organisations faced similar problems.[117] The youth groups (*Pioniere*) had no leadership at all in 30 per cent of cases, nine leaders in the space of a year in others and 'some in which the Pioneers simply do not know who the leader is because someone different turns up every time'.[118] Not for nothing did the Antifascist Action describe the KPD as a 'transit camp for thousands of workers'.[119] On the national scale the

KPD recruited 143 000 new members during 1930 while 95 000, no doubt often the same people, resigned or drifted away and there is scant evidence to suggest any improvement during the following two years.[120]

This chaotic situation reflected to a large degree the debilitating effects of mass unemployment on the KPD. The Communist movement's trenchant criticism of the capitalist order and particularly of Social Democracy's apparent accommodation with capitalism attracted many adherents from among the unemployed, but the party was, literally, destabilised organisationally as the jobless came to comprise 40 per cent of membership in mid 1930, 60 per cent by October, 80 per cent in 1931 and even 85 per cent in 1932.[121] The payment of monthly membership dues was beyond these impoverished members, their collection consequently impossible for the local party organisations, with a high turnover in party membership the inevitable result.[122]

This unemployment undoubtedly distinguished Communists from the SPD's core membership; indeed one writer has observed that 'lack of contact with SPD workers in the factories made it easy to regard them as enemies'[123] and, simultaneously, unemployment created a degree of sociological affinity between the KPD and the urban SA which was reinforced by a near-absence of female members in the KPD (none in the SA!) and the youthfulness of both organisations.[124] The violence between the two, far from amounting to a struggle between the disciplined revolutionary proletariat and some kind of bourgeois 'White Guard' had instead come to resemble a politicised brawl between elements of the unemployed working class. If the discussion is widened beyond the realm of paramilitary politics to include the electorate and the Nazi Party's membership then the unemployment question, it is true, becomes a less decisive aspect of Nazism's sociological profile,[125] but it was not negligible. Even in 1935 the NSDAP itself contained a higher proportion of unemployed than was to be found within the overall German population[126] and, as noted earlier, 13 per cent of the unemployed blue-collar electorate did vote Nazi in July 1932 as against 29 per cent for the KPD (abstention rates were doubtless high). These figures underline the futility of attempts to ascribe the bulk of the unemployed blue-collar vote to the KPD, or to deny any Nazi penetration thereof. Even in November 1932 only one in three unemployed workers cast a vote for the KPD, which must have made the one in eight still voting Nazi more than a minor irritant.[127]

These high levels of unemployment within the KPD had as their corollary a strikingly weak Communist presence within the factories of Germany, as opposed to the KPD's manifest strength, in terms of support at least, in certain poorer working-class neighbourhoods around them.[128] The Nazis' own weakness within the factories is well understood and will be discussed in due course,[129] but the Communists' shortcomings were sufficiently severe to compel a vigorous response to this modest, but growing, Nazi presence in the workplace. The turmoil and bloodletting of the years 1923 to 1926 had left the Communist movement vulnerable and exposed during the stabilisation era, for while the party contained 97 000 industrial workers in 1927[130] they represented a mere 0.59 per cent of workers in industry and crafts.[131] Even in the Ruhr District, where the KPD had attracted substantial support in the factory council elections of the early 1920s and would gain support in the early 1930s, its organisational capacity was suspect.[132] Fifty-four per cent of Ruhr Communists were factory workers in 1927, but they were only present, individually or collectively, in a fifth of the area's factories; largely in manufacturing rather than in heavy industry. Furthermore, the larger the factory the lower the proportion of Communists there tended to be, ranging from one in seventy in factories with between 500 and 1000 employees to one in 235 in factories with over 5000 employees.[133] Thus can be understood Arthur Rosenberg's complaint in 1927 that: 'We are extremely weak in the large factories and, therefore, in trade union activities. The largest part of our membership is unemployed or in small workshops; so we are on the periphery, not at the heart of the working class.'[134] Similarly Peterson notes that in November 1928 just 1200 of the 220 000 Ruhr metalworkers were in the KPD, of whom 987, in 33 factories, were members of the Free Trade Unions.[135]

Matters did not improve with the coming of the depression. In August 1930 only 0.73 per cent of factories with a workforce ranging from 11 to 5000 and above had Communist factory cells, which was about half the level achieved in 1925.[136] In March 1931 the KPD's Organisation Section complained that of 9000 factories employing more than 200 individuals only 1500 had an organised Communist presence and wrote of the 'colossal expenditure of political initiative and energy in future political and organisational work' that the situation demanded.[137] However, by the end of the year the rising proportion of unemployed within the party, high levels of membership turnover, and the non-collection or non-payment of dues testified to the failure of these attempts. The Prussian police estimated that the KPD's national membership of 250 000 included 72 500 factory workers,[138] but even this rather dismal 29 per cent of members might have been an overestimate. The Communist Party's Central Committee published figures in February 1932 which indicated that the number of due-paying factory workers in the KPD had declined from 47 046 in the first quarter of 1931 to 43 197 in the final quarter, or from 24.1 per cent to 16.8 per cent of total membership.[139] In individual regions the proportion of factory workers ranged from below 12 per cent to 38 per cent at best.[140] The *Kampfbund gegen den Faschismus*, which was intended to counter Nazi influence on the masses, was even less firmly rooted within the factories. In May 1931 it boasted 1289 District Groups, but only 68 Factory Groups and in December 1658 District and 109 Factory Groups.[141] Matters worsened further during 1932. Regional reports suggested a variation in the proportion of factory workers in the party from around 10 up to 20 per cent,[142] but the police had long observed a Communist predisposition to note new signings without recording the simultaneous flood of resignations from the party and its ancillary organisations.[143] By the fall of 1932 the Central Committee believed that just 10 per cent of KPD members were still active in the factories and concluded: 'It is out of the question for these 10 per cent to cope with our factory campaign'.[144] Even in the Ruhr the Central Committee noted 'serious organisational weaknesses' and, in addition to a huge turnover of members, a net loss thereof in certain cities.[145]

Therefore, despite the KPD's electoral strength in many industrial locations, it had failed to achieve a satisfactory balance between this passive, voting support and its organisational capacity.[146] The picture in individual factories emphasises this organisational weakness: a cell of 34 in the Phönix Works in Harburg which employed 2700 in April 1932,[147] or just 27 of the 1300 employees at Miag in Brunswick in October 1931 (although this figure had risen to 35 by February 1932).[148] In the Ruhr District the situation was even worse, with the metallurgical sector a case in point: 220 KPD members out of 22 000 workers at Krupp in Essen, 23 out of 11 000 at Thyssen in Hamborn, 60 out of 10 000 at the Bochumer Verein, 36 out of 7500 at the Dortmund-Hörder Hüttenunion and eight out of 5500 in the Hoesch-Werken in Dortmund.[149] These figures should be kept firmly in mind when noting the relative isolation of National Socialists in the factories. The proportion of factory workers in the KPD finally began to increase only after Hitler's takeover as the party's less committed, often unemployed, members either melted away or deserted to the Nazis[150] and even this, it must be stressed, was merely an increase in relative terms; the number of factory workers in the KPD fell at this time in absolute terms.

In November 1929 the KPD set up an oppositional trade union group, the Revolutionary Trade Union Opposition (RGO), in an attempt to undermine the ADGB and to attract factory workers to the KPD.[151] It failed on both counts, for although its membership did exceed 300 000 during 1932, it fell to 255 000 by January 1933.[152] Furthermore its membership was even more unstable than that of the KPD[153] and although a hostile reception from both employers and the ADGB must have affected its performance,[154] the fall in membership at the end of 1932 seems largely to have involved the unemployed.[155] Indeed, the presence of the unemployed within RGO was the great irony. The body was in part established to reduce the Communist movement's growing dependence on the unemployed, but its own rapid growth during 1931 was achieved precisely through recruitment of the jobless who came to comprise some 75 per cent of members.[156] There is some evidence to suggest that the proportion of unemployed fell during 1932, but only because of their own departure and not because of any increased recruitment of factory workers.[157] The RGO was strongest in Berlin and the Ruhr and attracted about half its membership from mining and metalworking alone,[158] but its weakness in many individual factories is unmistakeable from detailed local reports which indicate that only in exceptional cases did five per cent or more of a workforce belong to the RGO; in other cases no workers at all joined.[159]

The RGO fared less poorly in factory council elections, especially during 1931 when it performed respectably in selected industrial sectors and localities. Thus it gained 28 per cent of the mandates in the Ruhr mining industry, between 25 and 66 per cent of the vote in some of the larger chemical works and a fifth of the mandates in the Berlin metalworking industry.[160] When viewed across the board, however, the RGO's performance was much less impressive: 17 per cent of the mandates in coal-mining, five per cent in the metal industry, less than three per cent in manufacturing (although five per cent in the chemicals branch thereof). When this modest tally is contrasted with the Free Trade Unions' ability to win between 70 and 85 per cent of the mandates more or less across the board (although in mining the figure was 57 per cent), the RGO's efforts to mobilise even electoral support within the factories against the official unions must be adjudged a failure.[161] Over most of southern Germany the RGO had a lean time of it in 1931 and in Württemberg had to rely on workshops and medium-sized firms for its best results since the large factories remained an electoral wasteland.[162] In 1932 the deteriorating political situation led to the suspension of most factory council elections, but in those which were held the RGO experienced decidedly mixed fortunes. In the Ruhr it lost around half its 1931 support with its vote declining faster than the overall reduction in the workforce[163] and while the persecution of Communist activists by employers undoubtedly militated against the expansion, or even survival, of the small RGO cells,[164] it is less immediately clear that such persecution would affect the results of a secret ballot once candidates had presented themselves. Indeed in the Wurmrevier mines to the north of Aachen the RGO's vote held up well, or even rose, despite the organisation's vulnerable position.[165] Consideration of individual results in the postal industry underlines the patchiness of the RGO's electoral performance. In May 1930 it fared relatively well in the Reichspost's factory council elections in Berlin and Leipzig, but did not receive a single vote in fourteen cities, including Frankfurt-am-Main, Cologne and Hanover, nor in the entire states of Bavaria and Württemberg. In each of Konstanz, Magdeburg and Minden one single vote was cast for the RGO list.[166]

A discussion of the National Socialist Factory Cell Organisation's (NSBO) performance is better left to a later stage,[167] but it will demonstrate that increasingly significant support for this organisation means that even in the realm of factory politics the two main radical parties did not inhabit different planets. Thus, in sociological terms, numerous similarities existed between the Communist and Nazi movements alongside the widely recognised differences. The Social Democratic newspaper *Bremer Volkszeitung* alluded to these similarities and to certain ideological affinities when accusing the two movements of being two sides of the same coin:

> Through toying with illegality the KPD attracts all sorts of shady elements into its ranks who, at the first opportunity and in particular in return for better payment, go over at once to the Nazis, there to betray their knowledge of the Communist movement. . . . It is clear that a not inconsiderable proportion of former Red Front functionaries are active today as regimental and company leaders of the Nazi SA and SS. . . .
>
> On the other hand National Socialists transfer with the same ease to the Communists. . . . All these examples show how extraordinarily fluid the boundaries are between the parties of the two alleged

'extremes'. Nazis and Kozis share the same methods of political rowdyism, they share a common romantic-reactionary/revolutionary ideology, they have the same enemy – Social Democracy – and it is clear that many National Socialist members are strongly anti-capitalist. With so many points of contact it is understandable that members surge back and forth between the two parties.[168]

While this report was anything but detached or disinterested it is clear that transfers between the two radical extremes did occur, albeit on a more modest scale than that suggested by the *Bremer Volkszeitung*. There is wide agreement among historians that transfers between the SA and Red Front were common[169] and although precise figures are not available, and may never have been produced, evidence from official records and those of the SA and the Communist movement indicate that such transfers were part of the political life of late Weimar.[170] As one might expect, transfers between the Communist and Nazi *parties* were less common, but figures produced by the KPD nonetheless suggest that the proportion of erstwhile Nazis among their new recruits varied between 0.5 and 2.3 per cent, depending on the time and place, as compared with a slightly higher figure of 4 per cent from the SPD.[171] In the six months between July and December 1931 the Central Committee estimated that 450 former members of the NSDAP had joined the KPD.[172] The tenor of official reports and reports from within the Nazi movement indicate a higher rate of transfer in the other direction, thereby enhancing the overall impression of switching between the two sides.[173] The participation of Nazi party members in Communist-organised conferences, such as those of the RGO,[174] and the presence of Nazis on Anti-Fascist Action and United Front committees[175] doubtless reinforced the impression that relations between far left and far right could be relatively fluid, despite this occurring within strict numerical limits, and the sheer incongruity of the process when viewed from a conventional political perspective must have magnified its impact considerably.

This qualified element of sociological overlap between the National Socialist and Communist movements added a further and highly significant context within which relations, positive and negative, between these radical extremes would develop during the final years of Weimar. The final chapters of this study examine the specific nature of this relationship and its implications for the early months of 1933.

8 The Battle for the Unemployed and for Territory

From its beginnings the KPD had eschewed parliamentarianism and had sought to launch a revolution from within the factories. However, by the early 1930s the bankruptcy of this strategy was plain for all to see and the main focus of support for the Communists had shifted to the unemployed and to the neighbourhoods in which they lived. Here, away from parliament or the workplace, the Communist movement gained a significant following from more disadvantaged sections of the working class. These people were increasingly lost to, or inaccessible to, the Social Democratic or Centre Parties as the economic misery intensified, but by all accounts this did not make them into committed Marxist–Leninists. Many identified with the KPD either electorally or through transient membership of one Communist organisation or another but, as seen,[1] the KPD itself was very aware how ephemeral such recruits' commitment to the cause could be. In fairness to the unemployed themselves the KPD proved unable and for that matter unwilling to restructure its organisation to reflect the nature of its following.[2]

The KPD was also keenly aware that the Nazi movement was attracting some electoral support from the unemployed working class and, perhaps more crucially, was fashioning the urban SA from elements of the unemployed in particular. Although more unemployed workers probably supported the KPD than the NSDAP during the depression years, the fluidity of the political situation always threatened to reverse matters and, in any case, the SA's effectiveness suggested that the Nazis were utilising their unemployed supporters to better effect than did the Communists theirs. Competition between the two radical movements therefore became particularly intense in this context as both camps strove to organise as many of the unemployed as possible while simultaneously taking mighty side-swipes at each other in the process.

That said, the relationship between political radicalism and unemployment is not entirely straightforward. It has been argued with some justice that mass unemployment was in part indirectly rather than directly responsible for the upsurge in Nazism as members of the middle classes, terrified of the threat they believed the jobless posed to them, turned to the Nazis for protection.[3] Furthermore, looking at the jobless themselves, it has been observed that rather than fostering radicalism, mass unemployment induced political apathy and, on a personal level, resignation or cynicism. Many of the studies undertaken during the 1930s appear to support this contention,[4] with Eisenberg and Lazarsfeld's work remaining very influential. After an initial shock, they argue, the unemployed individual will undertake an active, optimistic search for work which, if unsuccessful, will be followed by anxiety, pessimism and distress. Then 'the individual becomes fatalistic and adapts himself to his new state with a narrower scope – he now has a broken attitude'.[5] The notable study of an Austrian industrial village, Marienthal, undertaken in 1931, seems to confirm these findings with high unemployment leading to declining levels of political and social activity and resignation prevailing within most unemployed households.[6]

Thus can be understood the observation that boredom and apathy, above all else, characterised unemployment,[7] but whether one can necessarily explain the KPD's failure to mould the unemployed working class into an effective, stable constituency in these terms is another matter.[8] Eisenberg and Lazarsfeld found that unemployment undermined people's emotional stability, resulting in mounting fear, a loss of sense of proportion and a collapse in self-esteem. This destabilisation of personality left some of the unemployed more suggestible politically than the employed, with a propensity to follow 'any political group or leader who appealed directly to their needs'.[9] This behaviour may not have stemmed from a feeling of heightened class consciousness, but it certainly revealed the presence of a less-clearly-defined criticism of the social order. A good quarter of the unemployed remained unbroken, being 'unresigned, aggressive individuals who are far from content with their present situation, who will not give up and sometimes go so far as to try to change the social order'. The unemployed young were most likely to go down this road,[10] in contrast to the middle aged and elderly who were fairly readily broken by unemployment. Thus the paramilitary formations of left and right in Weimar Germany for whom young, able-bodied men were indispensable, were provided with something of a ready-made constituency during the depression years[11] and this youthful, largely male membership became a vital element in the sociological affinity between the two radical extemes.[12]

The case of Austrian Marienthal was not considered as representative for Germany even by its authors[13] and studies by German contemporaries argued that unemployment had contributed decisively to Weimar's political radicalism. Neumann wrote of the KPD's attraction for 'youth and groups who have despaired in the present, but remain militant and expect everything from tomorrow',[14] an attraction which was reinforced by the Communists' fractious programme of agitation on the unemployment question.[15] The character of inter-war unemployment contributed to this distinctive political reaction. It was not just that unemployment levels rose, but that significant numbers of skilled workers and white-collar staff were affected who were not prepared to regard this as part of their lot. This was particularly so from 1929 onward as an upsurge in long-term employment undermined Weimar's social insurance system and threw many of the jobless back onto meagre local authority relief payments. In these circumstances millions of Germans suffered the dissipation of vocational skills, a loss of sense of position in society and a loss of self-esteem.[16] The unemployed came to inhabit a world apart and as one contemporary observer noted: 'The working class broke into two fundamentally different parts, those in work and the unemployed'.[17]

Unemployed youth in particular became outcasts as their life prospects faded, their apprenticeship training became useless or, if they were school-leavers, they confronted a world into which they had never been socialised through holding a job.[18] Then, as now, it has been argued, the seeds of radicalisation rather than apathy lay in this degrading process. As poverty at home drove unemployed youth onto the streets, devoid of either money or self-respect, they became ready recruits for street gangs which, in turn, were manipulated by extremist political parties – or they were recruited directly by the radical paramilitary formations:[19]

There the unemployed found what they needed. Uniforms gave them the feeling of superiority which compensated for their feeling of inferiority. They could march in file with the companions of their fate. They could fight against an enemy, they learned how to shoot and kill and they found an outlet for the painful tension of hate and resentment.[20]

This is not to say that unemployment had created either political radicalism or paramilitarism of course, but one can agree with Rosenhaft that both phenomena became more significant and adopted new forms in the specific socio-economic environment of the early 1930s.[21]

As a radical critic of the prevailing social order the KPD undoubtedly benefited, in terms of electoral support and a rising membership, from the severe strains imposed on German society by mass unemployment. The identification of the SPD with the political status quo and the Social Democrats' notorious reluctance to grant advancement within the party to younger members strengthened the appeal of the KPD to young, unemployed workers still further.[22] However, this same success was a mixed blessing for the Communist movement in a variety of ways. It is doubtful whether the radicalism of the unemployed could meaningfully be described as left-wing, for its basis lay, at best, in an ill-defined, quasi-socialist millenarianism and more often in a simple, despairing rejection of the existing society.[23] The KPD's recruitment methods among the unemployed reflected this. Rabble-rousing speeches at meetings provided the party with 'a certain following among those unemployed who wished, above all, to have their misery proclaimed far and wide', but such conversions were usually ephemeral and certainly did not 'provide the basis upon which a revolution can be achieved and a socialist community built'.[24]

The KPD, to be fair, appreciated that recruiting the unemployed posed dangers of many kinds. On the most mundane level jobless recruits were, as seen, reluctant to pay dues,[25] which often left them members in name only and made even the basic task of maintaining a coherent political organisation in being a nightmare for Communist functionaries.[26] With regard to political strategy, memories of the KPD's own disastrous utopian-anarchist phase during the German Revolution combined with Comintern directives to prevent any major concessions to the party's unemployed constituency.

Since the dispossessed alone would not make a Marxist–Leninist revolution, the unemployed movement was to be linked with the Communist factory movement which would topple capitalism through a general strike and a subsequent uprising. As *Pravda* put it: 'The workers' reserve army is the reserve army of the revolution'; it would be committed to battle at the decisive moment in the struggle between labour and capital and thereby obtain a revolutionary significance.[27] Thus, in a directive to a wide range of subordinate organisations, the KPD's Central Committee demanded closer links between the unemployed movement and the factory movement, warning:

The ongoing growth of unemployment and increasing deprivation among the unemployed . . . creates for us the danger that a section of the unemployed will fall prey to the psuedo-radical demagogy of the National Fascists or, out of revolutionary impatience, take premature, isolated, measures. . . . In recognition of these dangers, every unemployed comrade is obliged to contribute to the formation of Unemployed Committees at every Employment Office and to see that their delegates liaise closely with revolutionary shop stewards in the factories [and vice versa].[28]

Similar directives proliferated during the early 1930s, for the KPD's leaders were convinced that mobilising the unemployed had little value in itself.[29] However, the unemployed themselves were naturally insistent that something be done specifically for them, and since the Communist Party was unwilling, or unable, to transform itself accordingly,[30] it resorted instead to a range of expedients to try to square the circle.

On the most basic of levels the KPD sought to exploit the welfare issue as a means of mobilising the unemployed and tying them to the party. The Central Committee recognised that the sheer intensity and extent of material suffering provided the KPD with an excellent opportunity for mobilising mass support,[31] as often as not through applying pressure on local authorities to prevent cuts in benefits or to obtain supplies of food and fuel for the unemployed and destitute. This type of action succeeded more often than one might have supposed. The capably-led Offenbach KPD was able to negotiate with the authorities on behalf of the unemployed and became involved in community work,[32] while, from mid 1930, the Ruhr KPD concentrated increasingly on campaigning for improvements in the material conditions of the unemployed. Thus the KPD in Herne was able to resist cuts in benefits by combining debate inside the city parliament with demonstrations outside in May 1931,[33] while in May 1932 the KPD in Essen was able to obtain back pay for dismissed workers from labour schemes, reverse cuts in welfare benefits and achieve the distribution of grocery and meat tokens by the authorities to the needy.[34] Similarly the KPD obtained a partial reversal in benefits cuts in and around Chemnitz in the spring of 1932[35] and by the end of the year could list a range of individual successes of this kind.[36]

In broader political terms this tactic also paid off, not least as a means of mobilising mass support across party, and even class, lines in precisely the way the United Front From Below tactic demanded.[37] The standard approach involved the formation of United

Front Committees for the Unemployed to campaign locally on outstanding issues of the moment. In this way it was frequently possible to involve rank-and-file Nazis in Communist-led campaigns and thereby, as often as not, bring them into direct conflict with the local Nazi leadership.[38] Thus, when the authorities in Essen dismissed participants in public works schemes in May 1932, the KPD was able quickly to set up a Central Fighting Committee (ZKA) to extract material concessions for the workers concerned. Of the 88 committee members 62 were not politically active, but 16 were KPD members, set against five Nazis and five others – including members of the Centre Party and SPD. Thus far the KPD had achieved political dominance within a broad front and obtained modest participation by other parties, but matters quickly came to a head *vis à vis* the Nazis. The ZKA issued an initial proclamation which members of the individual parties were to present to their own party presses for publication. The Nazi leadership's response was predictable enough. Not only was publication refused, but a counter-leaflet denounced the ZKA as paid agitators and the Nazis, fearing they were losing the political initiative to the KPD, organised a counter meeting of the dismissed workers. Of the 7500 concerned, 400 attended, but the meeting ended in disaster. The ZKA had extracted concessions from the authorities and the Nazi workers put these material gains above their political allegiance.[39] They themselves therefore proposed a resolution supporting the ZKA's stance which was passed by 397 votes to three; a result the KPD could justly regard as a triumph for the United Front From Below tactic.[40] In Waltershausen, Thuringia, the KPD led a similar cross-party campaign against benefits cuts which eventually involved most of the community. Middle-class tradesmen were persuaded that cuts in benefits would simply reduce their custom. The mayor called in police units from Gotha, most of whom were allegedly NSDAP members, but when they opened fire on the crowds in Waltershausen their targets included the Nazis of the local community and even local middle-class town councillors suggested that the mayor himself should try facing a few police bullets.[41] Likewise in the Upper Silesian city of Hindenburg the KPD organised a mass welfare campaign in June 1932[42] and the success that this type of action could enjoy ensured that it remained a priority for the party until the final weeks of the Weimar Republic.[43]

The possibilities were obvious enough and contrasted starkly with the dwindling Communist presence in the factories and with the SA's growing superiority in the paramilitary field, but even among the unemployed success was qualified and limited. For one thing the KPD had a relatively small, unstable membership and even electoral support for it was modest. To put matters in perspective, the average level of support for the KPD nationally in the July 1932 Reichstag elections was lower than that for the NSDAP in its worst Berlin district, 'red' Wedding, and as a result of this weakness KPD campaigners often found that their efforts dissipated in political wastelands while in other cases even the activists were lacking.[44] Even where latent support did exist Communist officials admitted that they could not often deliver the results expected of them by the unemployed.[45] In part, as these functionaries sometimes recognised, this was because the KPD was a party of the unemployed, but not in the final analysis a movement for the unemployed and in addition the party confronted a range of practical obstacles about which it could do little. The ability of the Prussian and other state governments to impose cuts in welfare spending through local government commissars and the appalling financial difficulties that local government faced during the depression were bound to limit the KPD's success in extracting material concessions or resisting cuts. This was particularly debilitating politically, for the radicalised unemployed found their position too desperate to countenance gradualism or repeated setbacks. The momentum of the unemployed movement had to be maintained through repeated success, and the desire to maintain this momentum in the face both of Nazi competition and the threat of disillusionment could often lead the KPD down the blind alley of futile demonstrations, petitions and fights with rivals and the police.[46]

Attempts by the party to provide material assistance directly through soup kitchens and the like were hampered by the party's meagre resources and presented an unwelcome contrast with the achievements of the better-endowed Nazi movement.[47] The SA in particular was not simply a fighting organisation and propaganda vehicle, but also a form of surrogate welfare institution which distributed food and clothing collected from the Nazi movement's lower-middle and middle-class following, among its young, male, unemployed membership.[48] By 1932 in particular KPD leaders were aware that these welfare measures were contributing to Nazi recruitment in working-class circles, for instance in settings such as the settlements around the Wolfen film factory and in the Mansfeld countryside.[49] In more general terms too, the NSDAP's welfare drive was seen as having an effect. As the Red Front noted in January: 'Unemployed who join the SA receive clothing and sometimes accommodation and food',[50] while in May the RGO noted the transformation of SA hostels into soup kitchens for the unemployed and the provision of holidays for the latter's children.[51] By the summer of 1932 the International Workers' Aid (IAH) was contemplating a similar, KPD-led programme[52] and in isolated cases the KPD did set up soup kitchens in direct competition with those run by the Nazis, as in the Berlin district of Böhmisches Viertel in late 1932.[53] All in all, however, the KPD lacked any sufficiently well-endowed community or social group within its following from which to garner the necessary resources for a comprehensive welfare programme. It was left to watch as the Nazis made political capital from ameliorating a problem for which, the KPD believed, they were partly responsible in the first place: 'The Nazis organised emergency aid for malnourished communities in Thuringia after Nazi mayors and the Nazi delegates in the state parliament had cut benefits.'[54]

Thus, aside from welfare marches and demonstrations, the KPD's principal attraction for the young unemployed lay in its paramilitary formations which could compensate for the bitter experience of unemployment and which provided the party with a political tool for dominating the streets and tenement courtyards where the unemployed were forced to spend their days.[55] The keynote of life in any of the late Weimar paramilitary organisations was action. Where it was lacking the very cohesiveness of a particular outfit was put in question and the activism of the paramilitaries was, consequently, as much a matter of self-sustainment as of aggression against external bodies. The intermittent violence waged by the Communist-led paramilitaries against the authorities can be seen in this light. It was often easy enough to incite the unemployed to indulge in low-level rioting leading, inevitably, to fights with the police which Communist leaders perceived as a tool for disorientating and even paralysing the capitalist system's forces of law and order[56] while simultaneously training their members to overcome any inhibitions they might have had in confronting the police.[57] As a political tactic this offensive style of struggle was ultimately futile, but it did provide younger unemployed workers with a form of transient purpose which enhanced the KPD's credibility as long as the party could maintain its momentum. It also kept these same unemployed out of the clutches of Nazi organisations which were seeking recruits from the same social groups and which the Communist leaders saw as an ever-present threat in this regard. Thus the guidelines for the creation of the *Kampfbund gegen den Faschismus* (Fighting League against Fascism) in 1931 demanded 'struggle against Nazi propaganda and agitation at unemployment offices through the stringent organisation of the unemployed into units of the Fighting League against Fascism'[58] and similarly the RGO in Bremen saw the organising of the unemployed as essential in June 1932 if the KPD was not to be outpointed by the NSDAP and SPD in this regard.[59] Of course the NSDAP's followers among the unemployed were often anything but ideologically committed to their own movement, which allowed the KPD to adopt an aggressive as well as a defensive posture in the struggle with Nazism.[60] This could, as seen, entail the inclusion of Nazis in United Front actions designed to combat cuts in welfare relief [61] or, if possible, the involvement of rank-and-file Nazis in activities of which their own leaders disapproved, since the latter, in the KPD's view, 'had to stand openly on the side of the bourgeoisie and against the unemployed'.[62]

However, the KPD's effectiveness, even in this sphere, was limited. The banning of the paramilitary Red Front after the clashes between it and the Berlin police on May Day 1929 posed obvious problems which were compounded by the latitude sometimes afforded by the authorities to the SA. The character of the radicalism of the unemployed posed a further range of problems, for their ill-defined quasi-socialist millenarianism and, as often as not, their simple rejection of, and despair in, the existing society[63] could find the fascist message and the pull of the charismatic fascist *Führer* every bit as alluring as the convoluted theoretical basis of Stalinism.[64] The KPD itself might not have explained the many problems its unemployed campaign faced in these terms, but it was acutely aware of its own weaknesses and the potential and actual strengths of the Nazi movement.

Thus, while the KPD always understood the enormous political potential of the unemployment problem for its cause and could point to a range of local, individual successes, it was forced on balance to adjudge its unemployment campaign a relative failure. Regional party reports repeatedly complained during the depression years of their inability to exploit a potentially favourable situation and to transform a relatively high level of passive support into something more concrete.[65] Particularly ominous must have been the admission that even in Communist electoral strongholds such as the Ruhr and Upper Silesia the KPD was failing to organise the unemployed[66] and nationally the position was regarded as 'completely inadequate'.[67]

From the early days of 1930, therefore, until early 1933, the KPD observed Nazi advances into the ranks of the unemployed while acutely aware of its own inadequacies. In February 1930 the Baden

KPD acknowledged that the banning of the Red Front by the authorities had greatly assisted the Nazis' unemployed campaign[68] and during the following years internal Communist Party reports contrasted the KPD's organisational shortcomings with the increasingly effective Nazi performance.[69] In public the Communists had to be more optimistic, but it appears that many junior functionaries consequently fell victim to their own propaganda. In January 1932 the RGO's Central Council complained of the dangers inherent in this unjustified complacency:

> We believed we possessed a monopoly in organising the unemployed movement and therefore have not made any particular effort. Suddenly it appears that our monopoly had little substance. We must make every effort to retain our influence. The following example characterises our passiveness: in Frankfurt-am-Main a fascist joined the Unemployed Committee. While our comrades wasted time and didn't bother to get to work, this fascist signed up 1600 unemployed.[70]

The figure of 1600 might seem apocryphal, but a degree of substance doubtless underlay the complaint. Certainly, during 1932, the KPD saw fit to examine more closely the reasons for the Nazis' success in gaining support from the unemployed. The political and personal despair of the jobless was regarded as a crucial factor. Unemployed voters in Württemberg were quoted as saying: 'The SPD has betrayed us, you Communists are doing nothing, so we'll try voting for Hitler. Perhaps things will get worse; then we'll smash everything to pieces and Bolshevism can take over',[71] and the KPD itself regarded matters in comparable, if more dispassionate terms. The Nazis' welfare programme, while always considered important, was seen as secondary to the belief of stormtroopers and other Nazi activists that their campaign of terror would bring the Third Reich into being and provide them, 'without work or hope', with work and bread.[72] As the German Red Aid commented in the autumn of 1932:

> The fact that over a hundred thousand proletarian lads give themselves over to such activities, that their natural activity and activism are used against their own class, is a sign of the unspeakable deprivation into which the ruling class has pitched working youth.
> Among the SA proletarians in particular one finds young men

who have never worked in the production process . . . who became caught up in family conflicts at home, because the father was usually out of work himself . . .[73]

The KPD argued that there was a need to distinguish between the instigators and the executors of violence and to understand the process without excusing it.[74] In addition to this, the NSDAP had laid great emphasis on the issue of job creation and was committed to a major scheme of public and related works to soak up the unemployed. The KPD recognised that this constructive facet of Nazi politics had also done much to enhance its credibility among sections of the unemployed.[75]

This range of problems elicited a standard response from the Communist movement, the use of the United Front From Below tactic to win over misled class brothers from the National Socialists. This involved working together with Nazis on Communist-led cross-party (and non-party) Committees of the Unemployed and by the end of 1931 Nazi delegates were a common sight at district conferences. The majority of delegates belonged to no party and the Nazis were outnumbered decisively by Communists and comfortably by Social Democrats. Nonetheless, the presence of National Socialists in dozens or half-dozens at the mass delegate meetings was significant enough given the overall state of Nazi–Communist relations. Indeed, in strongly Catholic areas, such as the Lower Rhine district, Nazi delegates outnumbered those from the Centre Party.[76] With a National Socialist presence at delegate meetings normal, the question only remained of what level of seniority excluded Nazis from participation in the United Front. Despite the ongoing campaign of violence between the two radical movements, which kept the extent of fraternisation within limits, the use of the United Front tactic in this context served as a lightning rod by which people could contemplate changing sides in this violent political landscape.

The advent of mass unemployment was, therefore, crucial in initiating an open, territorial-style political struggle between radical left and right. Much has now been written on neighbourhood politics during the depression years, and the experiences of the working-class communities themselves, within which many Communist–Nazi street and meeting-hall battles occurred, are increasingly well understood.[77] Within the confines of this study, therefore, particular attention will be paid to three vehicles of the territorial conflict between the radical extremes; violence, meetings and marches, and, finally, the United

Front From Below tactic and variants thereof – rather than to neighbourhood politics *per se*.

It is a well-grounded commonplace of late Weimar history that relations between the Communists and Nazis were punctuated by violent confrontation. An incident in one of the Munich beer cellars, the Stadtkeller, in September 1929 can be taken as typical. On holding a meeting to found a local branch of the Anti-fascist Defence League, the KPD found that half of those attending were Nazis. As the police reported, trouble soon flared up:

> When the singing of a song with the words 'Hitler is our Leader' was followed by shouts of 'Heil Moscow', the two parties set upon each other with beer mugs, seats, plates, carpenters' nails, knives, steel rods, rubber coshes and the like. Police on hand cleared the room. Eight people were injured, two seriously. Two police officers also needed attention.[78]

Attacks on individual political enemies in the street, often after meetings, were also common[79] and even children were not necessarily immune from violent attention[80] Some impression of the overall scale of political violence can be obtained from Bavarian official figures for the year 1931.[81] There may have been certain inbuilt biases in the figures, but the massive implication of the Nazi movement in the violence (in 502 out of 509 incidents) revealed by Table 8.1 seems incontrovertible.[82] The NSDAP also suffered more than half the total reported casualties, as shown in Table 8.2[83] which probably reflected the Nazis' willingness to stage provocative street marches in politically hostile territory, often at considerable short-term cost. The Nazis' physical struggle was, almost unequivocally, offensive in nature. The relatively high Social Democratic involvement in Bavarian political violence (when compared with the KPD) likely stemmed from its strength and the KPD's weakness in Bavarian urban centres. In Prussia during 1928, by contrast, the NSDAP disrupted 60 meetings, the Social Democrats nine and the KPD between 103 and 234, and in Saxony the Communists disrupted at least forty-one meetings, the Nazis seven and the Social Democrats/Reichsbanner a mere four.[84] Allowing for some official bias towards the SPD, the latter was clearly outpointed by the Communists when it came to instigating violence in northern Germany, and taking Germany as a whole, it is telling that of 356 injuries inflicted on the SA between June and October 1932, 228 were attributed to the KPD.[85]

TABLE 8.1   *Pattern of political violence in Bavaria during 1931*

Perpetrator	Victim				Total perpetrated
	NSDAP	RB*	SPD	KPD	
NSDAP	8	110	57	38	213
RB*	115	–	–	1	116
SPD	50	–	–	–	50
KPD	111	1	2	3	117
Others	13	–	–	–	13
Total as victim	297	111	59	42	509

*RB: Reichsbanner.

TABLE 8.2   *Injuries received in Bavaria during 1931*

Victim	Frequencies
NSDAP	189
RB	63
SPD	21
KPD	27
Stahlhelm	4
Total	304

This familiar picture of continual petty violence between the left and the radical right has often been characterised as a form of class warfare.[86] The claim should not be dismissed out of hand, for it seems perfectly plausible that Social Democrats would have regarded Nazi violence as an assault on the organised working class and many rank-and-file Communists perceived their own violence as elemental and desirable which lent it an offensive dimension in certain localities at certain times.[87] The KPD's leaders, however, saw things differently. Their view of Social Democracy and the use of the United Front tactic to win over Nazis were bound to complicate the battle for territory.

In the earlier stages of Comintern's 'Third Period' and before the Nazis posed a major threat, the KPD painted an optimistic picture of their two-pronged strategy against fascism: ideological proselytisation working side by side with violent confrontation. Thus Werner Jurr, National Leader of the Red Youth Front, wrote in the autumn of 1928 in *Jugendinternationale* of the anti-fascist struggle in Germany:

The Red Youth Front is conducting a very energetic struggle against the [bourgeois] leagues. It is carrying out a comprehensive campaign of education so as to win over the misled youthful workers in these leagues to the Red Front, but it does not neglect the use of physical struggle. . . . Today the streets are dominated by the Red Front. Of course the streets had to be fought for initially. Red Youth Front groups patrolled the streets regularly during the evenings. Woe betide members of any fascist organisation who showed their faces.[88]

By 1932 this optimism had proved illusory. Nationally the KPD was forced to admit in September that: 'The political struggles this year have shown the KPD increasingly clearly that the weak leadership and reserves of the Red Front and the Fighting League against Fascism must be expanded and developed in the face of the superiority of rival organisations (SS, SA and Stahlhelm)'.[89] In certain cities matters had long been critical. Thus a report from Nazi-controlled Brunswick lamented in April 1932:

Even in Brunswick itself there are streets in which our comrades dare not be seen after dark. A Brunswick comrade reported to me that during the past few weeks he and his family could only leave the house after dark in disguise.[90]

This, of course, was an unpleasant premonition of what was to occur nationally in the spring of 1933 as the weak and ineffectual KPD faced up to a combination of Nazi-controlled state power and to the Nazi paramilitaries.

In essence the KPD demanded of its paramilitary forces a complex range of tasks which would, at best, be difficult to achieve and which, at worst, appear contradictory. From its formation in 1924 the Red Front was designed, in its own words: 'to organise and mobilise great masses against the republican indoctrination of workers by the Reichsbanner and against the fascist menace against which the Reichsbanner afforded no effective resistance'.[91] Thus, from the outset, it was very doubtful whether the KPD would be able to ally with the republican Reichsbanner to face the radical right in times of crisis, both because of its own antipathy to republicanism and because this same antipathy would always cause Social Democrats to doubt the Communists' bona fides.[92] When it came to facing the SA and other Nazi bodies matters were worse. Even in 1929 it was clear that the SA was not interested in gently persuading Communists of the error of their ways; aggressive violence and provocation was its hallmark. The KPD, therefore, was constrained to create a range of front organisations through which to conduct a physical defence against Nazi aggression[93] and the members of these defence leagues were later to take some persuading that the same Nazis were their misled class brothers. Although Communist leaders stressed from a very early stage that their own leagues were fundamentally different from those of the fascists,[94] they were forced to complain that their ordinary members often saw things differently and wished to respond to aggressive violence in kind. Thus the national leadership of the Fighting League against Fascism decried the tendency of their following to perceive the League as a sort of 'red SA': 'In spite of our unequivocal instructions, some local leaderships simply ignore the general line and play a *sectarian* [*sic*] role as a sort of red SA.'[95] In other words some sections of the League failed to function as a cross-party, class-based organisation and instead indulged in acts of individual terror against Nazis.[96] In December 1931 the Central Committee felt constrained to declare that 'attacks on individual National Socialists, on NSDAP meetings or bars, murders and shootouts . . . are incompatible with membership of the party'[97] and in the following month the KPD in Hamburg alluded to another Central Committee directive when trying to rein in anti-Nazi violence:

> We must oppose uncompromisingly the tendency to restrict the struggle against National Socialism to defence against fascist terror, for the ideological battle to win over the working supporters of the Nazis is, as before, one of our most important tasks without which we shall be unable to prevent the penetration of the factories by the Nazis.
>
> In line with the Central Committee's declaration of 13 November, we must wage a most intensive struggle against the unmarxist predilection for individual terror. Particular attention must be paid to all attempts to discredit this declaration as a 'concession' or 'surrender' to the class enemy.[98]

And yet the SA's terror campaign remained a fundamental problem. At times the Central Committee comforted itself by arguing that the Nazis' violence was a sign of desperation,[99] but both the national and regional leaderships recognised for the most part that the problem was not simply going to disappear on its own.[100] A campaign of physical defence continued to be promoted, even though the very same orders usually demanded 'an ideological struggle for the winning over of proletarian Nazi members for the red class front'[101] and declared that 'every National Socialist worker who recognises the treachery of his leaders' could join the Red Mass Self-Defence.[102] Yet again, therefore, many Nazis were seen as lost sheep rather than as rampaging wolves. As the KPD reminded its rural campaigners in August 1931: 'You will have difficulty winning over a young worker within a fascist organisation if you start off by saying that we are fighting to the death against fascism' and the party went on to suggest that such workers might well have joined the fascists to pursue their sporting interests rather than out of political conviction.[103] Similarly there was a general belief that many workers had been ensnared by a bourgeois militarist ideology propagated by the Reichsbanner, Stahlhelm, SA and SS[104] and 'a hundredfold greater effort to win back the proletarian elements there' was demanded from a relatively early stage.[105]

How successful, then, was the KPD's campaign of limited and purportedly defensive violence by the standards it set itself? The authorities for their part remained unimpressed by the Communists' didactic endeavours among pro-Nazi elements of the working class and were rather more concerned by apparent KPD preparations for an armed uprising against the state[106] (even if this remained a distant prospect both because of the KPD's own weakness[107] and Soviet disapproval for any premature, untimely military adventures in Germany[108]). The Communist Party's leaders also found that demanding a policy of defensive violence brought only limited rewards. It was occasionally possible to collaborate with Social Democrats against the Nazis;[109] the latter were sometimes shocked by individual acts of violence from their own side[110] and by December 1932 the Red Front claimed to detect signs that the proletarian elements of the SA were tiring of the constant fighting with the KPD and were sometimes even refusing to participate in such acts.[111] On balance, however, the SA's policy of combining terror and shows of strength against rivals with a rudimentary welfare programme proved both more single-minded and more logical. The SA also enjoyed advantages as party army of the NSDAP that its Communist rivals lacked. The authorities were not necessarily hostile and the NSDAP's electoral success made the utopian vision of the Third Reich with its work and bread for all more credible than the equally utopian Communist Germany for which there seemed only limited support.

The KPD's leaders therefore embraced two other methods of territorial struggle to try and overcome these problems. Mass marches were a way of demonstrating territorial strength or – more often in the Nazis' case – of striking a territorial claim in a working-class area. While Communist marches were often aggressive in both tone and outcome they also possessed, in a curious way, a defensive dimension as an assertion of communal solidarity, whether against the treacherous Social Democratic officialdom or against Nazi incursions into Communist-dominated territory.[112] To this extent marches stressed all that was different between Communists on the one hand and Socialists or more particularly Nazis on the other and although they were important, were not, therefore, an especially effective part of the United Front strategy. Here the public meeting was of greater importance.

The KPD's organisational weakness limited the number of formal meetings it could hold in most places. In provincial towns, such as Northeim in Lower Saxony, it was decisively outpointed by the Nazis and Social Democrats during the years 1930–32[113] and in more urban settings, such as Nuremberg or Fürth, the same usually applied. In the run-up to the July 1932 Reichstag elections the NSDAP held 245 meetings in and around Nuremberg, the Social Democrats 100, but the KPD only 68. In Fürth the figures were NSDAP 97, SPD 54 and KPD 10.[114] The KPD therefore visited other parties' meetings, often to obtain speaking time so as to put across its message without facing the organisational problems of setting up the meeting in the first place, although in areas where the KPD was strongest the temptation simply to wreck Nazi meetings was often irresistible.[115]

Of course it was no easy matter for Communist speakers to prevail at Nazi meetings. They were invariably allowed less, often far less, time to make their case than were the Nazi speakers, were never allowed the final word, and were often simply howled down as they tried to demolish their rivals' cases through considered argument or rhetorical appeal.[116] Nonetheless, the NSDAP was sometimes prepared to issue a formal invitation to the KPD to attend and speak at Nazi meetings, no doubt when it was especially confident of its speakers and audience. Thus the KPD in Demmin, Pomerania, appealed to the Central Committee to produce the Communist, ex-Freikorps leader, Beppo Römer, to speak against the Austrian Commnist-turned-Nazi Stephan Ehn at a meeting on 22 June 1932.[117] Sometimes the KPD could register an outright success and although the following reports have a self-congratulatory tone and were very probably often exaggerated, they nevertheless proved a useful insight into the KPD's way of thinking in this context. The Communist speaker, Richard Koppin, reported in November 1929 to the Central Committee that his speech at the first Nazi meeting to be held in Groß-Neuendorf on the River Oder in Brandenburg was a great success and effectively isolated the hard-core Nazis.[118] Likewise a Communist speaker at a Nazi local election meeting in the Palatine quarrying town of Kusel was reportedly so effective that the Nazis held no further meetings and even abandoned their electoral agitation at that time.[119]

The KPD's own meetings provided a more promising vehicle for promoting the United Front strategy, since on these occasions the Communists were more likely to be in control of events. At its most confident the KPD would actually invite Nazi speakers and their following to answer specific points or participate in a particular debate.[120] Subsequent Nazi non-attendance would (if it occurred) in itself be a propaganda victory of sorts,[121] which moved the Nazis sometimes to render apologies for absence,[122] but on other occasions Nazis attended with distinctly hostile intent. Even in the Ruhr District the NSDAP was able to wreck some Communist meetings in early 1931 which had been held to expose the Nazis as a pro-Young Plan [*sic*] movement[123] and, as is well documented in the existing literature, Nazi leaders did their best violently to disrupt KPD meetings or subject Communist speakers to ridicule.[124]

At other meetings the KPD were too firmly in control, or the speaker was occasionally too good an orator for the Nazis to make much impact and in these circumstances those National Socialists present became at worst passive and at best attentive listeners, even in cases where they had arrived in formation with the obvious intention of disrupting the meeting.[125] Just occasionally Communist speakers were able to achieve the best of all possible outcomes, when SA men in uniform defied their commanders and participated constructively in meetings. One such case occurred in July 1932 in Ratzebuhr, Pomerania, as the KPD's speaker, Rau, reported to the Central Committee:

> The Nazi leader from Neustettin spoke in the discussion; such rubbish that he was laughed down by the meeting. At the end he tried again to whip up his SA men into wrecking the meeting, but failed. It was noticed that a large proportion of the SA were extremely attentive and listened to my speech with visibly increasing interest. When the SA commander ordered them to leave the room, about a dozen SA men stayed behind and heard my concluding remarks.[126]

Similarly at a meeting in Rehna, Mecklenburg-Schwerin, in June 1932 a KPD speaker was able to prevent over fifty stormtroopers present from wrecking the event by appealing to their class solidarity: 'These working-class Nazis, who had wrecked all the SPD's meetings, desisted from this tactic for the first time, despite being urged on by the estate owners.' Indeed, so confident was the Communist speaker that he then felt able to allow the SA commander speaking time – a shrewd move since many present found him amusing, while the silence of the storm-troopers present suggested that they were at best embarrassed.[127] When Nazis attended Communist meetings in small groups, or individually, prospects were better still. In such cases it is reasonable to assume that genuine interest had prompted them to attend and these particular Nazis were the most likely to join Communist-led discussion groups or participate in other aspects of United Front work.[128] Thus a KPD speaker reported to the Central Committee that discussions had occurred with disillusioned Nazis in various Ruhr towns after a series of meetings in July 1932,[129] while in Grossenhain disgruntled Nazis and Social Democrats were targeted and brought into local discussion circles.[130] Joint meetings with Nazi renegades, such as Otto Strasser's group, were seen as a further means of bridge-building for which the Central Committee was prepared to commit a figure as illustrious as the propaganda specialist Willi Münzenberg in June 1932.[131]

Meetings clearly provided means of access to individual Nazis, but as with most aspects of United Front From Below work, the risks could be as great as the opportunities. The KPD inevitably came to feel that it was competing with the NSDAP for similar pools of support on some occasions and, therefore, felt it had to match the Nazis at particular times in particular places. This could involve the use of former Nazis as speakers at Communist meetings,[132] or could lead to the failure of a KPD meeting in a potentially promising area being explained by a strong local Nazi presence. Thus a Communist rally for the unemployed in the St Georg district of Hamburg in April 1932 attracted only a few dozen people because, as the speaker admitted, the Nazis dominated the area with 'between sixty and seventy swastika flags in individual streets'.[133] From this it was a short but logical step to try and match the Nazis meeting for meeting, as in the cases of Gross Umstadt and Gross-Zimmern in Hessen in June 1932. As the Central Committee wrote to the Reichstag Deputy Georg Schumann:

> Both towns lie in a rural setting in the Odenwald, but a goodly proportion of industrial proletarians live there. Since Hitler is speaking in Gross-Umstadt we must also hold a meeting there using an expert from headquarters. The comrades expect you to take both meetings.[134]

Given this attitude at the centre it is hardly surprising that many rank-and-file Communists or, more often, potential KPD supporters, came to regard the NSDAP and KPD as plausible alternatives and where the capacity of the Communists to get things done was doubted it seemed logical enough to back the Nazis. As two unaffiliated workers explained at a meeting in Silesia in April 1932: 'Although we are pro-

Communist we will therefore vote Nazi',[135] and as the speaker Handke reported to the Central Committee after a series of meetings in Lower Saxony in the same month: 'The contrast with the Nazis [here] is fairly blurred, which represents a great source of danger for us politically and organisationally.'[136]

The territorial dimension of the United Front From Below tactic was, therefore, unmistakable and required the creation of special front organisations designed specifically to avoid the kind of difficulties that inevitably arose when the KPD itself attempted to pursue United Front work. Of these the Fighting League against Fascism was the most significant. It was founded on 28 September 1930 in Berlin to function as a cross-party organisation for the conduct of the 'political and ideological mass struggle against fascism, particularly against the Nazis',[137] which would coordinate campaigns among the unemployed, in residential neighbourhoods, among youth and women and in the factories.[138] The Central Committee went to some lengths to disguise the Communists' predominant role in the League, reminding units sometimes to appoint non-Communists to positions of responsibility and forbidding the doubling up of KPD offices and rooms as League premises,[139] despite the practical and financial problems this must have created. The Nazis' electoral breakthrough in September 1930 had, evidently, impressed the Central Committee and while the League was undoubtedly intended also to fight Social Democracy, its main target was, as noted, the Nazis.[140] As with all United Front From Below work, the League was intended to conduct an ideological struggle so as 'to detach the working-class elements from the fascist and social fascist organisations and win them for the revolutionary class front'.[141] As always, this uncomfortable blending of reasoned persuasion with ever-present violent confrontation was going to create problems and the inherent confusion showed through in at least one Communist leaflet: 'Get fit for the fight against the murderous brown plague! Reclaim the misled working people from the claws of the fascist Hitler party!'.[142] Similarly in November 1931 the KPD in the Ruhr District observed that: 'SA and SS Terror and Murder Squads even here in the Ruhr District are organising so-called punitive expeditions in working-class areas, sealing off entire streets, ambushing workers and striking them down', against which the Communists sought to form cross-party defence committees. However the same paragraph of the report continued: 'Discussion groups are to be formed in order to detach in particular the proletarian element from the murderer's party through intensified ideological campaigning.'[143]

In addition to the obvious problems posed by this two-pronged strategy, the KPD demanded of the Fighting League a commitment to the widest possible range of campaigning: the recruitment of women to counter the right's women's organisations,[144] roaming the countryside agitating against Nazism in its most formidable strongholds,[145] capturing the factories from the SPD while holding off the Nazis[146] and mobilising youth while simultaneously attracting delegations from the Social Democratic and Nazi youth organisations, and from the SA, to KPD youth conferences.[147]

Bearing in mind the instability of the KPD's membership and the doubtful quality of many of its cadres, Communist leaders were remarkably sanguine about the Fighting League's prospects. The League's own leaders, it is true, recognised that the fresh-faced radicalism of the Nazi movement was a great asset which enabled it to mop up disillusioned Social Democrats and former bourgeois party supporters, from lower-middle-class and proletarian circles alike.[148] The League's leaders in the Ruhr were also worried that the Nazis' violence had forced the League to indulge in a 'mini civil war' on the NSDAP's terms which threatened its revolutionary character,[149] but these various practical doubts were outweighed by optimistic expectations. Thus, the Ruhr Fighting League boasted in May 1931: 'Leading National Socialists from the SA or SS are coming over to us daily; individual local groups must go about their work with fiery determination to win back [sic] as many as possible of these misled workers for the red class front.'[150] The national leadership perceived matters in similar terms during the following spring and urged its local groups to organise discussion circles, meetings and, as had already been achieved in the Lower Rhine area, to pass joint resolutions for political campaigning with workers from the Reichsbanner and the SA.[151] As morale in the SA and the wider Nazi movement declined during the autumn of 1932, the Fighting League urged its local formations on to greater efforts[152] and could cite isolated cases of entire Nazi or SA units transferring to the League, as in Chronstau near Oppeln in August.[153] Similarly the police in Bochum observed on 3 December that over forty SA men had joined the League in Dortmund and that many more were fraternising with or joining the United Front. In Recklinghausen both SA and SS members were changing sides in considerable numbers.[154] A meeting of League functionaries reflected in December on how counter-productive former Communist aggression towards the Nazis, and particularly the SA, had been:

The organisation has acknowledged the enormous harmfulness of the slogan 'Strike down the fascists wherever you find them'. Has not the slogan divided us from the misled proletarians and working people in the Hitler party? Has not the SA command used this to create a great gulf [between us and them]? Are we such idiotic 'strategists' as to allow the leaders of a hostile army to retain firm control over their proletarian soldiers and commit them, united, to battle against us?[155]

As the conference concluded: 'We want to beat Hitler with his own troops, by taking them away from him!'[156]

Despite this mood of optimism, it appears that in broader terms the League's success was less spectacular than its ambitions. The overall number of non-Communists who actually joined it were relatively limited, even if the situation had become potentially encouraging by late 1932 and even if contacts had been created with rival political groups. The League failed to expand much beyond an initial, largely Communist, membership of 100 000 and during 1931 this fell slightly from around 112 000 to 106 000;[157] by March 1932 matters still had not improved.[158] Still less satisfactory was the inability of district leaderships to collect dues from 50 per cent of members at best and 70 per cent at worst,[159] which opens to question these members' degree of commitment. A few thousand dedicated activists were never going to be a match for the SA. The high levels of unemployed within the Communist movement no doubt contributed to the miserable situation. The League only had 109 factory groups in December 1931 as against 1658 neighbourhood groups,[160] a position far removed from the Central Committee's idealised view of its own party. In this atmosphere of stagnation and frustration League members were every bit as likely to switch to the Nazis as the latter were to switch to the Communists when things were going badly for them. The Württemberg police noted the consequences of the League's shortcomings in November 1931, continuing:

Because of this situation, an irritable mood has arisen. This has found expression in continual personal disputes at the League's group evenings, and in many resignations from dissatisfied leaders and members and in desertions to the SA of the NSDAP. In September 1931, among other cases, the leader of the Stuttgart-Stockach group went over to the SA in unison with many of his men.[161]

In these circumstances orders to show some consideration for class brothers in the Nazi movement and in particular the SA must have appeared comic at best. Joint discussions and meetings could and did work where the KPD was strongly based, or during the Nazis' crisis months of late 1932, but during the spring of the same year the United Front tactic had sometimes had a devastating and unintended outcome. As the Munich authorities reported in April: 'Recently in particular, people have switched from the Communist paramilitary organisations to the SA because the Central Committee's instructions against "individual terror" had impinged on their activist leanings.'[162] Such events were an ominous portent of March 1933.

The KPD tried to circumvent its organisational weaknesses through the medium of the Anti-Fascist Action (Antifa) which was in practice little more than a logo attached to a wide variety of United Front From Below campaigning.[163] In other words the use of the term served to lend the impression of coherence to the KPD's activities even though this was often lacking. However, under these circumstances the Anti-Fascist Action, launched in June 1932, soon displayed the range of ambiguities and contradictions found in most aspects of United Front work. On the one hand it functioned, sometimes successfully, as a vehicle for cross-party campaigns of physical defence against the Nazis, claiming credit for a series of pitched street battles during the summer of 1932.[164] In this vein the KPD's Secretariat proclaimed in July: 'Drive the columns of Nazi murderers from their haunts, put paid to their murderous game through the solidarity of the Anti-Fascist Action.'[165] However, although the SA's campaign of terror obviously called for a physical response, the KPD's leaders, as always, did not want the physical struggle to overshadow their ideological work.[166] There were certainly instances where Nazis were drawn into Communist-led tenants' campaigns[167] and campaigns against cuts in benefits.[168] In September 1932 a KPD conference suggested dropping the term Anti-Fascist Action and replacing it with United Action so as not to alienate Nazi workers,[169] but this was not acted upon and the issue of whether or not to resort to violence against National Socialists always complicated matters. The party in Hamburg was accused by the Central Commitee of using too much violence, but the party in Berlin was not violent enough![170] The convoluted nature of the United Front campaign was further underlined in October when the KPD's Secretariat felt obliged to explain that attacks against the Reichsbanner were not permitted in conjunction with the Nazis, but that attacks on the Nazis jointly with the Reichsbanner were.[171] The very fact that Communists and Social Democrats could and did cooperate against the Nazis created further difficulties by prejudicing the prospects of a successful United Front campaign against the SPD's hierarchy. The Central Committee was, presumably, happy enough with areas such as Mecklenburg where Antifa had 'driven back the SPD'[172] or the Ruhr where Antifa was the 'decisive weapon' in the fight against the Social Democrats,[173] but the cross-party struggle against Nazism had sometimes allowed Communist and Social Democratic officials to become too friendly. The Central Committee therefore complained of insufficient clarity over day-to-day practice and broader strategy: 'In more than a few cases an opportunistic United Front From Above, as witnessed by a mass of discussions with SPD and Reichsbanner functionaries, has developed without our first achieving a basis among the masses.'[174] However, the KPD's leaders contained this problem with negative results for relations with the SPD that are well understood.[175] Not surprisingly the SPD accused the Communists of sowing confusion to no good purpose through their United Front From Below strategy.[176]

The qualified failure of the KPD's territorial and unemployed campaign was largely the result of circumstance. During the 1920s the KPD had, as seen, failed almost completely to become a major national force in the politics of the factory and the workplace. The economic catastrophe of 1929–32 did provide the party with new followers and a new lease of life, but Communist leaders appreciated that the unemployed and destitute were no guarantors of long-term political strength and were certainly not the revolutionary spearhead of an explicitly Bolshevik party. If the Communists had, indeed, dominated the great factories of Germany then, perhaps, their United Front campaign among the unemployed and in the neighbourhood might have ended successfully. Instead, with a small and unstable membership, the KPD's leaders devised a centrally-directed, explicit, long-term policy of bridge-building and rapprochment towards larger, far better organised movements: the Social Democratic and National Socialist. Had the Social Democrats alone been in the field, then the Communists' United Front campaign would probably have gone down as just another intriguing detail in the party's lacklustre history. With the Nazis involved, however, the KPD had created a witches' brew of grassroots political action which, as the weakest of the three main non-confessional popular parties, it was worst placed to exploit.

9   The Struggle in the Workplace

Little has been written of the conflict between Nazism and its left-wing enemies in the workplaces, and particularly the factories, of Weimar Germany. Nazism, it is commonly held, was too thinly represented on the shop floor to mount any effective challenge to the socialist working-class organisations, under which heading the Communists are often, implicitly, subsumed. Where Nazis did appear on the shop floor, it is argued, they played the role of strike-breakers and were thus set apart from the rest of the workers. The underlying assumptions about Nazi and, more especially, Communist organisational strength have been questioned in an earlier chapter, but equally telling are the assumptions regarding Communist and Nazi organisational objectives in the factories, some of which are questionable to say the least. For example, the aims of the Free Trade Unions (ADGB) differed so fundamentally from those of the Communist RGO that it seems profoundly unhistorical to regard them as respective wings of a single, 'Marxist', working-class factory movement. The RGO, after all, saw the destruction of the ADGB as its immediate priority, at least until early 1933.[1] Similarly, it is questionable whether a single standard can be applied to ascertain the success or failure of the RGO and NSBO respectively in factory politics. If their aims differed, then their definitions of success might also have differed, with considerable implications for our current understanding of relations between them.

For the KPD the factory, and the RGO within it, became the main focus of the revolutionary struggle, which made the success or failure of the RGO a matter of profound political importance. The origins of the NSBO, however, were very different. With Hitler and the Nazi leadership concentrating on the electoral struggle as their means to power, they found themselves engaged in factory politics contrary to their intentions and expectations.[2] Locally-based Nazi factory cells began to appear in the late 1920s in Berlin and other centres as a result of grassroots pressure from groups of salaried staff and manual workers. Local NSBO leaderships developed to accommodate this grassroots movement, but it was not until 1931 that the NSDAP felt obliged to allow the NSBO to campaign and organise on a national basis.[3] . The NSBO soon attracted the attention of the authorities and of political rivals as a vigorous exponent of National Socialism in the workplace and its 'Into the Factories Campaign' (*HIB-Aktion*) which it launched in September 1931 gave the impression of a determined Nazi assault on the citadels of Social Democratic trade unionism.[4] However, the Nazi party leadership perceived the NSBO and *HIB-Aktion* in terms which betrayed the relative lack of importance which they attached to factory politics.[5] The mobilisation of political support for the NSDAP through NSBO cells was certainly acceptable, but the cells were not intended to assume the welfare and industrial relations functions of the long-established official unions. Hitler saw this as an impossible task and the NSBO was starved of funds accordingly.[6] Despite this lukewarm response from their party leaders, rank-and-file Nazis in the factories saw things differently and, yet again, began to create new political facts from below.[7] Their demands for a 'genuine trade union organisation'[8] had helped precipitate the establishment of the NSBO on a national basis and in 1931 their insistence on a 'socialist' political stance combined with the politics of their leaders to bring about the expulsion of senior managers and employers from the organisation.[9] The NSBO came increasingly to support and mount strikes and, in as far as finance permitted, to develop the welfare functions commensurate with authentic trade unionism. As Mai comments:

> The more the NSBO was forced into a day-to-day position of conflict with the established unions and the more comprehensively it became committed in the factory and the world of work, the more it was unavoidably driven in the direction of classical trade unionism.[10]

In spite of the scepticism of the Nazi Party's leadership, therefore, the NSBO had engaged in a thoroughgoing two-front war; against the official unions and against the employers. Of its success in this regard more will be said presently, but for the RGO the emergence of this new factor in trade union politics was highly unwelcome.

In its origins the RGO was anything but a grassroots phenomenon. in late 1928, as part of the new Ultra-Leftist Strategy, the Red International Labour Union chief, Salomon Lozovsky, called for the creation of independent revolutionary trade union organisations. In response to this the KPD presented its own candidates for factory council elections in the spring of 1929 and subsequently established the RGO as the main focus of its campaign in the factories.[11] By July the Tenth ECCI Plenum observed that such moves had: 'enabled the communist parties and the adherents of the revolutionary trade union movement organisationally to consolidate large masses of workers against the social-democratic and the reformist trade union apparatus as was the case in the Ruhr',[12] but the new strategy was not without its problems. There was considerable opposition within the KPD to running independent lists of candidates in factory council elections which had to be suppressed from above[13] and in addition the Ultra-Left Strategy reinforced considerably Social Democratic hostility towards the KPD. Daycock observes that this precipitated a range of unforeseen consequences:

> As the oppositionist stance of the KPD hardened in the factories, the SPD dominated unions responded by withdrawing union rights. Deprived of protection, many Communist functionaries were made vulnerable to management reprisals and as unemployment rose, Communists were the first to lose their jobs.[14]

Thus the traumas inflicted by the KPD on its own trade union movement in the mid 1920s were now compounded by renewed and intensifying hostility on the part of employers and the official unions to any sign of Communist activity in the factories. Small wonder that the remaining rank-and-file Communists there were reluctant to become politically active.[15]

In these circumstances the KPD's attempt, on the instructions of the Comintern, to relocate its organisational focus in the factories was playing to its greatest weakness rather than to any latent strength – and the stakes were high. While the NSBO's modest advances were an unexpected bonus for the Nazi leadership, Communist party leaders were now, perforce, pinning their hopes for revolution on an intense campaign of politicisation within the factories. Economically motivated strikes would lead to political strikes from which would develop the ultimate general strike and armed insurrection through which capitalism would be toppled.[16] Parliamentary elections became a matter of secondary importance[17] (although their propagandistic value was recognised) and the factory, along with elections to works councils, became, as the Ruhr KPD put it: 'the locus of the most intense of political confrontations between Social Fascism, Fascism, and revolutionary theory and practice'.[18] Attempts to comply with Comintern instructions to trigger mass political strikes on May Day 1930[19] were perceived in comparable terms as: 'A decisive campaign of struggle *against* the knout of the Law for the Protection of the

Republic, *against* the brutal execution of the Young Plan at the expense of the working masses and *for* the defence of the Soviet Union.'[20] The KPD's attitude to the September Reichstag elections in 1930 confirmed this set of priorities. As the police in Nuremberg commented: 'The KPD fought an election campaign simply to conquer and mobilise the majority of the proletarian masses for the "extra-parliamentary economic and political mass struggles" it intended to pursue *after* the elections.'[21] Similarly the Ruhr KPD in its election campaign: 'declared to the workers that not parliament, but the extra-parliamentary struggle – the launching of mass strikes against the employers' offensive – can improve your situation'.[22]

This strategy called for nothing less than the establishment of a dominant organisational presence in the factories. The RGO was charged with building up its organisational strength to the point where it could initiate and lead economic struggles independently of the official unions[23] and eventually, as the ECCI demanded, prepare a general strike 'which must take in simultaneously all branches of German heavy industry from the Rhineland to Prussia'.[24] Orders and exhortations in this vein from both national and regional party leaderships continued throughout early 1931,[25] but with few concrete results. Thälmann was forced to admit at the Eleventh ECCI Plenum in the spring of 1931 that the number of revolutionary-led strikes in Germany fell far short of that in Russia in 1905 and that the political mood in the factories did not necessarily favour the KPD. The main tasks of organisation and education still lay in the future.[26] At regional level the party leaders in the Ruhr District observed that they had only been able to latch on to the miners' strikes of 1930 after they had started, with few political dividends to show for that.[27] Their plan of campaign for February 1931 urged the strengthening of the RGO to the point where it could 'destroy the reformist strike-breaking organisations' while putting up RGO candidates in every workplace for the approaching factory council elections.[28] Implicitly, however, they were forced to admit how organisationally weak the KPD remained within the factories of the Ruhr, for it was left to street cells to adopt an individual factory so as to divert party activity onto its self-selected battleground.[29] Later, in November, the Ruhr KPD demanded that 'the final traces of the old, traditional organisational form, based on the residential area, are eliminated and that, in their place, a reorganisation on the basis of the factory cell is accomplished',[30] but this was asking a great deal of its members.

The strategy also presumed the presence of an actual, or potential, mass following in the factories and since the KPD's existing strength lay, if anywhere, among the unemployed in the neighbourhood, the recruitment of new members in the workplace became a matter of fundamental importance. The authorities indeed observed in October 1931 that: 'The basic and most decisive element of the Communist campaign is ideological subversion, detailed spadework and above all the winning over of the decisive majority of the industrial working class',[31] which made confrontation with rival workers' organisations, from the ADGB to the NSBO, inevitable. The RGO spoke in September 1931 of engaging in the mass recruitment of Social Democratic trade unionists and of the liquidation of the NSDAP in the workplace,[32] but by June 1932 it was advocating a subtler and more ideologically-based campaign against the Nazis:

> The RGO must, through intensive propaganda among the proletarian elements of the NSDAP, divide them from the clique of Nazi leaders who are supported by the employers and win [them] for the class struggle. The liquidation of the NSDAP in the factories and the offices is one of the RGO's most important tasks.[33]

The Communist movement had recognised that attempts to remedy their chronic organisational weakness in the workplace and to gain mass support there had come up against a growing Nazi presence, which made the relationship between the KPD and Nazism important in this most unlikely of settings.

At the most basic of levels, the KPD's leaders sought to establish just how many Nazis there were in the factories and whether or not the problem was growing. In 1929 the Central Committee noted some Nazi recruitment of workers in areas with a radical tradition, but where the KPD, for one of several reasons, was weak. In other words the NSDAP seemed to profit when the KPD failed within its own potential constituency.[34] During 1930 reports of Nazi progress began to multiply and, again, it appeared that the NSDAP could benefit from Communist failings. Thus Berlin accused the KPD in Ludwigshafen and Mannheim of neglecting to address the question of wage cuts at the I.G. Farben chemical works: 'Is it surprising that the National Fascists in your district are winning ground when our [local] newspaper fails to demonstrate that the Party is prepared to act over a matter as decisively important as wage cuts for the dyestuff workers?'[35] In the spring the KPD estimated that the Nazis had established 1500 factory cells nationally[36] and although some areas were still free of a Nazi presence in the factories at this time,[37] in others (notably Berlin, the Erzgebirge and the Siegerland) the NSBO was beginning to gain some ground in factory council elections. The NSBO took six per cent of the workers' vote at the Berliner Verkehrsgesellschaft (BVG), 18 per cent at the Dynamowerk/Siemenskonzern,[38] and among the tram workers in Frankfurt-am-Main 19.5 per cent.[39] Salaried employees were even more inclined to vote for the NSBO which could poll 33 per cent or even 60 per cent in staff elections in isolated cases.[40]

The KPD's leaders, therefore, were aware that the Nazis had arrived in the factories, but subsequent attempts to establish the precise extent of Nazi penetration in individual cases were hampered by the Communists' own organisational weaknesses in the workplace.[41] The Fighting League against Fascism complained in March 1931 that although small numbers of Nazis were emerging, or being placed, in many larger factories in Berlin: 'Our cells usually know nothing about the presence of the Nazis.'[42] Many other individual reports made it clear that the NSBO was continuing to develop during 1931,[43] but again the KPD's own supporters appear either to have been remarkably unobservant or prepared to delude themselves that only salaried staff were involved.[44] In a notable example the Nazis had won two seats on the works council at the Wolfen Film Factory by early 1932 (the RGO had seven and the ADGB five) and yet, as a visiting official complained, the local RGO members 'could not provide any information as to whether a Nazi group exists or not, even though, with the help of management in this militarily strategic plant, a group undoubtedly does exist'.[45] The high level of electoral support for the RGO in this setting might, therefore, be judged as essentially passive and certainly not of the calibre needed to precipitate revolutionary struggle. Similarly in the surrounding communities the NSDAP had established voluntary welfare circles, collecting food and money from small tradesmen for redistribution among the poor and the SA and yet, the same official complained, 'the comrades knew nothing about this'.[46]

Nonetheless, the RGO was able by early 1932 to assess the extent of the NSBO's progress during the previous year, partly through reference to its own sources and partly to those of other political groups and trade unions.[47] The Communists believed that the NSBO's enhanced profile resulted from decisions on high, by the Nazi Party's leaders and their capitalist backers,[48] but the potential dangers posed for the RGO were still regarded as significant. For one thing the factory council election results for 1931 suggested that the NSBO was not an idle threat when it came to garnering popular support.

Estimates of the NSBO's performance nationally varied from around 0.5 per cent to 1.3 per cent of the votes cast specifically by the manual workers (with a slightly higher figure of 1.5 per cent in the larger factories)[49] which produced a tally of 710 mandates as against the RGO's 4664. However, the Nazi organisation was still in its infancy, the *HIB-Aktion* lay in the future,[50] so these apparently dreadful results appeared to many contemporaries to reflect the birth-pains of an infant movement rather than a negligible propensity for factory workers to vote Nazi.[51] The NSBO had been unable to put up candidates in most factories, but, where they had, the Nazi vote was often high among the manual workforce. Thus, at the first attempt in 1931, the NSBO took 16 per cent of the poll at the Friedrich-Alfred steel mill in Rheinhausen as the vote for all other unions (Communist, Liberal, SPD and Yellow) fell. The RGO's vote fell from 38.35 to 35.08 per cent which was not a decisive blow, but a move in the wrong direction for a body bent on seizing control of the industrial proletariat.[52] Similarly, in a number of the great chemical works, where the RGO was very strong, the NSBO burst onto the scene with great suddenness. At I.G. Farben Leverkusen it turned in a 13.32 per cent poll as the RGO's share of the vote fell from 39.65 to 32.96 per cent[53] and at the Leuna Works the NSBO took 11.6 per cent of the workers' vote.[54]

Recent research has confirmed this picture of NSBO candidates, where they stood, often doing rather well. Although the Nazis won just 1.74 per cent of the votes cast in the 10 190 factories of the metal industry in 1931,[55] the picture looks very different when one recognises that the NSBO put up candidates in just 147 of these factories. These workplaces provided 105 workers' votes each for the NSBO, as against 236 votes for the RGO in each of the 452 metalworking factories where it placed candidates.[56] In selected metal works around Duisburg the NSBO polled between seven and twenty-nine per cent.[57] Turning to the Ruhr mining industry, the NSBO increased its share of the workers' vote from a miserable 0.08 per cent in 1930 to 3.58 per cent in 1931,[58] but the results in individual pits where the NSBO actually had candidates were nearer 20 per cent[59] (although in selected pits around Duisburg the figure ranged from four to sixteen per cent[60]). Like the RGO, the NSBO fared poorly in the manufacturing sector,[61] but the latter's claim to have received 12 per cent of the working-class vote and 25 per cent of the white-collar vote where it actually contested elections was clearly by no means ludicrous.[62] The NSBO's particular success among salaried staff was no less feared, for it provided the organisation with relatively solid footholds within the factories from which the initial inroads into the workers' vote were sometimes achieved.[63]

The critical question, therefore, centred more on the NSBO's ability to extend its organisational base than on the propensity of a sizeable minority of workers to vote Nazi. The launching of the *HIB-Aktion* in September 1931 did subsequently enable the NSBO to build up its organisation and expand its membership to a significant degree in working-class circles as well as among salaried staff.[64] The RGO began to respond accordingly, recognising that the Nazis had definitely now become a factor to reckon with alongside the SPD and ADGB in the workplace.[65] The NSBO even seemed to be adopting a more positive view of trade unionism, which the RGO perceived as a cynical Nazi attempt to appeal to industrial workers,[66] but which has been interpreted more recently as the product of conviction rather than expediency.[67] Whatever the case, the NSBO was clearly gaining ground and by early 1932 the NSDAP's 'growing influence among the factory workers' in the traditionally radical city of Brunswick prompted a relatively detailed survey by the KPD of what it regarded as an acute situation.[68] As Table 9.1 shows, the KPD and RGO were being

TABLE 9.1 *Communist and Nazi presence in selected factories: Brunswick, early 1932*[69]

Firm	Workforce			Communists		Nazis(NSBO)	
	Workers	*Salaried*	*Combined*	*KPD*	*RGO*	*Workers*	*Salaried*
Büssing A.G.	480	200		7	18	18	100
Schmalbach			270	8	15	20	20
Jüdel			560	7	0	100	0
Voigtländer	450	220		12	0	0	100
Schlachthaus			51	2	0	2*	0
Westermann	315	50		6	1	4/5	30
Maschinenbau-anstalt			120	?	?	?	majority
Zuckerraf-finerie			300	6*	0	60	?
Union Blechwaren			150	0	0	20	0
Strassenbahn			400	8	25	20	?
Totals	1,245	470	1,851	56+	59+	245+	250+

* unorganised.

matched, if not outpointed, by the NSBO in Brunswick. The local Nazi party leaders had gained a promising organisational foothold in the factories which supplemented their electoral offensive, but the Communists were far short of organising sufficient numbers of workers to stage a political mass strike. These figures, taken from Communist sources, accord with fragmentary information from many parts of Germany. As the Nazis built up their organisational base in the factories potential support could be mobilised systematically for the first time, or new placements within the workforce organised. The KPD observed increased Nazi activity among salaried staff and wage-earners in a series of individual factories and towns across Germany,[70] with Bebra's railway workers, the factories of Halberstedt and Wernigerode, salaried staff and workers in the metallurgy, shipbuild-ing and port sectors of Bremen, and workers from all the major factories in the radical, working-class stronghold of Chemnitz singled out for special mention.[71] In the Wurmrevier, at three identified pits, the RGO gained fresh votes at one, but the NSBO polled strongly at two as the Christian and ADGB tally fell.[72] The RGO in the Ruhr lamented in January 1932 that: 'A neglect of youth work means that we have left the field wide open to the unions, the Nazis and the like'[73] and the Central Committee, on taking a broader view in March, concluded that: 'The underestimation of the Nazis' *HIB-Aktion* by the Party leadership has allowed the Nazis to gain ground in a series of factories.'[74] Recent research has identified Silesia as an area of rapid NSBO growth during early 1932[75] and Berlin, northern Westphalia, Silesia, Saxony and Cologne/Aachen have been identified as particular NSBO strongholds at the beginning of 1933.[76] The KPD itself regarded Westphalia as a region in which the NSBO was active, allegedly with support from employers,[77] although it should be remembered that in some instances the NSBO's growth stemmed from recruitment among the unemployed.[78]

The NSBO's considerable success in eliciting support from the white-collar, salaried staff of Germany's factories, shops and offices also impinged substantially on Communist-Nazi relations during the final years of the republic. The classification of salaried staff by the Nazis as workers (workers of the head, or brain!) was by no means an idiosyncratic deviation from the standards of the time. The British Labour Party predated the Nazis' use of this concept in clause Four of its constitution and the KPD, from its own perspective, was convinced that salaried staff were, objectively, workers the organisation of whom was as vital as that of blue-collar wage earners.[79] After all, the KPD argued, salaried staff were now present in such large numbers in the workplace that they could hardly be ignored. Indeed, in the state of Bremen and in the town of Oldenburg there were more salaried staff than wage earners in the working population.[80] It was recognised that many salaried staff had held aloof from the manual workers and had organised in separate unions which often behaved more like professional associations, but the depression, so the KPD argued, had stripped away these illusions of superiority.[81] Unfortunately for the Communists, the proletarianisation of salaried staff had driven them in the first instance to the Nazis,[82] so that the KPD's Central Committee began to express profound concern over the Nazi breakthrough into the lower middle classes in 1930 before it had become fully aware of Nazism's potential for attracting working-class support.

> The terrible danger posed by the National Socialist movement lies in its almost unlimited capacity to attract the working masses who are discontented with and despairing of bourgeois policies and who formerly supported bourgeois parties and to a degree the SPD. There is doubtless among the millions of Nazi supporters a majority of those groups who, in class terms, belong to the proletariat, are associated with it or can be won for the revolutionary proletariat as allies: salaried staff, civil servants, the *Mittelstand,* peasants and so on. The struggle between the KPD and National Socialists is in the first instance a struggle for hegemony over the working, non-proletarian groups.[83]

Even after the Communist movement became more concerned about Nazi inroads into the working class, the lower-middle-class question remained very much a live issue[84] and the RGO was given the task 'of organising the ideological and political proselytisation of these groups, so as to take the ground from under the Nazis' feet and transfer the radicalism present onto our own ground'.[85] However, the KPD was never able to organise more than a few thousand clerical staff.[86].

It was one thing to observe a rise in the Nazis' fortunes in the workplace, but another to develop appropriate responses and in the event the KPD swithered between outright confrontation and the gentler tactic of proselytisation. It seems clear that the KPD's leaders would have preferred to see no Nazis in the factories at all and where Nazis tried to organise in workplaces which had a significant Communist presence they often met with outright, violent, opposition.[87] Typical was a letter from the Central Committee of June 1930 to factory and street cells which declared:

> Out of the factories with the fascist plague! This slogan can, however, only be achieved through broadly-based mass struggle. It is therefore our duty to organise factory guards in all factories.[88]

Where the KPD was strong this tactic could lead to the forcible ejection of Nazis from their place of work,[89] but significantly the sheer volume of exhortation from the Communist Party's leaders to their thinly stretched activists on this matter revealed that the problem had grown beyond the point where it would be solved by outright confrontation. The danger was evident to the Central Committee even in mid 1930 and subsequently it sometimes attributed the National Socialists' success in this context to conspiratorial activities by the SPD's leaders.[90] In May 1932 the RGO in the Ruhr District echoed this complaint when observing that the 'Social Fascist leaders' wished to see Nazi factory cells established[91] and in August did provide evidence of a concrete grievance on this score.[92] However, it would have been futile and inaccurate to attribute the phenomenon simply to Social Democratic perfidy, and the struggle between the Communists and Nazis intensified. The Prussian police were in no doubt that the Nazis' increasingly prominent factory campaign was 'the deeper reason for the ever more bitter struggle between the exponents of the two ideologies and for the increasing bloodshed occurring in the course of this struggle'.[93]

Once the Nazis were well-established in particular workplaces, or where the Communists themselves were weak, violence became pointless from the KPD's point of view. As early as mid 1930 the Central Committee recognised that even in the factories the struggle would have to assume an ideological dimension[94] either by highlighting the alleged perfidy of Nazi factory politics,[95] or by fraternising with rank-and-file Nazis to achieve commonly-held concrete aims.[96] In late 1931 the RGO argued that 'a complete change to ideological work among Nazi supporters had to occur' and continued that even physical violence and strikebreaking activities by the Nazis could best be combated in this way.[97]

The situation demanded the extension of the United Front From

Below strategy to the anti-Nazi struggle in the workplace (where it had long since been employed against other elements of the radical right). Even before Hitler's electoral breakthrough in September 1930 the KPD had begun to move implicitly down this road, urging its members in April to fraternise with Nazis in the factories whenever expedient. Physical struggle was regarded as inevitable in some circumstances, but the Communist Party's leaders argued that beyond its considerable petty bourgeois following, the NSDAP had won over 'broad sections of disillusioned workers who were often very activist in outlook' and continued that 'an ideological struggle to separate [fascism] from its supporters and to subvert its active cadres' was necessary. The anti-fascist mass organisations in the factories were intended as much for this ideological campaign as they were for physical struggle.[98] In June the KPD again emphasised that 'the most intensive conduct of our ideological campaign to win over misled Nazi working-class supporters [in the factories] is the indispensable precondition for a physical struggle',[99] and in August both the Party[100] and the RGO put even greater stress on the ideological dimension, with the latter declaring that: 'Every worker must learn to understand that the National Socialist movement can only be worn down and weakened . . . through the broadest ideological mass struggle.'[101] The Central Committee detected straws in the wind which appeared to justify this ideological offensive. In June it commented that the contradictions between the promises made by Nazi leaders to their working-class supporters and these leaders' subsequent actions were creating tension within the National Socialist movement[102] and in July it reported on successful joint mass meetings with Nazi workers and white-collar staff, notably in Berlin and Hamburg.[103] Furthermore, the RGO mineworkers' conference, held in midsummer in the Ruhr, included not only five SPD delegates, but two from the NSDAP, which suggested that a United Front approach could achieve concrete results.[104]

After the September 1930 Reichstag elections the KPD strengthened its commitment to a United Front strategy in the factories and made it plain that the Nazis were not to be forgotten in this regard.[105] By October the Central Committee was evidently treating the problems posed by the Nazis in the workplace with the great urgency, declaring:

Everywhere in the factory and the neighbourhood we must above all identify the Nazi movement's proletarian elements and systematically influence them politically. We must succeed in detaching them from the fascist movement and thereby prevent the formation of Nazi cells in the factories.[106]

The KPD in Halle-Merseburg reported the recruitment of Nazis to the RGO in March 1931,[107] but the Fighting League recognised in the same month that Communist political strategy in the factories still left a lot to be desired. It appeared that many new recruits to the Communist movement were political virgins, for whom extensive political education was essential if they were to deal successfully with the National Socialists in the workplace. The Central Committee produced schooling material for new recruits which, therefore, paid specific attention to the problems posed by the growing Nazi presence in the workplace:

> *Example:* One comrade plays a Nazi worker. Another comrade is detailed to talk things over with the sham Nazi and educate him in a proletarian spirit. The remaining comrades form the audience. After ten minutes' discussion between the comrades, it is established whether the comrade has argued correctly, objectively and convincingly, and which mistakes have been made. The same can be done for the SPD, Christians and so on. It's good fun for the comrades and very educational.[108]

The use of the United Front strategy also required that individual Nazis play an organisational role in Communist front organisations located in the workplace. At first, this commitment was implicitly legitimated by exhortations from the Central Committee and the ECCI which urged local formations to forge organisational links with workers of all political persuasions.[109] The RGO reinforced this line in June, declaring that:

> Every militant worker must join the RGO which has the task of organising the Red United Front in every factory. The RGO must be a powerful organisation, with membership open to all workers, regardless of party political or religious affiliation.[110]

Similarly, in August, the Fighting League against Fascism argued that membership of its Factory Squads was open to workers of all political persuasions 'as long as they are honestly prepared to fight for the programme of revolutionary class struggle against fascism'.[111] It might appear that this proviso would, after all, exclude Nazis, but given the economistic definition of fascism employed by the Communists which regarded Social Fascism (the SPD) as a Siamese twin of National Fascism (the NSDAP),[112] the involvement of individual Nazis in Communist front organisations would, in theory, be restricted by their own scepticism rather than that of the Communists. As the RGO declared in December: 'The National Socialist-minded workers also belong in the United Front to fight for work, bread and freedom.'[113] As a corollary to this, the ECCI recommended that the KPD place 'sleepers' within the Nazi movement so as 'to be able to seize the leadership of the masses from the National Socialists at the appropriate moment.'[114]

The overall tenor of Communist ideology during the Third Period, at international and national level, lent an inherent logic to this particular aspect of United Front strategy and the involvement of working- and lower-middle-class Nazis in RGO committee work in certain areas[115] and the appearance of Nazis as delegates at some regional United Front congresses during late 1931[116] seemed to demonstrate the practicality of the tactic. However, the mounting threat posed by the Nazis in the factories (among other places!), the failure of the RGO to make decisive progress there[117] and the difficulties inherent in persuading some ordinary Communists to adopt a didactic, comradely tone with members of any other political party, let alone the Nazis, began to take their toll. As the Ruhr KPD complained in December:

> The more comradely the manner in which we speak with Social Democratic and otherwise organised class comrades, including the Nazis at the workbench and at the welfare office, the sooner these class comrades will join the right front. It is undeniable that the Red United Front could already have had substantial success if RGO members had not all too often blocked other class comrades' path to us through utterly uncomradely behaviour.[118]

In the same month the Central Committee emphasised the threat posed specifically by the Nazis and urged an intensification of ideological work within 'this rapidly growing people's movement'. It warned that failure 'would mean a great loss of momentum in our political fortunes, particularly in the Factory Council Elections'[119] and similar exhortations emphasised the significance of the Nazis' growing influence on young factory workers in particular.[120] In response to this threat the Communist Youth League (KJVD) planned five hundred meetings for factory workers to which young Nazi workers and their leaders were to be invited,[121] although it is unlikely that either the KJVD or the RGO was ever capable of an organisational effort on this scale.

The Communist movement therefore entered 1932 committed to a factory strategy that held out crumbs of hope, but was not going particularly well. Regional organisations issued a stream of orders urging rank-and-file Communists to enter the ideological struggle for the hearts and minds of Nazi factory workers[122] as matters deteriorated. In the Halle-Merseburg district the RGO acknowledged that Nazi penetration of the area's chemical works constituted a grave problem requiring a decisive response:

> Our members must find out, through comradely discussion with Nazi workers, why they entered Nazi organisations. Just as it is necessary to cultivate comradely discussion with Social Democratic and Free Trade Union members so as to detach them from the trade union bureaucracy and the SPD and win them for the class struggle, so too must we work on the Nazi workers and convince them of the RGO's strategy.[123]

It is evident that the RGO in Halle-Merseburg regarded the Social Democrats' and the Nazis' presence in the factories as inherently comparable problems and the Hamburg KPD took this line of argument further. The importance of the ideological battle against National Socialism was again stressed: 'Without the fulfilment of this task we will not be able to impede the Nazis' penetration of the factories'[124] and here the relationship between Nazism and Social Democracy was seen as significant. The Nazis, so the Hamburg KPD argued, were gaining support from factory workers and staff by presenting the 'treachery of the SPD's bureaucracy' as evidence of the bankruptcy of Marxism. The KPD had to demonstrate that Nazism and Social Democracy were, in fact, 'twin brothers'.[125] Yet again, therefore, the Communist movement sought to discredit Nazism by highlighting the alleged similarities between it and Social Democracy.[126] Ordinary workers had to be saved from both, but Nazi supporters were evidently not perceived as atypical or deviant elements of the factory-employed working class by this stage.

The United Front From Below strategy may have been clear enough in theory, but practice could be different. In Halle-Merseburg relations between Socialist, Nazi and Communist workers were generally bad[127] which made a strategy based on grassroots fraternisation at least questionable and the inherently violent mood of late Weimar politics did little to help. In January the KPD in Hamburg had to remind its members that abstention from a campaign of terror was not tantamount to surrender[128] and ordinary Communists throughout Germany were urged at this time to fraternise with Nazis on an individual basis. Given the Communists' own weakness in the factories it is understandable that misgivings would arise, reinforced, perhaps, by the apparent inability or reluctance of RGO 'Workers' Correspondents', even in the Ruhr, to provide detailed information on developments in the factories and on the mood among non-Communist workers;[129] a crucial prerequisite for the United Front campaign.

That said, the strategy enjoyed adequate success to permit its continuation. The Central Committee must have been pleased to learn that even in Halle-Merseburg, the United Front committee in the huge Leuna chemical works included workers of all political persuasions, with close fraternisation between Socialists, Nazis and Communists 'in all sections' of the plant. As one worker elaborated: 'We discuss things in our crew from early till late; there are nine of us, including two SPD and two Nazis.'[130] Similarly, discussions between Nazis and Communists in the Berlin Transport (BVG) depots began well before the notorious November strike when the NSDAP and KPD took action in the face of Social Democratic opposition. The Nazis here were not regarded as misfits, but as disillusioned Socialists who had consequently joined the NSDAP. Of course political deals with the Nazi Party (as with the SPD) were out of the question, but grassroots cooperation of a practical kind was the very stuff of the United Front strategy: 'There is a great deal of discussion with the Nazis and it has become evident that they are ready to strike against wage cuts and other attacks on conditions.'[131] Once the political radicals had sunk at least some of their immediate differences in this way, the possibility, or perhaps the danger, arose of their forming a new sort of United Front against the more cautious Social Democratic workers, just as Nazis and Communists had come together against the SPD at other times and in other settings.[132] A Central Committee official reported on the situation in the Appel foodstuffs factory in Hanover in Spring 1932 in this vein:

We can't do anything with the old, ossified SPD workers. The Nazis are much more lively intellectually. We have discussion evenings with the Nazis and the result is always a declaration by the National Socialists that: 'If things don't turn out as we expect in our party, then we'll come over to your side'. The comrade left the impression that activity among the Social Democrats had been almost wholly abandoned.[133]

As significant as the general tenor of the report was its observation that the Nazi cell contained just twelve men in a workforce of 470. The KPD probably had little more in the way of formal organisation, leaving the two small radical groups in intimate political contact out of which could develop a sense of shared interests and even shared values. Similarly in the Lower Saxon town of Groß Rühden, a sterile relationship between Communists and Socialists contrasted with close Communist-Nazi relations which was recognised as posing a substantial organisational and political threat to the integrity of the local KPD.[134] It would be mistaken to generalise from scattered instances of this sort, but they nonetheless demonstrate the potential for a United Front campaign to transmit Nazi values into the Communist movement as much as the opposite.[135]

   The July 1932 Reichstag elections changed the political environment sufficiently to heighten the significance of the United Front approach to Nazis in the factories. The failure to win an absolute majority in the Reichstag precipitated growing disarray in the SA and created mounting problems for the Nazi Party but, by contrast, seemed to trigger enhanced activity by the NSBO in the factories,[136] an enhanced NSBO involvement in strikes and similar actions[137] and a readiness on the part of the NSDAP's National Organisation Leader, Gregor Strasser, to ascribe a far greater significance to the NSBO than had hitherto been the case.[138] The KPD for its part detected the growing signs of disarray in the Nazi movement overall, which lent further credibility to the United Front From Below tactic, but precisely where it mattered most to the KPD, in the factories, it observed that the Nazis were not in retreat. The consequent flood of orders and correspondence concerning the problems posed by the National Socialists in the workplace bears eloquent testimony to the significance the KPD lent this development.

   In many cases individual pronouncements repeated earlier arguments. Factory squads had to win over Nazi proletarians,[139] working-class Nazis had to be convinced that National Socialism offered them nothing concrete,[140] be engaged in structured discussion sessions,[141] and so on. Articles in the Communist press continued to urge ordinary

Communists to forget or tone down their previous antagonism to working class Nazis and instead regard them as potential or even actual allies. Thus, in October, the Ruhr KPD's newspaper, *Pionier des Bolschewismus,* argued in a special edition that, exceptions apart, Nazi bashing was simply no longer on:

> It is perfectly clear *that without a serious campaign of subversion, without winning over or at least neutralising broad sections of the Nazi Party, we will not be in a position to carry through the proletarian revolution in Germany.*
>
> The fact that, in individual towns and in individual factories, the SA proletarians are fighting actively alongside our comrades against the attacks on living standards and working class rights shows that through a thorough proselytisation of these circles we can win them for the revolutionary class front. For this reason we cannot propagate the slogan *'Clear the factories of Nazis'* any longer.[142]

This was not an isolated instance, being part of a concerted press campaign. The KPD's Berlin-Brandenburg-Lausitz-Grenzmark [!] journal, *Der Funke,* also argued that the objective conditions for winning over vast sections of Nazism's mass support had never been better:

> In class terms millions of Nazi voters belong to us; our victory is impossible without winning them over. The further escalation of the crisis, rising unemployment, the broadening of the struggle in the factories, at welfare offices, have provided the preconditions for enrolling the Nazi voters who belong to us in class terms in the anti-fascist, anti-capitalist front.[143]

In the same edition of *Der Funke* specific attention was given to the question of factory politics and in this regard the plea for fraternisation was, if anything, more emphatic:

> Why is a slogan such as 'Throw the Nazis out of the Unions' wrong?
>
> Because it makes it impossible to win workers and employees who belong to the NSDAP for the revolutionary class struggle . . . *The slogan* 'Throw the Nazis out of the factories' *is equally wrong.* On the contrary, we must do everything possible to involve the NSDAP's supporters in the factory in the struggle for improved working conditions.[144]

The same article did not rule out punitive measures against individual Nazis where appropriate, but regarded such action as exceptional.

The KPD held true to this line to the very end of Weimar. Working-class Nazis were reassured that their goals were the KPD's goals; 'We all want socialism', as the *Arbeiter Zeitung* remarked in this context in November, but they were also reminded of the growing involvement of their leaders with the establishment,[145] which was nonetheless keeping Hitler out of power: 'Hindenburg asked Hitler if he'd join the firm as chief clerk; Hitler said he didn't want to be chief clerk, but the owner of the firm instead; the President rejected this and Hitler and Frick left the room somewhat depressed.'[146] The NSDAP's electoral road had, therefore, ended in failure and it was now incumbent on Communists to draw these misled Nazis into the United Front where they could fight both for immediate, concrete objectives and for the ultimate overthrow of capitalism.[147] In this vein it was considered vital that NSBO members be presented as United Front candidates in factory council elections once they had renounced their formal political adherence to Nazism,[148] and direct appeals were made to Nazis to join the United Front and repeat the 'achievements' of the Berlin Transport Strike.[149] By this time practice was coming to accord rather more closely with theory. The RGO in Westphalia claimed in October that: 'The ordinary NSDAP members in the factories are becoming radicalised and are prepared to join struggles against the wishes of their leaders',[150] and there was concrete evidence from elsewhere in Germany to support this contention. Nazis involved in welfare work schemes in Oldenburg, which was Nazi-governed, joined a Communist-led strike to protest against wage cuts the month before[151] and there were comparable events elsewhere at this time.[152]

Central to the KPD's United Front From Below tactic was the launching of strikes, but in this vital context the relationship between Communism and Nazism in the factories has most often been misunderstood. As often as not the NSBO has been characterised as a strikebreaking outfit, which operated precisely to undermine and even destroy working-class solidarity in the face of the layoffs and wage cuts that ravaged the industrial scene during the early 1930s. Implicitly at least, one is invited to draw parallels with the older-established company unions whose role certainly included the destruction of conventional trade union power in the workplace and perhaps also with the German Labour Front (DAF), established by the Nazis in May 1933, which organised workers, staff and management within single corporations, industry by industry. Its leader, Robert Ley, however, was careful to distinguish the DAF from the (by then defunct) NSBO in 1937 when dismissing the latter as 'every bit ideologically flawed as the [Free] Trade Unions'.[153] The NSBO, after all, set out to represent the class interests of workers and employees in the workplace even in the early 1930s. If the NSBO cannot be categorised among the 'economically peaceful', or non-striking unions, the RGO for its part cannot be compared unreservedly with the official unions. Both tactically and strategically it differed substantively from them and the precise objectives of the RGO need examining before the nature of RGO/NSBO relations can be fully understood.

The fundamental Communist attitude to the strike question was laid down by the Ninth ECCI Plenum on the Trade Union Question in February 1928, at which stage the incipient war against Social Democracy was uppermost in Comintern's mind. Social Democratic adherence to arbitration procedures, collective agreements and constructive relations with employers were branded as an 'industrial peace' which subjected the working class to the bourgeoisie. For the Comintern class warfare was the desirable norm in the workplace with any agreements between workers and management representing short-term ceasefires in this war. The official unions' mass following presented an obstacle to this strategy of course and it was 'therefore the job of Communists to pursue tactics which will enable them to seize strike leadership from the reformists'. As the ECCI continued:

> Every strike must be made the arena of struggle for leadership between communists and reformists. The communist attitude must therefore be designed to secure leadership in strikes. It is necessary to mobilize the masses under communist slogans . . . to expose the treacherous attitude of the reformists and, when the opportunity is favourable, organize strikes against the will of the trade union bureaucracy.[154]

By 1930, with the RGO in existence, the KPD set about putting these principles into practice. The RGO was to organise for, and prepare to lead, economic struggles in the face of 'the terror of the entrepreneurs and the social fascist bureaucracy'.[155] At the end of the day the RGO had to develop the capacity to lead strikes independently[156] and to do so in order to play for very high stakes indeed. As Ernst Thälmann declared at the Eleventh Plenum of the ECCI in 1931, the RGO, after completing the necessary ideological and organisational groundwork, would launch a growing wave of strikes with decidedly political, indeed revolutionary, objectives:

> A clear elaboration of the political dimension must always accompany the conduct of economic struggles; which in the nature of things will constantly enrich the working class's experience of strikes and thereby prepare the ground for the mass strike. There must be broad popularisation of all strike movements, especially political strikes, to strengthen the masses' support for political mass strikes.[157]

The final great political mass struggle was was intended to destroy the Weimar Republic and usher in a Bolshevik Germany, which made Social Democratic reluctance to participate in this grand design (far-fetched though the enterprise may have been) hardly surprising. That the NSBO's leadership was sceptical of the RGO's motives, to say the least, is equally understandable. Unlike the ADGB and the SPD, the NSBO had no interest in preserving the Weimar constitution, but the creation of a Marxist-Leninist Germany was most certainly not on the National Socialist agenda! Thus NSBO participation in RGO-led strikes on a formal basis was only likely to occur in the most exceptional of circumstances.[158]

The RGO's attitude to Nazi participation in their strike campaign made formal collaboration even more difficult and, indeed, made it more than likely that the NSBO's hierarchy would be actively hostile. Individual Nazis were to be welcomed into Communist-led strike campaigns, but their very participation, it was hoped, would divide them from their leaders and thereby undermine the NSBO as an organisation.[159] This determination to exclude Nazi organisations (as against individual members) from RGO-led strikes went as far as trying to exclude Nazis in uniform from performing picket duty and thereby making political capital on their own account.[160] The KPD's newspaper in Saxony, *Der Bolschewik*, included in its early December edition of 1932 a didactic account of a strike at the August Hoffmann textile works in Neugersdorf which no doubt reinforced the NSBO leadership's reserve, were this necessary:

> A strike committee consisting of Free Trade Union, Christian, unorganised, RGO and Nazi workers was elected. . . . The Nazis tried to offer cars to the strike committee in order to carry out joint collections. This was rejected by the strike committee.

The RGO here managed splendidly to organise the Nazi workers in the militant United Front under the leadership of the RGO. Striking Nazi workers participated in an Anti-fascist Struggle Congress as delegates. The Nazis participated in collections for the International Workers' Aid and in all strike duties.[161]

Similar successful strike campaigns were cited,[162] but the explicit politicisation of strikes by the RGO could often create as many problems as it solved. Thus *Der Bolschewik* reported on a strike in the Sörnewitz stoneware factory which failed not least because of RGO politicking. At the outset there was little Communist involvement in the strike. The RGO's cell had long since collapsed and its erstwhile leader was now convener of the NSBO group in the factory. The NSBO launched a strike against wage cuts, forming a committee with three NSBO, two ADGB and one KPD member, at which point the RGO sent in an external agitator to wrest control of the strike from the Nazis. This succeeded, but only at the cost of alienating the Social Democrats who pulled out of the strike, eventually agreed wage cuts, and thereby undermined the strike completely.[163] In this case the RGO had failed to win a strike and, once the Free Trade Unions had withdrawn, had been forced to conduct its campaign shoulder to shoulder with the NSBO as an organisation against the SPD. With the NSBO's leaders increasingly willing to participate in strikes where the KPD was involved, but not dominant, this situation where, de facto, Communists and Nazis were cooperating at organisational level rather than through the United Front From Below mechanism, worried Communist leaders. *Der Bolschewik* reported on a strike at the firm of Liebermann in the Flöha district in these terms in mid December:

> During the strike at Liebermann the Party did not succeed adequately in bringing the NSBO members, who were also striking, into conflict with their leaders and their party's policies. Thus the NSBO's factory cell exists as before. A systematic ideological struggle was not waged against the NSBO cell.[164]

Perhaps the KPD's own members on the ground forgot that Communist strikes were part of a longer-term political strategy and had become too involved in immediate shop-floor issues in their own right. Or perhaps the RGO was simply too weak to fulfil the ambitious tasks set for it.[165] Certainly the police in the Ruhr became increasingly sceptical of the RGO's capabilities by December and felt that the

Communists were exaggerating the extent of their successes.[166] In other cases the KPD press was remarkably frank about the strike campaign's problems in those major industrial centres where the NSBO was strong. Chemnitz was a case in point as *Der Bolschewik* complained in mid December 1932:

> Because the party organisation paid insufficient attention to the significance of the Central Committee's proclamation on national and social liberation, very grave weaknesses emerged on this section of the front, which also expressed itself in the NSDAP's strength in the city of Chemnitz and in the working class communities.
>
> A typical weakness in the struggle against the Nazis' social demagogy manifested itself during the strike by the Presto work-force. The NSBO joined the strike and succeeded in presenting itself as a workers' party while our factory cell has, so far, been unable to gain any influence over the Nazi workers and detach them from this party of strikebreakers.[167]

Of course it must have been especially difficult to brand the NSBO as a strikebreaking organisation just when it was showing an increasing proclivity to join or even mount strikes, as the KPD itself admitted.[168] Still worse were cases where the RGO, unable to control workforces politically, played the classic dog-in-the-manger. As *Der Bolschewik* admitted in mid December: 'In Ruppertsgrün [Saxony] things got to the point where the Nazis and SPD workers struck, while the workers who sympathised with us acted as strike-breakers'.[169]

Clearly, rather than being involved on the employers' side in a single-front war between labour and capital, the NSBO had become involved in a civil war within the labour movement as a relatively small, but increasingly prominent, participant. Thus by November 1932 the authorities noted that the RGO's National Committee was attaching 'particular significance to the National Socialists' present tendency to introduce their factory cell organisation as an independent trade union, as a negotiating force and a wage bargainer'.[170] The situation had become exceptionally complex for the Communist movement, as a more detailed consideration of the strike question illustrates.

As in other contexts, the KPD sought at the outset to meet the Nazis head on when it came to mounting strike campaigns. In an article entitled 'Down with the Fascist Murderers!', *Die Rote Fahne* declared in August 1929: 'Either you must organise defences against the fascist strikebreakers, or your struggle for better living conditions will be defeated by fascist terror.'[171] Similarly the *Arbeiter Zeitung* reported in January 1930 on a strike at the Nordsee-Werke in Emden where the introduction of Stalhelm and Nazi strikebreakers by the management had simply stiffened the resolve of the striker to bring the struggle to a successful conclusion.[172] By July, however, the RGO in the Ruhr District, while alluding to the Nazis' strikebreaking role in south-west Germany and the Mansfeld region, began to argue that the enemy was already within:

> Factory fascism is a dangerous enemy for the militant proletarian class. Therefore we must pursue an ideological campaign in the factories . . . to win over the workers who stand in its ranks.[173]

The same report attached particular importance to young workers in this context, presumably because their lack of political experience made them especially vulnerable to Nazism.[174] Soon after this the RGO admitted that alleged strikebreaking by the NSBO was related to the overt politicisation of strikes by the Communist movement. The Red Trade Union International's Fifth Congress reported in October 1930 that the Nazis had withdrawn from strikes in the Mansfeld area 'because the struggles have become political strikes under the leadership of the RGO'.[175] The Central Committee wrote in similar vein in November, but by then lumped the Nazis together with the Free Trade Unions as reprehensible bodies unwilling to further the political fortunes of the Communist movement; on this occasion in the context of the Berlin metalworkers' strike:

> The National Socialists' decision to participate in the strike proved to be a demagogic maneouvre to obscure from the masses their anti-working class character, as a means – as the NSDAP's leaders have explained to Saxon industrialists – of gaining influence within the working class. In fact, during the strike, the Nazis were merely an appendage of the reformist trade union bureaucracy and only agreed to strike when the DMV [German Metalworkers' Union] made the strike official [!].[176]

This identification of the Nazi movement with the Social Democrats was an equation to be repeated until the final days of Weimar,[177] but which effectively isolated the RGO politically in the factories at organisational level as the NSBO and ADGB edged towards the forging of tentative working agreements, particularly during early 1933.[178]

This is not to dismiss the RGO's United Front From Below strike campaign as a complete failure *vis à vis* the Nazis. Even when the NSBO pulled out of RGO-led 'political' strikes, the Communist movement could score propaganda points by presenting the move as strikebreaking pure and simple, often to the discomfiture of the Nazis themselves.[179] As previously intimated,[180] the RGO was able to recruit Nazis to strike committees on Communist terms, particularly from mid 1932 onwards.[181] Similarly it has been seen that the RGO could sometimes persuade Nazis to join Communist-led strikes even when their leaders were opposed to this.[182] As the Anti-Fascist Action's National Committee commented in October 1932, despite the terroristic inclinations of their leaders, 'the proletarian Nazi supporters and members are participating in various strike, rent and unemployment campaigns'.[183] On other occasions, as during the strike at the Zeiss-Ikon Filmworks in Berlin in the same month, the Nazis were dragooned into the strike by their workmates despite their initial wishes to to the contrary.[184] The notorious Berlin Transport Workers' strike of November 1932 was, therefore, no more than a single, albeit spectacular, example of the web of fraternisation and conflict that the Communist Party and the RGO had woven within the German labour movement.[185] On this occasion the ADGB leadership was quickly divided from much of its membership while the NSBO members also subsequently remained on strike even after their leaders had had second thoughts.[186] Small wonder then that Thälmann was greatly encouraged by the BVG strike[187] which was soon to be followed by significant United Front successes during the canal workers' strike on the Hunte in Oldenburg.[188]

By 4 November the International Workers' Aid in Berlin claimed that more than 600 political strikes had been launched since 15 September against the State of Emergency declared by the Papen government. Furthermore, it claimed that the majority had been successful, with failure only occurring when the ADGB or the National Socialists broke the United Front.[189] It does, however, remain a moot point as to how strong the Communist factory campaign really was and here the movement's own, more sober, testimony was especially damning. Political persecution of the Communists by the authorities and factory owners[190] had been compounded throughout the early 1930s by indifferent political campaigning by party activists, said by one district leadership to 'lack backbone' in the factories.[191]

Most worrying was the evident reluctance of activists to work the factories properly to gain a solid organisational base,[192] either through recruitment drives,[193] the holding of meetings[194] or even the distribution of news-sheets;[195] assuming these were produced at all. The exceptions to this dismal state of affairs were relatively few either in time or place and thus it is not surprising that factory workers, assuming they might have been receptive in the first place, were indifferent to, or even derisive of, most Communist attempts to effect the salvation of their class. Working was usually preferable to attending KPD meetings,[196] while during the political campaigning seasons factory workers could often find rival parties' meetings a more attractive option.[197] Thus can be understood the observation of the Reich Interior Ministry in October 1930 that 'the Party's capacity for action is much more limited than its vote,[198] as it surveyed the effects of the KPD's factory campaign in the Ruhr in particular.

This situation militated directly against any successful outcome to the KPD's strike campaign. With factory cells established in less than 18 per cent of medium-sized and larger-sized factories (200-plus employees), the KPD's Organisational Section in Berlin wrote in March 1931 of the 'colossal expenditure of political initiative and energy' necessary to remedy matters.[199] Yet, in October, the Central Committee admitted that the strike campaign was going badly and wrote that among the 'crass and damaging failings' was the 'complete inadequacy of factory work and the threatening decline in the proportion of factory workers in the party despite its furious growth overall'.[200] The full extent of the problem was graphically illustrated by reports from the Ruhr District where the KPD was, of course, electorally strong. In November 1930 the Ruhr KPD regarded the factory cells' performance as too weak to allow decisive support for any strike movement[201] and during 1931 the party here in Germany's industrial heartland doubted its capacity to launch political strikes at all.[202] By mid 1932 the Central Committee was openly critical of its Ruhr subordinates, complaining that 'the KPD's battle cry of political mass strikes has not been followed in a single [Ruhr] factory by the Young Communists',[203] while the September edition of the Ruhr KPD's newspaper, *Pionier des Bolschewismus,* admitted publicly that: 'Despite the objectively favourable situation, we have failed to precipitate significant struggles in the factories.'[204]

Thus, it is only fair to conclude, the United Front From Below strategy was, in the context of the strike campaign, pursued from a position of weakness rather than strength. This problem permeated

most dimensions of the KPD's factory campaign, including its relationship with Nazism in this context. The use of the United Front tactic, it
might be said, contained an inherent contradiction in the realm of
factory politics as elsewhere which left it fatally flawed. It had emerged
in the early 1920s out of the Communist movement's weakness, in
order to attain by stealth and in a circumvented manner the mass
working-class support that failed to materialise from any direct appeal
to the proletariat on Marxist-Leninist terms.[205] By-passing the rival
institutions of the labour movement in this way undoubtedly possessed
a certain logic in such circumstances, but the advisability of extended
attempts to fraternise with rank-and-file members of rival organisations must be questioned if and when these were proving, or were
becoming, stronger and more dynamic than the KPD and its affiliates.
Some ordinary Communists evidently baulked at applying the United
Front From Below strategy at all in these impropitious circumstances,
while others, in following their leaders' instructions, were, effectively,
brought to fraternise with the powerful and self-confident Nazi
movement. In the fall of 1932 the balance of power did temporarily tilt
towards the KPD, but after January, and more especially March, 1933
few radical factory workers could have entertained serious doubts as to
where the political initiative lay, at least for the foreseeable future.
The consequences for the KPD were to be catastrophic.

Conclusion

Before 1933 the KPD had made plans for working under conditions of illegality, but, like other oppositional groups it had not foreseen the rigours of operating in National Socialist Germany.[1] After the March 1933 elections, Hitler pushed the Enabling Act through the Reichstag which banned all non-Nazi political parties. Even before this, the authorities had used the notorious Reichstag fire as a pretext for rounding up some ten thousand Communist activists[2] and by the end of 1933 over 100 000 had been incarcerated in makeshift concentration camps (for a time at least) where several thousand were killed.[3] Most senior Communist leaders sought safety in exile although some, including Thälmann, were arrested and eventually killed. Under these circumstances it is remarkable that significant numbers of KPD members continued to resist as best they could, but by 1935 any form of organised, coherent resistance was becoming well-nigh impossible. The history of Communist resistance to Nazism becomes increasingly like a roll-call of martyrs with the passage of time.[4]

This history has, belatedly,[5] received deserved attention from Western historians in recent years,[6] but in order, perhaps, to compensate for past neglect and to emphasise the Communists' role in the resistance, the movement prior to 1933 is sometimes portrayed in idealised terms as a disciplined, coherent body which had experienced little or no contact with Nazism.[7] Its capacity and willingness to resist after January 1933 have, therefore, been seen as self-evident, but, as the preceding chapters have shown, the reality was very different. Although relations between the Communists and National Socialists were usually bad, the KPD's United Front From Below strategy meant that, at grassroots level, they were often intimate. Furthermore, the evidence used to argue otherwise has sometimes been presented in a highly selective and potentially misleading way. Much, for instance, is made of the evidence that only two out of 2825 recruits to the KPD in the Ruhr District and none of the 824 in the Lower Rhine district during December 1931 were former Nazis. This might appear to demonstrate the lack of contacts between the two movements, but in addition to the body of more elaborate evidence to the contrary, the inability of the KPD to attract more than sixteeen Social Democrats in the Ruhr and its inability to recruit a single Social Democrat in the Lower Rhine district during that December (indicated by the same

189

documentary source) is passed over in silence.[8] Yet without understanding that the KPD recruited few members from any rival mass party before 1933, the significance of the low Nazi figure could easily be misunderstood. At the other extreme it is claimed that perhaps a third of the SA's membership after Hitler's takeover were former Communists.[9] This may have been so in particular localities, but the scant statistical evidence which is available suggests that the proportion was much lower in Germany as a whole.[10]

Part of the problem undoubtedly lies with the enormous turnover in membership that the Communist movement had experienced before Hitler came to power, which leaves the historian hard put to define precisely who among the new recruits to the Nazi movement during 1933 were or were not former 'Communists'. Most of the KPD's members had been relative newcomers who were often politically uneducated and some hint of the problems this created for the Communist movement after Hitler's takeover are found in the contemporary observation that 'weaklings in our ranks capitulated',[11] or in the subsequent assessment that 'many . . . who had only recently joined . . . fell away and did not renew contact with the movement'.[12] However, the KPD suffered from more than a massive loss of members during the spring of 1933; it soon faced organisational paralysis which reduced the movement to a collection of scattered groups of individuals fighting against overwhelming odds.[13]

The records of three KPD sub-districts give a telling impression of the agonies the party suffered during this period. By mid April just two factory cells with a combined membership of fifteen survived in the Osnabrück sub-district; in its individual township groups matters were equally desperate. In Osnabrück itself a fear of persecution combined with an unwillingness to work for the party any longer and with a near-absence of funds to stymie the local KPD's prospects. In the outlying towns the situation was as bad. Things were tolerable in Gaste, where money could still be collected and 40 per cent of members were still active, but in Bramsche, despite an absence of arrests and only one house search, dues were no longer collected and, after the March elections, contact was lost with Osnabrück. In Lengerich, too, all activity had ended, because a threesome of members could not be assembled and the arrest of the treasurer with the consequent loss of all financial records prevented the collection of any dues. In the smaller towns of Wissingen and Vehrte matters were in a poor state, especially since some members had begun deserting to the Nazis even before the March election.[14] In the Lage sub-district things were no better:

'Because of arrests the whole party has been torn to shreds; we have re-established contact with twelve township groups with about 100 members as against a previous 500.'[15] In the Ruhr District waves of arrests combined with intensive recruitment by the NSBO[16] so that by May the RGO had all but collapsed. In the Essen and Düsseldorf districts just seven per cent of RGO dues could still be collected and the surviving party officials were forced to take over the running of the organisation. The collapse in party membership was also dramatic, to the point where Communist officials saw little future in overt resistance for the time being and, according to police sources, concluded that: 'The only solution is for KPD members who have been able to join the NSDAP to keep a watchful eye on all political developments and to report on any setbacks for the government.'[17]

One might be forgiven for suspecting that official reports of this kind contained an element of gleeful exaggeration, but in fact the transfer of Communists to the Nazi movement began to assume such proportions that the authorities became increasingly worried over the possible implications of this process. On some occasions the KPD was evidently hoping to infiltrate reliable members into Nazi organisations, sometimes to encourage or exploit discontent among working-class Nazi and at other times to win the confidence of local leaders and thereby gain access to weapons.[18] Individual Communist saboteurs were arrested on occasion[19] and the feeling grew among the public during 1933 and early 1934 that not just saboteurs, but also many of the wilder elements from the KPD had simply resurfaced in SA uniform, or come to dominate whole SA units.[20] The SA's leaders were unable to deny these accusations outright,[21] but, while disruptive, these ex-Communists were not in a position to pose any direct threat to the Nazi regime. The KPD itself understood this, arguing that the mass transfer of Communists to the National Socialist movement would not benefit the resistance in any way,[22] but it could not prevent such transfers which in these circumstances amounted to little more than mass desertions.[23] The Westphalian Police President became very concerned about developments in Germany's industrial heartland by late March 1933, urging extreme caution in dealing with these former Communists:

It has been established in numerous cases that former Communists, or people who were at least attached to the KPD as supporters, have transferred to the NSDAP or SA in substantial numbers. The SA Command is being informed immediately of such developments.

The transferred personnel are being closely observed and are being subjected to a particularly long period of probation. We shall have to be extremely careful about finally accepting [them].[24]

Contemporary accounts testify to desertions from the Communist to the Nazi movement in many parts of Germany[25] and oppositional observers did not try to disguise the scale of the phenomenon, although they attempted to put as favourable a gloss on events as possible.[26]

As one might have expected, the Communist movement also lost most of its passive supporters after the March elections and in the specific context of the factory council elections, the Nazis were the main beneficiaries of the collapsed RGO vote. On a national basis the NSBO did not do particularly well, receiving 11.7 per cent of the workers' votes as against 73.4 per cent for the ADGB. However, the RGO received just 4.9 per cent and in former RGO strongholds a veritable collapse in the Communist vote allowed the NSBO to chalk up some spectacular gains.[27] In the case of Duisburg, for instance, the RGO's share of the workers' votes fell from 33 to seven per cent as the NSBO's rose from 12 to 35 per cent (with the vote for the ADGB and the Catholic unions steady, or even rising).[28] It appears that a direct transfer of votes occurred from the RGO to the NSBO, which probably owed something to political terror,[29] but also bore eloquent testimony to the risks inherent in the Communist movement's attempts to pursue a United Front from Below policy from a narrow organisational base and with a mass of transient and often passive supporters.

What, then of the KPD's political strategy in these desperate circumstances? Its initial response to the burgeoning catastrophe had been to call a general strike upon the appointment of Hitler as Chancellor. The party had done the same when Papen had suspended the Prussian government in July 1932, but then, as in 1933, this appeal failed to elicit a response from factory workers.[30] Attempts to organise mass strikes and ultimately a general strike were not immediately abandoned, but the KPD recognised the scale of the NSDAP's electoral success in March which had seen many ex-Nazi converts to Communism switch back to the NSDAP.[31] This, Communist leaders felt, demanded a continuation of the previous policy of whipping up working-class resistance to Nazism on the one hand[32] and pursuing a United Front opening to ordinary Nazis on the other.[33] There were, therefore, frequent calls to meet the SA's violence in kind,[34] and some instances where this occurred,[35] but success was very limited. The balance of power was decisively with the Nazis who were now backed by the full rigour of the law. Furthermore, the SA's membership often came from the same neighbourhoods as their Communist rivals which made the latter's predicament all the more precarious in early 1933. Thus the Red Front reminded its members in late February that: 'The SA often knows our people in the working-class areas and also knows which organisations they belong to, which makes the task of denunciation an easy one.'[36] As for the United Front From Below tactic, it became far more defensive than hitherto. The KPD appealed, sometimes plaintively, to working-class Nazis to stop attacking their class brothers: 'SA comrades, don't let your leaders misuse you against the working class!'[37] or, as the Hamburg KPD warned:

> Working members of the Hitler Party, SA and SS! Recognise what's happening. You won't get bread and work, as Hitler has promised you a thousand times; instead you are going to be spurred on to fratricide against your fellow workers.[38]

Similarly, the KPD urged working-class Nazis to recognise that Hitler's government was a capitalist dictatorship and that his social programme was a sham:

> SA proletarians! Hitler and his lackeys have been in power since January. What was he going to give the workers? Work and bread! You got work from Hitler, but no bread! Instead he's given you the 'moral' value of work. You receive the 'moral' value and the top brass in the system take the profits![39]

There was undoubtedly a fair deal of this sort of discontent within the SA in particular which the KPD could and did address,[40] although it recognised that the expectations of many proletarian Nazi supporters would not dissipate overnight.[41] These appeals continued even after the Röhm purge of mid 1934 initiated a scaling down of the SA and the appointment of leaders who were prepared to stamp out the organisation's potential as an inchoate source of mass opposition to the government.[42] However, this tactic was of little more than nuisance value, given the KPD's weakness and the SA's isolation from much of the employed working class. Thus, at the time of the Röhm purge in mid 1934, the KPD distributed leaflets in Bavaria condemning Hitler's brutal action in which many senior SA leaders and other opponents of the regime were killed without trial, but the authorities noted that the workers in particular were relieved to see the disruptive SA brought to heel.[43] In effect the KPD found itself in the rather curious position of trying to encourage and even coordinate resistance to Hitler's government within dissident sections of the Nazi movement[44] rather than being able to lead any kind of mass struggle in its own right.

This marked the end of the road for the KPD's United Front From Below policy. It had sown distrust among Social Democrats and proved ultimately futile among National Socialists. Soon enough the KPD and Comintern began to re-establish relations with the Social Democratic leadership in order to initiate a low level, unarmed guerilla-style struggle against Hitler's regime. This struggle was troublesome for the authorities, but appears not to have attained critical dimensions[45] and Hitler's Reich was eventually to fall to the armed might of foreign adversaries after a bitterly contested struggle.

Despite the strenuous efforts of its leaders the KPD had failed to surmount the formidable obstacles which barred the way to its revolutionary objectives. The durability of the Social Democratic movement has long been acknowledged as crucial in this regard, but too little attention has been paid to the KPD's struggle against the radical Right and in particular against the National Socialists. The leaders of the Communist movement found that this relationship was conditioned by an exceptionally broad and complex range of factors which forced them to take the threat posed by the far right very seriously indeed. The KPD's inherent organisational weakness and the remarkably eclectic ideological and social appeal of the right-wing radicals created an ever-present threat of the far right stealing the Communist movement's radical thunder. The Russian government's wish to encourage anti-Western forces in Germany and the resonance of the national question right across Weimar society conspired to complicate matters all the more.

This is not to question the inherent hostility between the radical extremes. Although they shared many enemies and sometimes formed short-term tactical alliances, both determined to be the sole successor to Weimar. However, once their early putschist adventures had foundered, both radical left and right came to realise that the overthrow of Weimar would be no simple matter and would require the mobilisation of mass support. Hitler strove to win over 50 per cent of the vote (unheard of in German electoral history) while the KPD sought to mobilise the politically heterogeneous industrial labour force and as many other employees as possible within a single, revolutionary labour organisation. Both faced the opposition of republican and conservative groupings (although the latter was equivocal about the NSDAP) and both were always worried that the other might tap the pool of discontent that they themselves sought to exploit.

It was the KPD's particular misfortune that the working classes were the social group most supportive of the Republic, which made it very hard to confront the republican SPD head on. The KPD therefore employed its United Front From Below strategy to inveigle rank-and-file Socialists into collaboration with the Communist movement; a tactic the Social Democratic leadership rightly interpreted as a declaration of war. Once the radical right began to attract mass support, some of it working class, the KPD quite logically extended the United Front strategy further rightwards to destabilise and eventually destroy this new set of rival organisations. However, at least some Communist leaders appreciated that the weaker the KPD and the stronger its rivals, the riskier this strategy would become, since it contained the possibility of their own organisation being the worse disrupted. The seeds of the 1933 catastrophe were sown in profusion, well in advance.

The United Front From Below strategy was, therefore, inherently self-contradictory. It was a response to Communist weakness and yet the personal, often constructive, links it demanded with political rivals presumed a coherent, highly-motivated party organisation. This the KPD and its affiliates lacked, while the National Socialist movement by contrast was able to gain a sufficiently large and coherent working-class constituency to ride out the Communist assault. This lends credence to the hypothesis advanced recently of the National Socialists constituting a mass movement which represented an exceptionally broad coalition of social and ideological interests. Indeed the serious-ness with which the KPD had to take Nazism, and the history of their relationship, suggests that this coalition embraced even limited numbers of trade union-minded, revolutionary workers, some of whom had turned away from the SPD, exasperated by its moderation.

What, then, of traditional lines of historical inquiry which have sought to explain the origins and development of National Socialism by reference to the resentments, fears and aspirations of the lower middle classes? This study has not sought to invalidate this vast range of research and writing *tout court*, but indicates that attempts to account for the rise of Nazism solely through the politics of the lower middle classes can produce only a partial explanation for the phenomenon and might also, in some cases, unwittingly produce a distorted image of the crisis of inter-war Germany. Even some of the KPD's leaders possessed the courage and the insight to recognise that National Socialism had come to embrace a remarkably eclectic social constituency (a feat they sought to emulate in their own way) and that this social constituency displayed a remarkable degree of ideological eclecticism. Not all working-class Nazis, or even all of its petty bourgeois following, could, the KPD realised, be shoehorned into a reactionary, 'Pooterite' mould, for the rise of the Nazi movement resulted in part from the problems experienced by typical working-class Germans at that time. These Nazis the Communist movement wished to recruit, sought to recruit and even needed to recruit, so significant were their numbers. The KPD's leaders believed that National Socialism's ideological and social heterogeneity would, ultimately, prove to be its Achilles' heel. In the event, however, this very diversity, while not without its problems, was a vital factor in permitting the emergence of National Socialism as a mass movement sufficiently powerful first to undermine the Weimar Republic and then to set the Third Reich in its stead.

Notes

1   THE EARLY KPD: Responses to weakness

1. R. M. Watt, *The Kings Depart. The Tragedy of Germany: Versailles and the German Revolution* (London, 1968) p. 157.
2. O. K. Flechtheim, *Die KPD in der Weimarer Republik* (Frankfurt-am-Main, 1969) p. 116. Watt, op. cit. p. 198.
3. G. D. Feldman, *Vom Weltkrieg zur Weltwirtschaftskrise. Studien zur deutschen Wirtschafts- und Sozialgeschichte 1914–1932* (Göttingen, 1984) p. 71; M. Nolan, *Social Democracy and Society. Working-class Radicalism in Düsseldorf, 1890-1920* (Cambridge, 1981) Part II. cf. J. Gerber, 'From Left Radicalism to Council Communism: Anton Pannekoek and German Revolutionary Marxism', *Journal of Contemporary History*, 23 (2) (1988) pp. 172–7.
4. Feldman, *Weltkrieg*, p. 72; cf. D. Geary, *European Labour Protest 1848–1939* (London, 1981) p. 136 ff; Gerber, op. cit. p. 179; Nolan, op. cit. p. 260 ff.
5. J. A. Moses, *Trade Unionism in Germany from Bismarck to Hitler 1869-1933*, vol. I (Totowa, NJ, 1982) pp. 218–9.
6. Feldman, *Weltkrieg*, pp. 71,2. Geary, *European Labour*, p. 142.
7. Feldman, *Weltkrieg*, p. 79; Gerber, op. cit. pp. 174–7.
8. Gerber, op. cit. pp. 177–80; Nolan, op. cit. p. 267.
9. Nolan, op. cit. p. 262; Watt, op. cit. p. 128.
10. Watt, op. cit. p. 172.
11. F. L. Carsten, *Revolution in Central Europe 1918–1919* (Aldershot, 1988) pp. 130–3; Gerber, op. cit. p. 178; Nolan, op. cit. p. 267.
12. Carsten, *Revolution*, p. 134; cf. R. Rurup, 'Problems of the German Revolution 1918–1919', *Journal of Contemporary History*, 3 (4) (1968) p. 121.
13. A. J. Ryder, *The German Revolution of 1918. A Study of German Socialism in War and Revolt* (Cambridge, 1967) p. 194.
14. H. A. Winkler, *Von der Revolution zur Stabilisierung. Arbeiter und Arbeiterbewegung in der Weimarer Republik 1918 bis 1924* (Berlin, Bonn, 1984) p. 115.
15. B. Fowkes, *Communism in Germany under the Weimar Republic* (London, 1984) p. 19; cf. Ryder, op. cit. pp. 194–5.
16. Carsten, *Revolution*, p. 212; Ryder, op. cit. pp. 195, 196–7.
17. Winkler, *Revolution*, p. 116.
18. In full, the 'Communist Party of Germany, Spartacus League'.
19. Winkler, *Revolution*, pp. 116–7, 119; cf. Carsten, *Revolution*, p. 211.
20. F. Borkenau, *World Communism. A History of the Communist International* (Ann Arbor, Mich., 1962) p. 144; cf. Fowkes, op. cit. p. 21.

21. Carsten, *Revolution*, p. 211; A. Rosenberg, *Geschichte der Weimarer Republik*, 20th edn (Frankfurt-am-Main, 1980) p. 23.
22. Borkenau, op. cit. pp. 86–7; Winkler, *Revolution*, p. 118. See also; L. Kochan, *Russia and the Weimar Republic* (Cambridge, 1954) p. 16.
23. A. Klönne, *Die deutsche Arbeiterbewegung. Geschichte, Ziele, Wirkungen*, 3rd edn (Cologne, 1983) pp. 162–3; cf. Ryder, op. cit. p. 195.
24. Rosenberg, op. cit. pp. 51, 2.
25. Watt, op. cit. p. 125; Rosenberg, op. cit. p. 33.
26. Gerber, op. cit. p. 181; Ryder, op. cit. p. 198.
27. Rosenberg, op. cit. p. 52.
28. Carsten, *Revolution*, p. 214.
29. Quoted in Flechtheim, op. cit. p. 129; cf. Carsten, *Revolution*, p. 214; A. Dorpalen, *German History in Marxist Perspective. The East German Approach* (London, 1985) pp. 317–8.
30. The USPD members left the government at the end of December.
31. Ryder, op. cit. p. 201; Winkler, *Revolution*, pp. 121–2.
32. For a contemporary account; R. Müller, *Der Bürgerkrieg in Deutschland: Geburtswehen der Republik* (Berlin, 1925) pp. 35, 49, 58; cf. Rosenberg, op. cit. p. 56.
33. W. J. Mommsen, 'The German Revolution 1918–1920: Political Revolution and Social Protest Movement', in R. J. Bessel and E. J. Feuchtwanger (eds), *Social Change and Political Development in Weimar Germany* (London, 1981) pp. 43–4.
34. Ibid.
35. Rosenberg, op. cit. p. 76; Winkler, *Revolution*, pp. 159–78.
36. For accounts of these troubles: Nolan, op. cit. pp. 290–5; Ryder, op. cit. pp. 210–17; Winkler, *Revolution*, pp. 159–82.
37. Among general accounts of the SPD's role in the Revolution are; Ryder, op. cit. p. 165 ff.; Watt, op. cit. 203–389; Winkler, *Revolution*, pp. 68–205. See also; R. Rurup, 'Demokratische Revolution und „dritter Weg". Die deutsche Revolution von 1918/19 in der neueren wissenschaftlichen Diskussion', *Geschichte und Gesellschaft*, 9(2) (1983) p. 292 ff.
38. Ryder, op. cit. p. 194.
39. See Dorpalen, *German History*, pp. 313–24 for a general account of East German work in this area, and also Rurup, 'Demokratische Revolution', p. 283.
40. J. Petzold (ed.), *Deutschland im Ersten Weltkrieg*, 2nd edn, vol. 3 (Berlin, 1970) p. 590.
41. Ibid., pp. 590–1. For a more recent general account coached in these terms, at least regarding the SPD; S. Haffner, *1918–19. Eine deutsche Revolution* (Hamburg, 1981).
42. On this particular point East German historians would by and large concur; Dorpalen, *German History*, p. 323.
43. Geary, *European Labour* pp. 158–60. Geary also stresses the political potential of the middle classes, but cf. Ryder, op. cit. p. 217.
44. B. Moore Jr, *Injustice. The Social Bases of Obedience and Revolt* (London, 1978) pp. 183, 247, 255.

45. For instance; Geary, *European Labour*, p. 124; Gerber, op. cit. pp. 173–7; Nolan, op. cit. pp. 240–5.
46. Moore, op. cit. p. 260; cf. S. F. Hickey, *Workers in Imperial Germany. The Miners of the Ruhr* (Oxford, 1985) pp. 297–303.
47. Moore, op. cit. p. 274.
48. Hickey, op. cit. p. 295.
49. Ibid., p. 293.
50. K. Rohe, *Vom Revier zum Ruhrgebiet. Wahlen. Parteien. Politische Kultur* (Essen, 1986) esp. pp. 12–29, 43–59.
51. See pp. 2–3 above; cf. Feldman, *Weltkrieg,* p. 69.
52. cf. E. H. Tobin, 'War and the Working Class: The Case of Düsseldorf 1914–1918', *Central European History,* 18(3/4) (1985) pp. 257–98.
53. Mommsen, 'German Revolution', p. 32; cf. H. Mommsen, 'Sozialpolitik im Ruhrbergbau', in H. Mommsen, D. Petzina, B. Weisbrod (eds), *Industrielles System und Politische Entwicklung in der Weimarer Republik,* vol. I (Düsseldorf, 1977) pp. 312–13; Hickey, op. cit. p. 301; Moore, op. cit. pp. 323–6.
54. Mommsen, 'German Revolution', pp. 28, 35; cf. Gerber, op. cit. pp. 181, 183–4.
55. Mommsen, 'German Revolution', pp. 36–9.
56. Rosenberg, op. cit. pp. 41–2; cf. Borkenau, op. cit. p. 143.
57. Mommsen, 'German Revolution', pp.24–5; Rosenberg, op. cit. pp.41–2.
58. Borkenau, op. cit. p. 92.
59. J. Tampke, *The Ruhr and Revolution. The Revolutionary Movement in the Rhenish-Westphalian Industrial Region 1912–1919* (London, 1979) p. 161.
60. J. Kocka, *Facing Total War. German Society 1914–1918* (Leamington Spa, 1984) pp. 160–1.
61. Ibid., p. 160.
62. Tampke, op. cit. p. 162; cf. Gerber's discussion of developments in Bremen, op. cit. pp. 179–80, 184–5.
63. Winkler, *Revolution,* p. 182.
64. cf. Nolan, op. cit. p. 270, where she contrasts the more political radicalism of Düsseldorf with the economic radicalism of the Ruhr.
65. Ryder, op. cit. p. 210.
66. Tampke, op. cit. p. 161; cf. Rurup, 'Demokratische Revolution', p. 228.
67. cf. Moore, op. cit. pp. 318–20.
68. Rosenberg, op. cit. p. 24.
69. Borkenau, op. cit. pp. 145–6; cf. Gerber, op. cit. pp. 184–5.
70. See p.5 above.
71. Rosenberg, op. cit. p. 52.
72. Klönne, op. cit. pp. 162–3; Mommsen, 'German Revolution', pp. 40–1.
73. cf. Haffner, op. cit. pp. 206–9.
74. Ryder, op. cit. pp. 213–14; Fowkes, op. cit. pp. 30–4.
75. cf. Gerber, op. cit. pp. 181–2.
76. Flechtheim, op. cit. pp. 144, 146.
77. Fowkes, op. cit. pp. 36–7.
78. Flechtheim, op. cit. p. 144; Gerber, op. cit. p. 182. O.-E. Schüddekopf,

Linke Leute von rechts. Die nationalrevolutionären Minderheiten und der Kommunismus in der Weimarer Republik (Stuttgart, 1960) p. 115.

79. Kochan, op. cit. pp. 19–20; Schüddekopf, op. cit. p. 100.
80. Staatsarchiv Bremen (SB), Polizei-Direktion Bremen (4,65)/226/38. 'Die Spaltung der Kommunisten', *Vorwärts*, 26 October 1919; cf. Gerber, op. cit. pp. 182–3 who omits discussion of the national question.
81. Winkler, *Revolution*, pp. 477–8, but cf. the attitude of the left at the Heidelberg Conference; p.12 above.
82. For accounts of the merging of the USPD left with the KPD; Fowkes, op. cit. pp. 40-53. R. F. Wheeler, *USPD und Internationale. Sozialistischer Internationalismus in der Zeit der Revolution* (Frankfurt-am-Main, 1975) pp. 189–258. For an account of the KAPD's position; Winkler, *Revolution*, pp. 502-4.
83. Rosenberg, op. cit. p. 118; cf. Gerber, op. cit. p. 182.
84. J. Degras (ed.), *The Communist International 1919–1943. Documents*, vol. I (London, 1971) pp. 82–3; cf. Gerber, op. cit. p. 183.
85. R. N. Hunt, *German Social Democracy. 1918–1933* (Chicago, 1970) p. 224.
86. Kochan, op. cit. pp. 32–3; Winkler, *Revolution*, p. 470.
87. Fowkes, op. cit. p. 53; Winkler, *Revolution*, pp. 471–3.
88. Borkenau, op. cit. p. 200. Degras, op. cit., I, p. 196; Flechtheim, op. cit. p. 347; Fowkes, op. cit. p. 53; Winkler, *Revolution*, pp. 504–5.
89. Klönne, op. cit. p. 212.
90. Fowkes, op. cit. p. 53; Borkenau, op. cit. p. 200; Winkler, *Revolution*, pp. 473–4.
91. Winkler, *Revolution*, pp. 473–4, 503.
92. Borkenau, op. cit. p. 200; Rosenberg, op. cit. p. 119.
93. Hunt, op. cit. p. 100.
94. Ibid., pp. 199–200, 212.
95. Ibid., p. 169; cf. Borkenau, op. cit. p. 259, who gives a figure of 88.
96. Borkenau, op. cit. p. 259.
97. Bundesarchiv Koblenz (BA), Reichskommissar für die Überwachung der öffentlichen Ordnung und Nachrichtensammelstelle im Reichsministerium des Innern (RKo). Lageberichte (1920–1929) und Meldungen (1929–1933) (R134)/4(147), 18 January 1921. I.
98. Winkler, *Revolution*, pp. 510–11, 514.
99. For accounts of the March Action; Borkenau, op. cit. pp. 213–20; Flechtheim, op. cit. pp. 159–64; Fowkes, op. cit. pp. 63–8; Winkler, *Revolution*, pp. 515–18.
100. Quoted in Borkenau, op. cit. p. 216.
101. Borkenau, op. cit. p. 216.
102. Quoted in Winkler, *Revolution*, p. 518.
103. cf. Winkler, *Revolution*, pp. 518–19, note 260.
104. Degras, op. cit., I, p. 216.
105. BA R134/9 (62–3). RKo 38, 10 May 1921. I.
106. Fowkes, op. cit. pp. 68–73; Winkler, *Revolution*, p. 519.
107. cf. Winkler, *Revolution*, p. 520.

108. *For a full account of this strategy:* Winkler, *Revolution* pp. 537–49.
109. Kochan, op. cit. p. 71.
110. Quoted in Degras, op. cit., I, p. 224.
111. Flechtheim, op. cit. p. 236; cf. Winkler, *Revolution,* p. 538.
112. Rosenberg, op. cit. p. 121.
113. Paraphrased in Borkenau, op. cit. p. 224.
114. Flechtheim, op. cit. p. 347.
115. BA R134/17(31); RKo 69, 7 April 1922, 1; cf. Moses, op. cit., II, p. 439, note 77, where a strong Communist/Syndicalist presence in the Factory Councils in the Ruhr Mining District during 1921/22 is noted.
116. Fowkes, op. cit. pp. 82–3.
117. See pp. 46–9, 55–61, 68–9, 78–80, and ch.6, 8 and 9.
118. Winkler, *Revolution,* p. 545; cf. Kochan, op. cit. pp. 72–3.
119. Quoted in Degras, op. cit., I, p. 12. See also W. Bramke, 'Zum Verhalten der Mittelschichten in der Novemberrevolution', *Zeitschrift für Geschichtswissenschaft,* 31 (8) (1983) p. 698, for the initial German Communist attitude to the question.
120. Degras, op. cit., I, pp. 12, 15.
121. Borkenau, op. cit. p. 189.
122. Flechtheim, op. cit. p. 155. For further references to Comintern's concern over the peasant question; A. A. Anikeev, 'Zur marxistischen Historiographie über die Bauernpolitik des deutschen Faschismus', *Zeitschrift für Geschichtswissenschaft,* 19 (1971) pp. 1385–87.
123. Schüddekopf, op. cit. p. 56. See also; U. Rößling, 'Konferenz zum 60. Jahrestag der Novemberrevolution und zum 60. Jahrestag der Grüdung der KPD', *Zeitschrift für Geschichtswissenschaft,* 27 (2) (1979) p. 150.
124. Bramke, op. cit. p. 700.
125. Schüddekopf, op. cit. p. 110.
126. BA R134/4(3). RKo, 20 December 1920. I.

2 THE NATIONAL QUESTION 1918–1922

1. H. Mommsen, *Arbeiterbewegung und Nationale Frage. Aufgewählte Aufsätze* (Göttingen, 1979) p. 63; H.-U. Wehler, *Sozialdemokratie und Nationalstaat. Nationalitätenfragen in Deutschland 1840-1914* (Göttingen, 1971) pp. 19–20.
2. Mommsen, *Arbeiterbewegung,* pp. 71, 112.
3. Ibid., pp. 72, 74.
4. cf. W. J. Mommsen, *Max Weber and German Politics 1890–1920,* trans. J. Steinberg (Chicago, 1984) pp. 89–90.
5. Schüddekopf, op. cit. p. 39.
6. Royal Institute of International Affairs (RIIA), *Nationalism* (Oxford, 1939) p. 44.
7. Mommsen, *Arbeiterbewegung,* pp. 276–7. cf. RIIA, op. cit. p. 44.
8. F. Hertz, *Nationality in History and Politics. A Psychology and Sociology of National Sentiment and Nationalism* (London, 1966) p. 263; cf.

Wehler, op. cit. pp. 37–41.

9. T. S. Hamerow, *Restoration, Revolution, Reaction. Economics and Politics in Germany, 1815–1871* (Princeton NJ, 1966) chs. 11 and 12.

10. RIIA, op. cit. pp. 44, 172, 271–2; cf. M. C. Howard and J.E. King, 'The Revival of Revisionism: The Political Economy of German Marxism 1914–29', *European History Quarterly*, 18 (4) (1988) p. 411; M. van den Linden, 'The national integration of the European working classes 1871–1914', *International Review of Social History*, XXXIII (3) (1988) pp. 308–9.

11. Moses, *Trade Unionism*, I, chs 6 and 7, see esp. p. 200. For a briefer summary: J. Moses, 'Socialist Trade Unionism in Imperial Germany, 1871–1914', in R. Fletcher (ed.), *Bernstein to Brandt. A Short History of German Social Democracy* (London, 1987) pp. 25–34.

12. Paraphrased in Moses, *Trade Unionism*, I, p. 184. For a broader discussion see ch. 8. For similar thinking within French trade union circles see: J. Howarth, 'French Workers and German Workers: The Impossibility of Internationalism, 1900–1914', *European History Quarterly*, 15 (1) (1985) p. 82.

13. Thus, R. Michels, *A Sociological Study of the Oligarchical Tendencies of Modern Democracy* (London, 1962) p. 357.

14. cf. S. Tegel, 'The SPD in Imperial Germany, 1871-1914', in R. Fletcher (ed.), *Bernstein to Brandt*, pp. 16–24; S. Milner, 'The International Labour Movement and the limits of internationalism: The International Secretariat of National Trade Union Centres 1901-13', *International Review of Social History*, XXXIII (1) (1988) p. 24.

15. R. Fletcher, 'Revisionism and Wilhelmine Imperialism', *Journal of Contemporary History*, 23 (3) (1988) pp. 347–66. See also: R. Fletcher, 'The Life and Work of Eduard Bernstein', in R. Fletcher (ed.), *Bernstein to Brandt*, p. 50. But cf. H. Mommsen, *Arbeiterbewegung*, pp. 119–20, who stresses that Bernstein stopped well short of supporting Wilhelmine imperialism.

16. Fletcher, *Revisionism*, p. 357.

17. Wehler, op. cit. *passim*. For an interesting insight into the French labour movement's view of nationalism within the SPD and the German trade unions: Howorth, *French Workers, passim*.

18. Moore, op. cit. p. 225. cf. Mussolini's espousal of nationalism as well as socialism before the First World War; E. Weber, 'Fascism(s) and some Harbingers', *Journal of Modern History*, 54 (4) (1982) p. 752.

19. Borkenau, op. cit. p. 55; cf. L. L. Lorwin, *Labor and Internationalism* (New York, 1929) pp. 142–3; J. Howorth, 'The Left in France and Germany, Internationalism and War: A Dialogue of the Deaf 1900–1914', in E. Cahn and V. Fisera (eds), *Socialism and Nationalism in Contemporary Europe* (1848–1945), vol. 2 (Nottingham, 1979) p. 95: 'Both French and Germans were utterly convinced that socialist internationalism began at home'.

20. cf. Hertz, op. cit. p. 266–7.

21. Michels, op. cit. p. 359.

22. Paraphrased in Moses, *Trade Unionism*, I, p. 192; cf. Mommsen, *Max Weber*, pp. 287–8.
23. Quoted in R. Pore, *A Conflict of Interests: Women in German Social Democracy 1919-1933* (Westport, Conn., 1981) p. 30.
24. Moore, op. cit. pp. 223–4; cf. Howorth, *French Workers*, p. 76 for a discussion of (anti-German) chauvinism in France at this time.
25. Klönne, op. cit. p. 159; Mommsen, *Arbeiterbewegung*, p. 61.
26. Quoted in Mommsen, *Arbeiterbewegung*, p. 61.
27. Moore, op. cit. p. 231.
28. See pp. 2–3, 8 above.
29. G. D. Feldman, *Army, Industry and Labor in Germany, 1914–1918* (Princeton, NJ, 1966) p. 29.
30. C. E. Schorske, *German Social Democracy 1905–1917. The Development of the Great Schism* (London, 1955) p. 294.
31. Schüddekopf, op. cit. p. 88.
32. Edited by Johann Knief and the future KPD leader Paul Frölich. See Gerber, op. cit. p. 179 for a very positive assessment of the journal's significance.
33. Schüddekopf, op. cit. pp. 101–2.
34. Ibid., p. 100.
35. cf. A. Mohler, *Die Konservative Revolution in Deutschland 1918–1932. Grundriß ihrer Weltanschauungen* (Stuttgart, 1950) pp. 60–1.
36. Schüddekopf, op. cit. p. 112.
37. Quoted in Schüddekopf, op. cit. p. 44.
38. BA Reichskanzlei (R43I)/1326(159). Kabinettsitzung 23 January 1919.
39. BA R43I/1348(204). Sitzung des Reichsministeriums 21 March 1919.
40. cf. Max Weber, quoted in Mommsen, *Max Weber,* p. 313.
41. cf. Gerber, op. cit. pp. 181–2, who makes no mention of the nationalist dimension of left radicalism in the early KPD.
42. Schüddekopf, op. cit. p. 16.
43. Flechtheim, op. cit. p. 144; Gerber, op. cit. p. 182.
44. Borkenau, op. cit. p. 94.
45. See p.12 above.
46. Kochan, op. cit. pp. 19–20. Schüddekopf, op. cit. p. 100.
47. Schüddekopf, op. cit. pp. 56–9, 61; D. W. Daycock, 'The KPD and the NSDAP: A Study of the Relationship between Political Extremes in Weimar Germany 1923–1933', (PhD Dissertation, London School of Economics, 1980) pp. 96–8.
48. Schüddekopf, op. cit. p. 73.
49. Quoted in Degras, op. cit., I, p. 54.
50. Ibid., I, p. 3.
51. Ibid., I, p. 33.
52. Ibid., I, pp. 55–6.
53. Quoted in Schüddekopf, op. cit. p. 62.
54. Flechtheim, op. cit. pp. 139–40.
55. Quoted in Rosenberg, op. cit. p. 81.
56. Quoted in Schüddekopf, op. cit. p. 72.
57. Quoted in Degras, op. cit., I, p. 58. See also pp. 56–7.

Notes to Chapter 2

58. BA R134/1(20). Polizei-Direktion. 10 August 1920. I.
59. BA R134/1(23). Polizei-Direktion. 17 August 1920. I.
60. BA R134/2(1–2). RKo 1034/20. 31 August 1920. I.
61. BA R134/3(79). RKo. 17 November 1920. I.
62. BA R134/5(157). RKo 27. 8 February 1921. Inland. cf. K. M. Wilson (ed.), *George Saunders on Germany 1919–1920. Correspondence and Memoranda* (Leeds, 1987) p. 92.
63. BA R134/7(112). RKo 32. 15 March 1921. I.
64. BA R134/1(20). Polizei-Direktion. 10 August 1920. I. BA R134/3(88). RKo. 17 November 1920. 2a).
65. Schüddekopf, op. cit. p. 93.
66. BA R134/2(33). RKo. 16 September 1920. I.
67. BA R134/2(156). RKo 27. 8 February 1921. Inland.
68. Ibid.
69. G. A. Craig, *Germany 1866–1945* (Oxford, 1978) pp. 438–9. For a contemporary American assessment sympathetic to Germany's predicament: J. H. Williams, 'German Foreign Trade and the Reparation Payments', *Quarterly Journal of Economics*, (1922) pp. 482–503. For a recent, brief account of the problem: K. Hardach, *The Political Economy of Germany in the Twentieth Century* (Berkeley, Los Angeles, London, 1980) pp. 23–8.
70. BA R134/8(169–70). RKo 36. 26 April 1921. I.
     cf. H. J. Rupieper, *The Cuno Government and Reparations 1922–1923. Politics and Economics* (The Hague, 1979) pp. 86–7.
71. See pp. 15–16 above for details of the resulting struggle within the KPD, and of the 'March Action'.
72. Schüddekopf, op. cit. p. 134.
73. SB 4,65/228/39. 'Die Berliner Funktionärsammlung der V.K.P.D. zur politischen Lage', *Die Rote Fahne*, 10 February 1921.
74. SB 4,66/227/39. 'Proletarier aller Länder, vereinigt Euch!', *Hamburger Volkszeitung*, 6 December 1920.
75. SB 4,65/227/39. 'Der Vereinigungsparteitag der deutschen Kommunisten 1920', *Hamburger Volkszeitung*, 7 December 1920.
76. BA R134/4(105). RKo. 11 January 1921. I.
77. BA R134/7(109). RKo 32. 15 March 1921. I.
78. Quoted in Schüddekopf, op. cit. pp. 93–4.
79. SB 4,65/228/39. 'National-kommunistische Einheitsfront', *Vorwärts*, 8 February 1921.
80. SB 4,65/228/39. 'Hakenkreuz auf rotem Grund', *Vorwärts*, 9 February 1921.
81. BA R134/7(4). RKo 31. 9 March 1921. I.
82. Schüddekopf, op. cit. p. 94.
83. BA R134/6(166). RKo 30. 1 March 1921. I.
84. BA R134/7(4). RKo 31. 9 March 1921. I; Schüddekopf, op. cit. pp. 93–4.
85. SB 4,65/228/39 as in note 79 above; cf. BA R134/6(144). RKo 30. 1 March 1921. I.
86. BA R134/6(146). RKo 30. 1 March 1921. I.
87. SB 4,65/228/39. Auszug aus Z-1-gg. Ber. v. 19.II.21. Bremen. Betr.: Ausschluß der bayerischen Kommunistenführer . . .

88. See pp. 15–16 above.
89. BA R134/6(143). RKo 30. 1 March 1921. I.
90. Kochan, op. cit. p. 71.
91. Schüddekopf, op. cit. pp. 128-9.
92. BA R134/7(87-8). RKo 32. 15 March 1921. I.
    cf. Daycock, op. cit. p. 88, where Kopp's interest in German nationalism in the late 1920s is discussed.
93. Quoted in Degras, op. cit., I, p. 217.
94. Quoted in Degras, op. cit., I, p. 358.
95. Ibid.; cf. Degras, op. cit., I, p. 368.
96. Quoted in Degras, op. cit., I, p. 221.
97. Schüddekopf, op. cit. pp. 138–9.
98. SB 4,65/228/39. 'An das deutsche Proletariat!'. 4 March 1921.
99. BA R134/7(88) RKo 32. 15 March 1921. I.
100. SB 4,65/229/39. Auszug aus dem Lage-Bericht des St. K. Nr. 11554/21 v. 7.6.21. Bremen, 10 June 1921.
    BA R134/9(96) and (116). RKo 39. 17 May 1921. I.
101. SB 4,65/229/39. As in note 100.
102. SB 4,65/229/39. Vereinigte Kommunistische Partei Deutschlands. (Sektion III. Internationale). Pol. Rundschreiben Nr. 3. Berlin, 10 May 1921.
103. SB 4,65/230/39. Anlage zur Tagesmeldung v. 20.7.21. Auszug aus einem vertraulichen Rundschreiben der Vereinigten Kommunistischen Partei Deutschlands . . . Polizeidirektion Kdo der Abt. II. I. Nr. 1664. Bremen, 22 July 1921.
104. Quoted in Schüddekopf, op. cit. p. 130.
105. SB 4,65/230/39. 'Schaffende Männer und Frauen Deutschlands!', Die Rote Fahne, 1 September 1921.
106. BA R134/17(115). RKo 72. In. 15 May 1922. I.
107. SB 4,65/232/40. 'Die Beschlüsse des Zentralausschusses', Nordwestdeutsches-Echo, 244, 18 October 1922. 'Gemeinsamer Kampf...'
108. Rosenberg, op. cit. p. 126.
109. Borkenau, op. cit. p. 158. See also R. G. L. Waite, Vanguard of Nazism. The Free Corps Movement in Postwar Germany 1918–1923 (London, 1970) pp. 271–2.
110. B. Bond, War and Society in Europe, 1870–1970 (London, 1984) p. 138; cf. Waite, op. cit. pp. 271–2, and Weber, Fascism(s), p. 750.
111. Schüddekopf, op. cit. p. 73.
112. BA R134/15(60). RKo 56. 4 October 1921. I.
113. BA R134/17(139). RKo 74. 13 June 1922. Allgemeine Lage.
114. BA R134/18(145). RKo 81. 1 December 1922. I.
115. Schüddekopf, op. cit. p. 92.
116. G. Mai, 'Zwischen den Klassen? Zur Soziographie der SA', Archiv für Sozialgeschichte, 25 (1985) pp. 642–3.
117. Rosenberg, op. cit. p. 60.
118. BA R134/4(21). RKo. 20 December 1920. I. cf. F. L. Carsten, The Rise of Fascism (London, 1970) pp. 89–90.
119. Schüddekopf, op. cit. pp. 92, 94.

120. Waite, op. cit. p. 273.
121. Schüddekopf, op. cit. p. 93.
122. Quoted in Schüddekopf, op. cit. p. 77.
123. Schüddekopf, op. cit. pp. 123–4.
124. Ibid., pp. 103–4; cf. Waite, op. cit. pp. 176, 273.
125. BA R134/1(10). Undated [3.8.20] 12.
126. BA R134/5(154). RKo 27. 8 February 1921. Inland.
127. W. Laqueur, *Young Germany. A History of the German Youth Movement* (New Brunswick, London, 1984) pp. 125–7. Schüddekopf, op. cit. pp. 166-70.
128. Schüddekopf, op. cit. p. 94. Mohler, op. cit. pp. 59–65.
129. M. H. Kater, *The Nazi Party. A Social Profile of Members and Leaders, 1919–1945* (Oxford, 1983) pp. 22–3, 242–3 Table 2. J. C. Fest, *Hitler*, trans. R. and C. Winston (London, 1974) p. 147; cf. P. Madden, 'Some Social Characteristics of Early Nazi Party Members 1919–1923', *Central European History*, 15(1) (1982) p. 52.
130. R. Zitelmann, *Adolf Hitler. Eine politische Biographie* (Göttingen, 1989) p. 44.
131. Schüddekopf, op. cit. p. 93.
132. Carsten, *Rise of Fascism*, p. 101.
133. BA R134/2(39). RKo 16 September 1920. 2a).
134. Zitelmann, op. cit. p. 27; cf. A. J. Gregor, *Young Mussolini and the Intellectual Origins of Italian Fascism* (Berkeley, 1979) p. xi, where the ambivalence of early Italian fascism and its similarities with Marxism and also syndicalism are noted.
135. Fest, *Hitler*, p. 147.
136. Quoted in Schüddekopf, op. cit. p. 122.
137. Quoted in Schüddekopf, op. cit. p. 137.

3 THE 1923 CRISIS

1. Craig, op. cit. pp. 434–48. W. Fischer, 'Wirtschaftliche Rahmenbedingungen des Ruhrkonflikts', in K. Schwabe (ed.), *Die Ruhrkrise 1923. Wendepunkt der internationalen Beziehungen nach dem ersten Weltkrieg*, 2nd ed. (Paderborn, 1986) pp. 95–6.
2. Quoted in J. Bariéty, 'Die französische Politik in der Ruhrkrise', in K. Schwabe (ed.), as in note 1 p. 19.
3. Bariéty, op. cit. pp. 12, 13.
4. Ibid., p. 18. Fischer, *Rahmenbedingungen*, pp. 95, 99.
5. Bariéty, op. cit. p. 18.
6. Ibid., pp. 15–16, 19. Fischer, *Rahmenbedingungen*, p. 99; Rupieper, cit. pp. 81–4, 86–7, 125; cf. Kochan, op. cit. pp. 64–5.
7. Rupieper, op. cit. pp. 104–5. Winkler, *Revolution*, p. 558.
8. Fischer, *Rahmenbedingungen*, pp. 94–5. Winkler, *Revolution*, p. 566; cf. Mohler, op. cit. p. 61.
9. Rupieper, op. cit. pp. 86–7.
10. Kochan, op. cit. p. 69.

11. Winkler, *Revolution,* p. 556.
12. Rupieper, op. cit. pp. 98–9.
13. Kochan, op. cit. p. 69.
14. Rupieper, op. cit. pp. 101–2.
15. Winkler, *Revolution,* p. 556.
16. cf. Kochan, op. cit. pp. 73–4. Winkler, *Revolution,* pp. 561–2.
17. Quoted in Schüddekopf, op. cit. p. 142.
18. Quoted in Fowkes, op. cit. p. 89.
19. BA R134/19(15). RKo 84. 24 January 1923. I.
20. BA R134/19(53). RKo 86. 1 March 1923. I.
21. SB 4,65/233/40. 'Der räuberische Ueberfall des französischen Imperialismus auf das Ruhrgebiet und die Gefahr eines neuen Krieges', *Die Rote Fahne,* 68 (1. Beilage), 22 March 1923.
22. Winkler, *Revolution,* p. 564.
23. Quoted in Schüddekopf, op. cit. p. 146.
24. Winkler, *Revolution,* p. 564.
25. See pp. 51–6 below.
26. BA R134/20(25). RKo 89. 23 April 1923. I. cf. Winkler, *Revolution,* p. 567.
27. BA R134/20(47). RKo 90. 11 May 1923. I.
28. Rupieper, op. cit. pp. 178–9.
29. Winkler, *Revolution,* pp. 576–7. cf. BA R134/21(2). RKo 92. 15 June 1923. I.
30. Quoted in Winkler, *Revolution,* p. 578.
31. SB 4,65/233/40. Auszug aus dem Nachrichtenblatt der 6. Division Münster vom 5 Juni 1923.
32. BA R134/21(2). RKo 92. 15 June 1923. I.
33. BA R134/21(5). RKo 92. 15 June 1923. II; cf. Mohler, op. cit. pp. 61–2, where he notes the willingness of Communist workers in the Ruhr to engage in anti-French sabotage under the leadership of former Prussian front-line officers.
34. cf. Borkenau's contrary assertion; op. cit. p. 249.
35. SB 4,65/233/40. 'Manifest an das internationale Proletariat, an die Arbeiter und an die Arbeiterinnen Deutschlands!', *Die Rote Fahne,* 30 January 1923.
36. Quoted in Degras, op. cit., II, p. 22.
37. Daycock, op. cit. pp. 76–7.
38. J. M. Diehl, *Paramilitary Politics in Weimar Germany* (Bloomington, Ind. and London, 1977) pp. 133, 134.
39. Daycock, op. cit. pp. 78, 80.
40. BA R134/19(17-18). RKo 84. 24 January 1923. II.
41. See pp. 31–2, 37–9 above.
42. As note 40 above.
43. Daycock, op. cit. p. 75.
44. Ibid, p.69. See also p.48.
45. Quoted in Schüddekopf, op. cit. p. 145.
46. SB 4, 65/232/40. *Kommunistische Partei-Korrespondenz.* 3. Jahrg. Nr. 1. Berlin, 1 January 1923. 'Die Gegenrevolution. Der deutsche Faszismus' p. 3.

47. Quoted in Daycock, op. cit. p. 74.
48. Quoted in Schüddekopf, op. cit. p. 141. But cf. Degras, op. cit., II, p. 53, where ECCI assesses German fascism in much more negative terms.
49. Daycock, op. cit. p. 74.
50. SB 4,65/233/40. Auszug aus dem Lagebericht des St. K. Nr. 10354/23 vom 21. April 1923. Bremen, 23 April 1923.
51. Thus the problem was inherent in fascism *per se* as well as having roots in the specifics of the German situation.
52. SB 4,65/233/40. 'Resolution über den Kampf gegen den Faschismus', *Die Rote Fahne*, 68, 22 March 1923.
53. Quoted in Winkler, *Revolution,* p. 582. See also; W. Wippermann, '"Triumph des Willens" oder "kapitalistische Manipulation"? Das Ideologieproblem in Faschismus', in K.D. Bracher, M. Funke, H.-A. Jacobsen (eds), *Nationalsozialistische Diktatur 1933-1945. Eine Bilanz* (Bonn, 1983) p. 739.
54. Quoted in Winkler, *Revolution,* p. 582.
55. See; G. Dimitrov, *The Working Class against Fascism* (London, 1935) p. 10.
56. Quoted in Winkler, *Revolution,* p. 582.
57. SB 4,65/233/40. 'Die Taktik der Einheitsfront und die Arbeiterregierung' *Die Rote Fahne*, 27, 2 February 1923. 1. Beilage.
58. SB 4,65/233/40. 'Resolution über „Die politische Lage und die nächsten Aufgaben des Proletariats". . . .' *Nordwestdeutsches Echo*, 35, 10 February 1923. 8) Die faszistische Welle.
59. See pp. 46 above, and SB 4,65/232/40. Auszug aus dem Münster-Lagebericht vom 22.12.22. Kmdo. Abt. VI. Abt. N. Bremen, 2 January 1923. KPD. Aus der Zentrale. 4).
60. SB 4,65/233/40. As in note 58.
61. SB 4,65/233/40. Auszug aus dem Nachrichtenblatt Nr. 81 vom 15 Mai 1923. Bremen, 22 May 1923.
62. SB 4,65/233/40. Auszug aus dem Lagebericht des St. K. Nr. 12254/23 vom 15. Mai 1923. Bremen, 17 May 1923.
63. Ibid.
64. Winkler, *Revolution,* p. 579; cf. Daycock, op. cit. p. 71.
65. Daycock, op. cit. p. 74.
66. G. Eley, 'The Wilhelmine Right: How it Changed', in R. J. Evans (ed.), *Society and Politics in Wilhelmine Germany* (London, 1978) pp. 122–3, and G. Eley, *From Unification to Nazism. Reinterpreting the German Past* (Boston, 1986) ch. 10.
67. Flechtheim, op. cit. p. 176.
68. BA R134/19(76). RKo 87. 19 March 1923. Linksradikale Bewegung.
69. BA R134/21(123). RKo 97. 22 September 1923. II.
70. BA R134/25(17–18). RKo 108. 1 December 1924. II.
71. BA R134/29(62–3, 71). RKo 117. 1 April 1926. II.
72. Craig, op. cit. pp. 454–5.
73. Degras, op. cit., II p. 16.
    Klönne, op. cit. p. 213.
74. Rosenberg, op. cit. p. 137. Winkler, *Revolution*, p. 593.
75. Ibid., p. 136.

76. Borkenau, op. cit. p. 247.
77. Winkler, *Revolution*, p. 593; cf. Degras, op. cit., II, p. 1, where Zinoviev notes the continued popular support enjoyed by the SPD's leaders.
78. cf. Flechtheim, op. cit. p. 172.
79. Diehl, op. cit. p. 116.
80. cf. Daycock, op. cit. p. 81.
81. cf. Kochan, op. cit. p. 64.
82. Quoted in Kochan, op. cit. p. 68.
83. Quoted in Daycock, op. cit. p. 89.
84. Kochan, op. cit. p. 71.
85. Ibid., pp. 33, 75–6. Winkler, *Revolution*, p. 579.
86. Quoted in Degras, op. cit., II, pp. 7–8.
87. Degras, op. cit., II, p. 15.
88. Degras, op. cit., II, p. 6.
89. Quoted in Degras, op. cit., II, p. 10.
90. Schüddekopf, op. cit. p. 73; Winkler, *Revolution*, p. 579.
91. cf. Kochan, op. cit. pp. 74–5.
92. cf. Fowkes, op. cit. p. 92.
93. Quoted in Schüddekopf, op. cit. p. 145.
94. Winkler, *Revolution*, pp. 563–5.
95. Winkler, *Revolution*, pp. 578–9; Schüddekopf, op. cit. pp. 157–8.
96. Degras, op. cit., II, p. 29.
97. Quoted in Degras, as n.96.
98. Thus, Winkler, *Revolution*, p. 580; but cf. K. Sontheimer, *Antidemokratisches Denken in der Weimarer Republik. Die politischen Ideen des deutschen Nationalismus zwischen 1918 und 1933*, 2nd ed. (Munich, 1983) p. 128, who takes the speech to mark the actual shift in policy, rather than the earlier deals struck between the KPD and the ECCI.
99. The dates given for this speech vary. Fowkes, op. cit. p. 97: 20 June. Winkler, *Revolution* p. 580: 21 June. Degras, op. cit., II, p. 39: 23 June. The official German government report agrees with Fowkes. Thus, SB 4,65/233/40. Auszug aus dem Lagebericht des St. K. Nr. 15754/23. 26 June 1923. Eine bedeutsame Rede Radeks.
100. For a fuller account see Waite, op. cit. pp. 235–8.
101. Winkler, *Revolution*, p. 568.
102. Quoted in Degras, op. cit., II, p. 39. See also Wippermann, op. cit. pp. 739–40.
103. Degras, op. cit., II, pp. 39–40.
104. Degras, op. cit., II, p. 40.
105. Quoted in Degras, op. cit., II, p. 40.
106. Degras, op. cit., II, p. 27; Winkler, *Revolution*, p. 583.
107. Quoted in Degras, op. cit., II, p. 40.
108. Quoted in Winkler, *Revolution*, p. 581.
109. Winkler, *Revolution*, p. 582.
110. Quoted in Degras, op. cit., II, p. 40.
111. Quoted in Daycock, op. cit. p. 90.
112. Schüddekopf, op. cit. p. 151.
113. See p.46 above.

114. cf. Fowkes, op. cit. p. 97, who notes the KPD's leaders' acquiescence in the Radek line, but does not analyse the forces which, earlier in the year, had done much to convince them in advance.
115. SB 4,65/233/40. Auszug aus dem Lagebericht des St. K. Nr. 15754/23. 26 June 1923. Eine bedeutsame Rede Radeks.
116. BA R134/21(39–40). RKo 93. 1 July 1923. II.
117. BA R134/21(35). RKo 93. 1 July 1923. I. cf. BA R134/21(12), where it is noted that the KPD was now dead set against the separatist movements in the Rhineland.
118. cf. Sontheimer, op. cit. p. 128, where he argues that the national communist element within the KPD remained relatively small during 1923.
119. See p.46 above.
120. BA R134/21(8). RKo 92. 15 June 1923. II. cf. SB 4,65/233/40. 'An die Partei!', *Die Rote Fahne*, 12 July 1923.
121. BA R134/21(37). RKo 93. 1 July 1923. I.
122. Diehl, op. cit. p. 136.
123. Winkler, *Revolution*, p. 596; Rupieper, op. cit. p. 211; Flechtheim, op. cit. p. 177.
124. Winkler, *Revolution*, pp. 596–7.
125. Quoted in Flechtheim, op. cit. p. 177.
126. Thus; Winkler, *Revolution*, p. 597, where he describes the KPD's intention of waging a war of liberation against the West. One wonders quite what the SPD made of such declarations.
127. Winkler, *Revolution*, p. 594.
128. See pp. 41–5 above.
129. cf. R. Sarti, 'Fascist Modernization in Italy: Traditional or Revolutionary?', *American Historical Review*, LXXV (4) (1970) p. 1031, where he discusses comparable issues in the Italian context, but also takes issue with Nolte and Sauer for characterising German fascism as inherently reactionary.
130. Quoted in Winkler, *Revolution*, p. 596.
131. cf. the similar Comintern analysis in the same month on pp. 55–6 above.
132. Quoted in Winkler, *Revolution*, p. 598.
133. Ibid., p. 583.
134. See Winkler, *Revolution*, p. 583 note 69; cf. Kochan, op. cit. p. 78. In this much earlier work Fischer's version is accepted.
135. Quoted in Winkler, *Revolution*, p. 584.
136. Quoted in Daycock, op. cit. p. 84.
137. Winkler, *Revolution*, p. 584 note 70.
138. Flechtheim, op. cit. p. 179.
139. cf. K. D. Erdmann, 'Alternativen der deutschen Politik im Ruhrkampf', in K. Schwabe (ed.), *Die Ruhrkrise 1923. Wendepunkt der internationalen Beziehungen nach dem ersten Weltkrieg*, 2nd ed. (Paderborn, 1986) p. 29.
140. Quoted in Schüddekopf, op. cit. p. 150.
141. cf. Schüddekopf, as above.
142. Winkler, *Revolution*, p. 597.
143. See p.60 above.

144. cf. BA R134/21(77). RKo 95. 6 August 1923. IV, where Communist attitudes to various middle class groups are discussed.
145. Daycock, op. cit. p. 103.
146. cf. Schüddekopf, op. cit. pp. 141, 159.
147. cf. Daycock, op. cit. pp. 19–20, 99–100.
148. Rosenberg, op. cit. pp. 132–3.
149. Quoted in Schüddekopf, op. cit. p. 140.
150. Ibid., p. 139.
151. See pp. 44–5 above.
152. BA R134/19(89) RKo 87. 19 March 1923. III.
153. Quoted in BA R134/20(47–8). RKo.90. 11 May 1923. I.
154. Schüddekopf, op. cit. pp. 151–5, 161.
155. Winkler, *Revolution,* p. 154.
156. Schüddekopf, op. cit. p. 157; cf. Daycock, op. cit. p. 101.
157. Winkler, *Revolution,* pp. 584–5 and p. 597 note 101.
158. Borkenau, op. cit. p. 248.
159. BA R134/21(76–7). RKo 95. 6 August 1923. III.
160. BA R134/21(98). RKo 96. 25 August 1923. III.
161. cf. pp. 67–7 and 87 below, on Hitler's problems *vis à vis* the Communists also similar problems within Bund Oberland.
162. Schüddekopf, op.cit. pp. 156–7.
163. Ibid., p. 157.
164. Daycock, op. cit. p. 56.
165. Ibid, p. 100.
166. Winkler, *Revolution,* p. 599.
167. Kochan, op. cit. pp. 75–6.
168. Rosenberg, op. cit. p. 138.
169. Winkler, *Revolution,* pp. 600–4.
170. Kochan, op. cit. pp. 84–5; Fowkes, op. cit. p. 102.
171. For a full account: Fowkes, op. cit. ch. 5. Specifically on Hamburg, L. Peterson, 'A Social Analysis of KPD Supporters. The Hamburg Insurrectionaries of October 1923', *International Review of Social History,* XXVIII (2) (1983) pp. 200–39.
172. Borkenau, op. cit. p. 255.
173. Quoted in Degras, op. cit., II, p. 77.
174. Degras, op. cit., II, p. 72.
175. Quoted in Degras, op. cit., II, p. 1; cf. Winkler, *Revolution,* pp. 710–11, for KPD's acceptance of this in April 1924.
176. cf. Daycock, op. cit. pp. 25–7.
177. Flechtheim, op. cit. pp. 174–5.
178. BA R134/22(20). RKo 99. 17 December 1923. II; cf. Flechtheim, op. cit. pp. 195-6, 199-200.
179. Winkler, *Revolution,* pp. 701–2.
180. Flechtheim, op. cit. pp. 195–6.
181. Quoted in Carsten, *Rise of Fascism,* p. 112.
182. H. J. Gordon, *Hitler and the Beer Hall Putsch* (Princeton, NJ, 1972) pp. 449–51.
183. Carsten, *Rise of Fascism,* p. 113.
184. BA R134/22(11). RKo 98. 18 November 1923. III.

185. BA R134/22(22). RKo 99. 17 December 1923. II.
186. BA R134/22(39). RKo 99. 17 December 1923. III.
187. Gordon, op. cit. p. 427.
188. Schüddekopf, op. cit. p. 180.
189. Quoted in Daycock, op. cit. p. 134. For Radek's downfall see Kochan, op. cit. p. 91.
190. Quoted in Daycock, op. cit. p. 134.
191. cf. Wippermann, op. cit. p. 740.
192. Daycock, op. cit. p. 135.
193. Thus Nolte's assessment that the Comintern ignored the implications of fascism's mass support after 1923 is too harsh. E. Nolte, 'Zeitgenössische Theorien über den Faschismus', *Vierteljahreshefte für Zeitgeschichte*, 15 (3) (1967) pp. 253–4.
194. SB 4,65/234/40. 'Bezirksparteitag Berlin-Brandenburg', *Die Rote Fahne*, 21, Beilage, 25 March 1924.
195. cf. Winkler, *Revolution,* pp. 704–5.

4 THE STABILISATION ERA, 1924–1928: General Developments

1. E. H. Carr, *German-Soviet Relations between the two World Wars. 1919–1939* (Oxford, 1952) pp. 74–5. Kochan, op. cit. p. 92.
2. Kochan, op. cit. pp. 101–7.
3. Craig, op. cit. pp. 516–19. Of standard general accounts: H. L. Bretton, *Stresemann and the Revision of Versailles. A Fight for Reason* (Stanford, 1953), presents his policies in a sympathetic light. H. W. Gatzke, *Stresemann and the Rearmament of Germany* (Baltimore, 1954), is critically sympathetic. For a more biographical approach: A. Thimme, *Gustav Stresemann. Eine politische Biographie zur Geschichte der Weimarer Republik* (Hanover, Frankfurt-am-Main, 1957). See also H. Pogge von Strandmann, 'Imperialism and Revisionism in Interwar Germany', in W. J. Mommsen, J. Osterhammel (eds), *Imperialism and After. Continuities and Discontinuities* (London, 1986) pp. 90–119.
4. Carr, op. cit. pp. 81–2. Dorpalen, *German History,* pp. 351–2. Kochan, op. cit. pp. 96, 99–100, 107–14.
5. C. Höltje, *Die Weimarer Republik und das Ostlocarno-Problem 1919–1934 Revision oder Garantie der deutschen Ostgrenze von 1919* (Würzburg, 1958); Bretton, op. cit. pp. 120–1; Craig, op. cit. p. 520; Thimme, op. cit. pp. 106–11.
6. Carr, op. cit. pp. 80, 85; F. L. Carsten, *The Reichswehr and Politics 1918–1933* (Berkeley, Los Angeles, London, 1973) pp. 237–8; Kochan, op. cit. pp. 94, 116.
7. Carr, op. cit. pp. 93–4; Gatzke, op. cit. pp. 72–6.
8. Fowkes, op. cit. p. 127; cf. Carr, op. cit. p. 94; Kochan, op. cit. pp. 118–19.
9. See pp. 81–2 below.
10. Quoted in Degras, op. cit., II, p. 228.
11. BA R134/51(21). RKo Nr. 2357/26A. 18 March 1926.

12. Degras, op. cit., II, p. 352.
13. Quoted in Degras, op. cit., II, p. 356.
14. Schüddekopf, op. cit. p. 178.
15. BA R134/23(19). RKo 103. 16 April 1923. II. SB 4,65/239/42. 'Die politische Lage und die Aufgaben der KPD', *Bulletin des X. Parteitages der KPD,* 8, Berlin, 19 July 1925.
16. Quoted in Degras, op. cit., II, p. 165.
17. Ibid. pp. 288–9.
18. Schüddekopf, op. cit. p. 184.
19. cf. Schüddekopf, op. cit. p. 225.
20. Schüddekopf, op. cit. pp. 177, 179.
21. Ibid., pp. 183–4.
22. BA R134/31(67). RKo 120. 1 November 1926. III. SB 4,65/1250/208. 'Kommunisten und Völkische', *Bremer Volkszeitung,* 271?, 19 November 1927.
23. SB 4,65/1250/208. As above.
24. BA R134/29(41). RKo 116. 26 January 1926. III. 5.
25. Schüddekopf, op. cit. pp. 212–13.
26. BA R134/24(33). RKo 107. 11 October 1924. I.
27. Daycock, op. cit. pp. 141–2.
28. For instance, SB 4,65/1251/208. 'Sowjetstern am Stahlhelm . . .' *Vorwärts,* 617, 30 December 1927. The Red Front denial reported in *Berliner Tageblatt,* 31, 19 January 1928.
29. BA R134/41(23). RKo 127. 31 October 1928. II.
30. Diehl, op. cit. p. 216.
31. SB 4,65/234/40. Auszug: Pol. Rundschr. z. d. Reichstagswahlen vom 4.4.24. Abschrift. Die Bedeutung des kommenden Reichstagswahlkampfes f. d. 'KPD'. Zentrale der KPD . . . VIII.
32. SB 4,65/234/40. 'An die Partei! [. . .', *Die Rote Fahne,* 38, 13 April 1924.
33. SB 4,65/234/40. Polizeipräsident. Abteilung I A. Tgb.-Nr. 1454 I.A. 3.24. Betrifft: KPD. Berlin, 15 April 1924, p. 3.
34. SB 4,65/296/58. 'Was kann man aus den Reichstagswahlen lernen?', *Der Funke,* 7, Berlin, 12 May 1924.
35. SB 4,65/235/41. Zentrale der KPD. Polbüro. Berlin, 19 July 1924. b) Innerpolitische Lage.
36. Ibid. and SB 4,65/237/41. 'Die politische Lage und die Aufgaben der KPD', *Die Rote Fahne,* 10, 2. Beilage, 13 January 1925. II.
37. SB 4,65/1258/210. Auszug aus einem Monatsbericht der Politischen Abteilung des Polizeipräsidiums Hannover für die Zeit vom 1. bis 31.8.25/N. Stelle 2591 geh. v. 28.9.25. Roter Frontkämpferbund und Roter Jungsturm, p. 3.
38. SB 4,65/242/43. Auszug aus dem Stuttgarter Lagebericht W. 26 18 August 1926. Parteiarbeiterversammlung der KP Württemberg.
39. SB 4,65/1258/210. Ausschnitt aus dem L.B.W. 28 v. 27.7.27 des Pol. Präs. Stuttgart N. Stelle J. No. 1515/27 geh.
40. SB 4,65/246/44. Der Polizeipräsident. Tgb. Nr. 3218. I.A. 3.27. Berlin, 21 December 1927. Anlage. See ch. 5 above for a fuller discussion of these very important issues.

41. BA R134/56(165-6). RKo Nr. 3199 26II. 23 April 1926. cf. Diehl, op. cit. p. 188. Degras, op. cit.,II, p. 231.
42. BA R134/56(177,185) RKo. Abschrift. Jahresbericht der Bundesleitung des Roten Frontkämpferbundes.
43. SB 4,65/1262/210. Anlage zur Lagebericht No. 7 des Pol. Behörde Hamburg vom 19.7.26. N. Stelle 1944/26. cf. SB 4,65/1262/210. 'Kommunistische Spitzelarbeit', *Berliner Tageblatt*, 208, 4 May 1927, for use of identical tactics against republican organisations.
44. cf. Daycock, op. cit. p. 140.
45. SB 4,65/1259/210. Ausschnitt aus dem Lagebericht des Pol. Präs. Stuttgart, W. 30. 5 September 1928. Rundschreiben der Bundesführung des RFB Abteilung Rote Jungfront.
46. Quoted in Degras, op. cit., II, p. 138.
47. Degras, op. cit., II, p. 137.
48. Quoted in Degras, op. cit., II, p. 87.
49. SB 4,65/239/42. 'Die Schlußsitzung des Parteitags', *Bulletin des X Parteitages der KPD*, 12, 24 July 1925.
50. Quoted in Degras, op. cit., II, p. 139.
51. cf. Bordiga, in Degras, op. cit., II, p. 137.
52. Quoted in Degras, op. cit., II, p. 138.
53. For instance; R. F. Hamilton, 'Hitler's electoral support: recent findings and theoretical implications', *Canadian Journal of Sociology*, 11(1) (1986) pp. 22–3.
54. See pp. 47–9, 55–6 above.
55. SB 4,65/235/41. Zentrale der KPD. Polbüro. Berlin, 19 July 1924. b) Innerpolitische Lage. cf. Daycock, op. cit. pp. 127, 314.
56. BA R134/50(167). Niederschrift . . . Berlin, 23 and 24 January 1925. Anlage 4.
57. Kater, *Nazi Party*, pp. 244–5 table 3, pp. 35–6 and 248 table 5.
58. BA R134/32(75). RKo 121. 28 March 1927. III. 4 a).
59. SB 4,65/1249/207. Abschrift. Der Rote Frontkämpferbund 1926. Jahresbericht der Bundesführung. 11–13 March 1927. pp. 28–30.
60. BA R134/35(128–9). RKo 123. 15 October 1927. III. 4aO.
61. Schüddekopf, op. cit. p. 209. cf. BA R134/32(61). RKo 121. 28 March 1927. III. 2a).
62. SB 4,65/1262/210. Polizeidirektion: N.-Stelle B. Nr. 1813/26. Entnommen aus dem Lagebericht des Pol. Präsid. Abt. I.A. Berlin vom Juni 1926. Anlage A.
63. For instance: SB 4,65/241/43. Auszug aus dem Lagebericht W.21 des Pol. Präsidiums Stuttgart vom 9.6.26. Tätigkeitsbericht der Bezirksleitung der KPD Württemberg. SB 4,65/244/44. Ausschnitt aus einem Lagebericht aus Stuttgart vom 4.5.27. W 17 No. 967/27 geh. Kommunistische Parteiarbeiterversammlung.
64. BA R134/39(84). RKo 125. 14 April 1928. Abschrift.
65. SB 4,65/243/43. 'Genosse Denzel über die Arbeit der Partei', *Arbeiter Zeitung*, 53, 4 March 1927.
66. For instance; Degras, op. cit., II, pp. 139–40.
67. cf. Borkenau, op. cit. p. 259.
68. For instance: SB 4,65/241/43. As in note 63.

69. Quoted in Daycock, op. cit. p. 139. See also p.137.
70. SB 4,65/1250/208. Entnommen aus dem Monatsbericht des Pol. Präsidiums Hannover 1/28. Anlage 3. N. Stelle Nr. 60/28 geh. p. 6.
71. SB 4,65/235/41. Auszug aus dem Lagebericht Nr. 11 der Polizeibehörde Hamburg vom 16.9.24, diess. B. Nr. 3240/24 geh.
72. Schüddekopf, op. cit. pp. 194–5.
73. SB 4,65/244/44. 'Nette Bundesgenossen. . .', *Bremer Volkszeitung*, 87, 13 April 1927.
74. BA R134/35(129). RKo 123. 15 October 1927. III. 4a). Schüddekopf, op. cit. p. 195.
75. Schüddekopf, op. cit. p. 183.
76. Quoted in Schüddekopf, op. cit. p. 194. See also SB 4,65/235/41. As in note 71.
77. Daycock, op. cit. p. 137.
78. BA R134/28(103). RKo 114. 20 November 1925. III.
79. cf. pp. 71–2 above, where some *völkisch* leaders expressed similar views.
80. Quoted in BA R134/28(103) as in note 78.
81. Quoted in Schüddekopf, op. cit. p. 198.
82. Schüddekopf, op. cit. p. 189.
83. Quoted in Schüddekopf, op. cit. p. 190. cf. B. M Lane, 'Nazi Ideology: Some Unfinished Business', *Central European History*, VII (1) (1974) p. 25.
84. P. D. Stachura, *Gregor Strasser and the Rise of Nazism* (London, 1983) p. 61.
85. Thus, Strachura, *Strasser* pp. 46–51.
86. Schüddekopf, op. cit. pp. 200-2. cf. R. Kühnl, 'Zur Programmatik der Nationalsozialistischen Linken: Das Strasser-Programm von 1925/26', *Vierteljahreshefte für Zeitgeschichte*, 14 (1966) p. 323.
87. cf. Kühnl, op. cit. p. 323, and cf. Lane, op. cit. p. 20, who argues that Hitler had rejected the radicals' programme at Bamberg on the basis of its timing, not its content.
88. BA R134/41(128–9). RKo 127. 31 October 1928. III. 7bb).
89. Ibid.
90. cf. Daycock, op. cit. p. 124.

5   THE STABILISATION ERA, 1924–1928: The KPD and Right-Radicals

1. R. Breitman, *German Socialism and Weimar Democracy* (Chapel Hill, 1981) ch. 7; Moses, *Trade Unionism*, II, pp. 358–61.
2. cf. Fowkes, op. cit. pp. 122–3.
3. cf Klönne, op. cit. pp. 217–18.
4. For varying estimates see Degras, op. cit., II, p. 85; Flechtheim, op. cit. p. 148; Klönne, op. cit. p. 213; E. C. Schöck, *Arbeitslosigkeit und Rationalisierung. Die Lage der Arbeiter und die kommunistische Gewerkschaftspolitik 1920–28* (Frankfurt-am-Main, 1977) p. 226.
5. Diehl, op. cit. pp. 185, 186, 253; Flechtheim, op. cit. p. 214.
6. Flechtheim, op. cit. pp. 236, 237.
7. Moses, *Trade Unionism*, II, p. 439 note 77; Fowkes, op. cit. p. 138.

216 *Notes to Chapter 5*

8. Hunt, op. cit. p. 105; R. Wheeler, 'Zur sozialen Struktur der Arbeiterbewegung am Anfang der Weimarer Republik. Einige methodologischen Bemerkungen', in H. Mommsen, D. Petzina, B. Weisbrod (eds), *Industrielles System und Politische Entwicklung in der Weimarer Republik*, vol. I (Düsseldorf, 1977) pp. 184–5.
9. Moses, *Trade Unionism*, II, p. 439 note 77. cf. Schöck, op. cit. p. 101, who gives a figure of 41.5 per cent.
10. Borkenau, op. cit. p. 253. Schöck, op. cit. p. 57 estimates that 70 per cent of KPD members were unemployed in early 1924.
11. Hunt, op. cit. pp. 166–7.
12. Fowkes, op. cit. p. 119.
13. Degras, op. cit., II, p. 85; Schöck, op. cit. pp. 102–4.
14. Fowkes, op. cit. p. 120.
15. Degras, op. cit., II, p. 85.
16. Borkenau, op. cit. p. 267; Degras, op. cit., II, pp. 132–3; Fowkes, op. cit. pp. 121–2.
17. Fowkes, op. cit. p. 138. L. Preller, *Sozialpolitik in der Weimarer Republik* (Düsseldorf, 1978) p. 204.
18. Moses, *Trade Unionism*, II, p. 439 note 77; cf. Schöck, op. cit. pp. 105–6.
19. Hunt, op. cit. p. 169.
20. Fowkes, op. cit. p. 138.
21. Degras, op. cit., II, p. 207.
22. Ibid., and Hunt, op. cit. p. 169.
23. Quoted in Degras, op. cit., II, p. 228; cf. Schöck, op. cit. p. 113; Peterson, KPD Supporters pp. 232–3.
24. Quoted in Degras, op. cit., II, p. 231. cf. Schöck, op. cit., p. 59, 113, where she notes the high unemployment levels in the Ruhr KPD.
25. Degras, op. cit., II, p. 232.
26. For a specific discussion of Company Unions; K. J., Mattheier, 'Werkvereine und wirtschaftsfriedlich-nationale (gelbe) Arbeiterbewegung im Ruhrgebiet', in J. Reulecke (ed.), *Arbeiterbewegung an Rhein und Ruhr* (Wuppertal, 1974) pp. 173–204. See also: I. Hamel, *Völkischer Verband und nationale Gewerkschaft: Der DHV 1893–1933* (Frankfurt-am-Main, 1967); A Stupperich, *Volksgemeinschaft oder Arbeitersolidarität: Studien zur Arbeitnehmerpolitik in der Deutschnationalen Volkspartei 1918–1933* (Göttingen, 1982).
27. cf. Mattheier, op. cit. p. 174; M. Schneider, *Unternehmer und Demokratie. Die freien Gewerkschaften in der Unternehmer Ideologie der Jahre 1918 bis 1933* (Bonn-Bad Godesberg, 1975) pp. 33–7.
28. Mattheier, op. cit. pp. 177–8.
29. U. Nocken, 'Corporatism and Pluralism in Modern German History', in D. Stegmann, B.-J. Wendt, P.-C. Witt (eds), *Industrielle Gesellschaft und Politisches System. Beiträge zur politischen Sozialgeschichte* (Bonn, 1978) p. 47.
30. Mattheier, op. cit. pp. 193–9.
31. This change also upset many small and medium-sized firms who felt threatened both by the unions and by the advantages enjoyed by the larger firms in collective bargaining; G. D. Feldman, 'The large firm in the German Industrial System: The M.A.N. 1900–1925', in D. Stegmann

. . ., as in note 29 above p. 249. Preller, op. cit. p. 202; Schneider, op. cit. pp. 37–42.

32. cf. Schöck, op. cit. p. 99.
33. Feldman, M.A.N. p. 256; Mommsen, 'Sozialpolitik', pp. 307–8, 315; Preller, op. cit. p. 202; Schneider, op. cit. pp. 42–9.
34. Mattheier, op. cit. pp. 200–1.
35. Hamel, op. cit. pp. 208, 211; Feldman, M.A.N. p. 256.
36. Preller, op. cit. pp. 201, 203; cf. B. Weisbrod, *Schwerindustrie in der Weimarer Republik. Interessenpolitik zwischen Stablisierung und Krise* (Wuppertal, 1978) pp. 259–63.
37. Preller, op. cit. pp. 201, 203; S. Aufhäuser, 'Betriebsrat-Werkgemeinschaft', *Die Arbeit*, 1 (1924) pp. 272–5. This also had implications for the right-wing and white-collar organisations. cf. Hamel, op. cit. pp. 203-4; Mattheier, op. cit. pp. 203–4.
38. Schneider, op. cit. p. 69.
39. Nocken, op. cit. p. 50; Schneider, op. cit. p. 70; Weisbrod, op. cit. pp. 246–50.
40. Schneider, op. cit. pp. 70–1; Weisbrod, op. cit. pp. 251–68.
41. Nocken, op. cit. p. 51; Weisbrod, op. cit. pp 269–70.
42. Mattheier, op. cit. p. 177.
43. G. D. Feldman, 'The Social and Economic Policies of German Big Business 1918–1929', *American Historical Review*, LXXV (1) (1969) *passim;* Preller, op. cit. p. 200. For a contemporary account in a pro-employer vein, K. Vorwerck, *Die wirtschaftsfriedliche Arbeitnehmerbewegung Deutschlands in ihrem Werden und in ihrem Kampf um Anerkennung* (Jena, 1926). For a critical attitude: L. Erdmann, 'Gewerkschaften, Werkgemeinschaften und industrielle Demokratie', *Die Arbeit*, II (1925) esp. p. 138.
44. Feldman, *Big Business*, p. 53; Mommsen, 'Sozialpolitik'; pp. 316–18; Schneider, op. cit. pp. 76–85.
45. Moses, *Trade Unionism*, II, pp. 359–62, 366–70; cf. Schneider, op. cit. pp. 75, 85–92.
46. Schöck, op. cit. pp. 109–10; cf. Mattheier, op. cit. pp. 178–92, on comparable developments before the First World War.
47. F. Fricke, *Sie Suchen die Seele!* (Berlin, 1927) p. 30; cf. Schneider, op. cit. pp. 73–4.
48. Thus the DNVP's white collar union, the DHV, recognised, with reservations, the need to work within the framework of Weimar. Hamel, op. cit. pp. 184–7, 195–6; Preller, op. cit. 191–2.
49. Diehl, op. cit. pp. 152, 188–9, 202–3.
50. Diehl, op. cit. ch. 5.
51. cf. E. Posse, *Die politischen Kampfbünde Deutschlands* (Berlin, 1930) pp. 23, 26–7; Rosenberg, op. cit. pp. 171–2.
52. Diehl, op. cit. p. 171. A. Klotzbücher, 'Der politische Weg des Stahlhelm, Bund der Frontsoldaten, in der Weimarer Republik. Ein Beitrag zur Geschichte der "Nationalen Opposition" 1918–1933', (Inaugural Dissertation, Friedrich-Alexander-Universität, Erlangen-Nürnberg, 1965) p. 42.
53. K. Finker, 'Die militärischen Wehrverbände in der Weimarer Republik

und ihre Rolle bei der Unterdrückung der Arbeiterklasse und bei der Verbreitung eines neuen imperialistischen Krieges :1924–1929)', (Habilitationsschrift, Pädagogische Hochschule, Potsdam, 1964) pp. 147–9.

54. cf. Klotzbücher, op. cit. p. 44 note 43; Posse, op. cit. pp. 29–30.
55. V. R. Berghahn, *Der Stahlhelm, Bund der Frontsoldaten 1918–1935* (Düsseldorf, 1966) p. 107; Diehl, op. cit. pp. 174, 349 note 71; Finker, op. cit. p. 143; Klotzbücher, op. cit. p. 44; Posse, op. cit. p. 31. For similar, non-Stahlhelm activity: Vorwerck, op. cit. pp. 132–3.
56. cf. Preller, op. cit. p. 196. Schüddekopf, op. cit. p. 206.
57. Klotzbücher, op. cit. p. 44; Finker, op. cit. p. 161.
58. See Mattheier, op. cit. pp. 202–3; Diehl, op. cit. p. 349 note 71; Preller, op. cit. p. 196.
59. Finker, op. cit. pp. 159–60.
60. Even the DHV, as a right-wing, white-collar union accused the yellow unions in general of 'selling out to the employers'; Hamel, op. cit. pp. 199, 201–2.
61. See pp. 82–4 above.
62. See pp. 82–4 above.
63. Preller, op. cit. p. 204. Reich estimates yellow union membership in late 1930 as 193 340; N. Reich, *Labour Relations in Republican Germany* (New York, 1938) p. 80.
64. Moses, *Trade Unionism*, II, p. 439 note 77.
65. SB 4,65/289/57. 'Völkische Betriebsräte. Zum Wahlergebnis in der Knorr-Bremse', *Die Rote Fahne,* 13, 15 March 1924.
66. SB 4,65/268/51. 'Die „völkischen Kampfgewerkschaften"', *Mitteilungs-Blatt der Gewerkschaftsopposition,* 4/5, 20 March 1924 p.11. See also ch. 4 above.
67. SB 4,65/1246/207. 'Arbeitsnachweise der Reaktion', *Rote Front,* 6, 1 July 1925.
68. SB 4,65/239/42. Abschrift. Bezirk Ruhrgebiet Polbüro. Tgb. Nr. 1/1733. Essen, 1 August 1925, p. 3.
69. SB 4,65/1256/209. Anlage zum Lagebericht Nr. 24 v. 1.7.25 der Pol. Präsid. Stuttgart, Protokoll der 2. Reichskonferenz des R.F.B. am 22. und 23. Mai in Berlin. p. 10.
SB 4,65/1246/207. Auszug aus dem Lagebericht W.36 des Pol. Präsid. Stuttgart vom 21.10.25. Rundschreiben der Bundesleitung des RFB., Nr. 22/25. Berlin, 2 October 1925.
70. SB 4,65/1246/207. As in note 67 above.
71. SB 4,65/1246/207. Abschrift. Bundesleitung des RFB. Berlin, 30 November 1925 pp. 2–3; cf. the more sanguine assessment of the situation in Daycock, op. cit. p. 133.
72. SB 4,65/1246/207 as above.
73. SB 4,65/1262/210. Auszug aus dem Lagebericht d. Min. des Innern Dresden 20 December 1926. Anlage 1, p. 3. Cf. Diehl, op. cit. pp. 293–5; Posse, op. cit. p. 23.
74. SB 4,65/1262/210. As in note 73 above.
75. Finker, op. cit. p. 112.

76. Klotzbücher, op. cit. pp. 43–4. cf. Posse, op. cit. p. 31, who gives qualified acceptance to a figure of 65 per cent working class overall.
77. SB 4,65/1258/210. Auszug aus dem Lagebericht W.9 des Pol. Präsidiums Stuttgart vom 3.3.26. Referenten-Material . . . III).
78. SB 4,65/1256/209. Abschrift. Der Polizeipräsident zu Hannover. Nr. I.P. 329. N. Stelle Nr. 1012/26 geh. 9 April 1926. Abschrift. Jungfront Bericht . . . II).
79. SB 4,65/1258/210. Der Oberpräsident der Provinz Westfalen. No. 1411/ 26 III M. Betrifft: Richtlinien für die Organisierung. . . 19 August 1926.
80. SB 4,65/1254/209. Polizeidirektion. N-Stelle Nr. 270/26. Bremen, 28 January 1926. Abschrift. Richtlinien des Roten Frauenbundes. 1).
81. SB 4,65/1258/210. As in note 77 above.
82. SB 4,65/1262/210. Auszug aus dem Bericht d. Min. des Innern Dresden. 20 December 1926. Anlage 1 p. 2.
83. cf. Diehl, op. cit. pp. 219–22. Rosenberg, op. cit. pp. 171–2.
84. SB 4,65/1262/210. As in note 82 above.
85. Ibid. p. 1.
86. But cf. the more positive side of these relations discussed in ch. 4 above.
87. SB 4,65/1258/210. Auszug aus dem Lagebericht W.9 des Pol. Präsidiums Stuttgart vom 3.3.26. Referenten-Material für . . . RFB und . . . RJ. Einleitung, and VI.
88. SB 4,65/1262/210. Auszug aus dem Bericht d. Min. des Innern Dresden. 20 December 1926. Anlage 1 p. 9.
89. SB 4,65/1258/210. As in note 87 above. SB 4,65/1262/210. As in note 88 above. cf. S. Bahne, *Die KPD und das Ende von Weimar. Das Scheitern einer Politik 1932–1935* (Frankfurt-am-Main, 1976) p. 22; Degras, op. cit., II, pp. 72, 88; Fowkes, op. cit. p. 130.
90. SB 4,65/1262/210. Auszug aus dem Bericht d. Min. des Innern Dresden. 20 December 1926. Anlage 1 p. 3.
91. BA R134/56(148). RKo Nr. 3199/26II. 23 April 1926.
92. SB 4,65/1256/209. 'Unsere Gegner', *Rote Front,* early April 1926.
93. SB 4,65/1247/207. Polizeidirektion N-Stelle B. Nr. 428/27. Abschrift. RFB . . . Bremen, 14 May 1926. p. 4.
94. SB 4,65/1262/210. Auszug aus dem Bericht d. Min. des Innern Dresden. 20 December 1926. Anlage 1 pp. 8-9; SB 4,65/1256/209. Abschrift. Der Polizeipräsident zu Hannover. Nr. I.P. 329. N. Stelle Nr. 1012/26 geh. Hannover, 9 April 1926. Abschrift. Jungfront Bericht . . . II). Of these issues the nationalist leagues' attitude to economic crisis was regarded as the most important.
95. SB 4,65/1262/210. Auszug aus einem Rundschreiben des R.F.B. Gauleitung Württemberg vom 7.9.1926. Diess. B. Nr. 2495/26 geh. (3).
96. SB 4,65/242/43. Entnommen aus dem Lagebericht Nr. 25 vom 8. Sept. 1926 des Pol. Präsidiums Elberfeld-Barmen. N. Stelle B. Nr. 2355/26 geh. Vom ZK der KPD aufgestellte Richtlinien. II p. 4.
97. Schöck, op. cit. p. 110.
98. Ibid., pp. 250–1 Table 18.
99. Here the yellow vote had peaked in 1926, before the metalworkers' dispute: Schöck, op. cit. pp. 156–7 Table 23.

100. SB 4,65/1254/209. Auszug aus dem Lagebericht Januar 1927 des Pol. Präs. Abtl. I.A. Berlin. Roter Frauen- und Mädchenbund. 81. I.A. Allgem. 26. Anlage 1 p. 5.
101. SB 4,65/1256/209. 'Unsere 4. Reichskonferenz', *Rote Front*, 6, 15 March 1927. See also; SB 4,65/1258/210. Auszug aus dem Dresdener Lagebericht IPN 600/27 vom 14.3.27. Rote Jungfront.
102. SB 4,65/1249/207. Der Oberpräsident der Provinz Westfalen. Nr. 341/ 27 III M. Münster, 8 April 1927. Abschrift. Allgemeine Richtlinien für das Lagerleben der Roten Jungfront.
103. SB 4,65/1249/207. Auszug aus dem Stuttgarter Lagebericht W.13 vom 30.3.27. Mitgliederversammlung des RFB.
104. Ibid.
105. BA R134/33(7,10). RKo 121. 28 March 1927. Strafsache Otto Braun. IV. cf. Finker, op. cit. p. 327, who estimates a membership of 50 000 which was 70 per cent working class.
106. BA R134/33(9,10). RKo 121. As above. Finker, op. cit. p. 328.
107. SB 4,65/1249/207. Abschrift. Bundesführung des RFB. Rundschreiben Nr. 5/27. Berlin, 18 February 1927. III. SB 4,65/1248/207. Abschrift. Bundesführung RFB. Rundschreiben Nr. 4/27. Berlin, 29 January 1927. p. 9.
108. SB 4,65/1262/210. Entnommen aus dem L.B. Nr. 7/27 des Pol. Präs. Hannover. N. Stelle B. Nr. 2026/27. Anlage 1. mid July 1927.
109. The same company reportedly also had a strong Wehrwolf presence, with perhaps 70 per cent of the workforce so organised; Finker, op. cit. p. 327.
110. SB 4,65/1262/210. As in note 108 above.
111. Finker, op. cit. pp. 159–60.
112. Quoted in Fowkes, op. cit. p. 174.
113. SB 4,65/1262/210. As in note 108.
114. Ibid.
115. SB 4,65/1249/207. Abschrift. Bundesführung des RFB. Rundschreiben Nr. 5/27. Berlin, 18 February 1927. III pp. 1-2. BA R134/33(8). RKo 121. 28 March 1927. Strafsache Otto Braun. IV. cf. Posse, op. cit. p. 31.
116. BA R134/33(8). As above. cf. SB 4,65/1248/207. Abschrift. Bundesführung RFB. Rundschreiben Nr. 4/27. Berlin, 29 January 1927. p. 9.
117. SB 4,65/245/44. 'Stalhelm-Streikbrecher nach Berlin', *Die Rote Fahne*, 218, 16 September 1927. SB 4,65/1249/207. Abschrift. Bundesführung des RFB. Rundschreiben Nr. 5/27. Berlin, 18 February 1927. III p. 2.
118. SB 4,65/244/44. As in note 117 above; SB 4,65/1248/207. Abschrift. Bundesführung RFB. Rundschreiben Nr. 4/27. Berlin, 29 January 1927. p. 9; SB 4,65/1248/207. Polizeidirektion: N-Stelle B. Nr. 22/27. Abschrift. Der Aufbau des Gegner-Ressorts im RFB Bremen, 11 January 1927. pp. 4–5.
119. SB 4,65/244/44. Ausschnitt aus einem Lagebericht aus Stuttgart vom 4.5.27. W.17 N. Stelle No. 967/27 geh. Kommunistische Parteiarbeiterversammlung.
120. SB 4,65/1249/207. 'Was will der Rote Frontkämpferbund?', *Die Rote Fahne*, 124, 28 May 1927.
121. SB 4,65/1248/207. Polizeidirektion. As in note 118 above.

122. SB 4,65/1262/210. As in note 108 above.
123. SB 4,65/1251/208. Entnommen aus dem Monatsbericht 3/1928 des Polizei-Präs. Hannover. N. Stelle Nr. 476/28 geh. Berlin, 30 January 1928. Abschrift! Anlage 2; BA R134/39(83–4). RKo 125. 14 April 1928.
124. C. J. Fischer, 'The KPD and Nazism: A Reply to Dick Geary', *European History Quarterly*, 15 (4) (1985) p. 467.
125. BA R134/39(45). RKo 125. 14 April 1928. Anlage 1b.
126. SB 4,65/1259/210. Auszug aus dem Lagebericht W.9 des Pol. Präsidiums Stuttgart vom 29.2.28. J. Nr. 421/28 geh. Rundschreiben der Bundesführung des RFB Abt. Rote Jungfront; BA R134/39(91). RKo 125. 14 April 1928. Abschrift.
127. BA R134/39(111). RKo 125. 14 April 1928. Abschrift; SB 4,65/1262/210. Auszug aus dem Lagebericht Nr. 134/II 28 vom 11 9 1928 der Polizeidirektion Nürnberg-Fürth. Diess. B. Nr. 1852/28 geh; SB 4,65/1251/208. Anlage zu RKo No. 4474/28 II. Abschrift, Disposition. . .p. 3.
128. Thus, R. Weber, 'Werkgemeinschaft – Ein „wirtschaftsorganiatorischer Lösungsversuch" oder das sozialpolitische Programm der nationalistischen Diktatur?', *Die Arbeit*, V (1928) esp. pp. 546–7, where the potential political dangers are stressed. cf. Reich, op. cit. pp. 80–1, who, in common with many subsequent writers, has taken the contrary view.
129. In 1931 the yellow unions gained 5.77 per cent of the votes in mining and the Nazis a further 2.43 per cent. In the manufacturing sector the yellow and Nazi unions gained 270 mandates, as against the RGO's 492; Schöck, op. cit. pp. 252-2 Table 19, 255.
130. cf. G. Mai, 'Die Nationalsozialistische Betriebszellen-Organisation. Zum Verhältnis von Arbeiterschaft und Nationalsozialismus', *Vierteljahreshefte für Zeitgeschichte*, 31 (1983) pp. 604–5. W. L. Patch, Jr, 'German Social History and Labor History: A Troubled Partnership', *Journal of Modern History*, 56 (3) (1984) p. 490. A wider discussion of the difficulties inherent in 'categorising' the politics and ideology of the working class is to be found in D. Geary, 'Identifying Militancy: The Assessment of Working-Class Attitudes towards State and Society', in R. J. Evans (ed.), *The German Working Class 1888-1933. The Politics of Everyday Life* (London, 1982) pp. 220-46.
131. Mattheier, op. cit. p. 204; V. Kratzenberg, *Arbeiter auf dem Weg zu Hitler? Die nationalsozialistische Betriebszellen-Organisation. Ihre Entstehung, ihre Programmatik, ihr Scheitern 1927–1934* (Frankfurt-am-Main, Bern, New York, Paris, 1989) pp. 70–3.
132. Schöck, op. cit. pp. 250–3 Tables 18, 19. But cf. Mai, *Betriebszellen*, p. 605. Kratzenberg, op. cit. pp. 256–63, sees a closer link between the NSBO's salaried members and the non-Socialist white-collar unions.
133. cf. Schöck, op. cit. p. 110.

6 COMMUNIST—NAZI RELATIONS 1928–1932: The Ideological Dimension

1. Daycock, op. cit. p. 168.
2. Fowkes, op. cit. p. 148.
3. cf. the discussion of the contrasting aims of Socialist and Communist

education in Weimar, integration as against confrontation: D. Lange-wiesche, 'The Impact of the German Labor Movement on Workers' Culture', *Journal of Modern History*, 59(3) (1987) pp. 520–1.
4. Daycock, op. cit. p. 168. Fowkes, op. cit. p. 147.
5. SB 4,65/250/46. Referenten-Material. Kampf dem Faschismus. 20 September 1929. cf. BA R134/68(197). Abschrift IAN 2161a/3.8. Berlin, 3 August 1931. II, for similar KPD views, and Moses, *Trade Unionism*, II pp. 364-6 where the KPD's view of the Naphtali Programme is discussed.
6. Quoted in Degras, op. cit., III, pp. 27–8.
7. Degras, op. cit., III, pp. 36, 40–1. See also p. 152.
8. Quoted in Degras, op. cit., III, pp. 45–6.
9. Ibid., p. 215.
10. cf. Degras, op. cit., III, p. 154.
11. Degras, op. cit., III, pp. 27–8; cf. Bahne, *KPD und das Ende*, pp. 29, 30, 34, 36.
12. Within the party, the group around Heinz Neumann was the last to question the sense of according the primacy to the struggle against the SPD: J. J. Ward, '"Smash the Fasicsts..."'. German Communist Efforts to Counter the Nazis, 1930-31', *Central European History*, 14 (1) (1981) p. 40 ff.
13. Degras, op. cit., II, p. 565.
14. SB 4,65/1253/209. Ausschnitt aus dem Lagebericht des Pol. Präs. Stuttgart vom 6.3.29. W.5.N. Stelle No. 390/29 geh. Rundschreiben von Werner Jurr. cf. A. Dorpalen, 'SPD und KPD in der Endphase der Weimarer Republik', *Vierteljahreshefte für Zeitgeschichte*, 31 (1) (1983) pp. 84–5.
15. SB 4,65/2168/211. Auszug aus dem Lagebericht Nr. 3 aus Hamburg vom 19.10.1929. N. Stelle Nr. 2028/29 geh. 2).
16. Quoted in Degras, op. cit., III, p. 25. cf. BA R134/71(162); Zu IAN 2165e/3.3; Abschrift aus *Proletarische Sozialpolitik*. . . .
17. BA Kommunistische Partei Deutschlands (R45IV)/24. June? 1929. Anhang. Losungen gegen Demonstrationsverbot . . . cf. BA NSDAP Hauptarchiv(NS26)/1403. Berichte der Staatspolizei Württemberg zur politischen Lage. 22 January 1930. pp. 2–3.
18. Quoted in Degras, op. cit., III, pp. 26–7. cf. SB 4,65/1268/211. Auszug aus dem Lagebericht N/Nr. 85 aus München. 23 October 1929. N. Stelle Nr. 1983/29 geh., and Dorpalen, SPD und KPD, pp. 79–81.
19. SB 4,65/249/45. 'Das Referat des Genossen Thälmann auf dem 12. Parteitag der Kommunistischen Partei Deutschland', *Arbeiter Zeitung*, 134, 12 June 1929. Beilage. 'Die Gefahr des Faschismus'. cf. Flechtheim, op. cit. pp. 258–9.
20. Flechtheim, op. cit. p. 261. cf. BA NS26/1169. Pressebericht über die Hauptorgane der Gegner. *Die Rote Fahne*, 26 February 1932. 'Thälmann'. SB 4,65/260/49. Ekki-Plenum und 3. Reichs-Parteiarbeiter-Konferenz. Material für Referenten und Propagandisten. pp. 10–11. For a subsequent East German assessment: K. Gossweiler, 'Der Uebergang von der Weltwirtschaftskrise zur Rüstungskonjunktur in Deutschland 1933 bis 1934. Ein historischer Beitrag zur Problematik staatsmonopolis-tischer "Krisenüberwindung"', *Jahrbuch für Wirtschaftsgeschichte*, 2 (1968) pp. 64–5.

21. Daycock, op. cit. p. 324.
22. Quoted in Degras, op. cit., III, p. 40. cf. Daycock, op. cit. p. 180; Schüddekopf, op. cit. pp. 235–6.
23. Daycock, op. cit. p. 174.
24. Degras, op. cit., III, p. 100; cf. Bahne, *KPD und das Ende*, p. 68.
25. cf. Ward, op. cit. pp. 35–6.
26. BA NS26/1403. Berichte der Staatspolizei Württemberg zur politischen Lage. 17 September 1930. *Süddeutsche Arbeiterzeitung*, 185, 12 August 1930.
27. SB 4,65/252/46. 'Die Programmerklärung der KPD zeigt den Befreiungsweg', *Die Rote Fahne*, 233, 5 October 1930. BA NS26/1169. Pressebericht der Hauptorgane der Gegner. *Die Rote Fahne*, 12 March 1932. BA NS26/1169. Pressebericht der Hauptorgane der Gegner. *Die Rote Fahne*, 3 April 1932.
28. BA NS26/810. Resolution der KPD über die Lage in Deutschland und die Aufgaben der KPD. p. 6.
29. SB 4,65/252/46. As in note 27 above. cf. Bahne, *KPD und das Ende*, p. 60.
30. Quoted in Degras, op. cit., III, p. 166. cf. Ward, op. cit. p. 40.
31. BA NS26/810. Entwurf. Deklaration des Zentralkomitees der K.P.D. [1930] pp. 2–3.
32. Ibid. p. 4. cf. BA R45IV/32. An alle Parteimitglieder! Bezirksleitung der KPD. Niedersachsen. Sekretariat. 24 August 1932.
33. For a similar approach to factory politics see; BA R134/72(9–11). Abschrift. IAN 2162c^1/20.4. 26 March 1932.
34. Degras, op. cit., III, p. 101.
35. Schüddekopf, op. cit. p. 289.
36. Daycock, op. cit. p. 180; cf. Wippermann, op. cit. p. 743.
37. Schüddekopf, op. cit. p. 292.
38. Degras, op. cit., III., p. 100, and also 37, 212–17.
39. Bahne, *KPD und das Ende*, p. 25.
40. BA R45IV/21. Bericht über Versammlungstour in den Bezirken Mittelrhein, Saargebiet und Niederrhein – 30 June–30 July 1932. Allgemeines p. 2. gez. Daub.
41. Degras, op. cit., III, p. 155.
42. Schüddekopf, op. cit. p. 292.
43. Paraphrased in Daycock, op. cit. p. 170.
44. SB 4,65/252/46. 'Die Masken fallen!', *Vorwärts*, 417, 6 September 1930.
45. BA R45IV/21. KPD: Schivelbein (Pommern). May 1932. Unsigned.
46. BA R45IV/42. Lo/Er. 8 July 1932. [261 pp. transcript of discussions between SPD delegates and KPD leaders.] p. 152.
47. Ibid.
48. BA R45IV/42. As in note 46 above. p. 156.
49. BA R45IV/1. Kursus-Disposition zu den Problemen des Kampfes gegen Versailles – für soziale und nationale Befreiung. pp. 17,22,26. cf. SB 4,65/248/45. Anlage zu RKo 47/29II. Rededisposition für innerparteiliche Veranstaltungen [. . .] p. 11, (12).
50. SB 4,65/269/52. 'An das deutsche Proletariat!'. Das Reichskomitee zur Vorbereitung des Reichskongresses der revolutionären Gewerkschaftsopposition. Berlin, mid November 1929. cf. BA R45IV/40. Schluß mit

dem Volksbetrug!

51. SB 4,65/279/55. Abschrift. Der Polizei-Präsident in Bochum. (henceforward P-PB) Politische Nachrichtensammelstelle für die Provinz Westfalen (henceforward PNPW) I Nr. 86/32. Betrifft: Rededisposition für öffentliche und Mitgliederversammlungen der RGO. Bochum, 16 March 1932. Abschrift. p. 6.

52. Quoted in Daycock, op. cit. p. 187.

53. cf. T. Childers, *The Nazi Voter. The Social Foundations of Fascism in Germany, 1919–1933* (Chapel Hill, Ind., London, 1983) pp. 245–6.

54. SB 4,65/250/46. Referenten-Material. Kampf dem Faschismus. 20 September 1929. p. 3.

55. BA R45IV/36. 5 Monatsplan. Bezirk Pommern im Sturmangriff. 27 May 1932. p. 17.

56. SB 4,65/280/55. 'Das Programm der RGO. Sammelbecken aller klassenbewußten Straßenbahner', *Arbeiter Zeitung*, 105, 6 May 1932.

57. SB 4,65/280/55. P-PB. PNPW. I Nr. 124/32. 8 May 1932. Abschrift a) p. 8.

58. See pp. 73, 76–7 above.

59. SB 4,65/250/46. Referenten-Material. Kampf dem Faschismus. 20 September 1929. p. 3. See also; p. 17.

60. SB 4,65/226/38. Referentenmaterial zum Roten Volksentscheid am 9. August (1931). III. Wer hilft dem Faschismus?

61. Ibid.

62. BA R134/74(127). Nachrichtensammelstelle im Reichsministerium des Innern (henceforward NRI). IAN 2166a/23.12.31. Berlin, 14 January 1932. Abschrift. cf. C. Fischer, *Stormtroopers: A Social, Economic and Ideological Analysis 1929–35* (London, 1983) pp. 25–32, 45–8.

63. BA R134/74(127). As in note 62 above.

64. BA R45IV/8. Reorganisationsplan zur Schaffung von 13 Unterbezirken im Bezirk Niedersachsen. Bezirksleitung Niedersachsen, 17 March 1932. p. 4.

65. BA R45IV/16. Berichte der Arbeiterkorrespondenten über die Lage in den Großbetrieben unter der Militärdiktatur . . . 20-26 July (1932). p. 15.

66. SB 4,65/294/58. Polizei-Direktion: Zentralpolizeistelle B. Nr. 5984/31 geh. Bremen, 15 December 1931. cf. J. W. Falter, 'Warum die deutschen Arbeiter während des "Dritten Reiches" zu Hitler standen. Einige Anmerkungen zu Gunther Mais Beitrag über die Unterstützung des nationalsozialistischen Herrschaftssystems durch Arbeiter', *Geschichte und Gesellschaft*, 13 (1987) pp. 227–8.

67. SB 4,65/290/57. 'Eine rote Einheitsfront schlägt Hitler', *Die Rote Fahne*, 93, 30 April 1932.

68. R. F. Hamilton, *Who Voted for Hitler?* (Princeton, NJ, 1982) p. 387. See also Hamilton, *Electoral Support*, p. 23.

69. Fischer, *Stormtroopers*, chs. 6–8.

70. Hamilton, *Who Voted*, p. 609 note 73, 609–10 note 74.

71. For instance: BA NS26/1169. Reichsführer SS Abtg. Ic. Presseübersicht der Hauptorgane der Gegner. 16 December 1931. cf. Daycock, op. cit. pp. 146–7, where he observes that the same applied even during the Stabilisation Era.

72. BA R45IV/46. Bericht über Wahlversammlungen in Pommern, Erzge-
    birge und Hessen-Waldeck, 6–16 November 1929. gez. Edwin Hoernle.
    5).
73. Schüddekopf, op. cit. p. 288.
74. Quoted in Degras, op. cit., III, p. 120.
75. Schüddekopf, op. cit. p. 297; cf. E. Nolte, 'Marxismus und Nationalso-
    zialismus', *Vierteljahreshefte für Zeitgeschichte,* 31(3) (1983) p. 394;
    Ward, op. cit. pp. 45–7.
76. Flechtheim, op. cit. p. 276–7. Schüddekopf, op. cit. p. 299. cf. BA NS26/
    1405. Berichte der Staatspolizei Württembergs zur politischen Lage, 15
    July 1932. Rundschreiben des ZK der KPD Nr 11 v. 4.6.32.
77. Flechtheim, op. cit. pp. 276–7.
78. Quoted in Schüddekopf, op. cit. p. 303.
79. Schüddekopf, op. cit. 297–8.
80. Ibid. p. 305.
81. Mohler, op. cit. p. 63; cf. Dorpalen, SPD und KPD pp. 94–5; Ward, op.
    cit. pp. 53–4.
82. BA R45IV/35. Antifaschistische Aktion. Der Schulungsplan des Bez.
    Nordwest vom 1. Oktober bis 1. Febr. 1933. 6. cf. BA R134/89(41).
    Abschrift IAN 2162 c/27.7. [32]. Anlage 1.
83. Fischer, *Stormtroopers,* p. 210. C. Fischer, 'Class Enemies or Class
    Brothers? Communist-Nazi Relations in Germany, 1929–1933', *Euro-
    pean History Quarterly,* 15(3) (1985) p. 271.
84. BA R45IV/32. 'Durchbrecht den Naziblock', *Pionier des Bolschewis-
    mus,* October 1932, Sondernummer.
85. See pp. 153, 158–9 above.
86. Quoted in Degras, op. cit., III, p. 121.
87. Bahne, *KPD und das Ende,* p. 13.
88. Fowkes, op. cit. pp. 166–7; cf. Degras, op. cit., III, pp. 213–17.
89. SB 4,65/259/49. Abschrift. Rundschreiben Nr. 6. Anweisungen des
    Sekretariats. Berlin, 6 April 1932. cf. BA R45IV/24. Berlin 26 May 1932.
    Zentralkomitee der KPD. Rundtelefonat an alle Bezirksleitungen.
90. BA R45IV/36. 'Volle Klarheit über das Wesen des Faschismus', *Der
    Revolutionär,* May 1932, p. 8.
91. SB 4,65/281/56. 'Politische Massenstreiks als die entscheidende Kamp-
    form', *Die Rote Fahne,* 130, 15 June 1932.
92. BA R45IV/36. As in note 90 above. SB 4,65/259/49. As in note 89 above.
    cf. Degras, op. cit., III, pp. 213–17.
93. BA R45IV/17. 'Kampf gegen den Faschismus', *Der Funke.* Sonderaus-
    gabe zum Bezirksparteitag May 1930. p. 5.
94. BA R45IV/33. Anweisungen der Orgabteilung. Rundschreiben Nr. 10.
    Berlin, 17 July 1930.
95. BA R134/68(75). Abschrift IAN 2162/8.11. *Der revolutionäre Propagan-
    dist,* October 1930. cf. Dorpalen, SPD und KPD p. 88.
96. SB 4,65/253/47. Der Reichsminister des Innern. (henceforward RI) IAN
    2160d/31.10. Betreff: KPD – Kampf gegen Faschismus. Berlin, 7
    November 1930. cf. Dorpalen, SPD und KPD p. 92.
97. SB 4,65/255/47. Abschrift zu IAN 2160/7.4. Lehrbrief Nr. 2. Faschismus
    und Sozialfaschismus. II. p. 24.
98. SB 4,65/257/48. Zentralkomitee der Kommunistischen Partei Deutsch-

lands. Rundschreiben an alle Leitungen . . . Berlin, 8 December 1931. p. 11.

99. BA R45IV/13. Abschrift. 'Das Heranwachsen des revolutionären Aufschwunges in Deutschland', *Pravda*, 2 August 1932, p. 3.

100. BA R45IV/32. 'Revolutionärer Kampf und politischer Massenstreik gegen Notverordnung', *Die Schmiede*, 3 (3), July 1932, p. 1.

101. BA R45IV/13. As in note 99 above.

102. BA R45IV/1. 'Das XII. Plenum des EKKI und die KPD', *Die Internationale*, 15 (9/10), September/October 1932, pp. 398–9.

103. BA R45IV/17. Kampagne im Zeichen der ideologischen Offensive des revolutionären Marxismus-Leninismus. ZK-Agitprop-w. Berlin, 22 December 1932, p. 4.

104. BA R45IV/32. As in note 100 above. p. 4.

105. BA R45IV/32. 'Verstärkte ideologische Offensive gegen die Nazis', *Der Pionier des Bolschewismus*, August 1932.

7 THE SOCIOLOGY OF COMMUNIST–NAZI RELATIONS

1. For instance: M. Broszat, *The Hitler State. The Foundation and Development of the Internal Structure of the Third Reich*, trans. J. Hiden (London, 1981); I. Kershaw, *Popular Opinion and Political Dissent in the Third Reich: Bavaria 1933–1945* (Oxford, 1983); T.W. Mason, *Arbeiterklasse und Volksgemeinschaft. Dokumente und Materialien zur eutschen Arbeiterpolitik 1936–1939* (Opladen, 1975); T. W. Mason, *Sozialpolitik im Dritten Reich* (Opladen, 1977); D. Schoenbaum, *Hitler's Social Revolution. Class and Status in Nazi Germany 1933–1939* (London, 1967); G. Mai, '"Warum steht der deutsche Arbeiter zu Hitler?". Zur Rolle der Deutschen Arbeitsfront im Herrschaftssystem des Dritten Reiches', *Geschichte und Gesellschaft*, 12 (2) (1986) pp. 232-4, argues for a limited success in integrating the working class.

2. Among the many expositions: K. D. Bracher, *The German Dictatorship. The Origins, Structure and Consequences of National Socialism*, trans. J. Steinberg (London, 1973) pp. 195, 201, 203; M. Broszat, 'National ocialism, its Social Basis and Psychological Impact', in E. J. Feuchtwanger (ed.), *Upheaval and Continuity. A Century of German History* (London, 1973) pp. 134–51; H. H. Gerth, 'The Nazi Party: Its Leadership and Composition', *American Journal of Sociology*, XLV (4) (1940) pp. 517–41; S. Riemer, 'Zur Soziologie des Nationalsozialismus', *Die Arbeit*, 9 (1932) pp. 101–18; W. Sauer, 'National Socialism: Totalitarianism or Fascism?', *American Historial Review*, LXXIII (2) (1967) esp. p. 417; H. A. Winkler, 'Mittelstandsbewegung oder Volkspartei? Zur sozialen Basis der NSDAP', in W. Schieder (ed.), *Faschismus als soziale Bewegung. Deutschland und Italien im Vergleich*, 2nd ed. (Göttingen, 1983) esp. 113–14. More recently: Kater, *Nazi Party*, p. 236; P. D. Stachura, 'The Political Strategy of the Nazi Party, 1919–1933', *German Studies Review*, III (2) (1980) p. 279; P. D. Stachura, 'Who Were the Nazis? A Socio-Political Analysis of the National Socialist Machtübernahme', *European Studies Review*, 11 (3) (1981) pp. 303–4. Stachura, however,

would not now subscribe to the lower-middle-class hypothesis in the light of the latest evidence.

3. For instance: S. M. Lipset, *Political Man. The Social Bases of Politics* (Baltimore, Md, 1981).

4. M. Kele, *Nazis and Workers. National Socialist Appeals to German Labor, 1919–1933* (Chapel Hill, NC, 1972).

5. T. W. Mason, 'The Coming of the Nazis', *Times Literary Supplement*, 3752, 1 February 1974, p. 95.

6. For a critical survey of some late 1970s literature; T. Schnabel, '„Wer wählte Hitler". Bemerkungen zu einigen Neuerscheinungen über die Endphase der Weimarer Republik', *Geschichte und Gesellschaft*, 8 (1) (1982) pp. 116–33. For an authoritative survey of the entire range of recent literature: P. Manstein, *Die Mitglieder und Wähler der NSDAP 1919–1933. Untersuchungen zu ihrer schichtmäßigen Zusammensetzung* (Frankfurt-am-Main, Bern, New York, Paris, 1988).

7. Mason subsequently modified his earlier views and estimated that 3.5 million, or 25 per cent, of Nazi voters in July 1932 were working class; Mason, *Sozialpolitik*, pp. 62–78.

8. Childers, *Nazi Voter*, p. 245. cf. Kratzenberg, op. cit. pp. 61–2.

9. Childers, *Nazi Voter*, p. 268. He argues similarly in T. Childers, 'Who, Indeed, Did Vote for Hitler?', *Central European History*, 17 (1) (1984) p. 53.

10. Hamilton, *Who Voted*, pp. 91, 112, 122, 162, 179.

11. J. Falter, 'Unemployment and the Radicalisation of the German Electorate 1928–1933: An aggregate Data Analysis with Special Emphasis on the Rise of National Socialism', in P.D. Stachura (ed.), *Unemployment and the Great Depression in Weimar Germany* (London, 1986) p. 207.

12. Falter, 'Warum', pp. 229-30. See also Manstein, op. cit. pp. 182–93, 194 Table 7.

13. This issue is debated in *European History Quarterly;* D. Geary, 'Nazis and Workers: A Response to Conan Fischer's "Class Enemies or Class Brothers?"', *European History Quarterly*, 15 (4) (1985) pp. 453-64. Fischer, 'KPD and Nazism', *passim*.

14. Falter, 'Warum', pp. 222–5. J. Falter et al., 'Arbeitslosigkeit und Nationalsozialismus', *Kölner Zeitschrift für Soziologie und Sozial-psychologie*, 35 (1983) p. 535 Figure 6. Hamilton, *Who Voted*, pp. 78, 104.

15. Falter, 'Warum', pp. 227–8 and Table 5.

16. cf. E. Rosenhaft, 'The Unemployed in the Neighbourhood: Social Dislocation and Political Mobilisation in Germany 1929–33', in R. J. Evans, D. Geary (ed.), *The German Unemployed. Experiences and Consequences of Mass Unemployment from the Weimar Republic to the Third Reich* (London, 1987) pp. 194–227.

17. Thus, Geary, 'Nazis and Workers', pp. 454, 458–60.

18. Falter, 'Warum', p. 226 Table 4. Childers, *Nazi Voter*, pp. 186–7 Table 3.7, 254-5 Table 4.6.

19. Childers, *Nazi Voter*, pp. 254–5 Table 4.6.

20. Preller, op. cit. pp. 97–9; cf. Manstein, op. cit. pp. 12–13.

21. Childers, *Nazi Voter*, p. 225.

22. Ibid., pp. 254–5 Table 4.6.
23. cf. Falter, 'Warum', p. 226 Table 4. Falter, 'Arbeitslosigkeit', p. 535 Figure 6.
24. Childers, *Nazi Voter*, pp. 254–5 Table 4.6. cf. D. Hänisch, *Sozialstrukturelle Bestimmungsgründe des Wahlverhaltens in der Weimarer Republik* (Duisburg, 1983) p. 176 Table 42, where the Nazis' improving performance within the urban working class is indicated.
25. Childers, as in note 24 above.
26. Falter, 'Warum', pp. 227–8 esp. Table 5. cf. Manstein, op. cit. pp. 11–13.
27. Falter, 'Unemployment', p. 205 Table 8.6.
28. See pp.138–9 bèlow.
29. cf. Falter, 'Arbeitslosigkeit', p. 535 Figure 6. For a more general exposition; Falter, 'Warum', pp. 224–5.
30. Falter, 'Warum', p. 220–2. Manstein, op. cit. pp. 182–93, esp. p. 193.
31. Manstein, op. cit. p. 11.
32. Ibid., p. 165.
33. See pp. 76–7, 109–11 above.
34. Thus, I. Buchloh, *Die nationalsozialistische Machtergreifung in Duisburg. Eine Fallstudie* (Duisburg, 1980) p. 35; Falter, *Warum*, pp. 227–8 and Table 5. For similar trends in factory politics:Bahne, *KPD und das Ende*, p. 54.
35. See pp. 111–17 above and ch.8 and 9 below.
36. J. W. Falter, 'Die Wähler der NSDAP 1928-1933: Sozialstruktur und parteipolitische Herkunft', in W. Michalka (ed.), *Die nationalsozialistische Machtergreifung* (Paderborn, Munich, Vienna, Zürich, 1984) p. 54 Table 4.
37. Hamilton, *Who Voted*, p. 74 Table 4.2, 108 Table 5.2. cf. Bahne, *KPD und das Ende*, p. 29, where the fall in the KPD's working class support in Berlin, Hamburg and Merseburg is noted.
38. cf. J. Noakes, *The Nazi Party in Lower Saxony 1921-1933* (Oxford, 1971) pp. 139–46. cf. Ward, op. cit. pp. 34, 36.
39. For instance: BA R45IV/9. Bericht über Wahlversammlungen im Bezirk Thüringen vom 3. bis 7.12.29. BA R45IV/9. Bericht über Versammlungstour in Nordbayern (vom 9. November bis 8. Dezember 1929). Berlin 9 December 1929. gez. Ewert.
40. BA R45IV/15. 4. Plenar-ZK-Sitzung. 26/29 November 1929.
41. BA R134/58(176). Deutsche Nachrichtenkonferenz . . . 28 and 29 April 1930. 9).
42. BA R45IV/16. Bericht zum 1. Bezirksparteitag der KPD, Bezirk Sachsen – am 3. und 4. Mai in Dresden . . . 1. Sächsische Landtagswahlen. cf. Ward, op. cit. p. 34.
43. BA R134/58(177–8). Deutsche Nachrichtenkonferenz . . . 28 and 29 April 1930.
44. SB 4,65/253/47. Aus Mitteilungen Nr. 21 des Pol. Präs. Berlin, 1 November 1930. N. Stelle Nr. 2762/30 geh. v. 7.11.31. II. Linksradikale Bewegung p. 59.
45. SB 4,65/253/47. As above pp. 22-3. cf. Falter, 'Warum', p. 228 Table 5.
46. SB 4,65/253/47. As above p. 27. cf. Childers, *Nazi Voter*, pp. 186–7 Table 3.7.
47. SB 4,65/253/47. As above p. 26. cf. Falter, 'Warum', p. 228.

48. SB 4,65/253/47. As in note 44 above p. 28. cf. Geary's contrary assertion in 'Nazis and Workers', pp. 457–8.
49. BA R45IV/18. Abschrift. An das Zentralkomitee der KPD. Schriftlicher Vorbericht über das Resultat der Wahlen aus dem Bezirk Halle-Merseburg 12b). cf. Falter, 'Warum', p. 222, where he argues that the NSDAP had fared well electorally in working-class areas of Saxony.
50. SB 4,65/252/46. RI. IAN 2160/6.10. Betrifft: Kommunistische Bewegung. Berlin, 6 October 1930. Anlage p. 4.
51. SB 4,65/253/47. Aus Mitteilungen Nr. 21 den Pol. Präs., Berlin vom 1. November 1930. II. Linksradikale Bewegung p. 35.
52. SB 4,65/252/46. Ausschnitt aus den Mitteilungen Nr. 19 des Pol. Präs. Berlin vom Sept. 1930. N. Stelle Nr. 2498/30 geh. 7 October 1930. b. Stellungnahme Thälmanns zu den Wahlen.
53. BA R45IV/40. Pressedienst Nr. 112. Blatt 14. Die Oldenburger Landtagswahlen. 18 May 1931.
54. SB 4,65/259/49. Vertraulich! Linksbewegung. Kommunistische Partei. Allgemeines. München, 19 May 1932. BA R45IV/25. Protokoll der erweiterten Sekretariatssitzung der B.I. Pommern 26 April 1932. SB 4,65/260/49. L. Nr. 112. Ausschrift. Linksbewegung. Kommunistische Partei. Allgemeines. München, 3 October 1932. cf. SB 4,65/259/49. L. Nr. 110. Linksbewegung. Kommunistische Partei. München, 4 April 1932. BA NS26/1405. Berichte der Staatspolizei Württembergs zur politischen Lage. 13 May 1932. KPD und Landtagswahlen.
55. BA R45IV/21. Bericht Nr. 2 (Württemberg). 16 April 1932.
56. BA R45IV/25. Protokoll der erweiterten Sekretariatssitzung der B.L. Pommern vom 26. April 1932 p. 3. cf. Ward, op. cit. p. 37, for similar conclusions on Saxony.
57. BA NS26/1405. Berichte der Staatspolizei Württembergs zur politischen Lage. 25 June 1932.
58. SB 4,65/260/49. Rundschreiben Nr. 13. Anweisungen des Sekretariats. Berlin, 8 August 1932. I. Unser Wahlsieg.
59. A. Milatz, *Wähler und Wahlen in der Weimarer Republik* (Bonn, 1968) p. 151.
60. Geheimes Staatsarchiv München (GStAM), Monatsberichte der Regierungspräsidenten/Lageberichte (MA) 100 417/1. Linksbewegung. Kommunistische Partei. Allgemeines. München, 24 October 1930. BA NS26/1403. Landespolizei Württemberg. 1 October 1930. p. 3ff. Das Anwachsen der KPD . . . SB 4,65/252/46. Polizeidirektion Nürnberg-Fürth. Sonderbericht Nr. 181/II/30. Betreff: Arbeitsplan der KPD-Nordbayern für Oktober–November 1930. Nürnberg, 22 October 1930. cf. BA R134/40(18). RKo 126. 20 July 1928. II. A.2, noting the lack of any real progress by the KPD in the countryside in the 1928 election.
61. BA R45IV/21. Bezirk Pommern: Gesamtwahlergebnis. (July 1932). p. 1.
62. BA R45IV/21. Bezirk Mecklenburg, p. 7.
63. BA R45IV/21. Bezirk Oberschlesien, p. 3.
64. BA R45IV/21. Bezirk Halle-Merseburg pp. 5–6. cf. Bahne, *KPD und das Ende*, p. 29, who mentions KPD setbacks in working-class areas.
65. BA R45IV/21. Bezirk Großthüringen, p. 19.
66. BA R45IV/21. Bezirk Magdeburg-Anhalt, p. 2 (26).

67. BA R45IV/21. Bezirk Niederrhein, p. 8.
68. BA R45IV/21. Bezirk Niederrhein, pp. 8–9.
69. BA R45IV/21. Bezirk Ruhrgebiet, p. 23.
70. BA R45IV/21. Bezirk Mittelrhein, p. 11. Bezirk Hessen-Frankfurt, p. 13. Bezirk Baden-Pfalz, pp. 14–15. Bezirk Nordbayern, pp. 16–17.
71. SB 4,65/260/49. L. Nr. 112. Ausschrift. Linksbewegung. Kommunistische Partei. Allgemeines. München, 3 October 1932. SB 4,65/2039/ 362. Ausschrift aus L.B. Stuttgart vom 10.1.32. KPD und Reichstagwahlen.
72. BA R45IV/28(212–13). V–VI [Freiberg 3.8.32]. BA R45IV/28(250–5). Wahlergebnisse Chemnitz. 6 August 1932. pp. 5– 10. BA R45IV/22. UB 9. Einschätzung des Wahlergebnisses des UB 9, aus den Amtshauptmannschaften Plauen-Auerbach-Oelsnitz i/V. 1 August 1932.
73. BA R45IV/22. As above.
74. BA R45IV/28. Bericht des UB Chemnitz zur Durchführung der Reichstagwahl am 31.7.32.
75. Bahne, *KPD und das Ende*, p. 29.
    A. Milatz, 'Das Ende der Parteien im Spiegel der Wahlen 1930 bis 1933', in E. Matthias, R. Morsey (ed.), *Das Ende der Parteien 1933* (Düsseldorf, 1960) p. 778.
76. SB 4,65/260/49. Abschrift aus der Zeitschrift *Der Pionier des Bolschewismus . . .* August 1932, p. 2.
77. BA R45IV/21. Bezirk Ruhrgebiet, p. 24. cf. Bezirk Pommern, p. 1.
78. cf. Hunt, op. cit. p. 126. Rohe, Revier pp. 11–59.
79. cf. BA R45IV/21. Bezirk Großthüringen, p. 18.
    K. Rohe, 'Die Vorgeschichte: Das Parteiensystem in den preußischen Westprovinzen und in Lippe-Detmold 1871–1933', in U. von Alemann (ed.), *Parteien und Wahlen in Nordrhein-Westfalen* (Cologne, 1985 p. 36.
80. SB 4,65/260/49. Rundschreiben Nr. 13. Anweisungen des Sekretariats. Berlin, 8 August 1932. I. Unser Wahlsieg.
81. BA R45IV/21. Bezirk Großthüringen, p. 19.
82. BA R45IV/21. Bezirk Pommern p. 1. Bezirk Mittelrhein, p. 11. Bezirk Nordbayern, p. 17. cf. Milatz, Ende p. 780.
83. BA R45IV/13. Abschrift: 'Das Heranwachsen des revolutionären Aufschwunges in Deutschland', *Pravda* 2 August 1932, pp. 3–4.
84. cf. Milatz, *Ende*, p. 786.
85. BA R45IV/38. Materialien über Reichstagwahl, November 1932. KPD Bezirk Niederrhein, pp. 4, 8.
86. SB 4,65/261/49. Amt Butjadingen. Betrifft: KPD Nordenham, 13 January 1933.
87. SB 4,65/2040/362. '100 Prozent gewonnen. Die Früchte guter Landarbeit', *Arbeiter Zeitung*, 260, 8 November 1932.
88. SB 4,65/261/49. Bericht der Bezirksleitung des Bezirks Mecklenburg der KPD über die Arbeit der Partei 1931/32, p. 9. In Mecklenburg-Schwerin the rural vote also rose faster in relative terms, but, unlike M.-Strelitz, not in absolute terms.
89. SB 4,65/2039/362. Abschrift. Entwurf. Entschliessung der Plenar-B.L. des Bezirks Ruhrgebiet zu den Ergebnissen der Reichstagswahl am 6.11.32. pp. 2–3.

90. SB 4,65/2039/362. Ausschrift aus L.B. Stuttgart vom 10.11.32. KPD u. Reichstagswahlen.
91. BA R45IV/38. 'Niederrhein, rote Hochburg!', *Der Revolutionär*, November 1932.
92. BA R45IV/38. Materialien über Reichstagswahl November 1932. KPD Bezirk Niederrhein, pp. 4, 6, 8.
93. SB 4,65/283/56. Ausschrift aus dem Bericht der KPD über den Bezirksparteitag am 26./27.11.32. Z. St. 6932/32 geh. p. 40.
94. SB 4,65/2039/362. 'Ergebnisse aus Osthannover. . . .', *Bremer Volkszeitung*, 262, 7 November 1932. cf. Milatz, 'Ende', p. 786.
95. S. Neumann, *Die Parteien der Weimarer Republik*, 4th ed. (Stuttgart, 1977) p. 94.
96. cf. Neumann, op. cit. pp. 88–90. E. Rosenhaft, *Beating the Fascists? The German Communists and Political Violence 1929–1933* (Cambridge, 1983) p. 52. J. Wickham, 'The Working Class Movement in Frankfurt-am-Main during the Weimar Republic', (D. Phil. Dissertation, University of Sussex, 1979) p. 195.
97. cf. Dorpalen, 'SPD und KPD', p. 87.
98. BA R134/40(24). RKo 126. 20 July 1928. II. A3. See also Schöck, op. cit. pp. 226–27; Fowkes, op. cit. p. 173.
99. BA R45IV/36. 'Unser Bezirk im Aufgebot der 100,000', *Der Bolschewik*, 3 (10), Early June 1932, p. 157.
100. GStAM MA 101 241/1. Polizeidirektion Nürnberg-Fürth. Anlage zu Sonderbericht Nr. 191/II/31.
101. Thus; Institut für Zeitgeschichte (IfZ) MA-198/2 (Preußen 6). Abschrift. Die Ortspolizeibehörde. Minden, 27 April 1933. GStAM Reichsstatthalter (R) 283 and R281, where lists of Communists interned between 1933 and 1935 are found. cf. Bahne, *KPD und das Ende*, p. 52.
102. See pp.132 below, and Bahne, *KPD und das Ende*, p. 16.
103. Manstein, op. cit. pp. 164, 194.
104. Estimates vary between 252 000 and 360 000 for 1932. Bahne, *KPD und das Ende*, p. 16. Flechtheim, op. cit. p. 347. Fowkes, op. cit. p. 205 Table A2.
105. See p. 129 above.
106. Reichsorganisationsleiter der NSDAP (ed.), *Partei-Statistik. Stand 1. Januar 1935* (Munich, 1935) p. 70. These figures exclude those who had joined but then left again before 1935.
107. Extracted from Kater, *Nazi Party*, p. 250 Table 6, 255 Table 9, and Partei-Statistik p. 26.
108. SB 4,65/255/47. 'Die Lage in Deutschland und die Aufgaben der KPD', *Die Rote Fahne*, 142, 4 July 1931. cf. Fischer, *Stormtroopers*, pp. 25–9. Since the completion of this manuscript, P. Longerich, *Die braunen Bataillone. Geschichte der SA* (Munich 1989), has played down the working-class element in the SA, but D. Mühlberger, *Hitler's Followers* (London, 1990) ch. 7, produces considerable fresh statistical evidence that confirms and, if anything, reinforces the argument advanced in *Stormtroopers* that the SA was strongly working class.
109. Fischer, *Stormtroopers* pp. 19, 23 note 37. M. Jamin, 'Zur Rolle der SA im nationalsozialistischen Herrschaftssystem', in G. Hirschfeld, L. Kettenacker (ed.), *Der „Führerstaat": Mythos und Realität. Studien zur*

Struktur und Politik des Dritten Reiches (Stuttgart, 1981) pp. 332–3. Mühlberger, *Followers*, ch. 7.

110. H. W. Koch, *The Hitler Youth. Origins and Development 1922–1945* (London, 1975) pp. 85–6. P. D. Stachura, *Nazi Youth in the Weimar Republic* (Santa Barbara, Oxford, 1975) pp. 58–62.
111. See pp. 162–3, 166–71 below.
112. cf. Manstein, op. cit. pp. 11–13.
113. BA R45IV/26. Bezirksleitung Berlin-Brandenburg-Lausitz. An alle Strassenzellen in Gross-Berlin. Berlin, 2 June 1930 p. 4. BA R45IV/11. Bericht über die Kontrolle im Bezirk Halle-Merseburg. VI. Werbearbeit. Berlin, 16 March 1931.
114. SB 4,65/255/47. L. Nr. 100. Linksbewegung. Kommunistische Partei. München, 10 May 1931 p. 1.
115. SB 4,65/257/48. Aus den Mitteilungen des Landeskriminalpolizeiamts (henceforward MdL) (I) Berlin, 1 December 1931, Nr. 23. b) Werbekampagne . . . SB 4,65/1273/212. Reichsleitung des Kampfbundes gegen den Faschismus. Bundeskasse. Rundschreiben! Die Ursachen der Fluktuation . . . Berlin, 30 March 1932. SB 4,65/259/49. P-PB 12 June 1932. Abschrift. Arbeitsplan für Mai/Juni 32. p. 4.
116. SB 4,65/260/49. Badisches Landespolizeiamt. Die kommunistische Bewegung in Baden. Karlsruhe, 21 December 1932 pp. 4–5.
117. SB 4,65/260/49. As above, pp. 24–5. Daycock, op. cit. p. 183.
118. BA R134/89(90). IAN 2167/10.10. (18.10.32). cf. Fowkes, op. cit. p. 177.
119. BA R45IV/32. Kampf der Fluktuation! (24 August 1932).
120. Bahne, *KPD und das Ende,* pp. 16, 35. Daycock, op. cit. p. 183. Flechtheim, op. cit. p. 240. Hunt, op. cit. p. 102.
121. SB 4,65/257/48. MdL (I) Berlin, 1 December 1931, Nr. 23. b); Fowkes, op. cit. p. 176.
122. SB 4,65/257/48. As above. SB 4,65/260/49. Badisches Landespolizeiamt. Die kommunistische Bewegung in Baden. Karlsruhe, 21 December 1932. cf. Bahne, *KPD und das Ende,* p. 16; C. Fischer, 'Unemployment and Left-Wing Radicalism in Weimar Germany, 1930–1933', in P. D. Stachura (ed.), *Unemployment and the Great Depression in Weimar Germany* (London, 1986) p. 215.
123. Fowkes, op. cit. p. 176.
124. Fischer, 'Unemployment', pp. 214–21. cf. D. Peukert, 'The Lost Generation: Youth Unemployment at the End of the Weimar Republic', in R. J. Evans, D. Geary (eds), *The German Unemployed. Experiences and Consequences of Mass Unemployment from the Weimar Republic to the Third Reich* (London, 1987) pp. 188–9. The implications of this youthful, largely male profile are discussed more fully in Chapter 8 below.
125. Falter, 'Unemployment', *passim.*
126. Partei-Statistik pp. 297–9.
127. Falter, 'Unemployment', p. 205 Table 8.6; cf. Borkenau, op. cit. pp. 364, 366.
128. Rosenhaft, 'Unemployed', *passim;* Buchloh, op. cit. pp. 25–39; cf.

Borkenau, op. cit. pp. 361–2, who reveals a similar situation in most European communist parties at this time.

129. See discussion in ch. 9, p. 161ff below.
130. Hunt, op. cit. p. 105.
131. BA R134/40(24). RKo 126. 20 July 1928. II. A.3b. Bahne, *KPD und das Ende*, p. 15, also cites the figure of 0.59 per cent, but attributes it (too restrictedly) to industrial workers only.
132. Schöck, op. cit. pp. 101, 106, 250–2 Tables 18, 19; Buchloh, op. cit. pp. 56–8.
133. BA R134/40(26). RKo 126. 20 July 1928. II. A.3b.
134. Quoted in Flechtheim, op. cit. p. 241.
135. L. Peterson, 'Labor and the End of Weimar: The Case of the KPD in the November 1928 Lockout in the Rhenish-Westphalian Iron and Steel Industry', *Central European History*, 15(1) (1982) p. 65.
136. Flechtheim, op. cit. p. 239.
137. BA R134/81(125). Abschrift. IAN 2160/29.4 Berlin, 13 March 1931.
138. SB 4,65/257/48. MdL (I) Berlin, 1 December 1931, Nr. 23. b). The figure given was 29 per cent of 250,000 members; i.e. 72,500.
139. BA NS26/810. Anlage 1b. Anteil der betriebstätigen Mitglieder (nach Beitragsklassen). Anlage 1c. (Title as 1b).
140. SB 4,65/257/48. MdL (I) Berlin, 1 November 1931, Nr. 21. III. 1a.
141. SB 4,65/1273/212. NRI. IAN 2166 h/30.3. Betrifft: Kampfbund gegen den Faschismus. Berlin, 7 April 1932.
142. SB 4,65/261/49. Bericht der Bezirksleitung des Bezirks Mecklenburg der KPD über die Arbeit der Partei 1931/32. p. 9; BA R45IV/21. Extract from *Lenins Weg*, Hanover, June 1932; BA NS26/1405. Berichte der Staatspolizei Württembergs zur politischen Lage. 23 December 1932. Bezirksparteitag der KPD . . . .
143. SB 4,65/274/53. MdL (IA) Berlin, 15 August 1931, Nr. 16. II. p. 12; SB 4,65/257/48. MdL (I) Berlin, 1 November 1931, Nr. 12. III. 1a).
144. SB 4,65/260/49. Zu IAN 2162/11.10. Bericht von der Agitprop-Konferenz am 16. September 1932, p. 2.
145. SB 4,65/260/49. Abschrift. P-PB. PNPW. Betrifft: KPD. Bochum, 24 August 1932, p. 3. cf. S. Bahne, 'Die KPD im Ruhrgebiet in der Weimarer Republik', in J. Reulecke (ed.) *Arbeiterbewegung an Rhein und Ruhr. Beiträge zur Geschichte der Arbeiterbewegung in Rheinland-Westfalen* (Wuppertal, 1974) p. 343. Borkenau, op. cit. p. 364.
146. SB 4,65/260/49. As above p. 5.
147. BA R45IV/21. Versammlungsberichte – Wasserkante. Harburg, 22 April 1932. gez. Oskar Müller.
148. BA R45IV/21. Entwicklung der Partei und RGO in Braunschweig. February? 1932. b. Betriebszellen.
149. Bahne, *Ruhrgebiet*, p. 335.
150. Bahne, *KPD und das Ende*, p. 52; Fischer, 'Unemployment', pp. 220–1.
151. Bahne, *KPD und das Ende* pp. 18–19. Fowkes, op. cit. p. 159. See also pp. 163–66 below.
152. Bahne, *KPD und das Ende*, p. 18. But cf. SB 4,65/281/56. Polizei-Direktion. Zentralpolizeistelle B. Nr. 6106/32 geh. MdL (I). Berlin, 15

October 1932, Nr. 20, f; which gives a rather higher figure (322 000) for August 1932.

153. Bahne, *KPD und das Ende*, p. 18. cf. SB 4,65/280/55. P-PB. PNPW I Nr. 143/32. Betrifft: Zunehmende Aktivität der RGO. Bochum, 11 June 1932. Abschrift c. p. 5.

154. Bahne, *KPD und das Ende*, p. 19.

155. SB 4,65/283/56. Ausschrift aus dem Bericht der KPD über den Bezirksparteitag am 26./27.11.32. Z. St. 6932/32 geh. . . . Mitgliederbewegung der RGO im Bez. Weser-Ems 1931/32.

156. Bahne, *KPD und das Ende*, p. 18. See also; BA R45IV/21. Bericht über Instrukteurreise nach Thüringen 5 March 1931. VII R.G.O. cf. the very different impression given in Degras, op. cit., III, p. 153.

157. SB 4,65/283/56. As in note 155 above. SB 4,65/281/56. Polizei-Direktion. Zentralpolizeistelle. B. Nr. 6106/32 geh. MdL (I). Berlin, 15 October 1932, Nr. 20. SB 4,65/281/56. Polizei-Direktion: Zentralpolizeistelle. B. Nr. 4610/32 geh. MdL (I). Berlin, 1 August 1932. Nr. 15. 2. RGO.

158. SB 4,65/281/56. 15 October 1932, as in note 157 above.

159. BA R45IV/21. Entwicklung der Partei und RGO in Braunschweig Feb? 1932. BA R45IV/21. Versammlungsberichte – Wasserkante. Harburg. 22 April 1932. gez. Oskar Müller. cf. Bahne, 'Ruhrgebiet', p. 347.

160. Bahne, *KPD und das Ende*, pp. 31–2. Schöck, op. cit. p. 254 Table 21.

161. Schöck, op. cit. pp. 250–1 Table 18, 255, 256–7 Table 23. cf. C. Seifert, 'Die deutsche Gewerkschaftsbewegung in der Weimarer Republik', in F. Deppe, G. Fülberth, J. Harrer (ed.), *Geschichte der deutschen Gewerkschaftsbewegung*, 3rd eds. (Cologne, 1981) p. 192.

162. SB 4,65/274/53. Auszug aus L.B. Nr. 102 v. 12.7.31 der Pol. Dir. München. Revolutionäre Gewerkschaftsopposition. BA NS26/1404. Berichte der Staatspolizei Württembergs zur politischen Lage. 25 March 1931. Betriebsrätewahlergebnisse.

163. SB 4,65/280/55. 'Schwerer Schlag für die RGO . . .', *Bremer Volkszeitung*, 103, 3 May 1932.

164. Bahne, 'Ruhrgebiet', p. 348.

165. BA R45IV/13. Nr. 386. Inform. Tagesnotizen vom 23. Juni 1932. Innenpolitik p. 7.

166. BA R134/81(35-6). IAN 2160e/16.7. Berlin 16 July 1930. Anlage.

167. See ch. 9 below.

168. SB 4,65/1270/211. 'Hakenstern und Sowjetkreuz . . .', *Bremer Volkszeitung*, 67, 20 March 1931.

169. Bahne, *KPD und das Ende*, p. 16. Buchloh, op. cit. p. 35. J. Fest, *The Face of the Third Reich*, trans. M. Bullock (London, 1972) p. 220. Schüddekopf, op. cit. p. 375.

170. Fischer, *Stormtroopers*, ch. 9.

171. SB 4,65/255/47. Aus L. B. Stuttgart Nr. W.8 – N. Stelle Nr. 2325/31 geh. 17 June 1931. 18. Aus der KPD. BA R45IV/21. 'Ergebnisse des Aufgebots der 100 000' (for Thuringia). BA R45IV/25. Bezirksleitung Südbayern. An das Zentralkomitee. Abt. Org. und Sekretariat. München, 19 May 1932. See also; SB 4,65/256/48. '14 402 Neuaufnahmen für die KPD', *Die Rote Fahne*, 160, 25 August 1931. BA R134/93(4-4a). NRI. IAN 2160a/8.12. Berlin, 16 December 1932.

172. BA NS26/810. Die organisatorische Entwicklung der Partei im Jahre 1931. Anlagen 6a, 6b.
173. BA R134/58(207). Deutsche Nachrichtenkonferenz, 28 and 29 April 1930. SB 4,65/259/49. Die Lage in der KPD (München 20 April 1932). BA NS26/1404. Berichte der Staatspolizei Württembergs zur politischen Lage, 25 November 1931. See also Fischer, *Stormtroopers*, pp. 211–12.
174. SB 4,65/270/52. Abschrift. Nachrichtensammelstelle (henceforward Na) I Nr. 829/30. Betr.: Bergbau-Konferenz (der RGO) Ruhrgebiet. Bochum, 10 July 1930. SB 4,65/278/55. Polizei-Direktion. Zentralpolizeistelle. B. Nr. 5991/31 geh. Betr.: RGO-Kongress am 5. u. 6.12.31 in Sielers Festsälen. Bremen, 14 December 1931. BA R134/94(42). NRI. IAN 2160^5/29.12. Berlin, 6 January 1933. SB 4,65/282/56. 'Streiks, Lohnbewegungen und Erwerbslosenkämpfe. Bezirk Weser-Ems', *Die Information!*, 7, 3. Januarwoche 1933. p. 4.
175. BA R45IV/23. Bezirk Baden-Pfalz. An das ZK der KPD, Sekretariat Berlin. Bericht über die Vorbereitung und Durchführung der Antifaschistischen Aktion. Mannheim, 11 June 1932. BA R45IV/23. Abschrift. Bezirksleitung Mittelrhein. An das ZK/Sekretariat. Bericht über den Stand der Antifaschistischen Aktion im Bezirk Mittelrhein. Köln, 14 June 1932. BA R45IV/23. Abschrift. Bezirksleitung der KPD Groß-Thüringen. An das Sekretariat des ZK. Bericht des Bezirks Thüringen über die Antifaschistische Aktion. Erfurt, 10 June 1932. BA R45IV/23. Bezirksleitung Oberschlesien der KPD. An das Zentralkomitee Abt. Sekretariat, Berlin. Betr.: Bericht über die Einleitung zur Antifaschistischen Aktion. Hindenburg, 10 June 1932.

8 THE BATTLE FOR THE UNEMPLOYED AND FOR TERRITORY

1. See pp. 132-5 above.
2. A. McElligott, 'Mobilising the Unemployed: The KPD and the Unemployed Workers' Movement in Hamburg-Altona during the Weimar Republic', in R. J. Evans, D. Geary (eds.), *The German Unemployed. Experiences and Consequences of Mass Unemployment from the Weimer Republic to the Third Reich* (London, 1987) esp. IV. For an isolated Communist advocacy of the creation of a genuine unemployed movement; BA R45IV/11. Protokoll über die Sitzung der engeren BL . . . Halle, 21 March 1932, p. 17 Gen: Sch.-Erwerbslose.
3. Falter, 'Unemployment', p. 206.
4. For instance: E. W. Bakke, *The Unemployed Man* (Nisbet, 1933) p. 149. See also; E. W. Bakke, 'The Cycle of Adjustment to Unemployment', in N. W. Bell, E. F. Vogel (eds), *A Modern Introduction to the Family* (Glencoe, Ill., 1960) pp. 113, 121.
5. P. Eisenberg, P. F. Lazarsfeld, 'The Psychological Effects of Unemployment', *Psychological Bulletin* (1938), p. 378.
6. M. Jahoda, P. F. Lazarsfeld, H. Zeisel, *Die Arbeitslosen von Marienthal* (Bonn, 1960) pp. 37–41, 54. (First published Leipzig, 1933).
7. Thus; D. Geary, 'Unemployment and Working Class Solidarity in Germany, 1929–1933', in R. J. Evans, D. Geary (eds), *The German*

236   *Notes to Chapter 8*

Unemployed (as in note 2 above) p. 261.
8. As in Geary, 'Unemployment', esp. p. 275, but cf. McElligott, 'Mobilising', pp. 252–3.
9. Eisenberg, Lazarsfeld, op. cit. pp. 359, 364.
10. Ibid. pp. 369–72, 375, 384.
11. cf. A. Sinfield, *What Unemployment Means* (Oxford, 1981) p. 68.
12. Neumann, op. cit. pp. 80–2, 87.
13. Jahoda et al., op. cit. p. 42; cf. Wickham, op. cit. p. 218.
14. Neumann, op. cit. p. 87.
15. Rosenberg, op. cit. p. 199. McElligott, 'Mobilising', esp. III.
16. F. Wunderlich, 'New Aspects of Unemployment in Germany', *Social Research*, I (1934) pp. 97, 99, 100–4.
17. Quoted in C. Severing, *Mein Lebensweg*, vol. 2 (Cologne, 1950) p. 357. cf. Wickham, op. cit. p. 189.
18. Wunderlich, op. cit. pp. 105, 108. cf. R. J. Geary, 'Jugendarbeitslosigkeit und politischer Radikalismus in der Weimarer Republik', *Gewerkschaftliche Monatshefte,* (May 1983) p. 307.
19. cf. Peukert, Lost Generation pp. 183–4. Rosenhaft, 'Unemployed', p. 210.
20. Wunderlich, op. cit. pp. 108-9. cf. Sinfield, op. cit. p. 68. BA R45IV/39. 'Schluß mit dem SA Terror' pp. 4–5. 'Die wahren Schuldigen'. Here, the KPD explains the SA's success in recruiting so many workers in terms remarkably similar to Wunderlich's.
21. Rosenhaft, *Beating the Fascists?,* p. 49.
22. cf. Fischer, 'Unemployment', pp. 214–15.
23. H. Möller, 'Die nationalsozialistische Machtergreifung. Konterrevolution oder Revolution?', *Vierteljahreshefte für Zeitgeschichte,* 31 (1) (1983) p. 42. Rosenberg, op. cit. pp. 199–200. Wunderlich, op. cit. pp. 108–9. These sentiments are vividly expressed in Bertolt Brecht's poem 'Das Lied vom SA-Mann', esp. Verse 2: 'Da sah ich viele marschieren/ Sie sagten: ins Dritte Reich/Ich hatte nichts zu verlieren/Und lief mit, wohin war mir gleich'.
24. Rosenberg, op. cit. p. 200; Neumann, op. cit. p. 88.
25. See pp. 131–4 above, and; SB 4,65/257/48. Aus den Mitteilungen des Landeskriminalpolizeiamts (I) Berlin, 1 December 1931, Nr. 23 b). cf. Neumann, op. cit. p. 88.
26. cf. D. Watts, 'Electoral Success and Political Failure: The KPD in Mannheim in the Last Years of the Weimar Republic', *European History Quarterly,* 18 (4) (1988) pp. 446–50.
27. SB 4,65/251/46. Imprekorr. Nr. 11. 31 January 1930. cf. SB 4,65/251/46. Abschrift aus dem Lagebericht der Pol. Dir. München, 7 February 1930. Br. B. Nr. 375/30 geh. N.-Stelle.
28. SB 4,65/251/46. Zentralkomitee der Kommunistischen Partei Deutschlands. Sekretariat. Brief des Zentralkomitees. Berlin, early June 1930 p. 3.
29. SB 4,65/251/46. Imprekorr Nr. 11. 31 January 1930. 'Der Verlauf der Lenin-Tage in den kapitalistischen Ländern'. BA R45IV/24. Zentralkomitee der KPD. Sekretariat. Rundschreiben Nr. 8. Berlin, 4 July 1930. Anweisungen der Agitpropabteilung p. 3. SB

4,65/255/47. MdL (IA) Berlin, 15 May 1931, Nr. 10. IV. p. 1. SB
4,65/260/49. Abschrift. P-PB. Betrifft: *Pionier des Bolschewismus.*
Bochum, 5 October 1932.
30. cf. McElligott, 'Mobilising', passim.
31. BA R134/62(237). Abschrift IAN 2160/2.6. Berlin, 8 May 1931. 3).
32. Wickham, op. cit. pp. 194–5.
33. B. Herlemann, *Kommunalpolitik der KPD im Ruhrgebiet 1924–1933*
(Wuppertal, 1977) p. 178.
34. BA R134/83(160–2). NRI. IAN 2164 d/8.6. Berlin, 18 June 1932.
Anlage.
35. Ibid.
36. BA R134/92(11a) Abschrift IAN 2165b/9.12. Berlin, 11 April 1932.
37. cf. SB 4,65/253/47. Rundschreiben Nr. 14. Anweisungen des
Sekretariats. Berlin, 6 October 1930. II.
38. BA R134/83(159). NRI. IAN 2164 d/8.6. Berlin, 18 June 1932.
39. cf. BA R134/62(237). Abschrift IAN 2160/2.6. Berlin, 8 May 1931. 3),
where the KPD discusses the identity of material interests between
workers of different political persuasions.
40. BA R134/83(161–2). As in note 34.
41. BA R134/83(164). As in note 34.
42. BA R45IV/23. Bezirksleitung Oberschlesien der KPD. Betr: Bericht
über die Einleitung zur Antifaschistischen Aktion. Hindenburg, 10 June
1932.
43. BA R45IV/44. 'Wir lauten die Sturmglocken zum Millionen-Angriff!
. . .', November 1932 p. 3. BA R134/92(49, 51). NRI. IAN 2160[7]/3.12a.
44. BA NS26/1404. Berichte der Staatspolizei Württembergs zur politischen
Lage. 21 January 1931. SB 4,65/1272/212. Ausschnitt aus dem L.B. Nr.
104 München, 28 September 1931. Z.-St. Nr. 4298/31 geh. Kampfbund
gegen den Faschismus.
45. BA R134/83(164–5). NRI. IAN 2164 d/8.6. Berlin, 18 June 1932.
46. Herlemann, op. cit. pp. 91-107, 175, 179, 183-6. cf. Flechtheim, op. cit.
p. 279. McElligott, 'Mobilising', esp. pp. 249–54. See also; BA
NS26/1404. Berichte der Staatspolizei Württembergs zur politischen
Lage. 21 January 1931.
47. Rosenhaft, *Beating the Fascists?* p. 52. Fischer, *Stormtroopers,* p. 209.
48. Fischer, *Stormtroopers,* pp. 115–22.
49. BA R45IV/11. Bericht über die Ermittlung der Arbeit in der Filmfabrik
Wolfen 1932, p.6; BA R45IV/11. Bericht über den Bezirk Halle-
Merseburg (2–6 May 1932) p. 3. gez. Werner.
50. BA R134/74(127). NRI. IAN 2166a/23.12.31. Berlin, 14 January 1932.
Abschrift.
51. BA R45IV/45. Reichsfraktionsleitung der Kommunisten in der RGO.
Betr. Herstellung der praktischen Einheitsfront . . . . Berlin, 11 May
1932, p. 6.
52. SB 4,65/260/49. Abschrift. Internationale Arbeiterhilfe. Landesvorstand
Wasserkante. Schafft Solidaritäts-Kommissionen! Hamburg, 30 August
1932.
53. BA R134/92(106). NRI. IAN 2160/14.11. Berlin, 15 December 1932.
Abschrift. V.

54. BA R134/84(61). Ministerium des Innern. Oldenburg, August 1932. Anlage 2. VI.
55. Rosenhaft, *Beating the Fascists?*, pp., 43, 45; Rosenhaft, 'Unemployment', esp. VII; Wickham, op. cit. p. 218; Wunderlich, op. cit. p. 108.
56. SB 4,65/255/47. Abschrift. P-PB I Nr. 239/31. Betrifft: KPD, Bezirksleitung Ruhrgebiet . . . . Bochum, 11 May 1931. Anlage. SB 4,65/255/47. Abschrift. RI. IA 2130/15.7. Betrifft: Kommunistische Partei. Berlin, 25 July 1931. BA R45IV/28. Arbeitsplan der Ortsgruppe Grossenhain für Monat Juni (1932). Erwerbslosenbewegung. See also; BA NS26/1403. Berichte der Staatspolizei zur politischen Lage. [Württemberg]. Stuttgart, 22 January 1930 p. 7. SB 4,65/253/47. RI. IAN 2160/26.11. Betrifft: Kommunistische Bewegung. Berlin, 26 November 1930.
57. BA R134/62(267). NRI. IAN 2160/6.7. Berlin, 6 July 1931.
58. SB 4,65/272/53. Polizei-Direktion: N.-Stelle B. Nr. 580/31 geh. Bremen, 21 February 1931. Abschrift: Richtlinien für den Aufbau des Kampfbundes gegen den Faschismus, p. 4.
59. SB 4,65/281/56. Polizei-Direktion: Zentralpolizeistelle. B. Nr. 3413/32 geh. Betr. Bezirkskonferenz der RGO. Bremen, 22 June 1932, pp. 4–5.
60. BA R134/82(224). Abschrift. IAN 2164d 3/6.1. Richtlinien . . . 4.
61. BA R134/84(4). NRI. IAN 2164 d/6.6. Berlin, 9 July 1932.
62. BA R134/84(111). Abschrift zu IAN 2164d/1.9. Berlin, August 1932. VI. See also; BA R45IV/23. Bezirk Baden-Pfalz. Bericht über die Vorbereitung und Durchführung der Antif. Aktion. Mannheim, 11 June 1932. BA R45IV/32. 'Enge Verbindung des Kampfes der Betriebsarbeiter mit den Kampfaktionen der Erwerbslosen', *Der Bolschewik*, 3 (16) p. 265.
63. Rosenberg, op. cit. pp. 199-200. Wunderlich, op. cit. pp. 108–9.
64. Eisenberg, Lazarsfeld, op. cit. p. 370; A. Gorz, *Farewell to the Working Class. An Essay on Post-Industrial Socialism*, trans. M. Sonenscher (London, 1982) pp. 58-9, 62; Möller, op. cit. p. 42; cf. Neumann, op. cit. p. 88.
65. SB 4,65/251/46. Ausschnitt aus dem Lagebericht der Pol. Dir. Nürnberg vom 6.5.30. N.-Stelle Br. B. Nr. 1137/30 geh. Bezirksparteitag der KPD-Nordbayern in Fürth, 14 April 1930. SB 4,65/251/46. Abschrift. Betrifft: Bezirksparteitag der KPD. Der Polizei-Präsident. Landeskriminalpolizeistelle. Hannover, 3 July 1930. BA NS26/1404. Berichte der Staatspolizei Württembergs zur politischen Lage. 21 January 1931. SB 4,65/274/53. Auszug aus L.B. Nr. 102 v. 12.7.31 der Pol. Dir. München. Revolutionäre Gewerkschaftsopposition. SB 4,65/281/56. Ausschrift aus L.B. München am 3.10.32. No. 112. ZB No 5813/32 geh. Revolutionäre Gewerkschaftsopposition. p. 15.
66. SB 4,65/251/46. Abschrift! Bezirksleitung Ruhrgebiet. Sekretariat. Arbeitsplan für die Monate Februar/März. Essen, 31 January 1930 pp. 5–6. SB 4,65/280/55. P-PB. I Nr. 121/32. Bochum, 2 May 1932. Abschrift b. SB 4,65/280/55. P-PB I Nr. 124/32. Betrifft: 3. Ruhrkongress der RGO Ruhrgebiet. Bochum, 8 May 1932. Abschrift e. p. 7. BA R45IV/35. Bericht über die erweitete Agitpropabteilungssitzung Oberschlesien, 25 September 1932, p. 3.

67. SB 4,65/274/53. MdL (IA) Berlin, 15 August 1931, Nr. 16. II. Reichskonferenz am 20. u. 21. Juni 1931 in Berlin p. 12. SB 4,65/260/49. Zu IAN 2162/11.10 Bericht von der Agitprop-Konferenz, 16 September 1932. Anlage 1, p. 4.
68. SB 4,65/1268/211. Auszug aus dem Bericht aus Karlsruhe, 20 February 1930. N. Stelle Nr. 425/30 geh. p. 2.
69. BA R45IV/17. Kommunistische Partei Deutschlands. Bezirk Baden. Bericht der Bezirksleitung an den Bezirks Parteitag . . ., 24/25 May 1930 in Karlsruhe. 4c). SB 4,65/271/52. Der Polizeipräsident. Abt. IA. Betrifft: Bezirkskongress der revolutionären Gewerkschaftsopposition. Hannover, 5 August 1930. Abschrift. Bericht des Erwerbslosenausschuß! SB 4,65/1272/212. Auszug aus dem Lagebericht W.10 der Polizeidirektion Stuttgart, 25 November 1931. Vom Kampfbund gegen den Faschismus – Bez. Württemberg.
70. SB 4,65/278/55. 'Einige Schwächen der RGO-Arbeit . . .', *Arbeiter Zeitung*, 5, 7 January 1932.
71. BA R45IV/21. Bericht Nr. 2. Württ. 16 April 1932.
72. BA R45IV/39. 'Schluß mit dem SA Terror'. Herausgegeben von der Roten Hilfe Deutschlands. 2. Die wahren Schuldigen pp. 4–5.
73. Ibid.
74. Ibid.
75. BA R134/83(129). Abschrift IAN 2164d/20.5. München, 17 May 1932. cf. R. A. Gates, 'Von der Sozialpolitik zur Wirtschaftspolitik? Das Dilemma der deutschen Sozialdemokratie in der Krise 1929–1933', in H. Mommsen, D. Petzina, B. Weisbrod (eds), *Industrielles System und politische Entwicklung in der Weimarer Republik,* vol. 1 (Düsseldorf, 1977) p. 223.
76. BA R134/82(182-5). NRI. IAN 2164d/3.12. Berlin, 3 December 1931. See also; BA R45IV/28. An die Bezirksleitung. Bericht über den Einheitskongress am 18. Juni in Chemnitz. Chemnitz, 21 June 1932. BA R45IV/8. An das ZK. Die BL Nieder-Sachsen. Die UBL Peine. gez. Franz Schabek. After 31 July 1932 p. 2. SB 4,65/282/56. *Die Information!,* 7, 3. Januarwoche 1933 p. 4.
77. The work of Eve Rosenhaft is among the more notable in the English language – as cited above.
78. SB 4,65/1268/211. Auszug aus dem Lagebericht der Pol. Direktion-München, 12 September 1929. N.-Stelle Br. B. Nr. 1772/29 geh. p. 2.
79. For example; SB 4,65/289/57. Ausschnitt aus dem Lagebericht Nr. 2, 17 April 1930. Br. Nr. 955/30 geh. The secondary literature is also replete with examples of such violence.
80. Thus; BA R45IV/32. 'Rote Wehrhaftigkeit der Arbeiterkinder!',- *Rundschreiben der Kommunistischen Partei Deutschlands. Bezirk Sachsen, 19,* Sept/Oct 1932.
81. GStAM MA 100 426. Zu Nr. 2013 g. 11. Uebersicht über die in Bayern in der Zeit vom 1. Januar bis 31. Dezember 1931 verübten politischen Gewalttaten.
82. Ibid.
83. Ibid. In addition, one Nazi and one Communist were killed.
84. Bayerisches Hauptstaatsarchiv München (BHStA) Abteilung I (Abt.I)/

Staatsministerium des Innern, Band 22 (M.Inn)/73 721. Report of the Prussian Ministry of the Interior, 8 January 1929, concerning political violence, etc. and Sachsen, Polizeibericht, III. Zusammenstösse (January–September 1928).

85. IfZ MA 616/20, 73 796-73 819 (SA III – Ausschreitungen). (June–October 1932).
86. For instance; A. McElligott, '. . . und so kam es zu einer schweren Schlägerei". Straßenschlachten in Altona und Hamburg am Ende der Weimarer Republik', in M. Bruhns et al. (eds), *"Hier war doch alles nicht so schlimm"*. *Wie die Nazis in Hamburg den Alltag eroberten* (Hamburg, 1984) pp. 58–85.
87. SB 4,65/252/46. MdL (IA Berlin), 1 July 1930, Nr. 13. Die linksradikale Bewegung. 2). SB 4,65/256/48. Auszug aus dem 10. Lagebericht des Freistaates Sachsen, 24 October 1931. I. Allgemeines.
88. BA R134/42(14–15). RKo 128. 20 February 1929. II. 1).
89. SB 4,65/1267/211. Abschrift. NRI. IAN 2166i/15.9. Betrifft: Proletarischer Massenselbstschutz. Berlin, 15 September 1932.
90. BA R45IV/25. An das ZK. Pol. Sekr. Braunschweig, 29 April 1932. gez. Adolf Bescheid.
91. SB 4,65/1253/209. Ausschnitt aus dem Lagebericht des Pol. Präs. Stuttgart, 6 March 1929. W.5. N. Stelle No. 390/29 geh. Rundschreiben von Werner Jurr. cf. SB 4,65/1268/211. Auszug aus dem Lagebericht Nr. 3 aus Hamburg, 19 October 1929. N. Stelle Nr. 2028/29 geh. (2) Norddeutscher Arbeiterschutzbund, where the latter was created to 'protect' workers as much from the Reichsbanner as from the Nazis.
92. See also; SB 4,65/1268/211. Auszug aus dem Lagebericht N/Nr. 85 aus München, 23 October 1929. N. Stelle Nr. 1983/29 geh. Fortführung des Roten Frontkämpferbundes . . . .
93. SB 4,65/1268/211. 'Niederrheinische Arbeiterwehren gebildet', *Arbeiter Zeitung*, 178, 2 August 1929. SB 4,65/1268/211. Ausschnitt aus dem Lagebericht des Min. des Innern Dresden, 10 August 1929. N.-Stelle Br.-B. Nr. 1533/29 geh. SB 4,65/1268/211. As in note 91 above. SB 4,65/1268/211. As in note 92 above.
94. BA R134/74(29). Abschrift. Anlage zu IAN 2160d/31.10. 8 October 1930.
95. SB 4,65/1272/212. Abschrift. IAN 2166h/17.12. Kampfbund gegen den Faschismus Reichsleitung. Rundschreiben Nr. 34. Berlin, 6 November 1931. (4) pp. 1–2.
96. SB 4,65/1273/212. Abschrift. P-PB PNPW. I Nr. 50/32. Bochum, 2 February 1932. Abschrift (a) *Alarm*, 16. a) Politische Unklarheiten. cf. Ward, op. cit. pp. 39–40.
97. BA R134/64(143-4). Abschrift IAN 2160/28.12. Berlin, 8 December 1931. cf. McElligott, Mobilising pp. 249–50.
98. BA R45IV/39. "Kampf dem Opportunismus', *Der Leninist,* January 1932. Rundbrief Nummer 1.
99. BA R134/62(43). Abschrift zu IAN 2160/4.4. Berlin, 25 March 1931. SB 4,65/250/46. Polizeidirektion Nürnberg. 19 June 1929. Beilage I zu Sonderbericht 153/II/29. Abschrift. KPD Bezirk Nordbayern.
100. BA R45IV/27. ZK der KPD. 8 August 1932. Transcript of meeting.

Notes to Chapter 8

241

Fritz speaking. BA R134/92(46). NRI. IAN 2160'/3.12.a. Anlage 1. 1c). BA R45IV/26. Bezirksleitung Berlin-Brandenburg-Lausitz. KPD. An alle Strassenzellen in Gross-Berlin. Berlin, 2 June 1930. p. 2.
101. SB 4,65/258/48. P-PB. PNPW. Betrifft: Rundschreiben der Bezirksleitung der KPD Ruhrgebiet. Bochum, 6 February 1932. For a narrative account of SA terror in Eastern Germany; R. Bessel, *Political Violence and the Rise of Nazism. The Storm Troopers in Eastern Germany 1925–1934* (New Haven, Conn., London, 1984) ch. VI.
102. BA R134/74(305). Abschrift IAN 2166i/11.7. 27 July 1932.
103. BA R134/77(112). NRI. IAN 2164h/8.8. Berlin, 8 August 1931.
104. BA R134/92(14a). NRI. IAN 2166a/5.12. Berlin, 10 December 1932. Anlage 1. BA R134/89(157a). NRI. IAN 2167. 30.11. Berlin, 13 December 1932.
105. BA R134/74(262). NRI. IAN 2162c/28.4. Abschrift.
106. BA R134/82(67). Denkschrift. . . . Undated. [Late 1931].
107. BA R134/74(20). Abschrift. IAN 2160c/2.7. Undated [July 1932].
108. SB 4,65/256/48. NRI. IAN 2160/1.10.a. Betrifft: Kommunistische Bewegung. Berlin, 1 October 1931. See also H. Pogge von Strandmann, 'Industrial Primacy in German Foreign Policy? Myths and Realities in German–Russian Relations at the End of the Weimar Republic', in R. Bessel, E.J. Feuchtwanger (eds), *Social Change and Political Development in Weimar Germany* (London, 1981) pp. 241–67.
109. For instance: BA R45IV/32. 'Einheitsfront auf der Straße – gegen Naziterror', *Mitteilungsblatt für alle Mitglieder der KPD, Bez. Württemberg*, 7(5) Early August 1932, p. 3.
110. BA R134/80(146). Zu IAN 2165a/3.12. Anlage 2. (Z.V. 30.10.32).
111. BA R134/76(86-9). Abschrift. IAN 2166a/31.1. Anlage 1. pp. 15–18.
112. For instance; SB 4,65/252/46. 'Das rote Heer Berlins marschiert für den Sieg', *Die Rote Fahne*, 198, 1. Beilage. 26 August 1930. SB 4,65/256/48. Abschrift. P-PB. Betrifft: Parteiarbeiterkonferenz, 6 September [1931] in Gelsenkirchen. SB 4,65/256/48. Abschrift. P-PB. Betrifft: KPD Rundschreiben der Bezirksleitung Ruhrgebiet. Bochum, 10 September 1931. BA R45IV/21. Wolfenbüttel (Jan/Feb. 1932).
113. W. S. Allen, *The Nazi Seizure of Power. The Experience of a single German Town 1930–1935* (London, 1966) pp. 294–5 Table 6: NSDAP 95, SPD 61, Nationalists 21, Others 22 meetings.
114. GStAM MA 101 241/2. Polizeidirektion Nürnberg-Fürth. Nr. 200/II/32. Lagebericht. Nürnberg, 3 August 1932.
115. For the Ruhr; SB 4,65/252/46. P-PB I Nr. 912/30. Abschrift. Betrifft: Referentenmaterial des Zentralkomitees der Kommunistischen Partei. Bochum, 8 August 1930. For attacks on NS meetings in Hagen-Haspe; BA R45IV/46. Bericht über die Wahlversammlungen im Bezirk Niederrhein vom 9. bis 16.11. Berlin, gez. Oberdörster. This same report also details the KPD's more conciliatory attitude in Mettmann where the Nazis were stronger.
116. BA R45IV/46. Bericht des Genossen Albrecht über die Wahlversammlungen in Schlesien [Nov. 1929]. SB 4,65/1271/212. Aus L.B. Pol. Dir. München – N. Stelle Nr. 893/31 geh., 12 March 1931. (3).
117. BA R45IV/12. Sekretariat R. An Genossen Dr. Beppo Römer. Berlin,

16 June 1932.
118. BA R45IV/46. Abschrift. An die Zentralleitung der KPD. Berlin. Groß-Neuendorf, 14 November 1929. gez. Richard Koppin.
119. BA R45IV/27. Bericht über die Versammlung in der Pfalz, 28 April – 1 May, 5–9 May [1932]. Steinarbeitergebiet Kusel.
120. SB 4,65/252/46. Ausschnitt aus dem Lagebericht Nr. 6 Dresden. – N. Stelle Nr. 2072/30 geh., 30 August 1930. II. Linksbewegung.
121. SB 4,65/294/58. 'Der Aufmarsch der Bremer roten Mieterfront', *Arbeiter Zeitung* 20, 25 January 1932.
122. BA R45IV/21. Bericht über meine Versammlungen zum preuss. Landtagswahlen. Bohnsdorf bei Grünau. Berlin, 26 April 1932. gez. Kasper.
123. SB 4,65/1271/212. Abschrift. Kampfbund gegen den Faschismus. Bezirksverband Ruhrgebiet. Essen, 7 February 1931.
124. See also; BA R45IV/21. Paul Hoffmann. An das Sekretariat des Z.K. Versammlungsbericht vom 13.4 bis 23.4 in Pommern (Landtagswahl). Berlin, 29 April 1932. (9). BA R45IV/21. Bericht über Wahlversammlungen in Hessen. Mannheim, 19 June 1932. Oeffentliche Versammlung in Niederflörsheim, 15 June 1932. gez. Paul Schreck. BA R45IV/21. Fortsetzung der Schlussbemerkung aus Walldorf.
125. BA R45IV/21. Bericht über durchgeführte Wahlversammlungen zur Preussenwahl im Bezirk Thüringen. Für den Bericht: Paul Otto. BA R45IV/21. Bericht über die Versammlungen zum II. Präsidentenwahlkampf. Sonnabend den 9 April – Bebra, Hessen-Waldeck. Berlin, 13 April 1932. Willi Weiss. BA R45IV/6. Beppo Römer. Dienstag, 14.6.32. Oeffentliche Versammlung in Finkenbach-Hinterbach. BA R45IV/6. Karl Schulz – Neukölln. An das ZK der KPD, Berlin. Bericht über Versammlungstour im Hessen-Wahlkampf v. 10.–18. Juni 1932. Berlin, 22 June 1932, pp. 1–2.
126. BA R45IV/21. Bericht über Versammlungen im Bezirk Pommern, 13–17 July 1932. gez. Rau. p. 2.
127. BA R45IV/30. Bericht über Mecklenburg-Schwerin. 17 – ? June 1932.
128. For instance; BA R45IV/21. 18. – 23.4. Bez. Hessen-Frankfurt. Versamml. 21 April 1932. Biedenkopf. gez. Steinfurth.
129. BA R45IV/21. An das ZK der KPD, Berlin. 'Nachstehend ein kurzer Bericht über meine bisherigen Versammlungen'; Bottrop. Bremen, 22 July 1932. gez. Schneider?
130. BA R45IV/28. Arbeitsplan der Ortsgruppe Grossenhain für Monat Juni (1932). Gegnerarbeit.
131. BA R45IV/12. Sekretariat R. An Genossen Willi Münzenberg, M.d.R. Berlin, 13 June 1932.
132. BA R45IV/21. Bericht über die Wahlversammlungen in Hessen in der Zeit vom 12. bis 18.6.32. XIX.
133. BA R45IV/21. Bericht über die Versammlungstournee des Genossen Weiss . . . in den Bezirken Niedersachsen, Wasserkante und Nordwest. Berlin, 27 April 1932. Montag den 18.4. Erwerbslosenversammlung in Sk. Georg.
134. BA R45IV/12. Sekretariat R. An Genossen Georg Schumann, M.d.R. Berlin, 31 May 1932.

135. BA R45IV/21. Abschrift. Bericht für die BL Schlesien über den Unterbezirk Langenbielau. April 1932. gez. Z.K. Instrukteur Richard Schulz.
136. BA R45IV/21. Bericht über die Versammlungen im Bezirk Niedersachsen. April 1932. Groß-Rühden. gez. Handke.
137. SB 4,65/252/46. KPD Bezirk Nordbayern. Nürnberg, 17 October 1930. Richtlinien für die Arbeit der Kommunisten zum Aufbau des Kampfbundes gegen den Faschismus. p. 1.
138. SB 4,65/1269/211. Ausschnitt aus L.B. Nr. 179/30 der Pol. Dir. Nürnberg-Fürth, 6 October 1930. N.-Stelle Nr. 2519/30 geh., 9 October 1930. (5). SB 4,65/1271/212. Aus Mitteilungen Nr. 2 des Pol. Präs. Berlin, 21 January 1931. N. Stelle Nr. 206/31 geh., 21 January 1931. Anlage L. 1. II.
139. SB 4,65/1271/212. As in note 138 above. I.
140. SB 4,65/252/46. Sonderbericht Nr. 181/II Anlage 2. KPD Bezirk Nordbayern. . . . Richtlinien . . . . Nürnberg, 17 October 1930, p. 1.
141. SB 4,65/253/47. RI IAN 2160d/31/10. Betreff: KPD – Kampf gegen Faschismus. Berlin, 7 November 1930.
142. SB 4,65/1271/212. Mitteilungen des Pol. Präs. Berlin Nr. 21, 1 November 1930. N. Stelle Nr. 2762/30 geh., 7 November 1930. Kampfbund gegen den Faschismus.
143. SB 4,65/257/48. Abschrift c). Bezirksleitung Ruhrgebiet. Abtlg. Org. 'Schafft Einheitsfrontorgane'. Essen, 26 November 1931, pp. 1–2.
144. SB 4,65/1271/212. Abschrfit. Alarm, Nr. 1, January 1931, pp. 3–4.
145. SB 4,65/255/47. Abschrift. KPD Bez. Nordbayern. Sonderanweisung zur Verbreitung der Unterbezirks-Parteitage. Nürnberg, 7 May 1931, p. 7.
146. SB 4,65/255/47. As above. pp. 2, 7.
147. BA R134/74(155). Abschrift. IAN 2166h/11.1. Berlin, 23 January 1932. Anlage 1.
148. BA R134/74(47–8). RI IAN 2166h. SH. 1/22.4. Berlin, 22 April 1931. Anlage 1.
149. SB 4,65/1272/212. P-PB I Nr. 509/31. Bochum, 12 November 1931. Abschrift c. p. 4.
150. SB 4,65/1271/212. Abschrift. P-PB I Nr. 246/31. Betrifft: Arbeits- und Sturmplan . . . . [Ruhrgebiet]. Bochum, 18 May 1931.
151. SB 4,65/1273/212. Abschrift (a). Rundschreiben Nr. X. Reichsleitung des Kampfbundes . . . . Berlin, 20 April 1932. (4) p. 6.
152. For instance; SB 4,65/1274/213. Arbeitsrichtlinien. Beschlossen von der Führertagung des Kampfbundes . . ., 5 August 1932. p. 4. BA R134/93(42a). NRI. IAN 2166h/9.12. Berlin, 20 December 1932. BA R45IV/32. Bezirksleitung der KPD. Niedersachsen. Sekretariat. 24 August 1932. 'Entschliessung der Bezirksleitung . . .'. (5).
153. SB 4,65/1274/213. 'Nazi-Ortsgruppe mit SA-Führer tritt zum Kampfbund gegen den Faschismus über', Arbeiter-Zeitung, 181, 4 August 1932.
154. Dr Detlef Mühlberger of the Department of Humanities, Oxford Polytechnic, very kindly provided me with details derived from the Staatsarchiv Münster (StAM) I PA VII-66 Bd.2.

155. BA R134/93(48). Zu IAN 2166h/9.12. December 1932.
156. Ibid.
157. SB 4,65/1273/212. NRI. IAN 2166h/30.3. Berlin, 7 April 1932. Mitgliederbewegung des Kampfbundes gegen den Faschismus 1931.
158. SB 4,65/1273/212. Reichsleitung des Kampfbundes gegen den Faschismus. Bundeskasse. Rundschreiben! Die Ursachen der Fluktuation in unserer Organisation. Berlin, 30 March 1932.
159. Ibid.
160. SB 4,65/1273/212. NRI. IAN 2166h 30.3. Berlin, 7 April 1932. Zahl der Ortsgruppen und Betriebsstaffeln im Kampfbund gegen den Faschismus.
161. SB 4,65/1272/212. Auszug aus dem Lagebericht W.10 der Polizeidirektion Stuttgart, 25 November 1931. Vom Kampfbund gegen den Faschismus – Bez. Württemberg. p. 19.
162. SB 4,65/259/49. Die Lage in der KPD. München 20 April 1932. For a comparable argument with regard to voting behaviour, see; W. S. Allen, 'Farewell to Class Analysis in the Rise of Nazism: Comment', *Central European History,* 17 (1) (1984) pp. 61–2.
163. BA R45IV/20. Rundschreiben Nr. 11. Anweisungen des Sekretariats. Berlin, 4 June 1932. II. Die Antifaschistische Aktion. p. 7.
164. BA R45IV/28. Antifaschistische Massenaktion auf dem Hecht (Stadtteil 3). June? 1932. BA R45IV/40. 'Genosse Sandtner über die Aufgaben der antifaschistischen Aktion', *Arbeiter-Zeitung für Schlesien,* 14(131), 7 June 1932.
165. BA R134/66(54-5). Abschrift IAN 2160/5.8. Anlage 1. Berlin, 14 June 1932.
166. SB 4,65/1694/285. ZK/Org. Rundschreiben der Org. Abteilung des ZK an alle Bezirksleitungen. Berlin, 19 July 1932.
167. SB 4,65/294/58. 'Proletarische Einheitsfront verhindert Massenermission . . .', *Arbeiter Zeitung,* 198, 3 November 1931. SB 4,65/294/58. 'Staatswohnungsmieter zahlen nur noch 65 Proz. Miete . . .', *Arbeiter Zeitung,* 218, 27 November 1931. BA R45IV/39. Kampferfahrungen. Die Instrukteure in der Großstadt . . . ZK der KPD, January 1933, p. 9, (3).
168. BA R45IV/23. Bezirksleitung Oberschlesien der KPD. An das Zentralkomitee. Betr.: Bericht über die Einleitung zur Antifaschistischen Aktion. Hindenburg, 10 June 1932.
169. SB 4,65/260/49. Zu IAN 2162/11.10. Bericht von der Agitprop-Konferenz, 16 September 1932. Anlage 1.
170. SB 4,65/260/49. Abschrift. P-PB, PNPW. Betrifft: KPD. Bochum, 24 August 1932, p. 5.
171. BA NS26/809. Information über den Gegner. KPD Antif. Aktion. [SPD report]. October 1932, p. 4. cf. J. Valtin, *Out of the Night* (London, 1941) pp. 225–6, where examples of earlier NS–KPD cooperation in Hamburg are given.
172. BA R45IV/30. Abschrift. Bericht über Mecklenburg, 15 June – 1 August 1932. Rote Front. gez. Ziegler.
173. SB 4,65/260/49. Abschrift aus der Zeitschrift: *Der Pionier des Bolschewismus.* Referat des Gen. Max Opitz, . . ., 7 and 8 August 1932, p. 2.

See; BA R45IV/23. Plan des Bezirks Pommern zum Reichstagswahl im Rahmen der Antifaschistischen Aktion [mid 1932], for a similar attitude in Pomerania.
174. BA R45IV/21. Aufruf zur antifasch. Aktion! July? 1932. cf. Valtin, op. cit. pp. 305–6.
175. For instance: Fowkes, op. cit. pp. 166–8.
176. SB 4,65/2037/362. 'Der Schädling der Arbeiterklasse. Nachdenkliches zur KPD-Einheitsfrontaktion', *Bremer Volkszeitung*, 238, 10 October 1932; cf. Ward, op. cit. p. 61, who makes a much more optimistic assessment.

9 THE STRUGGLE IN THE WORKPLACE

1. For instance: SB 4,65/251/46. Zentralkomitee der Kommunistischen Partei Deutschlands. Sekretariat. Berlin, early June 1930. pp. 2, 5. SB 4,65/283/56. Abschrift. Strategie und Taktik des Streikkampfes. Antifaschistische Aktion. Bezirksleitung Ruhrgebiet. September 1932. p. 6. cf. Degras, op. cit., III, pp. 58, 142. Moses, *Trade Unionism*, II, pp. 364–6.
2. cf. Kratzenberg, op. cit. pp. 74–76.
3. cf. Kratzenberg, op. cit. p. 79.
4. cf. BA R134/59(61–2). Preußisches Polizeiinstitut. (Zum Erl. vom 30.11.1931).
5. cf. M. H. Kater, 'Sozialer Wandel in der NSDAP im Zuge der nationalsozialistischen Machtergreifung', in W. Schieder (ed.), *Faschismus als soziale Bewegung* (Göttingen, 1983) p. 31. Lane, op. cit. pp. 20–1.
6. Mai, Betriebszellen p. 577. cf. Kratzenberg, op. cit. pp. 49–51, 67–9.
7. cf. Bracher, *German Dictatorship,* p. 200, who takes little account of this grassroots factor.
8. Mai, 'Betriebszellen', p. 579.
9. Ibid., pp. 584–5. See also; Kratzenberg, op. cit. pp. 39–47, but cf. Bracher, *German Dictatorship,* p. 201, where it is suggested that employers remained in the NSBO throughout the pre-1933 period.
10. Mai, 'Betriebszellen', p. 593. cf. Dorpalen, 'SPD und KPD', p. 103. Kratzenberg, op. cit. pp. 86–8, 99.
11. Fowkes, op. cit. p. 153.
12. Degras, op. cit., III, p. 58.
13. Ibid., pp. 27–8, 143.
14. Daycock, op. cit. p. 183.
15. cf. Degras, op. cit., III, p. 143–4; Watts, op. cit. p. 445.
16. SB 4,65/257/48. Denkschrift über die kommunistische Bewegung. Berichterstatter: R.R. ieR. von Lengriesser. [Nov. 1931]. esp. pp. 17, 19. cf. SB 4,65/251/46. Zentralkomitee der Kommunistischen Partei Deutschlands. Sekretariat. Berlin, early June 1930. p. 2. SB 4, 65/256/48. NRI. IAN 2160/1.10.a. Betrifft: Kommunistische Bewegung. Berlin, 1 October 1931. BA R134/94(116a–118). NRI. IAN 2160/30.12. Berlin, 17 January 1933, pp. 8–11.

17. SB 4,65/251/46. Abschrift! Bezirksleitung Ruhrgebiet. Sekretariat. Arbeitsplan für die Monate Februar/März. Essen, 31 January 1930, p. 4.
18. SB 4,65/251/46. Abschrift. Bezirksleitung Ruhrgebiet. Abtlg. Org. Arbeitsplan für den Monat März und April. Essen, 25 February 1930 p. 1. cf. BA R134/60(228). IAN 2160/26.6. Berlin, 7 July 1930.
19. SB 4,65/251/46. Polizei-Direktion: N.-Stelle. B.Nr. 767/30. Bremen, 28 March 1930.
20. BA NS26/1403. Berichte der Staatspolizei Württembergs zur pol. Lage. 7 May 1930. cf. SB 4,65/252/46. Nr. 174/II. Polizeidirektion Nürnberg-Fürth. Sonderbericht Nr. 174/II/30.
21. SB 4,65/252/46. Polizeidirektion Nürnberg-Fürth. Lagebericht Nr. 179/ II/30, Betreff: Kommunistische Bewegung. Nürnberg, 6 October 1930, p. 4.
22. SB 4,65/253/47. Abschrift. Bezirksleitung Ruhrgebiet. Essen, 7 October 1930.
23. SB 4,65/252/46. RI IAN 2160/6.10. Betrifft: Kommunistische Bewegung, Berlin, 6 October 1930, p. 2.
24. SB 4,65/255/47. Abschrift. RI IA 2130/15.7. Betrifft: Kommunistische Partei. Berlin, 25 July 1931, p. 2.
25. For instance; SB 4,65/254/47. Abschrift. Bezirksleitung Ruhrgebiet. Abtlg. Org. Essen, 24 February 1931. SB 4,65/255/47. Abschrift zu IAN 2160/7.4. Lehrbrief Nr. 2. Faschismus und Sozialfaschismus [1931] pp. 26–7. SB 4,65/255/47. Abschrift. P-PB. Na. Betrifft: Rundschreiben der KPD Abt. Org. Bochum, 22 April 1931. SB, 4,65/255/47. Auszug aus dem L. B. No. 33040/4 des Minist. des Innern. Dresden, 24 April 1931. II. Linksbewegung. KPD. SB 4,65/255/47. Abschrift. KPD Bez. Nordbayern. Sonderanweisung zur Vorbereitung der Unterbezirks-Parteitage. Nürnberg, 7 May 1931, p. 2. SB 4,65/255/47. Abschrift. P-PB. Na. I Nr. 239/31. Betrifft: KPD, Bezirksleitung Ruhrgebiet. Arbeitsplan für den Monat Mai 1931. Bochum, 11 May 1931.
26. SB 4,65/255/47. 'Die Lage in Deutschland und die Aufgaben der KPD', *Die Rote Fahne*, 142, 4 July 1931.
27. SB 4,65/253/47. P-PB.Na I Nr. 55/31. Abschrift. Bezirksleitung Ruhrgebiet. Abtlg. Org. Essen, 15 January 1931.
28. SB 4,65/254/47. Abschrift. P-PB. Na. Betrifft: Rundschreiben der kommunistischen Bezirksleitung Ruhrgebiet mit Arbeitsplan für den Monat Februar 1931. Bochum, 11 February 1931, p. 2.
29. Ibid.
30. SB 4,65/257/48. Abschrift. Arbeitsplan des Bezirks Ruhrgebiet für November–Dezember 1931. 'Reorganisierung der Partei'.
31. SB 4,65/256/48. Abschrift. Vertraulich. O-Dienst. Nachrichten über die bolschewistische Bewegung. 3 October 1931, p. 5. cf. SB 4,65/259/49. Zu IAN 2160/30.3. Rundschreiben Nr. 2. Anweisungen zu den Reichspräsidenten- u. Landtagswahlen. Berlin, 18 February 1932, pp. 1–2.
32. SB 4,65/276/54. Ausschrift aus dem L. B. Nr. 104 München, 28 September 1931. Z-St. Nr. 4298/31 geh. Revolutionäre Gewerkschaftsopposition.

33. BA R134/82(60). Abschrift. Anlage 2. 20, 21 June 1932.
34. SB 4,65/250/46. Referenten-Material. Kampf dem Faschismus. IV, p. 11.
35. BA R45IV/19. Agitprop. Betr. Kopfblatt für die Pfalz. An die Redaktion der *Arbeiterzeitung* Mannheim. Berlin, 15 December 1930.
36. SB 4,65/1268/211. RI Nr. IAN 2166 b/8.4. Betrifft: Merkblatt für die Schaffung und Zusammenfassung antifaschistischer Schutz – (Abwehr) – Organisation. Berlin, 17 April 1930. Abschrift. I.
37. BA R45IV/17. Kommunistische Partei Deutschlands, Bezirk Baden. Bericht der Bezirksleitung an den Bezirks-Parteitag . . . 25 May 1930 in Karlsruhe. (4c). BA R134/58(176–7). Deutsche Nachrichtenkonferenz in Berlin, 28, 29 April 1930. (9).
38. BA R134/58(180). Deutsche Nachrichtenkonferenz; as above.
39. Mai, Betriebszellen p. 599.
40. As note 38 above.
41. For instance: BA R45IV/24. Zentralkomitee der KPD. Sekretariat. Rundschreiben Nr. 8. Berlin, 4 July 1930. Anweisungen der Agitpropabteilung.
42. SB 4,65/1271/212. Abschrift. *Alarm* Nr. 6. Funktionärprogramm des Kampfbundes gegen den Faschismus. March 1931.
43. For instance; SB 4,65/1272/212. P-PB Na I Nr. 370/31. Bochum, 20 August 1931. Abschrift. *Alarm* Nr. 11 – July 1931. 'Gegen den Werkfaschismus'. BA R45IV/39. 'Die HIB-Aktion der Nazis', *Der Leninist*, January 1932. Rundbrief Nr 1.
44. BA R45IV/26. Bericht über die Ermittlung der Arbeit in dem Betrieb Wasag (Piesteritz). Unterschätzung der Nazi.
45. BA R45IV/11. Bericht über die Ermittlung der Arbeit in der Filmfabrik Wolfen (1932). Unterschätzung der Nazi und Stahlhelm.
46. Ibid.
47. SB 4,65/278/55. P-PB. PNPW. I Nr. 58/32. Bochum, 19 February 1932. Abschrift! R.G.O. Hieb gegen 'Hib'. (22pp). SB 4,65/1273/212. Abschrift. Kampfbund gegen den Faschismus. Bezirksverband Ruhrgebiet. *Der Revolutionäre Antifaschist*. February 1932.
48. SB 4,65/278/55. As in note 47 above, p. 1. cf. Reuter, quoted in Kratzenberg, op. cit. p. 18.
49. SB 4,65/1273/212. As in note 47 above, pp. 2–3.
50. It was launched in September 1931, after the factory council elections.
51. SB 4,65/278/55. As in note 47 above, esp. p. 18. See also police preamble. SB 4,65/1273/212. As in note 47 above, p. 3.
52. SB 4,65/278/55. As in note 47 above, p. 18.
53. Ibid.
54. Schöck, op. cit. p. 254 Table 21. cf. Buchloh, op. cit. p. 59, who argues that the NSBO's gains in Duisburg were largely at the RGO's expense, and Kratzenberg, op. cit. pp. 177–8, where he notes that many NSBO functionaries were former Communists.
55. Mai, Betriebszellen p. 597. But cf. W. Böhnke, *Die NSDAP im Ruhrgebiet, 1920–1933* (Bonn-Bad Godesberg, 1974) p. 173, where he estimates that the NSBO received 5 per cent of the workers' vote in the North-West group of the metal industry.

56. Mai, Betriebszellen p. 597.
57. Buchloh, op. cit. pp. 57–8.
58. Mai, Betriebszellen p. 597. The figure for the whole of Germany was 1.67 per cent; Schöck, op. cit. pp. 250–1 Table 18.
59. Mai, Betriebszellen p. 597. Böhnke, op. cit. p. 173, stresses the universal figure of 3.58 per cent mentioned immediately above.
60. Buchloh, op. cit. pp. 56–7.
61. Schöck, op. cit. p. 255.
62. Mai, Betriebszellen p. 597. But cf. Kratzenberg, op. cit. p. 186, who argues that these figures are probably rather high.
63. BA R45IV/21. Zusammenfassender Bericht über die Kontrolle in Braunschweig (Jan./Feb. 1932) p. 10.
64. Mai, Betriebszellen pp. 593–607.
65. SB 4,65/278/55. P-PB. PNPW. I Nr. 58/32. Bochum, 19 February 1932. Abschrift! R.G.O. Hieb gegen 'Hib'. pp. 2, 17.
66. As above, p. 6.
67. Mai, Betriebszellen p. 579.
68. BA R45IV/21. Die NSDAP in Braunschweig. February? 1932. cf. Noakes, op. cit. p. 32, who notes that proto-Nazi groups in Brunswick had derived much of their early membership from 'discontented Independent Socialists'.
69. BA R45IV/21. As in note 63 above pp. 9–10, 12, 17–19. BA R45IV/21. As in note 68 above, pp. 1–3. cf. BA R45IV/21. Versammlungsberichte – Wasserkante. Harburg, 22 April 1932, where the RGO's and KPD's weakness in selected factories in Hamburg and its neighbourhood is demonstrated.
70. BA R45IV/21. As in note 69 above. BA R45IV/21. Versammlungsberichte. Ffm. 7–9 April 1932. gez. Werner. BA R45IV/26. Bericht über die Kontrolle im Bezirk Nordwest, 19 September 1932. BA R45IV/27. Bericht der Betriebszelle Film-Wolfen, 28 October 1932.
71. BA R45IV/35. An das Zentralkomitee der KPD, Sekr. Agitprop., Berlin. Magdeburg, 10 September 1932, p. 2. BA R45IV/21. Bericht über die Versammlungen zum II. Präsidentenwahlkampf. Saturday 9 April – Bebra – Hessen-Waldeck. Berlin, 13 April 1932. gez. Willi Weiss. SB 4,65/283/56. Ausschrift aus dem Bericht der KPD über den Bezirksparteitag, 26/27 November 1932. Z. St. 6932/32 geh. Bericht der kommunistischen Fraktion in der RGO. Bezirk Weser-Ems. pp. 67–70. BA R45IV/39. 'Die Stellungnahme der 26 Unterbezirke', *Der Bolschewik*, 3(20), mid December [1932] p. 393. For NSBO successes in the public sector works in Dresden; same source p. 390.
72. BA R45IV/13. 'Soziale Lage und Kämpfe. Betriebsratswahlen im Wurmrevier', *Die Rote Fahne*, 23 June 1932, quoted in Nr. 386 *Inform. Tagesnotizen*, 23 June 1932. Innenpolitik p. 7.
73. SB 4,65/279/55. Bezirkskomitee der RGO. I. Gr. Metall. Abtl. Jugend, Essen, 20 January 1932.
74. BA R45IV/8. Abschrift. ZK der KPD. Berlin, 1 March 1932. 'Welches sind die Hauptschwächen und Unterlassungen, die in der Arbeit der Partei in Erscheinung traten?'. (3).
75. Kratzenberg, op. cit. p. 216.

76. Mai, Betriebszellen p. 596. cf. Kratzenberg, op. cit. pp. 184, 195 ff, 217–18.
77. SB 4,65/281/56. P-PB. PNPW. I Nr. 160/32. Betrifft: Rundschreiben des Bezirkskomitees der RGO. Bochum, 12 July 1932. Abschrift (d). cf. BA R45IV/22. UB IX Instrukt. Becher. Betrieb Thorey. Falkenstein, 21 July 1932, where employers' measures against the RGO in an NSBO and Stahlhelm-dominated Bavarian factory are discussed.
78. Kratzenberg, op. cit. p. 215.
79. cf. the earlier syndicalist Union der Hand und Kopfarbeiter.
80. SB 4,65/283/56. Ausschrift aus dem Bericht der KPD über den Bezirksparteitag, 26/27 November 1932. Z. St. 6932/32 geh. Bericht der kommunistischen Fraktion in der RGO. Bezirk Weser-Ems. p. 51.
81. For instance; SB 4,65/277/54. Abschrift. P-PB. Na I Nr. 543/31. Betrifft: Rundschreiben des Reichskomitees der RGO. Early November. Bochum, 30 November 1931.
82. SB 4,65/252/46. Rundschreiben Nr. 14. Anweisungen des Sekretariats. Berlin, 6 October 1930. II. SB, 4,65/278/55. Abschrift. Bezirkskomitee der RGO. Angestellten-Kommission. Essen, 4 December 1931. BA R45IV/11. Protokoll über die Sitzung der engeren BL mit den Polleitern . . . Halle, 21 March 1932, p. 4.
83. SB 4,65/252/46. RI. IAN 2160/6.10. Betrifft: Kommunistische Bewegung. Berlin, 6 October 1930. Anlage. p. 4.
84. BA R45IV/38. 'Nazis bekennen sich offen für Lohnabbau', *Post und Staat*, 2(8), September 1932, p. 3. BA R134/67(58). Abschrift zu IAN 2160a^8/28.10. 10 November 1932. SB 4,65/261/49. Disposition zur Durchführung von Einführungs-Abenden für neu eingetretene Parteimitglieder. . . . B.-L. Schlesien der KPD Agitprop. (c) Einheitsfrontaktion. cf. Rößling, op. cit. 150. Degras, op. cit., III, p. 151.
85. SB 4,65/277/54. Abschrift. P-PB. Na I Nr. 543/31. Betrifft: Rundschreiben des Reichskomitees der RGO. Bochum, 30 November 1931.
86. BA R134/83(91) Abschrift zu IAN 2163f 17/10.5. Berlin, 28 April 1932. BA R45IV/39. Entschließung des Bezirksparteitages des Bezirks Großthüringen, 19, 20 November 1932. III.
87. Thus, SB 4,65/1268/211. Entnommen aus den Mitteilungen Nr. 20/1929 des Pol. Präsident Berlin, 15 November 1929. N.-Stelle Br. B. Nr. 2140/29 geh. SB 4,65/254/47. Abschrift. P-PB. Na Betrifft: Rundschreiben der KPD, Unterbezirksleitung Oberhausen. Bochum, 23 March 1931. SB 4,65/257/48. Zentralkomitee Kommunistischen Partei Deutschlands. Rundschreiben an alle Leitungen . . .! Berlin, 8 December 1931. BA R134/81(45). Oldenburg, August 1932. Anlage 1.
88. BA R134/81(25). Abschrift IAN 2160/25.6. Anlage 1.
89. SB 4,65/252/46. Abschrift. P-PB. Na I Nr. 912/30. Bochum, 8 August 1930. BA R45IV/38. 'Nazis bekennen sich offen für Lohnabbau', *Post und Staat*, 2(8) September 1932, p. 3. See also; Fischer, *Stormtroopers*, p. 95.
90. SB 4,65/278/55. P-PB. PNPW I Nr. 587/31. Bochum, 31 December 1931. Abschrift. . . . RGO. Gruppe Chemie, pp. 2–3. SB 4,65/280/55. 'Das Programm der RGO. Sammelbecken aller klassenbewußter Straßenbahner', *Arbeiter Zeitung*, 105, 6 May 1932. SB 4,65/280/55. P-PB.

PNPW I Nr. 124/32. Bochum, 8 May 1932. Abschrift(b). IX.
91. SB 4,65/280/55. P-PB. PNPW I Nr. 124/32. Bochum, 8 May 1932.
   Abschrift(a) pp. 7–8.
92. SB 4,65/281/56. P-PB. PNPW I Nr. 187/32. Bochum, 1 September 1932.
   Abschrift(a) p. 4.
93. BA R134/59(61–2). Preußisches Polizeiinstitut. (Zum Erl. 30
   November
94. SB 4,65/251/46. Abschrift IAN 2160/1.8. Zentralkomitee der KPD.
   Sekretariat. Berlin, 17 July 1930. Rundschreiben Nr. 10. Anweisungen
   des Sekretariats . . ., p. 5. Anweisungen der Orgabteilung, p. 8.
95. For instance; SB 4,65/272/53. P-PB Na I Nr. 154/31. Abschrift. Bezirkskomitee der RGO Ruhrgebiet. Essen, 13 March 1931. SB 4,65/272/53.
   P-PB. Na I Nr. 128/31. Bochum, 21 February 1931. Abschrift. Bezirkskomitee der RGO. Industriegruppe Metall. Early February 1931.
   Vestag Ruhrort-Meiderich, p. 5. BA R134/82(60). Abschrift. Anlage 2.
   20, 21 June 1932. SB 4,65/1694/285. Reichsausschuss der Betriebsräte.
   Rote Betriebsräte mobilisiert die Belegschaften [Nov. 1932] p. 4.
96. BA R45IV/11. Bericht über die Kontrolle im Bezirk Halle-Merseburg.
   Berlin, 16 March 1931, p. 7. SB 4,65/278/55. 'RGO zum neuen
   Kampfjahr . . .', *Arbeiter Zeitung*, 245, 31 December 1931.
97. BA R134/82(170). IAN 2163a/7a/26.11. Berlin, 26 November 1931.
98. SB 4,65/1268/211. RI. Nr. IAN 2166b/8.4. Berlin, 17 April 1930.
   Abschrift. I. Warum Antifaschistische Organisationen? pp. 2–3.
99. BA R134/60(228). IAN 2160/26.6. Berlin, 7 July 1930. Abschrift.
100. SB 4,65/252/46. P-PB. Na I Nr. 912/30. Abschrift. Betrifft:
   Referentenmaterial des Zentralkomitees der Kommunistischen Partei.
   Bochum, 8 August 1930.
101. SB 4,65/271/52. Der Polizeipräsident. Landeskriminalpolizeistelle.
   Abt. IA. Betrifft: Bezirkskongress der revolutionären
   Gewerkschaftsopposition. Hannover, 5 August 1930. Abschrift.
   Richtlinien für die Organisierung Roter Betriebswehren.
102. BA R134/81(26). Abschrift. IAN 2160/25.6 Anlage 1. Berlin, early
   June 1930.
103. SB 4,65/251/46. Abschrift IAN 2160/1.8. Zentralkomitee der KPD.
   Sekretariat. Berlin, 17 July 1930. Rundschreiben Nr. 10, p. 8.
104. SB 4,65/270/52. Abschrift. P-PB. Na I Nr. 829/30. Betr.: Bergbau
   Konferenz . . . . Bochum, 10 July 1930.
105. SB 4,65/253/47. Rundschreiben Nr. 14. Anweisungen des Sekretariats.
   Berlin, 6 October 1930. II.
106. BA R134/61(98). Abschrift IAN 2160/3.11. Berlin, early October 1930.
107. BA R45IV/11. Bericht über die Kontrolle im Bezirk Halle-Merseburg.
   Berlin, 16 March 1931, p. 7. By contrast no Social Democratic workers
   had been recruited.
108. SB 4,65/1271/212. Abschrift. *Alarm* Nr. 6. Funktionärprogramm des
   Kampfbundes gegen den Faschismus. pp. 2–3.
109. SB 4,65/255/47. Abschrift. Resolution des Zentral-Komitees über die
   Beschlüsse des XI Plenums des Ekki. May? 1931. I. cf. Degras, op. cit.,
   III pp. 206–7.
110. SB 4,65/273/53. P-PB. Na. Bochum, 11 June 1931. Abschrift.

Streikführer-Kursus-Material Nr. 2. p. 6. cf. SB 4,65/257/48. Abschrift.
Arbeitsplan des Bezirks Ruhrgebiet für November–Dezember 1931 p.
3, where the Ruhr KPD makes a similar commitment.

111. SB 4,65/1272/212. P-PB. Na I Nr. 370/31. Bochum, 20 August 1931.
Abschrift. *Alarm* Nr. 11–July 1931, p. 3.

112. cf. Degras, op. cit., I, p. 12, on Lenin's twelfth thesis on bourgeois
democracy, and p. 15, Lenin's twenty-first thesis.

113. SB 4,65/278/55. P-PB. PNPW. I Nr. 582/31. Bochum, 31 December
1931. Abschrift. 'Trägt die revolutionäre Theorie in die Massen der
Betriebe . . .', Kursusmaterial Nr. 2 – RGO . . . Ruhrgebiet . . ., p. 6.
See also, p. 10.

114. SB 4,65/255/47. RI. IA 2130/15.7. Berlin, 25 July 1931. Betrifft:
Kommunistische Partei. Abschrift, p. 2.

115. BA R134/82(169–71). NRI. IAN 2163a/7a/26.11. Berlin, 26 November
1931.

116. For instance, SB 4,65/278/55. 'RGO zum neuen Kampfjahr . . .',
Arbeiter Zeitung, 245, 31 December 1931.

117. Thus, SB 4,65/1272/212. Auszug aus dem Lagebericht W.10 der
Polizeidirektion Stuttgart, 25 November 1931. (Z. St. Nr. 5674/31 geh.
. . .). Vom Kampfbund gegen den Faschismus – Bez. Württemberg.

118. SB 4,65/278/55. As in note 113 above, p. 10.

119. SB 4,65/257/48. Zentralkomitee Kommunistischen Partei
Deutschlands. Rundschreiben an alle Leitungen . . . . Berlin, 8
December 1931, p. 11.

120. BA R134/87(7–8). NRI. IAN 2167/17.12. Berlin, 17 December 1931. cf.
Kratzenberg, op. cit. pp. 236, 244.

121. BA R134/87(7–8) as above. cf. SB 4,65/280/55. 'Verstärkt die
Mobilisierung der Erwerbslosen! . . .', *Die Rote Fahne*, 118, 1 June
1932.

122. SB 4,65/258/48. Abschrift. P-PB. PNPW. Betrifft: Arbeitsplan für den
Monat Januar der KPD. Bezirksleitung Ruhrgebiet. Bochum, 16
January 1932. See also original document, p. 9. SB 4,65/281/56.
'Kampfkonferenz der RGO', *Arbeiter Zeitung*, 142, 20 June 1932. BA
R134/83(56–7). NRI. IAN 2163/27.4. Berlin, 6 May 1932.

123. BA R45IV/11. Stand der Arbeit in den Betrieben und unter den
Erwerbslosen und die wichtigsten Aufgaben der RGO im Bezirk Halle-
Merseburg. (1932) p. 9. (18).

124. BA R45IV/39. 'Kampf dem Opportunismus', *Der Leninist*, Hamburg,
January 1932. Rundbrief Nr 1.

125. BA R134/72(10–11). Abschrift. IAN 2162c^1/20.4. Hamburg, 26 March
1932. See also; Kratzenberg, op. cit. pp. 54–8, for evidence of a similar
NSBO tactic nationally.

126. cf. pp. 106, 108-11 above, and Klönne, op. cit. p. 256.

127. BA R45IV/11. As in note 123 above, p. 13.

128. BA R45IV/39. As in note 124.

129. SB 4,65/280/55. P-PB. PNPW. I Nr. 146/32. Bochum, 13 June 1932.
Abschrift!(a). cf. Degras, op. cit., III pp. 143–4.

130. BA R45IV/11. Bericht über den Bezirk Halle-Merseburg (2–6 May
1932). gez. Werner. pp. 4–5.

131. BA R45IV/16. Berichte der Arbeiterkorrespondenten über die Lage in den Großbetrieben . . . 20–26 July (1932). BVG-Weissensee – Omnibus, p. 15. cf. SB 4,65/280/55. 'Das Programm der RGO. Sammelbecken aller klassenbewußten Straßenbahner', *Arbeiter Zeitung*, 105, 6 May 1932.

132. See, for instance, pp. 59-61, 72 above.

133. BA R45IV/21. Besprechung mit den Polleitern der Betriebszellen und Stadtteilen in Hannover. April/Mai 1932. Appel; Nahrungsmittel. ZK/ Org. – M. Olbrich.

134. BA R45IV/21. Bericht über die Versammlungen im Bezirk Niedersachsen. April 1932. Groß-Rühden, gez. Handke.

135. cf. Kratzenberg, op. cit. pp. 264–9.

136. For instance, BA R45IV/39. 'Die Stellungnahme der 26 Unterbezirke', *Der Bolschewik*, 3(20), mid December 1932, p. 390, Unterbezirk Dresden.

137. Mai, Betriebszellen pp. 585–6, 597–9, but cf. the more modest estimates by Daycock, op. cit. p. 288.

138. Mai, Betriebszellen p. 581. cf. BA R45IV/32. 'Verstärkte ideologische Offensive gegen die Nazis', *Der Pionier des Bolschewismus*, August 1932.

139. SB 4,65/260/49. Abschrift! Plan für unsere Massenarbeit für August/ September 1932. Entnommen aus dem Landespol. Mitteilungsblatt u. Fahndungsblatt des Pol.-Präs, Harburg-Wilhelmsburg, 6 September 1932.

140. SB 4,65/2038/362. Betriebs Presse Dienst. Oktober 1932, 5. 'Gegen die Nazi', pp. 8–9. BA R134/89(166). Auszugsweise Abschrift zu IAN 2167/24.11. Early October 1932.

141. SB 4,65/260/49. Abschrift. P-PB. PNPW. Betrifft: *Pionier des Bolschewismus*. Bochum, 5 October 1932, p. 2. BA R134/67(73). NRI. IAN 2160/4.11. Berlin, 10 November 1932.

142. BA R45IV/32. 'Durchbrecht den Naziblock', *Pionier des Bolschewismus*, October 1932, Sondernummer.

143. BA R45IV/32. 'Verstärkt die ideologische Offensive gegen die NSDAP!', *Der Funke*, 10 (6), October 1932, p. 11.

144. BA R45IV/32. 'Die Demagogie der Nazis', *Der Funke*, 10 (6), October 1932, p. 4.

145. SB 4,65/282/56. 'Postler fliegen auf die Straße', *Arbeiter Zeitung*, 259, 7 November 1932.

146. SB 4,65/2039/362. Polizei-Direktion. Zentralpolizeistelle. Betr.: Oeffentliche Wählerversammlung der KPD. Bremen, 24 October 1932, pp. 2–3.

147. SB 4,65/1694/285. Antifaschistische Aktion, Politische Information Nr. 2 des Reichseinheitsausschusses der Antifaschistischen Aktion. Berlin, 26 October 1932. III. p. 3.
BA R45IV/39. 'Die Stellungnahme der 26 Unterbezirke', *Der Bolschewik*, 3(20), mid December, p. 393; Unterbezirk Chemnitz, where a weak performance in this regard is discussed.
SB 4,65/282/56. Abschrift A. Bezirkskomitee der RGO. Jugend-Kommission. Essen, 12 December 1932, p. 6.

148. BA R134/94(116a–118). Anlage 1. esp. 117a. SB 4,65/261/49. Abschrift. Material zur Vertiefung unseres politischen Einflusses u. Verstärkung der Organisationsbasis der Partei. January? 1933, p. 11.
149. BA R134/94(114a). NRI. IAN 2160/30.12. Berlin, 17 January 1933.
150. SB 4,65/281/56. Abschrift. P-PB. PNPW I Nr, 209/32. Betrifft: Arbeitsplan der RGO für den Monat Oktober. Bochum, 14 October 1932. 'Die Manöver der Nazis', p. 4. cf. BA R45IV/32. 'Neue Manöver der Nazis', *Der Revolutionär*, Sondernummer, September [1932].
151. BA R45IV/38. '600 Notstandsarbeiter im Streik gegen die Naziregierung in Oldenburg', *Der Pionier*, 3(17), early Setpember 1932, p. 1. BA R45IV/26. Auszug aus den Berichten der BL über die Durchführung der Antifaschistischen Betriebswoche. Bezirk Nordwest. Undated.
152. For instance; BA R45IV/13. 'Internationale Arbeiterkämpfe. Deutschland', *Internationale Gewerkschafts-Pressekorrespondenz*, 73, 13 September 1932, pp. 899, 900.
153. Kratzenberg, op. cit. p. 13. See also; W. Jasper, 'Nicht nur Streikbrechertruppe. Die NS-Betriebszellen und der Gewerkschaftsbund – ein Tabu Thema', *Die Zeit*, 6 May 1988.
154. Quoted in Degras, op. cit., II, p. 433.
155. SB 4,65/251/46. Zentralkomitee der Kommunistischen Partei Deutschlands. Sekretariat. Berlin, early June 1930, p. 2. cf. SB 4,65/257/48. Abschrift. Arbeitsplan des Bezirks Ruhrgebiet für November-Dezember 1931.
156. SB 4,65/252/46. RI. IAN 2160/6.10. Betrifft: Kommunistische Bewegung. Berlin, 6 October 1932, p. 2.
157. SB 4,65/255/47. 'Die Lage in Deutschland und die Aufgaben der KPD', *Die Rote Fahne*, 142, 4 July 1931. cf. SB 4,65/1272/212. P-PB. Na I Nr. 370/31. Bochum, 20 August 1931. Abschrift. *Alarm* Nr. 11 – July 1931, p. 1.
158. See; BA R45IV/39. 'Die HIB-Aktion der Nazis', *Der Leninist*, January 1932. Rundbrief Nr 1. SB 4,65/278/55. P-PB. PNPW. I Nr. 58/32. Bochum, 19 February 1932. Abschrift! RGO Hieb gegen 'Hib'. pp. 10–16. cf. Kratzenberg, op. cit. p. 113.
159. BA R45IV/32. 'Neue Manöver der Nazis', *Der Revolutionär*, Sondernummer, September [1932]. cf. SB 4,65/281/56. P-PB. PNPW I Nr. 209/32. Bochum, 14 October 1932. Abschrift. Bezirks-Arbeitsplan der RGO. p. 4. BA R45IV/45. Reichsfraktionsleitung der Kommunisten in der RGO. Betr.: Herstellung der politischen Einheitsfront . . . . Berlin, 11 May 1932, p. 7. BA R134/89(166). Auszugsweise Abschrift zu Nr. IAN 2167/24.11. ZK der KJVD. Early October 1932.
160. BA R45IV/32. As in note 159 above.
161. BA R45IV/39. 'Streikerfahrungen! Streik bei August Hoffmann – Neugersdorf', *Der Bolschewik*, 3 (19), early December [1932] p. 357.
162. As above, pp. 357–8.
163. BA R45IV/39. 'Streik bei der Steingutfabrik Sörnewitz . . .', *Der Bolschewik*, 3 (19), early December [1932] pp. 359–60.
164. BA R45IV/39. 'Die Stellungnahme der 26 Unterbezirke', 'Unterbezirk Flöha', *Der Bolschewik*, 3 (20), mid December [1932] p. 394.

165. cf. BA R45IV/39. 'Die HIB-Aktion der Nazis', *Der Leninist*, January 1932. Rundbrief Nr 1.
166. SB 4,65/282/56. Abschrift. P-PB. PNPW. I Nr. 252/32. Betrifft: RGO. Bochum, 30 December 1932.
167. BA R45IV/39. 'Die Stellungnahme der 26 Unterbezirke', 'Unterbezirk Chemnitz', *Der Bolschewik*, mid December [1932] p. 393.
168. BA R45IV/32. 'Die Demagogie der Nazis', *Der Funke*, 10 (6), October 1932, p. 3. cf. SB 4,65/119/18. 'Schmiedet die Einheitsfront im Betriebsrätewahlkampf!', and Kratzenberg, op. cit. p. 106, who estimates that the NSBO participated in 101 strikes between April 1932 and the BVG strike.
169. BA R45IV/39. 'Die Stellungnahme der 26 Unterbezirke', *Der Bolschewik*, 3 (20), mid December [1932] p. 396.
170. BA R134/93(171). IAN 2163/12.12. Anlage 1, 23/24 November 1932.
171. SB 4,65/250/46. 'Nieder mit den faschistischen Mördern!', *Die Rote Fahne*, 165, 29 August 1929.
172. SB 4,65/270/52. 'Emden wählt drei Delegierte zum Betriebskongreß . . .', *Arbeiter Zeitung*, 11, 14 January 1930.
173. SB 4,65/270/52. Abschrift. P-PB. Na I Nr. 831/30. Betrifft: Politisches Informationsmaterial der Leitung der Roten Gewerkschaftsopposition. Bezirk Ruhrgebiet. Bochum, 19 July 1930.
174. cf. Kratzenberg, op. cit. p. 236.
175. SB 4,65/271/52. V. R.G.I. Kongress. Referenten-Material. II. Teil. Streikführung und Streikerfahrung der RGO. Berlin, 10 October 1930. (5).
176. BA R134/81(64). Abschrift IAN 2160/4.12. 15 November 1930.
177. For instance; SB 4,65/281/56. P-PB. PNPW. I Nr. 209/32. Bochum, 14 October 1932. Abschrift. Bezirks-Arbeitsplan der RGO, p. 1. SB 4,65/282/56. Abschrift (b). Resolution zur Plenartagung des Bezirkskomitees der RGO, 4 December 1932; Situation im Ruhrgebiet, p. 10. SB 4,65/282/56. 'Der Angestelltenkampf 1933 in Einheitsfrontaktion mit der Arbeiterklasse', *Arbeiter Zeitung*, 10 January 1933. (4). SB 4,65/280/55. P-PB. PNPW. I Nr. 124/32. Bochum, 8 May 1932. Abschrift (a).
178. Kratzenberg, op. cit. p. 123.
179. For instance; SB 4,65/272/53. 'Resolution zu den Wirtschaftskämpfen und den Aufgaben der RGO', *Die Rote Fahne*, 51, 1. Beilage, 1 March 1931. 'Der Ruhrkampf . . .'.
180. See pp. 174, 177, 180.
181. Thus; BA R45IV/23. Bezirk Baden-Pfalz. Mannheim, 11 June 1932. Bericht über . . . Antif. Aktion. Aktionen der Erwerbslosen und Pflichtarbeiter. BA R45IV/23. Abschrift. Bezirksleitung Mittelrhein. Köln, 14 June 1932. Bericht über . . . Antifasch. Aktion . . . . BA R45IV/13. 'Internationale Arbeiterkämpfe. Deutschland', *Internationale Gewerkschafts-Pressekorrespondenz*, 73, 13 September 1932, p. 899.
182. See pp. 142–3, 182–3 above, and BA R45IV/35. Kommunistische Partei Deutschlands. Bezirk Schlesien. Bericht von der Bezirks-Agitprop-Konferenz, 18 September 1932. Breslau, 26 September 1932, p. 1. SB

4,65/2038/362. Betriebs Presse Dienst. October 1932. 'Gegen die Nazi', pp. 8–9.
183. SB 4,65/1694/285. Antifaschistische Aktion. Politische Information Nr. 2 des Reichseinheitsausschusses der Antifaschistischen Aktion. Berlin, 26 October 1932. III. p. 3.
184. SB 4,65/2038/362. Betreibs Presse Dienst. Early November 1932. 'Neue Streiks', p. 6.
185. cf. Dorpalen, 'SPD und KPD', p. 103.
186. SB 4,65/2038/362. Betriebs Presse Dienst. Early November 1932. 'Reformisten und NSBO gegen streikende Kraftfahrer', p. 3. BA Sammlung Schumacher (Sch) 330. 'Kameraden: Im letzten Briefe . . .'. HEIL! Die oppositionellen SA der Standarten 9, 15, 31, 45 u. 76. Undated.
187. See p. 177 above.
188. SB 4,65/283/56. Ausschrift aus dem Bericht der KPD über den Bezirksparteitag, 26/27 November 1932. p. 12, Der Hunterarbeiterstreik Oldenburg. SB 4, 65, as above. Der Einfluß der NSBO in den Betrieben des Weser-Ems Geb., p. 68.
189. BA R134/92(4). IAN 2165b/9.12. Berlin, 4 November 1932.
190. For instance; SB 4,65/1268/211. Auszug aus dem Lagebericht N/Nr. 85 aus München, 23 October 1929. N. Stelle Nr. 1983/29 geh. Fortführung des Roten Frontkämpferbundes . . . . BA R45IV/21. Versammlungsberichte. Ffm. 7–9 April 1932. Zellstofffabrik Kostheim.
191. BA R45IV/28. An B.L. und U.B. Chemnitz. Bericht von der Konferenz des U.B. Einsiedel. August 1932, p. 2.
192. BA NS26/1405. Berichte der Staatspolizei Württembergs zur politischen Lage. 23 December 1932. Bezirksparteitag der KPD, Bezirk Württemberg. 10/11 December 1932. SB 4,65/1267/211. Abschrift. IAN 2166i/15.9. Betrifft: Proletarischer Massenselbstschutz. Berlin, 15 September 1932. SB 4,65/252/46. Polizeidirektion Nürnberg-Fürth. Sonderbericht Nr. 181/II/30. Nürnberg, 22 October 1930. Abschrift. Bezirk Nordbayern. Arbeitsplan – Oktober–November. p. 2. BA R45IV/9. Bericht über die Wahlkampagne zu den Thüringer Landtagswahlen im Unterbezirk Greiz (December 1929) gez. Gippel. BA R45IV/8. Reorganisationsplan – Niedersachsen, 17 March 1932, p. 3. SB 4,65/254/47. Abschrift. Bezirksleitung Ruhrgebiet. Abtlg. Org. Essen, 3 February 1931.
193. SB 4,65/253/47. Abschrift. Bezirksleitung Ruhrgebiet. Sekretariat (Agitprop). Essen, 9 October 1930. SB 4,65/254/47. Abschrift. Bezirksleitung Ruhrgebiet. Abtlg. Org. Essen, 24 February 1931. BA R45IV/15. 4 Plenar-ZK-Sitzung. 26–29 November 1929.
194. Thus, BA R45IV/21. Versammlungsberichte. Ffm. 7–9 April 1932. 7 April, Betriebsversammlung I.G. Höchst.
195. BA R134/89(6). IAN 2167/23.7. Berlin, 22 June 1932. SB 4,65/251/46. Ausschnitt aus dem Lagebericht der Pol. Dir. Nürnberg, 6 May 1930. Bezirksparteitag der KPD-Nordbayern in Fürth. 14 April 1930. Organisationsbericht.
196. SB 4,65/251/46. Ausschnitt aus dem Lagebericht des sächsischen Ministeriums des Innern in Dresden, 25 May 1932. KPD.

197. Thus; BA R45IV/21. Suhl, 18 April 1932. gez. Jahnke. Berlin, 2 May 1932.
198. SB 4,65/252/46. RI. IAN 2160/6.10. Betrifft: Kommunistische Bewegung. Berlin, 6 October 1930, p. 4.
199. BA R134/81(125). IAN 2160/29.4 Berlin, 13 March 1931.
200. SB 4,65/256/48. Abschrift. IAN 2160/27.10. Zentralkomitee der KPD. Sekretariat. Sonderanweisungen! Berlin, 7 October 1931, p. 5.
201. SB 4,65/253/47. Abschrift. P-PB. Na. Betrifft: Arbeitsplan des Bezirks Ruhrgebiet der KPD. Bochum, 15 November 1930, p. 2.
202. SB 4,65/254/47. Abschrift. P-PB. Na. Betrifft: Rundschrieben der kommunistischen Bezirksleitung Ruhrgebiet . . . . Bochum, 11 February 1931. SB 4,65/274/53. P-PB. Na. Bochum, 1 August 1931. Abschrift. 'Geht unsere Betriebsarbeit vorwärts oder zurück?'. SB 4,65/257/48. Abschrift. Arbeitsplan des Bezirks Ruhrgebiet für November-Dezember 1931. 'Reorganisierung der Partei'.
203. SB 4,65/260/49. P-PB. PNPW. I Nr. 183/32. Betrifft: KPD. Bochum, 24 August 1932, p. 2. See also; p. 1.
204. SB 4,65/260/49. Abschrift. P-PB PNPW. I Nr. 241/32. Betrifft: *Pionier des Bolschewismus*. Bochum, 5 October 1932, p. 3.
205. See pp. 17-19 above.

CONCLUSION

1. D. Peukert, 'Der deutsche Arbeiterwiderstand 1933–1945', in K. D. Bracher, M. Funke, H. -A. Jacobsen (eds), *Nationalsozialistische Diktatur. Eine Bilanz* (Bonn, 1983) p. 642.
2. A. Merson, *Communist Resistance in Nazi Germany* (London, 1985) p. 32.
3. Bahne, *KPD un das Ende*, p. 44
4. Merson, op. cit. chs. 7, 8. R. O. Paxton, 'The German Opposition to Hitler: A Non-Germanist's View', *Central European History*, 14(4) (1981) p. 363. Peukert, Arbeiterwiderstand p. 643.
5. For a discussion of this reluctance; Peukert, *Arbeiterwiderstand*, p. 634.
6. Thus, Merson, op. cit. D. Peukert, *Die KPD im Widerstand. Verfolgung und Untergrundarbeit an Rhein und Ruhr, 1933 bis 1945* (Wuppertal, 1980), and the earlier work by K. Duhnke, *Die KPD von 1933 bis 1945* (Cologne, 1972).
7. Thus, Merson, op. cit. p. 35.
8. Peukert, *KPD im Widerstand*, quoted in Merson, op. cit. p. 316 note 22. For figures on SPD; BA NS26/810. 20 February 1932. Die organisatorische Entwicklung der Partei im Jahre 1931, p. 3 and Anlage 5a/b.
9. Waite, op. cit. p. 274
10. Fischer, *Stormtroopers*, pp. 55–8.
11. Valtin, op. cit. p. 345.
12. Merson, op. cit. p. 35.
13. cf. K. Repgen, 'Ein KPD-Verbot im Jahre 1933?', *Historiche Zeitschrift*, 240(1) (1985) p. 79.
14. SB 4, 65/262/50. Bericht über die im U. B. Osnabrück vom 9. – 14. IV. dürchgeführten Arbeiten. p. 1.
15. As above, p. 2.
16. SB 4,65/262/50. Berichte von der Instrukteursitzung am 17. u. 24.4. (Telegrammstil) [1933].
17. SB 4.65/284/56. Abschrift. P-PR. PNPW. N.St. Geh. Nr. 126/33. (a)

Betrifft: RGO. Recklinghausen, 24 May 1933. See also; SB 4,65/262/50.
P-PR. PNPW. Betrifft: KPD. Recklinghausen, 13 March 1933. cf.
Bahne, *KPD und das Ende*, pp. 52, 53.

18. SB 4, 65/262/50. P-PR. PNPW. Betrifft: KPD. Recklinghausen, 13
March 1933. SB 4,65/284/56. P-PR. PNPW. I. Geheim Nr. 68/33.
Betrifft: Funktionärsitzung der RGO. Recklinghausen, 4 April 1933. SB
4,65/262/50. Abschrift! P-PR. PNPW. Sammelbericht. Recklinghausen,
16 May 1933. Staatsarchiv München (SM) NSDAP 798. SA der NSDAP.
Der OSAF. Der Chef des Stabes. Betr.: Kommunistische Zersetzungs
versuche in der SA. München, 22 October 1934. SB 4.65/1253/209. Der
Politische Polizeikommandeur. B. Nr. 61931. II 1A1/J. Betrifft: R.F.B.
BA SA Archiv (NS23)/9. Sturmbann III/53. An C93. Opladen, 15 June
1933. BA NS23/298. Hessisches Staatspolizeiamt. Betr.: Komm.
Zersetzungsarbeit in SA und SS. Darmstadt, 19 November 1934.
19. GStAM R293. Politische Nachrichten der Polizeidirektion Nürnberg-
Fürth. Nr. 2. Nürnberg, 21 October 1933.
20. BA NS23/9. Sturmbann III/53. An C93. Opladen, 15 June 1933. BA
NS23/383. SA der NSDAP. Reiterstandarte der Brigade 12. B.B. Nr. III
33/34. Betr.:Schrb. d. OSAF v. 2.3.34. Hamburg, 12 March 1934.
GStAM R276/2. Halbmonatsbericht des Regierungspräsidiums von
Niederbayern und der Oberpfalz. Nr. 366. Regensburg, 20 April 1934.
BA NS23/158. Anon. An das Braune Haus. München, 3 June 1934. BA
NS23/158. An die Oberste SA Stelle. Straubing, 4 July 1934. gez. L.
Kraus. BA NS23/158. An den Chef des Stabes der SA. Berlin, 9 July
1934. gez. Ein alter Nationalsozialist. GStAM R280/1. Präsidium der
Regierung von Niederbayern und der Oberpfalz. Betreff: Lagebericht
. . . . Regensburg, 8 August 1934.
21. BA NS23/126. OSAF I Nr. 1748/33. München, 22 December 1933. gez.
v. Kraußer. BA NS26/1240. 'Was wird aus der SA? – Unterredung mit
dem Chef des Stabes', *Frankfurter Oder-Zeitung*, 6 July 1934.
22. SB 4,65/284/56. P-PR. PNPW. I, Geheim Nr. 63/33. Betrifft: RGO.
Recklinghausen, 18 April 1933, p. 1. SB 4,65/284/56. Entnommen aus
OD – Spezialbericht vom 24. Juni 1933. Bremen, 26 June 1933. 'An alle
Gewerkschaftsorganisationen . . .', p. 3.
23. cf. Bahne, *KPD und das Ende*, p. 41. Fest, *Third Reich*, p. 220.
24. SB 4,65/262/50. Abschrift. P-PR. PNPW. Betrifft: KPD. Recklinghausen, 22 March 1933. p. 5.
25. Quoted in Fischer, *Stormtroopers*, pp. 58, 198, 211–2. See also R. Diels,
Lucifer ante Portas. Zwischen Severing und Heydrich (Zurich, 1949)
pp. 153, 334–5.
26. Thus: K. Bredow, *Hitlerrast. Die Bluttragödie der 30. Juni 1934. Ablauf,
Vorgeschichte und Hintergründe* (Saarbrücken, 1935). *Weissbuch über
die Erschiessungen der 30. Juni 1934* (Paris, 1935).
27. Bahne, *KPD und das Ende*, p. 54.
28. Buchloh, op. cit. pp. 145–53, esp. 151–2.
29. This factor should not be exaggerated; cf. Moses, *Trade Unionism*, II, p. 426.
30. Flechtheim, op. cit. p. 273.
31. SB 4,65/262/50. P-PR. PNPW. Betrifft: KPD. Recklinghausen, 16
March 1933. Anlage. Zum Wahlergebnis und unseren nächsten
Aufgaben, p. 2.
32. BA R134/85(150). Zu IAN 2162c^1/12.4. 27 March 1933. BA NS23/8.
'Alarm! Lesen und weitergeben! Alarm!'. Undated.

258   *Notes to Conclusion*

33. cf. Daycock, op. cit. p. 294.
34. Thus, BA R134/67 (Between 319 and 320). 14 February 1933. BA R134/95(2). IAN 2166a/20.2. Berlin, 1 March 1933.
35. Bahne, *KPD und das Ende* p. 35. Valtin, op. cit. pp. 345–6.
36. BA R134/95(116). IAN 2166a/4.3. Berlin, 16 March 1933.
37. SB 4,65/2044/364. 'SA-Kameraden!', *Der SA Prolet*, 3, Undated [March 1933].
38. BA Sch 331. 'Arbeiter, Antifaschisten Hamburgs. Alarm!', Roter Frontkämpferbund. cf. BA R45IV/3. 'Durch Klassenkampf zum Klassensieg . . .', *Die Rote Front*, 9(12), 35. illegale Nummer. BA Sch 331. '. . . SA Proleten sei gesagt', *Die Rote Front*, March 1933. BA Sch 331. Mitteilung des Gaues Wasserkante. R.F.B. Wasserkante. April 1933.
39. BA Sch 331. 'Pflichtarbeiter!! Erwerbslose!! SA Proleten!!', KPD und KJVD Wandsbek. Undated. cf. SB 4,65/2045/364. Betr. Oeffentliche Wahlversammlung des Stadtteils IIa der KPD am 27.2. bei Heide. . . . Bremen, 3 March 1933.
40. SB 4,65/2044/364. 'SA Kameraden! Augen auf!', *Kleine Arbeiterzeitung*, March 1933, pp. 4–6. BA Sch 331. 'Nazi-Prolet, Augen auf!', *Hamburger Volkszeitung*, 26 March 1933. BA Sch 330. 'Geht es dem Volk besser?'. Undated [May 1933]. BA NS23/401. OSAF. Betr.: Kommunistische Bewegung. Abschrift. Min. des Innerns. München, 24 April 1933. GStAM MA 106 670. Halbmonatsbericht des Regierungs-Präsidiums von Oberbayern (15. mit 31. Januar 1933) Nr. 283. München, 6 February 1933. See also Fischer, *Stormtroopers*, pp. 188-90. 191–6.
41. BA R134/95(96a). IAN 2164d/7.3. Berlin, 15 March 1933.
42. GStAM R280/1. Abdruck. Präsidium der Regierung der Pfalz. Lagebericht. Speyer, 9 August 1934. BA NS23/295. 'Männer der SA und SS! Kameraden der HJ!', September 1934. BA NS23/262. OSAF Stabsabteilung No, 1070 geh. Auszug aus den Tagesmeldungen des Gestapa . . ., 1–28 February 1935. München, 8 April 1935.
43. GStAM MA 106 669. Abdruck. Nr. 2577/Abt.1. Polizeidirektion München. Betreff: Lageberichte; hier Monat Juli 1934 München, 8 August 1934. I. cf. Bahne, *KPD und das Ende* p. 61. Kershaw, op. cit. p. 75.
44. cf. Bahne, *KPD und das Ende*, p. 58.
45. This is an area of heated controversy which remains unresolved, but on balance those arguing for a limited, containable crisis seem to have the stronger case. For one recent debate, focusing on the implications of working-class resistance to Nazism and on the economic problems faced by the Third Reich during the late 1930s: R. J. Overy, 'Germany, "Domestic Crisis" and War in 1939', *Past and Present*, 116 (1987) pp. 138–68; R. J. Overy, 'Debate. Germany, "Domestic Crisis" and War in 1939. Reply', *Past and Present*, 122 (1989) pp. 221–40; Overy qualifies heavily the extent of the crisis. But cf. D. Kaiser, 'Debate. Germany, "Domestic Crisis" and War in 1939. Comment 1', *Past and Present*, 122 (1989) pp. 200–5, and T. W. Mason, Debate. Germany, "Domestic Crisis" and War in 1939. Comment 2', *Past and Present*, 122 (1989) pp. 205–21. Kershaw, op. cit. pp. 95–110 argues for a limited crisis, as do: M. Knox, Conquest, Foreign and Domestic, in Fascist Italy and Nazi Germany', *Journal of Modern History*, 56 (1) (1984) pp. 49–57, esp. 52–4, and A. Adamthwaite, 'War Origins Again', *Journal of Modern History*, 56 (1) (1984) esp. 110–11, 112–13. See also Zitelmann, op. cit. pp. 95–6, where he notes the degree of working-class support for the Third Reich in the Saar plebiscite in 1935.

Sources

PRIMARY SOURCES

Bayerisches Hauptstaatsarchiv München (BHStA)
Abteilung I (Abt. I).
Staatsministerium des Innern, Band 22 (M. Inn).
Geheimes Staatsarchiv München (GStAM).
Monatsberichte der Regierungspräsidenten/Lageberichte (MA).
Reichsstatthalter Epp, 1933–1945 (R).
Staatsarchiv München (SM).
NSDAP
Bundesarchiv Koblenz (BA)
R43I   (Reichskanzlei).
R134   (Reichskommissar für die Überwachung der öffentlichen Ordnung und Nachrichtensammelstelle im Reichsministerium des Innern. Lageberichte (1920–1929) und Meldungen (1929–1933) (RKo)).
R45IV   (Zentralkomitee der Kommunistischen Partei Deutschlands).
NS23   (SA der NSDAP).
NS26   (NSDAP Hauptarchiv).
Sammlung Schumacher (Sch).
Institut für Zeitgeschichte (IfZ)
SA.
Staatsarchiv Bremen (SB)
Polizei-Direktion Bremen (Rep. 4,65).

SECONDARY SOURCES

These have been cited as follows:

Adamthwaite, A., 'War Origins Again', *The Journal of Modern History*, 56 (1) (1984) 100–15.
Alemann, U. von (ed.), *Parteien und Wahlen in Nordrhein-Westfalen* (Cologne, 1985).
Allen, W. S., 'Farewell to Class Analysis in the Rise of Nazism: Comment', *Central European History*, 17 (1) (1984) 54–62.
Allen, W. S., *The Nazi Seizure of Power. The Experience of a single German Town 1930–1935* (London, 1966).
Anikeev, A. A., 'Zur marxistischen Historiographie über die Bauernpolitik des deutschen Faschismus', *Zeitschrift für Geschichtswissenschaft*, 19 (1971) 1385–94.
Aufhaüser, S., 'Betriebsrat – Werksgemeinschaft', *Die Arbeit*, 1 (1924) 272–5.
Bahne, S., 'Die KPD im Ruhrgebiet in der Weimarer Republik', in J. Reulecke (ed.), *Arbeiterbewegung an Rhein und Ruhr. Beiträge zur Geschichte der Arbeiterbewegung in Rheinland-Westfalen* (Wuppertal, 1974) 315–53.

259

260 *Sources*

Bahne, S., *Die KPD und das Ende von Weimar. Das Scheitern einer Politik 1932–1935* (Frankfurt-am-Main, 1976).

Bakke, E. W., 'The Cycle of Adjustment to Unemployment', in N. W. Bell, E. F. Vogel (ed.), *A Modern Introduction to the Family* (Glencoe, Ill., 1960)

Bakke, E. W., *The Unemployed Man* (Nisbet, 1933).

Bariéty, J., 'Die französische Politik in der Ruhrkrise', in K. Schwabe (ed.), *Die Ruhrkrise 1923. Wendepunkt der internationalen Beziehung nach dem Ersten Weltkrieg*, 2nd ed. (Paderborn, 1986) 11–27.

Bell, N. W., Vogel, E. F. (eds), *A Modern Introduction to the Family* (Glencoe, Ill., 1960).

Berghahn, V. R., *Der Stahlhelm, Bund der Frontsoldaten 1918–1935* (Düsseldorf, 1966).

Bessel, R., *Political Violence and the Rise of Nazism. The Storm Troopers in Eastern Germany 1925–1934* (New Haven, Conn., London, 1984).

Bessel, R., Feuchtwanger, E. J. (eds), *Social Change and Political Development in Weimar Germany* (London, 1981).

Böhnke, W., *Die NSDAP im Ruhrgebiet, 1920–1933* (Bonn, Bad Godesberg, 1974).

Bond, B., *War and Society in Europe, 1870–1970* (London, 1984).

Borkenau, F., *World Communism. A History of the Communist International* (Ann Arbor, Mich., 1962).

Bracher, K. D., *The German Dictatorship. The Origins, Structure and Consequences of National Socialism*, trans. J. Steinberg (London, 1973).

Bracher, K. D., Funke, M., Jacobsen, H. -A. (eds), *Nationalsozialistische Diktatur 1933–1945. Eine Bilanz* (Bonn, 1983).

Bramke, W., 'Zum Verhalten der Mittelschichten in der Novemberrevolution', *Zeitschrift für Geschichtswissenschaft*, 31 (8) (1983) 691-700.

Bredow, K., *Hitlerrast. Die Bluttragödie des 30. Juni 1934. Ablauf, Vorgeschichte und Hintergründe* (Saarbrücken, 1935).

Breitman, R., *German Socialism and Weimar Democracy* (Chapel Hill, NC, 1981).

Bretton, H. L., *Stresemann and the Revision of Versailles. A Fight for Reason* (Stanford, Calif., 1953).

Broszat, M., *The Hitler State. The Foundation and Development of the Internal Structure of the Third Reich*, trans. J. Hiden (London, 1981).

Broszat, M., 'National Socialism, its Social Basis and Psychological Impact', in E. J. Feuchtwanger (ed.), *Upheaval and Continuity. A Century of German History* (London, 1973) 134–51.

Bruhns, M. et al. (eds), *„Hier war doch alles nicht so schlimm". Wie die Nazis in Hamburg den Alltag eroberten* (Hamburg, 1984).

Buchloh, I., *Die nationalsozialistische Machtergreifung in Duisburg. Eine Fallstudie* (Duisburg, 1980).

Cahn, E., Fisera, V. (eds), *Socialism and Nationalism in Contemporary Europe (1848–1945)* (Nottingham, 1979).

Carr, E. H., *German–Soviet Relations between the two World Wars, 1919–1939* (Oxford, 1952).

Carsten, F. L., *The Reichswehr and Politics 1918–1933* (Berkeley, Los Angeles, London, 1973).

Carsten, F. L., *Revolution in Central Europe 1918–1919* (Aldershot, 1988).

Carsten, F. L., *The Rise of Fascism* (London, 1970).

Childers, T., *The Nazi Voter. The Social Foundations of Fascism in Germany, 1919–1933* (Chapel Hill, NC, London, 1983).

Childers, T., 'Who, Indeed, Did Vote for Hitler?', *Central European History*, 17 (1) (1984) 45–53.

Craig, G. A., *Germany. 1866–1945* (Oxford, 1978).

Daycock, D. W., 'The KPD and the NSDAP: A Study of the Relationship between Political Extremes in Weimar Germany 1923–1933', (PhD Dissertation, London School of Economics, 1980).

Degras, J. (ed.), *The Communist International 1919–1943. Documents.* (3 vols.) (London, 1971).

Deppe, F., Fülberth, G., Harrer, J. (eds), *Geschichte der deutschen Gewerkschaftsbewegung*, 3rd edn (Cologne, 1981).

Diehl, J. M., *Paramilitary Politics in Weimar Germany* (Bloomington, Ind., London, 1977).

Diels, R., *Lucifer ante Portas. Zwischen Severing und Heydrich* (Zurich, 1949).

Dimitrov, G., *The Working Class against Fascism* (London, 1935).

Dorpalen, A., *German History in Marxist Perspective. The East German Approach* (London, 1985).

Dorpalen, A., 'SPD und KPD in der Endphase der Weimarer Republik', *Vierteljahreshefte für Zeitgeschichte*, 31 (1) (1983) 77–107.

Duhnke, K., *Die KPD von 1933 bis 1945* (Cologne, 1972).

Eisenberg, P., Lazarsfeld, P. F., 'The Psychological Effects of Unemployment', *Psychological Bulletin*, (1938).

Eley, G., *From Unification to Nazism. Reinterpreting the German Past* (Boston, Mass., 1986).

Eley, G., 'The Wilhelmine Right: How it Changed', in R. J. Evans (ed.), *Society and Politics in Wilhelmine Germany* (London, 1978).

Erdmann, K. D., 'Alternativen der deutschen Politik im Ruhrkampf', in K. Schwabe (ed.), *Die Ruhrkrise 1923. Wendepunkt der internationalen Beziehungen nach dem Ersten Weltkrieg*, 2nd edn (Paderborn, 1986) 29–38.

Erdmann, L., 'Gewerkschaften, Werksgemeinschaften und industrielle Demokratie', *Die Arbeit*, II (1925) 131–42.

Evans, R. J., Geary, D. (eds), *The German Unemployed. Experiences and Consequences of Mass Unemployment from the Weimar Republic to the Third Reich* (London, 1987).

Evans, R. J. (ed.), *The German Working Class 1888–1933. The Politics of Everyday Life* (London, 1982).

Evans, R. J. (ed.), *Society and Politics in Wilhelmine Germany* (London, 1978).

Falter, J. et al., 'Arbeitslosigkeit und Nationalsozialismus', *Kölner Zeitschrift für Soziologie und Sozialpsychologie*, 35 (1983) 525–54.

Falter, J., 'Unemployment and the Radicalisation of the German Electorate 1928–1933: An Aggregate Data Analysis with Special Emphasis on the Rise of National Socialism', in P. D. Stachura (ed.), *Unemployment and the Great Depression in Weimar Germany* (London, 1986) 187–208.

Falter, J., 'Die Wähler der NSDAP 1928–1933: Sozialstruktur und parteipolitische Herkunft', in W. Michalka (ed.), *Die nationalsozialistische*

Machtergreifung (Paderborn, Munich, Vienna, Zurich, 1984) 47–59.

Falter, J., 'Warum die deutschen Arbeiter während des „Dritten Reiches" zu Hitler standen. Einige Anmerkungen zu Gunther Mais Beitrag über die Unterstützung des nationalsozialistischen Herrschaftssystems durch Arbeiter', *Geschichte und Gesellschaft*, 13 (1987) 217–31.

Feldman, G. D., *Army, Industry and Labor in Germany, 1914–1918* (Princeton, NJ., 1966).

Feldman, G. D., 'The large Firm in the German Industrial System: The M.A.N. 1900–1925', in D. Stegmann, B.-J. Wendt, P.-C. Witt (eds), *Industrielle Gesellschaft und Politisches System. Beiträge zur politischen Sozialgeschichte* (Bonn, 1978) 241–57.

Feldman, G. D., 'The Social and Economic Policies of German Big Business, 1918–1929', *The American Historical Review*, LXXV (1) (1969) 47–55.

Feldman, G. D., *Vom Weltkrieg zur Weltwirtschaftskrise. Studien zur deutschen Wirtschafts- und Sozialgeschichte 1914–1932* (Göttingen, 1984).

Fest, J. C., *Hitler*, trans. R. and C. Winston (London, 1974).

Fest, J. C., *The Face of the Third Reich*, trans. M. Bullock (London, 1972).

Feuchtwanger, E. J. (ed.), *Upheaval and Continuity. A Century of German History* (London, 1973).

Finker, K., 'Die militaristischen Wehrverbände in der Weimarer Republik und ihre Rolle bei der Unterdrückung der Arbeiterklasse und bei der Vorbereitung eines neuen imperialistischen Krieges (1924–1929)', (Habilitationsschrift, Pädagogische Hochschule, Potsdam, 1964).

Fischer, C. J., 'Class Enemies or Class Brothers?' Communist–Nazi Relations in Germany, 1929–1933', *European History Quarterly*, 15 (3) (1985) 259–79.

Fischer, C. J., 'The KPD and Nazism: A Reply to Dick Geary', *European History Quarterly*, 15 (4) (1985) 465–71.

Fischer, C. J., *Stormtroopers: A Social, Economic and Ideological Analysis 1929–35* (London, 1983).

Fischer, C. J., 'Unemployment and Left-Wing Radicalism in Weimar Germany, 1930–1933', in P. D. Stachura (ed.), *Unemployment and the Great Depression in Weimar Germany* (London, 1986) 209–25.

Fischer, W., 'Wirtschaftliche Rahmenbedingungen des Ruhrkonflikts', in K. Schwabe (ed.), *Die Ruhrkrise 1923. Wendepunkt der internationalen Beziehungen nach dem Ersten Weltkrieg*, 2nd edn (Paderborn, 1986) 89–101.

Flechtheim, O. K., *Die KPD in der Weimarer Republik* (Frankfurt-am-Main, 1969).

Fletcher, R. (ed.). *Bernstein to Brandt. A Short History of German Social Democracy* (London, 1987).

Fletcher, R., 'The Life and Work of Eduard Bernstein', in R. Fletcher (ed.), *Bernstein to Brandt. A Short History of German Social Democracy* (London, 1987) 45–53.

Fletcher, R., 'Revisionism and Wilhelmine Imperialism', *Journal of Contemporary History*, 23 (3) (1988) 347–66.

Fowkes, B., *Communism in Germany under the Weimar Republic* (London, 1984).

Fricke, F., *Sie Suchen die Seele!* (Berlin, 1927).

Gates, R. A., 'Von der Sozialpolitik zur Wirtschaftspolitik? Das Dilemma der deutschen Sozialdemokratie in der Krise 1929–1933', in H. Mommsen, D. Petzina, B. Weisbrod (eds). *Industrielles System und politische Entwicklung in der Weimarer Republik*, vol. 1 (Düsseldorf, 1977) 206–25.

Gatzke, H. W., *Stresemann and the Rearmament of Germany* (Baltimore, Md, 1954).

Geary, D., *European Labour Protest 1848–1939* (London, 1981).

Geary, D., 'Identifying Militancy: The Assessment of Working-Class Attitudes towards State and Society', in R. J. Evans (ed.), *The German Working Class 1888–1933. The Politics of Everyday Life* (London, 1982) 220–46.

Geary, R. J. (D.), 'Jugendarbeitslosigkeit und politischer Radikalismus in der Weimarer Republik', *Gewerkschaftliche Monatshefte*, (1983) 304–9.

Geary, D., 'Nazis and Workers: A Response to Conan Fischer's "Class Enemies or Class Brothers?" ', *European History Quarterly*, 15 (4) (1985) 453–64.

Geary, D., 'Radicalism and the Worker: Metalworkers and Revolution 1914–23', in R. J. Evans (ed.), *Society and Politics in Wilhelmine Germany* (London, 1978) 267–86.

Geary, D., 'Unemployment and Working-Class Solidarity: The German Experience 1929–33', in R. J. Evans, D. Geary (eds), *The German Unemployed. Experiences and Consequences of Mass Unemployment from the Weimar Republic to the Third Reich* (London, 1987) 261–80.

Gerber, J., 'From Left Radicalism to Council Communism: Anton Pannekoek and German Revolutionary Marxism', *Journal of Contemporary History*, 23 (2) (1988) 169–89.

Gerth, H. H., 'The Nazi Party: Its Leadership and Composition', *American Journal of Sociology*, XLV (4) (1940) 517–41.

Gordon, H. J., *Hitler and the Beer Hall Putsch* (Princeton, NJ, 1972).

Gorz, A., *Farewell to the Working Class. An Essay on Post-Industrial Socialism*, trans. M. Sonenscher (London, 1982).

Gossweiler, K., 'Der Übergang von der Weltwirtschaftskrise zur Rüstungskonjunktur in Deutschland 1933 bis 1934. Ein historischer Beitrag zur Problematik staatsmonopolistischer "Krisenüberwindung" ', *Jahrbuch für Wirtschaftsgeschichte*, 2 (1968) 55–116.

Gregor, A. J., *Young Mussolini and the Intellectual Origins of Italian Fascism* (Berkeley, Calif., 1979).

Haffner, S., *1918/19. Eine deutsche Revolution* (Hamburg, 1981).

Hamel, I., *Völkischer Verband und nationale Gewerkschaft: Der DHV 1893–1933* (Frankfurt-am-Main, 1967).

Hamerow, T. S., *Restoration, Revolution, Reaction, Economics and Politics in Germany, 1815–1871* (Princeton, NJ, 1966).

Hamilton, R. F., 'Hitler's electoral support: recent findings and theoretical implications', *Canadian Journal of Sociology*, 11 (1) (1986) 1–34.

Hamilton, R. F., *Who Voted for Hitler?* (Princeton, NJ, 1982).

Hänisch, D., *Sozialstrukturelle Bestimmungsgründe des Wahlverhaltens in der Weimarer Republik* (Duisburg, 1983).

Hardach, K., *The Political Economy of Germany in the Twentieth Century* (Berkeley, Los Angeles, London, 1980).

Herlemann, B., *Kommunalpolitik der KPD im Ruhrgebiet 1924–1933*

(Wuppertal, 1977).

Hertz, F., *Nationality in History and Politics. A Psychology and Sociology of National Sentiment and Nationalism*, 5th imp. (London, 1966).

Hickey, S. H. F., *Workers in Imperial Germany. The Miners of the Ruhr* (Oxford, 1985).

Hirschfeld, G., Kettenacker, L. (eds), *Der „Führerstaat": Mythos und Realität. Studien zur Struktur und Politik des Dritten Reiches* (Stuttgart, 1981).

Höltje, C., *Die Weimarer Republik und das Ostlocarno-Problem 1919–1934. Revision oder Garantie der deutschen Ostgrenze von 1919* (Würzburg, 1958).

Howard, M. C., King, J. E., 'The Revival of Revisionism: The Political Economy of German Marxism 1914–29', *European History Quarterly*, 18 (4) (1988) 409–26.

Howorth, J., 'French Workers and German Workers: The Impossibility of Internationalism, 1900–1914', *European History Quarterly*, 15 (1) (1985) 71–97.

Howorth, J., 'The Left in France and Germany. Internationalism and War: A Dialogue of the Deaf 1900–1914', in E. Cahn, V. Fisera (eds), *Socialism and Nationalism in Contemporary Europe (1848–1945)*, vol. 2 (Nottingham, 1979) 81–100.

Hunt, R. N., *German Social Democracy 1918–1933* (Chicago, Ill., 1970).

Jahoda, M., Lazarsfeld, P. F., Zeisel, H., *Die Arbeitslosen von Marienthal* (Bonn, 1960). First published Leipzig, 1933.

Jamin, M., 'Zur Rolle der SA im nationalsozialistischen Herrschaftssystem', in G. Hirschfeld, L. Kettenacker (eds), *Der „Führerstaat": Mythos und Realität. Studien zur Struktur und Politik des Dritten Reiches* (Stuttgart, 1981) 329–60.

Jasper, W., 'Nicht nur Streikbrechertruppe. Die NS-Betriebszellen und der Gewerkschaftsbund – ein Tabu Thema', *Die Zeit*, 6 May 1988.

Kaiser, D., 'Debate. Germany, "Domestic Crisis" and War in 1939. Comment 1', *Past and Present*, 122 (1989) 200–5.

Kater, M., *The Nazi Party. A Social Profile of Members and Leaders, 1919–1945* (Oxford, 1983).

Kater, M., 'Sozialer Wandel in der NSDAP im Zuge der nationalsozialistischen Machtergreifung', in W. Schieder (ed.), *Faschismus als soziale Bewegung* (Göttingen, 1983) 25–67.

Kele, M., *Nazis and Workers. National Socialist Appeals to German Labor, 1919–1933* (Chapel Hill, NC, 1972).

Kershaw, I., *Popular Opinion and Political Dissent in the Third Reich: Bavaria 1933–1945* (Oxford, 1983).

Klönne, A., *Die deutsche Arbeiterbewegung. Geschichte, Ziele, Wirkungen*, 3rd edn (Cologne, 1983).

Klotzbücher, A., 'Der politische Weg des Stahlhelm, Bund der Frontsoldaten, in der Weimarer Republik. Ein Beitrag zur Geschichte der „Nationalen Opposition" 1918–1933', (Inaugural Dissertation, Friedrich-Alexander-Universität, Erlangen-Nürnberg, 1965).

Knox, M., 'Conquest, Foreign and Domestic, in Fascist Italy and Nazi Germany', *The Journal of Modern History*, 56 (1) (1984) 1–57.

Koch, H. W., *The Hitler Youth. Origins and Development 1922–1945* (London, 1975).

Kochan, L., *Russia and the Weimar Republic* (Cambridge, 1954).

Kocka, J., *Facing Total War. German Society 1914–1918* (Leamington Spa, 1984).

Kratzenberg, V., *Arbeiter auf dem Weg zu Hitler? Die nationalsozialistische Betriebszellen-Organisation. Ihre Entstehung, ihre Programmatik, ihr Scheitern 1927–1934* (Frankfurt-am-Main, Bern, New York, Paris, 1989).

Kühnl, R., 'Zur Programmatik der Nationalsozialistischen Linken: Das Strasser-Programm von 1925/26', *Vierteljahreshefte für Zeitgeschichte*, 14 (1966) 317–33.

Lane, B. M., 'Nazi Ideology: Some Unfinished Business', *Central European History*, VII (1) (1974) 3–30.

Langewiesche, D., 'The Impact of the German Labor Movement on Workers' Culture', *Journal of Modern History*, 59 (3) (1987) 506–23.

Laqueur, W., *Young Germany. A History of the German Youth Movement* (New Brunswick, London, 1984).

Linden, M. van den, 'The national integration of the European working classes 1871–1914', *International Review of Social History*, XXXIII (3) (1988) 285–311.

Lipset, S. M., *Political Man. The Social Bases of Politics* (Baltimore, Md, 1981).

Longerich, P., *Die braunen Bataillone. Geschichte der SA* (Munich, 1989).

Lorwin, L. L., *Labor and Internationalism* (New York, 1929).

Madden, P., 'Some Social Characteristics of Early Nazi Party Members', *Central European History*, 15 (1) (1982) 34–56.

Mai, G., 'Die Nationalsozialistische Betriebszellen-Organisation. Zum Verhältnis von Arbeiterschaft und Nationalsozialismus', *Vierteljahreshefte für Zeitgeschichte*, 31 (1983) 573–613.

Mai, G., '„Warum steht der deutsche Arbeiter zu Hitler?" Zur Rolle der Deutschen Arbeitsfront im Herrschaftssystem des Dritten Reiches', *Geschichte und Gesellschaft*, 12 (2) (1986) 212–34.

Mai, G., 'Zwischen den Klassen? Zur Soziographie der SA', *Archiv für Sozialgeschichte*, 25 (1985) 634–46.

Manstein, P., *Die Mitglieder und Wähler der NSDAP 1919–1933. Untersuchungen zu ihrer schichtmäßigen Zusammensetzung* (Frankfurt-am-Main, Bern, New York, Paris, 1988).

Mason, T. W., *Arbeiterklasse und Volksgemeinschaft. Dokumente und Materialien zur deutschen Arbeiterpolitik 1933–1939* (Opladen, 1975).

Mason, T. W., 'The Coming of the Nazis', *Times Literary Supplement*, 3752 (1974) 93–6.

Mason, T. W., 'Debate. Germany, "Domestic Crisis" and War in 1939. Comment 2', *Past and Present*, 122 (1989) 205–21.

Mason, T. W., *Sozialpolitik im Dritten Reich* (Opladen, 1977).

Mattheier, K. J., 'Werkvereine und wirtschaftsfriedlich-nationale (gelbe) Arbeiterbewegung im Ruhrgebiet', in J. Reulecke (ed.), *Arbeiterbewegung an Rhein und Ruhr* (Wuppertal, 1974) 173–204.

Matthias, E., Morsey, R., (eds), *Das Ende der Parteien 1933* (Düsseldorf, 1960).

McElligott, A., 'Mobilising the Unemployed: The KPD and the Unemployed Workers' Movement in Hamburg-Altona during the Weimar Republic', in R. J. Evans, D. Geary (eds), *The German Unemployed. Experiences and Consequences of Mass Unemployment from the Weimar Republic to the Third Reich* (London, 1987) 228–60.

McElligott, A., '„. . . und so kam es zu einer schweren Schlägerei". Straßenschlachten in Altona und Hamburg am Ende der Weimarer Republik', in M. Bruhns et al. (eds), *„Hier war doch alles nicht so schlimm". Wie die Nazis in Hamburg den Alltag eroberten* (Hamburg, 1984) 58–85.

Merson, A., *Communist Resistance in Nazi Germany* (London, 1985).

Michalka, W. (ed.), *Die nationalsozialistische Machtergreifung* (Paderborn, Munich, Vienna, Zurich, 1984).

Michels, R., *A Sociological Study of the Oligarchical Tendencies of Modern Democracy* (London, 1962).

Milatz, A., 'Das Ende der Parteien im Spiegel der Wahlen 1930 bis 1933', in E. Matthias, R. Morsey (eds), *Das Ende der Parteien 1933* (Düsseldorf, 1960).

Milatz, A., *Wähler und Wahlen in der Weimarer Republik* (Bonn, 1968).

Milner, S., 'The International Labour Movement and the limits of internationalism: The International Secretariat of the National Trade Union Centres 1901–13', *International Review of Social History*, XXXIII (1) (1988) 1–24.

Mohler, A., *Die Konservative Revolution in Deutschland 1918–1932. Grundriß ihrer Weltanschauungen* (Stuttgart, 1950).

Möller, H., 'Die nationalsozialistische Machtergreifung. Konterrevolution oder Revolution?', *Vierteljahreshefte für Zeitgeschichte*, 31 (1) (1983) 25–51.

Mommsen, H., *Arbeiterbewegung und Nationale Frage. Aufgewählte Aufsätze* (Göttingen, 1979).

Mommsen, H., 'Sozialpolitik im Ruhrbergbau', in H. Mommsen, D. Petzina, B. Weisbrod (eds), *Industrielles System und Politische Entwicklung in der Weimarer Republik*, vol. 1. (Düsseldorf, 1979) 303–21.

Mommsen, H., Petzina, D., Weisbrod, B. (eds), *Industrielles System und politische Entwicklung in der Weimarer Republik* (Düsseldorf, 1977).

Mommsen, W. J., 'The German Revolution 1918–1920: Political Revolution and Social Protest Movement', in R. Bessel, E. J. Feuchtwanger (eds), *Social Change and Political Development in Weimar Germany* (London, 1981) 21–54.

Mommsen, W. J., *Max Weber and German Politics 1890–1920*, trans. J. Steinberg (Chicago, Ill., 1984).

Mommsen, W. J., Osterhammel, J. (eds), *Imperialism and After. Continuities and Discontinuities* (London, 1986).

Moore, B. Jr, *Injustice. The Social Bases of Obedience and Revolt* (London, 1978).

Moses, J. A., *Trade Unionism in Germany from Bismarck to Hitler 1869–1933* (Totowa, NJ, 1982).

Moses, J. A., 'Socialist Trade Unionism in Imperial Germany, 1871–1914', in R. Fletcher (ed.), *Bernstein to Brandt. A Short History of German Social Democracy* (London, 1987) 25–34.

Mühlberger, D., *Hitler's Followers* (London, 1990).

Mühlberger, D., 'The Sociology of the NSDAP: The Question of Working-Class Membership', *Journal of Contemporary History* 15 (3) (1980) 493–511.

Müller, R., *Der Bürgerkrieg in Deutschland: Geburtswehen der Republik* (Berlin, 1925).

Neumann, S., *Die Parteien der Weimarer Republik* (Stuttgart, 1977).

Noakes, J., *The Nazi Party in Lower Saxony 1921–1933* (Oxford, 1971).

Nocken, U., 'Corporatism and Pluralism in Modern German History', in D. Stegmann, B.-J. Wendt, P.-C. Witt (eds), *Industrielle Gesellschaft und Politisches System. Beiträge zur politischen Sozialgeschichte* (Bonn, 1978) 37–56.

Nolan, M., *Social democracy and society. Working-class radicalism in Düsseldorf, 1890–1920* (Cambridge, 1981).

Nolte, E., 'Marxismus und Nationalsozialismus', *Vierteljahreshefte für Zeitgeschichte*, 31 (3) (1983) 389–417.

Nolte, E., 'Zeitgenössische Theorien über den Faschismus', *Vierteljahreshefte für Zeitgeschichte*, 15 (3) (1967) 247–68.

Overy, R. J., 'Debate. Germany, "Domestic Crisis" and War in 1939. Reply', *Past and Present*, 122 (1989) 221–40.

Overy, R. J., 'Germany, "Domestic Crisis" and War in 1939', *Past and Present*, 116 (1987) 138–68.

Patch, W. L. Jr, 'German Social History and Labor History: A Troubled Partnership', *Journal of Modern History*, 56 (3) (1984) 483–98.

Paxton, R. O., 'The German Opposition to Hitler: A Non-Germanist's View', *Central European History*, 14 (4) (1981) 362–8.

Peterson, L., 'Labor and the End of the Weimar: The Case of the KPD in the November 1928 Lockout in the Rhenish-Westphalian Iron and Steel Industry', *Central European History*, 15 (1) (1982) 57–95.

Peterson, L., 'A Social Analysis of KPD Supporters: The Hamburg Insurrectionaries of October 1923', *International Review of Social History*, XXVIII (2) (1983) 200–39.

Petzold, J. (ed.), Deutschland im Ersten Weltkrieg, vol. 3, 2nd edn (Berlin, 1970).

Peukert, D., 'Der deutsche Arbeiterwiderstand 1933–1945', in K. D. Bracher, M. Funke, H.-A. Jacobsen (eds), *Nationalsozialistische Diktatur 1933–1945. Eine Bilanz* (Bonn, 1983) 633–54.

Peukert, D., *Die KPD im Widerstand. Verfolgung und Untergrundarbeit an Rhein und Ruhr, 1933 bis 1945* (Wuppertal, 1980).

Peukert, D., 'The Lost Generation: Youth Unemployment at the End of the Weimar Republic', in R. J. Evans, D. Geary (eds), *The German Unemployed. Experiences and Consequences of Mass Unemployment from the Weimar Republic to the Third Reich* (London, 1987) 172–93.

Pogge von Strandmann, H., 'Imperialism and Revisionism in Interwar Germany', in W. J. Mommsen, J. Osterhammel (eds), *Imperialism and After. Continuities and Discontinuities* (London, 1986) 90–119.

Pogge von Strandmann, H., 'Industrial Primacy in German Foreign Policy? Myths and Realities in German-Russian Relations at the End of the Weimar Republic', in R. Bessel and E. J. Feuchtwanger (eds), *Social Change and*

Political Development in Weimar Germany (London, 1981) 241–67.

Pore, R., *A Conflict of Interests: Women in German Social Democracy 1919–1933* (Westport, Conn., 1981).

Posse, E., *Die politischen Kampfbünde Deutschlands* (Berlin, 1930).

Preller, L., *Sozialpolitik in der Weimarer Republik* (Düsseldorf, 1978).

Reich, N., *Labour Relations in Republican Germany* (New York, 1938).

Reichsorganisationsleiter der NSDAP (ed.), *Partei-Statistik. Stand 1. Januar 1935* (Munich, 1935).

Repgen, K., 'Ein KPD-Verbot im Jahre 1933?', *Historische Zeitschrift*, 240 (1) (1985) 67–99.

Reulecke, J. (ed.), *Arbeiterbewegung an Rhein und Ruhr. Beiträge zur Geschichte der Arbeiterbewegung in Rheinland Westfalen* (Wuppertal, 1974).

Reuter, E., 'Die Politik der NSDAP zur Einbeziehung der Arbeiterklasse in der faschistischen Massenanhang (1930–1934)', (Dissertation, East Berlin, 1976).

Riemer, S., 'Zur Soziologie des Nationalsozialismus', *Die Arbeit*, 9 (1932) 101–18.

Rohe, K., 'Die Vorgeschichte: Das Parteiensystem in den preußischen Westprovinzen und in Lippe-Detmold 1871–1933', in U. von Alemann (ed.), *Parteien und Wahlen in Nordrhein-Westfalen* (Cologne, 1985) 22–47.

Rohe, K., *Vom Revier zum Ruhrgebiet. Wahlen Parteien Politische Kultur* (Essen, 1986).

Rosenberg, A., *Geschichte der Weimarer Republik*, 20th edn (Frankfurt-am-Main, 1980).

Rosenhaft, E., *Beating the Fascists? The German Communists and Political Violence 1929–1933* (Cambridge, 1983).

Rosenhaft, E., 'The Unemployed in the Neighbourhood: Social Dislocation and Political Mobilisation in Germany 1929–33', in R. J. Evans, D. Geary (eds), *The German Unemployed. Experiences and Consequences of Mass Unemployment from the Weimar Republic to the Third Reich* (London, 1987) 194–227.

Rößling, U., 'Konferenz zum 60. Jahrestag der Novemberrevolution und zum 60. Jahrestag der Gründung der KPD', *Zeitschrift für Geschichtswissenschaft*, 27 (2) (1979) 149–50.

Royal Institute of International Affairs, *Nationalism*, (Oxford, 1939).

Rupieper, H. J., *The Cuno Government and Reparations 1922–1923. Politics and Economics* (The Hague, 1979).

Rurup, R., 'Demokratische Revolution und „dritter Weg". Die deutsche Revolution von 1918/19 in der neueren wissenschaftlichen Diskussion', *Geschichte und Gesellschaft*, 9 (2) (1983) 278–301.

Rurup, R., 'Problems of the German Revolution 1918–1919', *Journal of Contemporary History*, 3 (4) (1968) 109–36.

Ryder, A. J., *The German Revolution of 1918. A Study of German Socialism in War and Revolt* (Cambridge, 1967).

Sarti, R., 'Fascist Modernisation in Italy: Traditional or Revolutionary?', *The American Historical Review*, LXXV (4) (1970) 1029–45.

Sauer, W., 'National Socialism: Totalitarianism or Fascism?', *The American Historical Review*, LXXIII (2) (1967) 404–24.

Schieder, W. (ed.), *Faschismus als soziale Bewegung. Deutschland und Italien im Vergleich*, 2nd edn (Göttingen, 1983).

Schnabel, T., '„Wer wählte Hitler?" Bemerkungen zu einigen Neuererscheinungen über die Endphase der Weimarer Republik', *Geschichte und Gesellschaft*, 8 (1) (1982) 116–33.

Schneider, M., *Unternehmer und Demokratie. Die freien Gewerkschaften in der Unternehmer Ideologie der Jahre 1918 bis 1933* (Bonn-Bad Godesberg, 1975).

Schöck, E. C., *Arbeitslosigkeit und Rationalisierung. Die Lage der Arbeiter und die kommunistische Gewerkschaftspolitik 1920–28* (Frankfurt-am-Main, 1977).

Schoenbaum, D., *Hitler's Social Revolution. Class and Status in Nazi Germany 1933–1939* (London, 1967).

Schorske, C. E., *German Social Democracy, 1905–1917: The Development of the Great Schism* (London, 1955).

Schüddekopf, O.-E., *Linke Leute von rechts. Die nationalrevolutionären Minderheiten und der Kommunismus in der Weimarer Republik* (Stuttgart, 1960).

Schwabe, K. (ed.), *Die Ruhrkrise 1923. Wendepunkt der internationalen Beziehungen nach dem Ersten Weltkrieg*, 2nd edn (Paderborn, 1986).

Seifert, C., 'Die deutsche Gewerkschaftsbewegung in der Weimarer Republik', in F. Deppe, G. Fülberth, J. Harrer (eds), *Geschichte der deutschen Gewerkschaftsbewegung*, 3rd edn (Cologne, 1981).

Severing, C., *Mein Lebensweg* (Cologne, 1950).

Sinfield, A., *What Unemployment Means* (Oxford, 1981).

Sontheimer, K., *Antidemokratisches Denken in der Weimarer Republik. Die politischen Ideen des deutschen Nationalismus zwischen 1918 und 1933*, 2nd edn (Munich, 1983).

Stachura, P. D., *Gregor Strasser and the Rise of Nazism* (London, 1983).

Stachura, P. D., *Nazi Youth in the Weimar Republic* (Santa Barbara, Calif., Oxford, 1975).

Stachura, P. D., 'The Political Strategy of the Nazi Party, 1919–1933', *German Studies Review*, III (2) (1980) 261–88.

Stachura, P. D., (ed.), *Unemployment and the Great Depression in Weimar Germany* (London, 1986).

Stachura, P. D., 'Who were the Nazis? A Socio-Political Analysis of the National Socialist Machtübernahme', *European Studies Review*, 11 (3) (1981) 293–324.

Stegmann, D., Wendt, B.-J., Witt, P. C. (eds), *Industrielle Gesellschaft und Politisches System. Beiträge zur politischen Sozialgeschichte* (Bonn, 1978).

Stupperich, A., *Volksgemeinschaft oder Arbeitersolidarität: Studien zur Arbeitnehmerpolitik in der Deutschnationalen Volkspartei 1918–1933* (Göttingen, 1982).

Tampke, J., *The Ruhr and Revolution. The Revolutionary Movement in the Rhenish-Westphalian Industrial Region 1912–1919* (London, 1979).

Tegel, S., 'The SPD in Imperial Germany, 1871–1914', in R. Fletcher (ed.), *Bernstein to Brandt. A Short History of German Social Democracy* (London, 1987) 16–24.

Thimme, A., *Gustav Stresemann. Eine politische Biographie zur Geschichte* der Weimarer Republik (Hannover, Frankfurt-am-Main, 1957).

Tobin, E. H., 'War and the Working Class: The Case of Düsseldorf 1914–1918', *Central European History*, 18 (3/4) (1985) 257–98.

Valtin, J., *Out of the Night* (London, 1941).

Vorwerck, K., *Die wirtschaftsfriedliche Arbeitnehmerbewegung Deutschlands in ihrem Werden und in ihrem Kampf um Anerkennung* (Jena, 1926).

Waite, R. G. L., *Vanguard of Nazism. The Free Corps Movement in Postwar Germany 1918–1923* (London, 1970).

Ward, J. J., ' "Smash the Fascists . . .". German Communist Efforts to Counter the Nazis, 1930–31', *Central European History*, 14 (1) (1981) 30–62.

Watt, R. M., *The Kings Depart. The Tragedy of Germany: Versailles and the German Revolution* (London, 1968).

Watts, D., 'Electoral Success and Political Failure: The KPD in Mannheim in the Last Years of the Weimar Republic', *European History Quarterly*, 18 (4) (1988) 439–54.

Weber, E., 'Fascism(s) and some Harbingers', *Journal of Modern History*, 54 (4) (1982) 746–65.

Weber, R., 'Werkgemeinschaft – Ein „wirtschaftsorganisatorischer Lösungsversuch" oder das sozialpolitische Programm der nationalistischen Diktatur?', *Die Arbeit*, V (1928) 533–46.

Wehler, H.-U., *Sozialdemokratie und Nationalstaat. Nationalitätenfragen in Deutschland 1840–1914* (Göttingen, 1971).

Weisbrod, B., *Schwerindustrie in der Weimarer Republik. Interessenpolitik zwischen Stabilisierung und Krise* (Wuppertal, 1978).

Weissbuch über die Erschiessungen des 30. Juni 1934 (Paris, 1935).

Wheeler, R. F., *USPD und Internationale. Sozialistischer Internationalismus in der Zeit der Revolution* (Frankfurt-am-Main, 1975).

Wheeler, R. F., 'Zur sozialen Struktur der Arbeiterbewegung am Anfang der Weimarer Republik. Einige methodoligischen Bemerkungen', in H. Mommsen, D. Petzina, B. Weisbrod (eds), *Industrielles System und Politische Entwicklung in der Weimarer Republik*, vol 1 (Düsseldorf, 1977) 179–89.

Wickham, J., 'The Working Class Movement in Frankfurt-am-Main during the Weimar Republic', (D. Phil. Dissertation, University of Sussex, 1979).

Williams, J. H., 'German Foreign Trade and the Reparation Payments', *Quarterly Journal of Economics*, (1922) 482–503.

Wilson, K. M. (ed.), *George Saunders on Germany. Correspondence and Memoranda* (Leeds, 1987).

Winkler, H. A., 'Mittelstandsbewegung oder Volkspartei? Zur sozialen Basis der NSDAP', in W. Schieder (ed.), *Faschismus als soziale Bewegung. Deutschland und Italien im Vergleich*, 2nd edn (Göttingen, 1983) 97–118.

Winkler, H. A., *Von der Revolution zur Stabilisierung. Arbeiter und Arbeiterbewegung in der Weimarer Republik 1918 bis 1924* (Berlin, Bonn, 1984).

Wippermann, W., „Triumph des Willens" oder „kapitalistische Manipulation"? Das Ideologieproblem in Faschismus', in K. D. Bracher, M. Funke, H. A. Jacobsen (eds), *Nationalsozialistische Diktatur 1933–1945. Eine Bilanz* (Bonn, 1983) 735–59.

Wunderlich, F., 'New Aspects of Unemployment in Germany', *Social Research*, I (1934) 97–110.

Zitelmann, R., *Adolf Hitler. Eine politische Biographie* (Göttingen, 1989).

Glossary of German Words and Terms Used in the Text

Anschluß	Union (of Germany and Austria)
Arbeitsgemeinschaft Nord-West	North-Western Working Association
Berliner Verkehrsgesellschaft	Berlin Transport Company
Bund der Kommunisten	League of Communists
Bund Oberland	Oberland League
bürgerlich	bourgeois
Burgfriede	political truce (in wartime)
Deutsche Freiheitsbund	German Freedom League
Deutsche Volkshochschule	German People's College
Freideutsche Jugend	Free German Youth
Freikorps	Volunteer Corps
Führer	(Fascist) leader
Großdeutsche Volksgemeinschaft	Greater German Ethnic Community
Hansa-Bund	Hanseatic League (of industrialists)
HIB-Aktion	Into The Factories Campaign (of NSDAP)
Kampfbund gegen den Faschismus	Fighting League Against Fascism
Kozi	Communist (Social Democratic term of abuse for)
Landtag	Lower house of state parliament
Mittelstand	(traditional) middle class
Norddeutscher Arbeiterschutzbund	North German Workers' Defence League
Pioniere	Pioneers (KPD youth group)
Reichspost	national postal service
Reichstag	Lower house of German parliament
Reichsverband der deutschen Industrie	National Association of German Industry
Reichswehr	German Army (in Weimar Republic)
Revolutionäre Obleute	Revolutionary Shop Stewards
Rote Frontkämpferbund	Red Front Fighters' League (Red Front)
Rote Lanzen	Red Lances
Schutzstaffel	Guard Squadron
Spartakusbund	Spartacus League
Stahlhelm-Selbsthilfe	Stahlhelm Self-Help
Sturmabteilung	Storm Section
Union der Hand und Kopf Arbeiter	Union of Manual and Intellectual Workers
Verbände	Paramilitary Leagues

völkisch	populist racist
Völkische	populist racist parties
Volksgemeinschaft	Ethnic populist community
Volksgenossen	Ethnic comrades
Volksrevolution	People's revolution
Volksschule	Junior basic school
Westorientierung	Westward orientation (in foreign policy)
Zentrale	Central Committee (of the KPD)

Index

274　　　　*Index*

and Allies, 18, 27–8, 30–2, 39,
　43–5, 53, 56, 57, 59, 70, 71, 79,
　105–6, 108, 112, 113, 165
and army, 67, 106, 111
authorities' views of, 18–19, 32, 36,
　56–7, 63, 66–7, 115, 121, 124,
　126, 128, 133–4, 137, 153, 159–
　60, 165–6, 172, 183–4, 187, 191–2
and Bolshevism, 10, 12, 19, 58, 76,
　107, 161
Central Committee of, xiii, 12, 15,
　30, 32, 34–5, 43–4, 49, 53–4, 59,
　60, 65, 73–4, 104, 107–9, 114,
　116, 122–3, 134, 137, 141–2, 152,
　154–7, 159–61, 166, 170–1, 173–
　5, 177, 184–5, 187
and Comintern, 12–13, 15–16, 19,
　21, 27, 32, 35, 43, 65–6, 71, 76,
　84, 96, 103, 107, 114, 141, 163–5,
　174–5
in countryside, 20–1, 124–9, 152–3,
　158
and demonstrations, marches,
　142–5, 148, 153–4
discipline in, 107, 111
and elections, 15, 51, 72, 82, 118ff,
　141, 144, 156–7, 164–5, 178, 187,
　228 n37
and employers, management, 79,
　89, 106, 135–6, 164–5, 181, 186,
　249 n77
in factories, industry, 13, 16–18,
　50, 82–4, 89ff, 102–4, 110, 115–
　17, 123, 129, 132–6, 138, 141–3,
　152, 157–9, 161, 162ff, 190, 192
factory cells of, 17–18, 133ff, 162ff
and factory council elections, 82–4,
　90, 94, 133, 135–6, 163–5, 167–9,
　175
and fascism, fascists, 45–9, 51–7,
　61, 64, 66, 68, 76–8, 104–8, 111,
　114–15, 150–3, 157, 164, 175, 179
finances of, 131–4, 141, 144–5, 157,
　159, 190
and Freikorps, *see* radical right
and German Revolution, 11–13,
　26, 114, 141
historians' views of, 7, 11, 26, 45,
　129, 162, 189–90

and insurgency, 3, 5–6, 12, 14–16,
　30, 32, 36, 39, 44, 58, 65, 140,
　144–5, 150, 153, 164–5, 194
and Jews, 59–61, 79
and lower middle classes, 19–21,
　43, 49–50, 54–5, 59, 60–1, 125,
　171, 175
and meetings, 46, 59–60, 64, 79,
　107, 121, 141, 143, 148–9, 154ff,
　173, 176, 187
membership, social composition
　of, 12, 14–15, 18, 82, 84, 89,
　129ff, 139, 141, 144, 187
membership turnover in, 129, 131–
　5, 138, 144, 158, 190
and middle classes, 19, 30, 42–4,
　49, 59, 67, 73, 77, 112–13, 115,
　122–3, 127, 129–31, 143
morale in, 124, 164
and national bolshevism/
　communism, 12, 26–7, 31–3, 43,
　53, 56, 59, 68, 210 n118, n126
and nationalism, 12, 21, 22ff, 42ff,
　71–2, 76, 105–8, 111–13, 117
and Nazi takeover, 189ff
and Nazism, NSDAP, xi–xiv, 21,
　45–7, 59–61, 64, 67, 70, 72,
　77–80, 82, 91, 100–1, 103–4,
　106–17, 118ff, 138ff, 162ff, 189ff,
　240 n91, 247 n54
in neighbourhood, 133–4, 138, 145,
　148ff, 165–6, 173, 190, 193
organisational capacity of, 84, 98–
　9, 123, 129, 131, 133–4, 141, 147,
　151, 153–4, 156–62, 165–7, 176–
　7, 183, 186–7, 190–5
and peasantry, 20, 49, 50, 125–6
Proletarian Hundreds of, 46, 57–8,
　65
and radical right, xi–xii, 19, 21, 25,
　29, 31–3, 35–9, 44–6, 50–1, 54–5,
　57–64, 66–8, 70–5, 77, 82, 84,
　90ff, 109, 113, 173, 194, 207 n33
and Reichsbanner, 104, 106–7,
　149–51, 153, 240 n91
and revolution, 17, 22, 28, 31, 33,
　43, 49, 51, 56, 60, 63–6, 70–1, 77,
　81–2, 85, 99, 112, 131, 138, 141,
　164–5, 179, 181–2, 194–5

Index

280 *Index*